THE

BUCCANEERS OF AMERICA

THE

BUCCANEERS OF AMERICA

A TRUE ACCOUNT OF THE MOST REMARKABLE ASSAULTS COMMITTED OF LATE YEARS UPON THE COASTS OF THE WEST INDIES BY THE BUCCANEERS OF JAMAICA AND TORTUGA (BOTH ENGLISH AND FRENCH)

Wherein are contained more especially the Unparalleled Exploits of Sir Henry Morgan, our English Jamaican Hero, who sacked Porto Bello, burnt Panama, etc.

BY

JOHN ESQUEMELING

One of the Buccaneers who was present at these tragedies

ISBN: 978-93-5128-950-0(PB)

First Published in 1911
Indian Reprint in 2017

Published by

Kalpaz Publications
C-30, Satyawati Nagar,
Delhi – 110052
E-mail: kalpaz@hotmail.com
Website: kalpazpublications.com
Ph.: +91-9212142040

EDITOR'S NOTE

THE first three PARTS of this work were originally written in Dutch by Alex. Olivier Exquemelin (1645–1707)—anglicized as JOHN ESQUEMELING; and published in Amsterdam in 1678 under the title *De Americaensche Zeerovers*. A Spanish translation by A. de Buena-Maison, under the title *Piratas de la America*, appeared in small 4to, at Colonia Agrippina 1681, and translations into other European languages followed, each magnifying the deeds of its own national hero, sometimes at the expense of Esquemeling's text.

The FOURTH PART consists of the *Journal* of Basil Ringrose, "gent.", one of the English Buccaneers; and gives an account of their principal exploits in the South Seas, with which Esquemeling dealt only in outline. Ringrose was with the Buccaneers at Darien in 1680, and returned to England in 1682: his *Journal* appeared as the second volume of Esquemeling's work in 1685. He sailed in 1684 for the South Seas in the *Cygnet*, whose Captain joined the Buccaneers: he was killed by the Spaniards in Mexico in 1686.

The present edition is a *verbatim* reprint—modernized in respect of punctuation, and obsolete spellings and verbal and typographic eccentricities—of the second edition of the English translation (London: printed for William Crooke, at the Green Dragon without Temple-bar, 1684), which contains two additional chapters (XI and XII) to the first edition (also 1684) relating the adventures of Captain Cook, Captain Sharp, and others. Ringrose's FOURTH PART is reprinted from the first edition, which is excessively rare, valued to-day at about £60 (in good condition). A few notes have been added at the foot of the pages where obscurities—chiefly verbal—occur.

The essay on this book from the pen of the late Mr Andrew Lang is reprinted from his *Essays in Little*, by kind permission of Messrs Longmans, Green and Co., its publishers.

W. S. S.

CONTENTS

PAGE

EDITOR'S NOTE v
ESSAY BY ANDREW LANG xiii
ADVERTISEMENT TO THE READER 1
THE TRANSLATOR TO THE READER 3

CHAPTER

PART I

I: The author sets forth towards the Western Islands, in the service of the West India Company of France. They meet with an English frigate, and arrive at the island of Tortuga 9
II: Description of the island of Tortuga: of the fruits and plants there growing: how the French settled there, at two several times, and cast out the Spaniards, first masters thereof. The author of this book was twice sold in the said Island 14
III: Description of the great and famous Island of Hispaniola 23
IV: Of the Fruits, Trees, and Animals that are found at Hispaniola 27
V: Of all sorts of quadruped animals and birds that are found in this island. As also a relation of the French Buccaneers 39
VI: Of the origin of the most famous Pirates of the coasts of America. A notable exploit of Pierre le Grand 55
VII: After what manner the Pirates arm their vessels, and how they regulate their voyages 59

PART II

I: Origin of Francis L'Ollonais, and beginning of his robberies 81
II: L'Ollonais equips a fleet to land upon the Spanish islands of America, with intent to rob, sack, and burn whatever he met 87
III: L'Ollonais makes new preparations to take the city of St James de Leon; as also that of Nicaragua, where he miserably perishes 101
IV: Of the origin and descent of Captain Henry Morgan—his exploits and a continuation of the most remarkable actions of his life 119
V: Some account of the island of Cuba. Captain Morgan attempts to preserve the isle of St Catharine as a refuge and nest to Pirates; but fails of his designs. He arrives at and takes the village of El Puerto del Principe 127
VI: Captain Morgan resolves to attack and plunder the city of Porto Bello. To this effect he equips a fleet, and with little expense and small forces, takes the said place 135

CHAPTER PAGE

VII: Captain Morgan takes the city of Maracaibo, on the coast of New Venezuela. Piracies committed in those seas. Ruin of three Spanish ships that were set forth to hinder the robberies of the Pirates 143

PART III

I: Captain Morgan goes to the isle of Hispaniola to equip a new fleet, with intent to pillage again upon the coasts of the West Indies 173

II: What happened in the river De la Hacha 175

III: Captain Morgan leaves the island of Hispaniola, and goes to that of St Catharine, which he takes 179

IV: Captain Morgan takes the Castle of Chagre, with four hundred men sent for this purpose from the Isle of St Catharine 185

V: Captain Morgan departs from the Castle of Chagre, at the head of twelve hundred men, with design to take the city of Panama 192

VI: Captain Morgan sends several canoes and boats to the South Sea. He sets fire to the city of Panama. Robberies and cruelties committed there by the Pirates till their return to the Castle of Chagre 208

VII: Of a voyage made by the author along the coasts of Costa Rica, at his return towards Jamaica. What happened most remarkable in the said voyage. Some observations made by him at that time 224

VIII: The author departs towards the Cape of Gracias á Dios. Of the commerce which here the Pirates exercise with the Indians. His arrival at the Island De los Pinos; and, finally, his return to Jamaica 233

IX: The relation of the shipwreck which Monsieur Bertram Ogeron, Governor of the isle of Tortuga, suffered near the Isles of Guadanillas. How both he and his companions fell into the hands of the Spaniards. By what arts he escaped their hands, and preserved his life. The enterprise which he undertook against Porto Rico to deliver his people. The unfortunate success of that design 242

X: A relation of what encounters lately happened at the islands of Cayana and Tobago between the Count de Estres, Admiral of France, in America, and the Heer Jacob Binkes, Vice-Admiral of the United Provinces, in the same parts 249

XI: Adventures of Captain Cook, in the year 1678. He is taken by the Spaniards. Bold exploits, and revenge of his losses, performed by some few Buccaneers that were on board his ship 254

XII: A brief account of Captain Sharp and other his companions; their voyage from Jamaica unto the province of Darien and South Sea; with the robberies and assaults they committed there for the space of three years, till their return for England in the year 1682. Given by one of the Buccaneers who was present at those transactions 257

PART IV

CHAPTER PAGE

THE PREFACE TO THE READER 289

I: Captain Coxon, Sawkins, Sharp, and others set forth in a fleet towards the province of Darien, upon the continent of America. Their designs to pillage and plunder in those parts. Number of their ships, and strength of their forces by sea and land 297

II: They march towards the town of Santa Maria with design to take it. The Indian King of Darien meets them by the way. Difficulties of this march, with other occurrences till they arrive at the place 301

III: They take the town of Santa Maria with no loss of men, and but small booty of what they fought for. Description of the place, country, and river adjacent. They resolve to go and plunder for the second time the city of Panama 306

IV: The Buccaneers leave the town of Santa Maria, and proceed by sea to take Panama. Extreme difficulties, with sundry accidents and dangers of that voyage 309

V: Shipwreck of Mr Ringrose, the author of this narrative. He is taken by the Spaniards, and miraculously by them preserved. Several other accidents and disasters which befel him after the loss of his companions till he found them again. Description of the Gulf of Vallona 312

VI: The Buccaneers prosecute their voyage, till they come within sight of Panama. They take several barks and prisoners by the way. Are descried by the Spaniards before their arrival. They order the Indians to kill the prisoners 318

VII: They arrive within sight of Panama. Are encountered by three small men-of-war. They fight them with only 68 men, and utterly defeat them, taking two of the said vessels. Description of that bloody fight. They take several ships at the Isle of Perico before Panama 321

VIII: Description of the state and condition of Panama, and the parts adjacent. What vessels they took while they blocked up the said Port. Captain Coxon with seventy more returns home. Sawkins is chosen in chief 327

IX: Captain Sawkins, chief commander of the Buccaneers, is killed before Puebla Nueva. They are repulsed from the said place. Captain Sharp chosen to be their leader. Many more of their company leave them and return home overland 333

X: They depart from the island of Cayboa to the island of Gorgona, where they careen their vessels. Description of this isle. They resolve to go and plunder Arica, leaving their design of Guayaquil 338

XI: The Buccaneers depart from the isle of Gorgona, with design to plunder Arica. They lose one another by the way. They touch at the Isle of Plate, or Drake's Isle, where they meet again. Description of this isle. Some memoirs of Sir Francis Drake. An account of this voyage and the coasts all along. They sail as far in a fortnight as the Spaniards usually do in three months 345

CONTENTS

CHAPTER PAGE

XII: Captain Sharp and his company depart from the Isle of Plate in prosecution of their voyage towards Arica. They take two Spanish vessels by the way, and learn intelligence from the enemy. Eight of their company destroyed at the Isle of Gallo. Tediousness of this voyage, and great hardships they endured. Description of the coast all along, and their sailings 354

XIII: A continuation of their long and tedious voyage to Arica, with a description of the coasts and sailings thereunto. Great hardship they endured for want of water and other provisions. They are descried at Arica, and dare not land there—the country being all in arms before them. They retire from thence, and go to Puerto de Hilo, close by Arica. Here they land, take the town with little or no loss on their side, refresh themselves with provisions; but in the end are cheated by the Spaniards, and forced shamefully to retreat from thence 367

XIV: The Buccaneers depart from the Port of Hilo, and sail to that of Coquimbo. They are descried before their arrival. Notwithstanding they land; are encountered by the Spaniards; and put them to flight. They take, plunder, and fire the City of la Serena. A description thereof. A stratagem of the Spaniards, in endeavouring to fire their ship, discovered and prevented. They are deceived again by the Spaniards, and forced to retire from Coquimbo, without any ransom for the City or considerable pillage. They release several of their chief prisoners 380

XV: The Buccaneers depart from Coquimbo for the isle of Juan Fernandez. An exact account of this voyage. Misery they endure, and great dangers they escape very narrowly there. They mutiny among themselves, and choose Watling to be their chief commander. Description of the island. Three Spanish men-of-war meet with the Buccaneers at the said island, but these outbrave them on the one side and give them the slip on the other 390

XVI: The Buccaneers depart from the isle of Juan Fernandez to that of Iquique. Here they take several prisoners, and learn intelligence of the posture of affairs at Arica. Cruelty committed upon one of the said prisoners who had rightly informed them. They attempt Arica the second time, and take the town, but are beaten out of it again before they could plunder—with great loss of men, many of them being killed, wounded, and made prisoners. Captain Watling, their chief Commander, is killed in this attack, and Captain Sharp presently chosen again, who leads them off, and through mountains of difficulties makes a bold retreat to the ship 401

XVII: A description of the Bay of Arica. They sail hence to the Port of Guasco, where they get provisions. A draft of the said port. They land again at Hilo to revenge the former affronts, and take what they could find 410

CHAPTER		PAGE
XVIII:	They depart from the Port of Hilo to the Gulf of Nicoya, where they take down their decks and mend the sailing of their ship. Forty-seven of their companions leave them, and go home over land. A description of the Gulf of Nicoya. They take two barks and some prisoners there. Several other remarks belonging to this voyage	416
XIX:	They depart from the Gulf of Nicoya to Golfo Dulce, where they careen their vessel. An account of their sailings along the coast; also a description of Golfo Dulce. The Spaniards force the Indians of Darien to a peace by a stratagem contrived in the name of the English	423
XX:	They depart from Golfo Dulce, to go and cruise under the equinoctial. Here they take a rich Spanish vessel with 37,000 pieces-of-eight, besides plate and other goods. They take also a packet-boat bound from Panama to Lima. An account of their sailings and the coast along	428
XXI:	They take another Spanish ship richly laden under the equinoctial. They make several dividends of their booty among themselves. They arrive at the Isle of Plate, where they are in danger of being all massacred by their slaves and prisoners. Their departure thence for the port and bay of Paita, with design to plunder the said place	433
XXII:	They arrive at Paita, where they are disappointed of their expectations, as not daring to land, seeing all the country alarmed before them. They bear away for the Strait of Magellan. Description of the bay and port of Paita, and Colan. An account of their sailings towards the Strait aforementioned	439
XXIII:	The Buccaneers arrive at a place incognito, to which they give the name of the Duke of York's Islands. A description of the said islands and of the gulf, or lagoon, wherein they lie, so far as it was searched. They remain there many days by stress of weather, not without great danger of being lost. An account of some other remarkable things that happened there	447
XXIV:	They depart from the English Gulf in quest of the Strait of Magellan, which they cannot find. They return home by an unknown way, never navigated before	455
XXV:	The Buccaneers continue their navigation, without seeing any land, till they arrive at the Caribbean Islands in the West Indies. They give away their ship to some of their companions that were poor, and disperse for several countries. The author of this Journal arrives in England	466

LIST OF FULL-PAGE ILLUSTRATIONS

Sir Henry Morgan	*Frontispiece*
	PAGE
Bartholomew Portugues	65
Rock Brasiliano	71
Francis L'Ollonais	83
L'Ollonais' Brutalities	105
Puerto del Principe Taken and Sacked	149
The Spanish Armada Destroyed by Capt. Morgan	163
The Country and City of Panama	193
Battle before Panama	209
Map of the South Seas and Coasts	287

ADVENTURES OF BUCCANEERS

BY ANDREW LANG[1]

MOST of us, as boys, have envied the buccaneers. The greatest of all boys, Canon Kingsley, once wrote a pleasing and regretful poem in which the Last Buccaneer represents himself as a kind of picturesque philanthropist :

" There were forty craft in Aves that were both swift and stout,
All furnished well with small arms, and cannons round about ;
And a thousand men in Aves made laws so fair and free,
To choose their valiant captains and obey them loyally.
Thence we sailed against the Spaniard with his hoards of plate and gold,
Which he wrung with cruel tortures from Indian folk of old ;
Likewise the merchant captains, with hearts as hard as stone,
Who flog men and keel-haul them, and starve them to the bone."

The buccaneer is " a gallant sailor ", according to Kingsley's poem—a Robin Hood of the waters, who preys only on the wicked rich, or the cruel and Popish Spaniard, and the extortionate shipowner. For his own part, when he is not rescuing poor Indians, the buccaneer lives mainly " for climate and the affections " :

" Oh, sweet it was in Aves to hear the landward breeze,
A swing with good tobacco in a net between the trees,
With a negro lass to fan you, while you listened to the roar
Of the breakers on the reef outside that never touched the shore."

This is delightfully idyllic, like the lives of the Tahitian shepherds in *The Anti-Jacobin*—the shepherds whose occupation was a sinecure, as there were no sheep in Tahiti.

Yet the vocation was not really so touchingly chivalrous as the poet would have us deem. One Joseph Esquemeling, himself a buccaneer, has written the history and described the exploits of his companions in plain prose, warning eager

[1] Reprinted, by kind permission of Messrs Longmans, Green and Co., from his *Essays in Little*.

youths that "pieces-of-eight do not grow on every tree", as many raw recruits have believed. Mr Esquemeling's account of these matters may be purchased, with a great deal else that is instructive and entertaining, in *The History of the Buccaneers in America*. My edition (of 1810) is a dumpy little book, in very small type, and quite a crowd of publishers took part in the venture. The older editions are difficult to procure if your pockets are not stuffed with pieces-of-eight. You do not often find even this volume, but "when found make a note of", and you have a reply to Canon Kingsley.

A charitable old Scotch lady, who heard our ghostly foe evil spoken of, remarked that "If we were all as diligent and conscientious as the Devil, it would be better for us". Now, the buccaneers were certainly models of diligence and conscientiousness in their own industry, which was to torture people till they gave up their goods, and then to run them through the body, and spend the spoils over drink and dice. Except Dampier, who was a clever man, but a poor buccaneer (Mr Clark Russell has written his life), they were the most hideously ruthless miscreants that ever disgraced the earth and the sea. But their courage and endurance were no less notable than their greed and cruelty, so that a moral can be squeezed even out of these abandoned miscreants. The soldiers and sailors who made their way within gunshot of Khartoum, overcoming thirst, hunger, heat, the desert, and the gallant children of the desert, did not fight, march, and suffer more bravely than the scoundrels who sacked Maracaibo and burned Panama. Their good qualities were no less astounding and exemplary than their almost incredible wickedness. They did not lie about in hammocks much, listening to the landward wind among the woods—the true buccaneers. To tell the truth, most of them had no particular cause to love the human species. They were often Europeans who had been sold into slavery on the West Indian plantations, where they learned lessons of cruelty by suffering it. Thus Mr Joseph Esquemeling, our historian, was beaten, tortured, and nearly starved to death in Tortuga, "so I determined, not knowing how to get any living, to enter into the order of the pirates or robbers of the sea". The poor Indians of the isles, much pitied by Kingsley's buccaneer, had a habit of sticking their prisoners all over with thorns, wrapped in oily cotton, whereto they then set fire. "These cruelties many Christians have seen while they lived among these barbarians". Mr Esquemeling was to see, and inflict, plenty of this kind of torment, which was not out of the way nor unusual. One planter alone had killed over a hundred of his servants—"the English did the same with theirs".

A buccaneer voyage began in stealing a ship, collecting desperadoes, and torturing the local herdsmen till they gave up their masters' flocks, which were salted as provisions. Articles of service were then drawn up, on the principle "no prey, no pay". The spoils, when taken, were loyally divided as a rule, though Captain Morgan, of Wales, made no more scruple about robbing his crew than about barbecuing a Spanish priest. "They are very civil and charitable to each other, so that if any one wants what another has, with great willingness they give it to one another". In other matters they did not in the least resemble the early Christians. A fellow nicknamed The Portuguese may be taken as our first example of their commendable qualities.

With a small ship of four guns he had taken a great one of twenty guns, with 70,000 pieces-of-eight. . . . He himself, however, was presently captured by a larger vessel, and imprisoned on board. Being carelessly watched, he escaped on two earthen jars (for he could not swim), reached the woods in Campechy, and walked for a hundred and twenty miles through the bush. His only food was a few shell-fish, and by way of a knife he had a large nail, which he whetted to an edge on a stone. Having made a kind of raft, he struck a river, and paddled to Golpho Triste, where he found congenial pirates. With twenty of these, and a boat, he returned to Campechy, where he had been a prisoner, and actually captured the large ship in which he had lain captive! Bad luck pursued him, however: his prize was lost in a storm; he reached Jamaica in a canoe, and never afterwards was concerned as leader in any affair of distinction. Not even Odysseus had more resource, nor was more long-enduring; but Fortune was The Portuguese's foe.

Braziliano, another buccaneer, served as a pirate before the mast, and "was beloved and respected by all". Being raised to command, he took a plate ship; but this success was of indifferent service to his otherwise amiable character.

" He would often appear foolish and brutish when in drink ", and has been known to roast Spaniards alive on wooden spits " for not showing him hog yards where he might steal swine ". One can hardly suppose that Kingsley would have regretted *this* buccaneer, even if he had been the last, which unluckily he was not. His habit of sitting in the street beside a barrel of beer, and shooting all passers-by who would not drink with him, provoked remark, and was an act detestable to all friends of temperance principles.

François L'Olonnois, from Southern France, had been kidnapped, and sold as a slave in the Caribbee Islands. Recovering his freedom, he plundered the Spanish, says my buccaneer author, " till his unfortunate death ". With two canoes he captured a ship which had been sent after him, carrying ten guns and a hangman for his express benefit. This hangman, much to the fellow's chagrin, L'Olonnois put to death like the rest of his prisoners. His great achievements were in the Gulf of Venezuela or Bay of Maracaibo. The gulf is a strong place ; the mouth, no wider than a gun-shot, is guarded by two islands. Far up the inlet is Maracaibo, a town of three thousand people, fortified and surrounded by woods. Yet farther up is the town of Gibraltar. To attack these was a desperate enterprise ; but L'Olonnois stole past the forts, and frightened the townsfolk into the woods. As a rule the Spaniards made the poorest resistance ; there were examples of courage, but none of conduct. With strong forts, heavy guns, many men, provisions, and ammunition, they quailed before the desperate valour of the pirates. The towns were sacked, the fugitives hunted out in the woods, and the most abominable tortures were applied to make them betray their friends and reveal their treasures. When they were silent, or had no treasures to declare, they were hacked, twisted, burned, and starved to death.

Such were the manners of L'Olonnois ; and Captain Morgan, of Wales, was even more ruthless.

Gibraltar was well fortified and strengthened after Maracaibo fell ; new batteries were raised, the way through the woods was barricaded, and no fewer than eight hundred men were under arms to resist a small pirate force, exhausted by debauch, and having its retreat cut off by the forts at the mouth of the great salt-water loch. But L'Olonnois did not blench: he told the men that audacity was their one hope, also that he would pistol the first who gave ground. The men cheered enthusiastically, and a party of three hundred and fifty landed. The barricaded way they could not force, and in a newly cut path they met a strong battery which fired grape. But L'Olonnois was invincible. He tried that old trick which rarely fails, a sham retreat, and this lured the Spaniards from their earthwork on the path. The pirates then turned, sword in hand, slew two hundred of the enemy, and captured eight guns. The town yielded, the people fled to the woods, and then began the wonted sport of torturing the prisoners. Maracaibo they ransomed afresh, obtained a pilot, passed the forts with ease, and returned after sacking a small province. On a dividend being declared, they parted 260,000 pieces-of-eight among the band, and spent the pillage in a revel of three weeks.

L'Olonnois "got great repute" by this conduct, but I rejoice to add that in a raid on Nicaragua he "miserably perished", and met what Mr Esquemeling calls "his unfortunate death". For L'Olonnois was really an ungentlemanly character. He would hack a Spaniard to pieces, tear out his heart, and "gnaw it with his teeth like a ravenous wolf, saying to the rest 'I will serve you all alike if you show me not another way'" (to a town which he designed attacking). In Nicaragua he was taken by the Indians, who, being entirely on the Spanish side, tore him to pieces and burned him. Thus we really must not be deluded by the professions of Mr Kingsley's sentimental buccaneer, with his pity for "the Indian folk of old".

Except Denis Scott, a worthy bandit in his day, Captain Henry Morgan is the first renowned British buccaneer. He was a young Welshman, who, after having been sold as a slave in Barbadoes, became a sailor of fortune. With about four hundred men he assailed Puerto Bello. "If our number is small", he said, "our hearts are great", and so he assailed the third city and place of arms which Spain then possessed in the West Indies. The entrance of the harbour was protected by two strong castles, judged as "almost impregnable", while Morgan had no artillery of any avail against fortresses. Morgan had the luck to capture a Spanish soldier, whom he compelled to parley with the garrison of the castle. This he stormed and blew up, massacring all its defenders, while with its guns he disarmed the sister fortress. When all but defeated in a new assault, the sight of the English colours animated him afresh. He made the captive monks and nuns carry the scaling ladders; in this unwonted exploit the poor religious folk lost many of their numbers. The wall was mounted, the soldiers were defeated, though the Governor fought like a Spaniard of the old school, slew many pirates with his own hand, and pistolled some of his own men for cowardice. He died at his post, refusing quarter, and falling like a gentleman of Spain. Morgan, too, was not wanting in fortitude: he extorted 100,000 pieces-of-eight from the Governor of Panama, and sent him a pistol as a sample of the gun wherewith he took so great a city. He added that he would return and take this pistol out of Panama; nor was he less good than his word. In Cuba he divided 250,000 pieces-of-eight, and a great booty in other treasure. A few weeks saw it all in the hands of the tavern-keepers and women of the place.

Morgan's next performance was a new sack of Maracaibo, now much stronger than L'Olonnois had found it. After the most appalling cruelties, not fit to be told, he returned, passing the castles at the mouth of the port by an ingenious stratagem. Running boatload after boatload of men to the land side, he brought them back by stealth, leading the garrison to expect an attack from that quarter. The guns were massed to landward, and no sooner was this done than Morgan sailed up through the channel with but little loss. Why the Spaniards did not close the passage with a boom does not appear. Probably they were glad to be quit of Morgan on any terms.

A great Spanish fleet he routed by the ingenious employment of a fire-ship. In a later expedition a strong place was taken by a curious accident. One of the buccaneers was shot through the body with an arrow. He drew it out, wrapped it in cotton, fired it from his musket, and so set light to a roof and burned the town.

His raid on Panama was extraordinary for the endurance of his men. For days they lived on the leather of bottles and belts. "Some, who were never out of their mothers' kitchens, may ask how these pirates could eat and digest these pieces of leather, so hard and dry? Whom I answer—that could they once experience what hunger, or rather famine is, they would find the way, as the pirates did". It was at the close of this march that the Indians drove wild bulls among them; but they cared very little for these new allies of the Spaniards: beef, in any form, was only too welcome.

Morgan burned the fair cedar houses of Panama, but lost the plate ship with all the gold and silver out of the churches. How he tortured a poor wretch who chanced to wear a pair of taffety trousers belonging to his master, with a small silver key hanging out, it is better not to repeat. The men only got two hundred pieces-of-eight each, after all their toil, for their Welshman was indeed a thief, and bilked his crews, no less than he plundered the Spaniards, without remorse. Finally, he sneaked away from the fleet with a ship or two; and it is to be feared that Captain Morgan made rather a good thing by dint of his incredible cruelty and villainy.

And so we leave Mr Esquemeling, whom Captain Morgan also deserted; for who would linger long when there is not even honour among thieves? Alluring as the pirate's profession is, we must not forget that it had a seamy side, and was by no means all rum and pieces-of-eight. And there is something repulsive to a generous nature in roasting men because they will not show you where to steal hogs.

AN ADVERTISEMENT TO THE READER CONCERNING THIS SECOND EDITION

The first edition of this History of the Buccaneers was received with such general applause of most people, but more especially of the learned, as to encourage me towards obliging the public with this second impression, though within the space of three months of time. This I have completed with the same cuts and maps, and all the other embellishments which the former had; and yet rendered it by the closeness of its character more easy to be purchased, as being comprehended in a fewer number of sheets of paper. Unto this second edition I have also added some relations which have been imparted to me from good and authentic hands; wherein are contained several other bold exploits and attempts, performed of late years by the same Buccaneers, especially since the time that the author of the first impression left those parts of the West Indies, and published his book in Holland. These are comprehended in two or three chapters at the latter end of this second edition, and do chiefly relate unto the adventures of Captain Cook in the year 1678, and the hazardous and bold attempts of Captain Sharp and others; who lately, setting forth from Jamaica, penetrated into the South Sea, and there ransacked and pillaged, for the space of three years, all they could meet, returning at last homewards about the Tierra del Fuego, commonly called Terra Australis Incognita, beyond the Strait of Magellan; and thus performing one of the boldest and longest voyages that ever was attempted in the world. Of all which voyage, and especially of all the soundings, ports, harbours, rivers, creeks, islands, rocks, towns, and cities belonging unto the whole navigation of the South Sea, he hath brought home such an exact description, and such complete maps, taken from the Spaniards themselves, who only navigate that ocean, as were never seen in these parts of the world before.

The very Journal of this triennial navigation, I am informed, is now in the press, being published by a worthy gentleman of my acquaintance ; the perusal whereof I hope will acquit what I have said to be nothing more nor less than the very truth itself.

What I here give my reader concerning Captain Sharp and his companions is only a short account of his transactions, which may serve for an accomplishment of this History of the Buccaneers (he being one of the same profession) ; which I received from the very hand of one of his seamen who was present at these exploits (and which was printing before I heard of the Journal of Captain Sharp): the which likewise how far it will agree with the Journal itself (as I hear is almost ready to be published) I cannot easily declare, as having not seen nor perused the said book. Yet thus much I am induced to believe of this narrative, though never so shortly compiled, that it will not much deviate from the substance of what matter of fact will be there rehearsed, and that the said Journal, when published, will appear, for its novelty and curiosity, to be as it were a Second Part of this History of the Buccaneers. All which notwithstanding, something may be yet remaining behind of this nature, wherewith in due time I may chance to pleasure the public, but not to be added to this volume, but to be a volume of itself, this first volume of the Buccaneers being as full as it can be made. Whatever shall for the future be published by me shall be put into another volume.

THE TRANSLATOR TO THE READER

The present volume, both for its curiosity and ingenuity, I dare recommend to the perusal of our English nation, whose glorious actions it contains. What relates to the curiosity hereof, this piece, both of natural and human history, was no sooner published in the Dutch original than it was snatched up for the most curious libraries of Holland: it was translated into Spanish (two impressions thereof being sent into Spain in one year); it was taken notice of by the learned Academy of Paris; and finally recommended as worthy of our esteem by the ingenious author of the 'Weekly Memorials for the Ingenious', printed here at London about two years ago. Neither all this undeservedly, seeing it enlarges our acquaintance of natural history, so much prized and inquired for by the learned of this present age, with several observations not easily to be found in other accounts already received from America; and, besides, it informs us (with huge novelty) of as great and bold attempts in point of military conduct and valour as ever were performed by mankind, without excepting here either Alexander the Great or Julius Cæsar or the rest of the Nine Worthies of Fame. Of all which actions, as we cannot but confess ourselves to have been ignorant hitherto (the very name of 'Buccaneers' being as yet known but to few of the ingenious, as their lives, laws, and conversation are in a manner unto none), so can they not choose but be admired, out of this ingenious Author, by whosoever is curious to learn the various revolutions of human affairs. But, more especially by our English nation, as unto whom these things more narrowly do appertain—we having here more than half the book filled with the unparalleled if not inimitable adventures and heroic exploits of our own countrymen and relations, whose undaunted and exemplary courage, when called upon by our King and Country, we ought to emulate.

From whence it has proceeded that nothing of this kind was ever as yet published in England I cannot easily determine, except, as some will say, from some secret 'Ragion di Stato'. Let the reason be as it will, this is certain, so much the more we are obliged to this present author, who, though a stranger to our nation, yet with that candour and fidelity has recorded our actions, as to render the metal of our true English valour to be the more believed and feared abroad than if these things had been divulged by ourselves at home. From hence peradventure will other nations learn that the English people are of their genius more inclinable to act than to write; seeing as well they as we have lived unacquainted with these actions of our nation, until such time as a foreign author to our country came to tell them.

Besides the merit of this piece for its curiosity, another point of no less esteem is the truth and sincerity wherewith everything seems to be penned. No greater ornament or dignity can be added to history, either human or natural, than truth. All other embellishments, if this be failing, are of little or no esteem; if this be delivered, are either needless or superfluous. What concerns this requisite in our author, his lines do everywhere declare the faithfulness and sincerity of his mind. He writes not by hearsay, but was an eye-witness, as he somewhere tells you, to all and every one of the bold and hazardous attempts which he relates. And these he delivers with such candour of style, such ingenuity of mind, such plainness of words, such conciseness of periods, so much divested of rhetorical hyperboles or the least flourishes of eloquence, so hugely void of passion or national reflections, that he strongly persuades all along to the credit of what he says—yea, raises the mind of the reader to believe these things far greater than what he has said; and, having read him, leaves only this scruple or concern behind, that you can read him no longer. In a word, such are his deserts that some persons peradventure would not stickle to compare him to the Father of Historians, Philip de Comines: at least, thus much may be said with all truth imaginable, that he resembles that great author in many of his excellent qualities.

I know some persons have objected to the greatness of these prodigious adventures, intimating that the resistance our Buccaneers found in America was everywhere but small. For the Spaniards, say they, in the West Indies are become of late years nothing less, but rather much more, degenerate than in Europe, the continual peace they have enjoyed in those parts, the defect of military discipline, and European soldiers for their commanders, much contributing hereunto. But more especially and above all other reasons the very luxury of the soil and riches, the extreme heat of those countries and influence of the stars being such as totally incline their bodies to an infinite effeminacy and cowardice of mind.

Unto these reasons I shall only answer in brief: This History will convince them to be manifestly false. For, as to the continual peace here alleged, we know that no peace could ever be established 'beyond the Line,' since the first possession of the West Indies by the Spaniards till the burning of Panama. At that time, or a few months before, Sir William Godolphin by his prudent negociation in quality of Ambassador for our most Gracious Monarch concluded at Madrid a peace to be observed even beyond the Line and through the whole extent of the Spanish Dominions in the West Indies. This transaction gave the Spaniards new causes of complaint against our proceedings, that no sooner a peace had been established for those parts of America but our Forces had taken and burnt both Chagre, St Catharine, and Panama. But our reply was convincing: That, whereas eight or ten months had been allowed by Articles for the publishing of the said peace through all the dominions of both monarchies in America, those hostilities had been committed, not only without orders from his Majesty of England but also within the space of the said eight or ten months of time. Until that time the Spanish inhabitants of America being, as it were, in a perpetual war with Europe, certain it is that no coasts nor kingdoms in the world have been more frequently infested or alarmed with the invasions of several nations than theirs. Thus, from the very beginning of their conquests in America, both English, French, Dutch, Portuguese, Swedes, Danes, Courlanders, and all other nations that navigate the ocean have frequented the West Indies, and filled them with their robberies and assaults. From these occasions have they been in continual watch and ward, and kept their militia in constant exercise, as also their garrisons pretty well provided and paid; as fearing every sail they discovered at sea to be pirates of one nation or another. But much more especially, since that Curaçoa, Tortuga, and Jamaica have been inhabited by English, French, and Dutch, and bred up that race of huntsmen than which no other ever was more desperate nor more mortal enemies to the

Spaniards, called Buccaneers. Now shall we say that these people, through too long continuation of peace, have utterly abolished the exercises of war, having been all along incessantly vexed with the tumults and alarms thereof?

In like manner is it false to accuse their defect of military discipline for want of European commanders. For who knows not that all places, both military and civil, through those vast dominions of the West Indies are provided out of Spain? And those of the militia most commonly given to expert commanders trained up from their infancy in the Wars of Europe, either in Africa, Milan, Sicily, Naples, or Flanders, fighting against either English, French, Dutch, Portuguese, or Moors? Yea, their very garrisons, if you search them in those parts, will peradventure be found to be stocked three parts to four with soldiers both born and bred in the kingdom of Spain.

From these considerations it may be inferred what little difference ought to be allowed betwixt the Spanish soldiers, inhabitants of the West Indies, and those of Europe. And how little the soil or climate has influenced or caused their courage to degenerate towards cowardice or baseness of mind. As if the very same arguments, deduced from the nature of that climate, did not equally militate against the valour of our famous Buccaneers, and represent this to be of as degenerate metal as theirs.

But nothing can be more clearly evinced than is the valour of the American Spaniards, either soldiers or officers, by the sequel of this history. What men ever fought more desperately than the garrison of Chagre—their number being 314, *and of all these only* 30 *remaining; of which number scarce* 10 *were unwounded, and among them not one officer found alive? Were not* 600 *killed upon the spot at Panama,* 500 *at Gibraltar, almost as many more at Puerto del Principe, all dying with their arms in their hands and facing bravely the enemy for the defence of their country and private concerns? Did not those of the town of San Pedro both fortify themselves, lay several ambuscades, and lastly sell their lives as dear as ever any European soldier could do,* L'Ollonais *being forced to gain step by step his advance unto the town with huge loss both of blood and men? Many other instances might be produced out of this compendious volume of the generous resistance the Spaniards made in several places, though fortune favoured not their arms.*

Next, as to the personal valour of many of their commanders, what man ever behaved himself more briskly than the Governor of Gibraltar, than the Governor of Puerto del Principe, both dying for the defence of their towns; than Don Alonso del Campo, and others? Or what examples can easily parallel the desperate courage of the Governor of Chagre, who, though the palisades were fired, the terrepleins [ramparts] *were sunk into the ditch, the breaches were entered, the houses all burnt about him, the whole castle taken, his men all killed, yet would not admit of any quarter, but chose rather to die under his arms, being shot into the brain, than surrender himself as a prisoner to the Buccaneers? What lion ever fought to the last gasp more obstinately than the Governor of Porto Bello, who, seeing the town entered by surprisal in the night, one chief castle blown up into the air, all the other forts and castles taken, his own assaulted several ways, both religious men and women placed at the front of the enemy to fix the ladders against the walls, yet spared not to kill as many of the said religious persons as he could; and at last, the walls being scaled, the castle entered and taken, all his own men overcome by fire and sword, who had cast down their arms and begged mercy from the enemy, yet would admit of none for his own life? Yea, with his own hands killed several of his soldiers, to force them to stand to their arms though all were lost. Yea, though his own wife and daughter begged of him upon their knees that he would save his life by craving quarter, though the enemy desired of him the same thing, yet would hearken to no cries nor persuasions, but they were forced to kill him, combating with his arms in his hands, being not otherwise able to take him prisoner as they were desirous to do. Shall these men be said to be influenced with cowardice, who thus acted to the very last scene of their own tragedies? Or shall we rather say that they wanted not courage, but fortune?—it being certainly true that he who is killed in a battle may be equally courageous with him that kills. And that whosoever derogates from the valour of the Spaniards in the West Indies diminishes in like manner the courage of the Buccaneers, his own countrymen, who have seemed to act beyond mortal men in America.*

Now, to say something concerning John Esquemeling, the first author of this history. I take him to be a Dutchman, or at least born in Flanders, notwithstanding that the Spanish translation represents him to be native of the kingdom of France—his printing this history originally in Dutch, which doubtless must be his native tongue, who otherwise was but an illiterate man, together with the very sound of his name, convincing me thereunto. True it is, he set sail from France, and was some years at Tortuga, but neither of these two arguments, drawn from the history, are prevalent. For, were he a Frenchman born, how came he to learn the Dutch language so perfectly as to prefer it to his own—especially that not being spoken at Tortuga nor Jamaica, where he resided all the while?

I hope I have made this English translation something more plain and correct than the Spanish. Some few notorious faults, either of the printer or of the interpreter, I am sure I have redressed. But, the Spanish translator complaining much of the intricacy of style in the original (as flowing from a person who, as hath been said, was no scholar) as he was pardonable, being in great haste, for not rendering his own version so distinct and elaborate as he could desire—so must I be excused from the one, that is to say elegance, if I have cautiously declined the other, I mean confusion.

THE BUCCANEERS OF AMERICA

PART I

CHAPTER I

The author sets forth towards the Western Islands, in the service of the West India Company of France. They meet with an English frigate, and arrive at the island of Tortuga

WE set sail from Havre de Grace, in France, in a ship called *St John*, the second day of May, in the year 1666. Our vessel was equipped with eight-and-twenty guns, 20 mariners, and 220 passengers, including in this number those whom the Company sent as free passengers, as being in their service. Soon after we came to an anchor under the Cape of Barfleur, there to join seven other ships of the same West India Company, which were to come from Dieppe under the convoy of a man-of-war, mounted with seven-and-thirty guns and 250 men Of these ships two were bound for Senegal, five for the Caribbee Islands, and ours for the island of Tortuga. In the same place there gathered unto us about twenty sail of other ships that were bound for Newfoundland, with some Dutch vessels that were going for Nantes, Rochelle, and St Martins; so that in all we made a fleet of thirty sail. Here we prepared to fight, putting ourselves into a convenient posture of defence, as having notice that four English frigates, of three-score guns each, did lie in wait for us about the Isle of Ornay. Our admiral, the Chevalier Sourdis, having distributed what orders he thought convenient, we set sail from thence with a favourable gale of wind. Presently after, some mists arising, these totally impeded the English frigates from discovering our fleet at sea. We steered our course as near as we could under the coast of France for fear of the enemy. As we sailed along, we met a vessel of Ostend, who complained to our admiral that a French privateer had robbed him that very morning. This complaint being heard, we endeavoured to pursue the said pirate ; but our labour was in vain, as not being able to overtake him.

Our fleet, as we went along, caused no small fears and alarms to the inhabitants of the coasts of France, these judging us to be English and that we sought some convenient place for landing. To allay their frights, we used to hang out our colours ; but, notwithstanding, they would not trust us. After this we came to an anchor in the Bay of Conquet, in Brittany, nigh unto the Isle of Ushant, there to take in water. Having stored ourselves with fresh provisions at this place, we prosecuted our voyage, designing to pass by the Ras of Fonteneau and not expose ourselves to the Sorlingues, fearing the English vessels that were cruising thereabouts to meet us. This river Ras is of a current very strong and rapid, which, rolling over many rocks, disgorges itself into the sea on the coast of France, in the latitude of eight-and-forty degrees and ten minutes. For which reason this passage is very dangerous, all the rocks as yet being not thoroughly known.

Here I shall not omit to mention the ceremony which at this passage, and some other places, is used by the mariners, and by them called ' Baptism ', although it may seem either little to our purpose or of no use. The master's mate clothed himself with a ridiculous sort of garment that reached unto his feet, and on his head he put a suitable cap, which was made very burlesque. In his right hand he placed a naked wooden sword, and in his left a pot full of ink. His face was horribly blacked with soot, and his neck adorned with a collar of many little pieces of wood. Being thus apparelled, he commanded to be called before him every one of them who never had passed that dangerous place before. And then, causing them to kneel down in his presence, he made the sign of the Cross upon their foreheads with ink, and gave each one a stroke on the shoulders with his wooden sword. Meanwhile the standers-by did cast a bucket of water upon every man's head; and this was the conclusion of the ceremony. But, that being ended, every one of the baptized is obliged to give a bottle of brandy for his offering, placing it nigh the main-mast, and without speaking a word, even those who have no such liquor being not excused from this performance. In case the vessel never passed that way before, the Captain is obliged to distribute some wine among the mariners and other people in the ship. But, as for other gifts which the newly baptized do frequently offer, they are divided among the old seamen, and of them they make a banquet among themselves.

The Hollanders likewise do use to baptize such as never passed that way before. And not only at the passage above-mentioned, but also at the rocks called Berlingues, near the coast of Portugal, in the latitude of 39 degrees and 40 minutes, as being a passage very dangerous, especially by night, when through the obscurity thereof the rocks are not distinguishable, by reason the land is very high, they use some such ceremony. But their manner of baptizing is quite distinct from that which we have described above as performed by the French. He, therefore, that is to be baptized is fastened, and hoisted up three times at the main-yard's end, as if he were a criminal. If he be hoisted the fourth time, in the name of the Prince of Orange or of the captain of the vessel, his honour is more than ordinary. Thus they are dipped, every one, several times into the main ocean. But he that is the first dipped has the honour of being saluted with a gun. Such as are not willing to fall are bound to pay twelve pence for their ransom; if he be an officer in the ship, two shillings; and, if a passenger, according to his pleasure. In case the ship never passed that way before, the captain is bound to give a small runlet of wine, which, if he does not perform, the mariners may cut off the stem of the vessel. All the profit which accrues by this ceremony is kept by the master's mate, who, after reaching their port, doth usually lay it out in wine, which is drunk amongst the ancient seamen. Some will say this ceremony was instituted by the Emperor Charles the Fifth; howsoever, it is not found amongst his Laws. But here I leave these customs of the sea, and shall return to our voyage.

Having passed the river Ras, we met with very good weather

until we came to Cape Finisterre. Here a huge tempest of wind surprised us, and separated our ship from the rest that were in our company. This storm continued for the space of eight days, in which time it would move compassion to see how miserably the passengers were tumbled to and fro on all sides of the ship; insomuch as the mariners in the performance of their duty were compelled to tread upon them everywhere. This uncouthsome weather being spent, we had again the use of very favourable gales until we came unto the Tropic of Cancer. This Tropic is nothing else but an imaginary circle which astrologers have invented in the heavens, and serves as a period to the progress of the sun towards the North Pole. It is placed in the latitude of 23 degrees and 30 minutes under the line. Here we were baptized the second time, after the same manner as before. The French do always perform this ceremony at this Tropic, as also under the Tropic of Capricorn, towards the South. In this part of the world we had very favourable weather, at which we were infinitely gladdened by reason of our great necessity of water. For at this time that element was already so scarce with us that we were stinted unto two half-pints per man every day.

Being about the latitude of Barbados, we met an English frigate, or privateer, who first began to give us chase; but, finding himself not to exceed us in strength, did presently steer away from us. This flight gave us occasion to pursue the said frigate, as we did, shooting at him several guns of eight-pound carriage. But at length he escaped, and we returned to our course. Not long after, we came within sight of the isle of Martinique. Our endeavours were bent towards the coast of the Isle of St Peter. But these were frustrated by reason of a storm which took us hereabouts. Hence we resolved to steer to the island of Guadaloupe. Yet neither this island could we reach by reason of the said storm, and thus we directed our course to the isle of Tortuga, which was the very same land we were bound unto. We passed along the coast of the isle of Porto Rico, which is extremely delicious and agreeable to the view, as being adorned with beautiful trees and woods, even to the tops of the mountains. After this, we discovered the island Hispaniola[1] (of which I

[1] The English corruption of *Española* [" Little Spain "], the name given by Columbus to the island of Haiti, discovered by him in 1492,

shall give a description in this book), and we coasted about it until we came unto the isle of Tortuga, our desired port. Here we anchored the seventh day of July in the same year, not having lost one man in the whole voyage. We unladed the goods that belonged unto the Company of the West Indies, and soon after the ship was sent to Cul de Sac with some passengers.

whereon he established the first Spanish colony in the New World. Subsequently it was neglected and became the prey of freebooters and Buccaneers. In old Latin maps it is called *Hispaniae Insula.* Next to Cuba, it is the largest of the West Indian islands. It was later divided politically into the republics of Haiti and Santo Domingo, the latter called after the city of that name.

CHAPTER II

Description of the island of Tortuga: of the fruits and plants there growing; how the French settled there, at two several times, and cast out the Spaniards, first masters thereof. The author of this book was twice sold in the said island

THE island of Tortuga is situated on the North side of the famous and great island called Hispaniola [Haiti], nigh unto the continent thereof and in the latitude of twenty degrees and thirty minutes. Its just extent is threescore leagues about. The Spaniards, who gave name to this island, called it so from the shape of the land, which in some manner resembles a great sea-tortoise, called by them *tortuga de mar*. The country is very mountainous and full of rocks, yet, notwithstanding, hugely thick of lofty trees that cease not to grow upon the hardest of those rocks without partaking of a softer soil. Hence it comes that their roots, for the greatest part, are seen all over entangled among the rocks, not unlike unto the branching of ivy against our walls. That part of this island which stretches towards the North is totally disinhabited. The reason is, first, because it has proved to be very incommodious and unhealthy, and, secondly, for the ruggedness of the coast, that gives no access to the shore, unless among rocks almost inaccessible. For this cause it is populated only on the Southern part, which has only one port that may be esteemed indifferently good. Yet this harbour has two several entries, or channels, which afford passage unto ships of 70 guns, the port itself being without danger and capable of receiving a great number of vessels. That part which is inhabited is divided into four other parts, of which the first is called the Low-Land, or Low-Country. This is the chiefest among the rest, because it contains the aforesaid port. The town is called Cayona, and here do live the chief and richest planters of the island. The second part is called the Middle Plantation. Its territory, or soil, is hitherto almost new, as being only known to be good for the culture of tobacco. The third is named Ringot. These places are situated towards the Western part of the island. The fourth, and last, is called The Mountain, in which place were made the first plantations that were cultivated upon this island.

As to the wood that grows on the island, we have already said that the trees are exceedingly tall and pleasing to the sight; whence no man will doubt but they may be applied unto several uses with great benefit. Such is the Yellow Saunder, which tree by the inhabitants of this country is called *bois de chandelle*, or in English Candlewood, because it burns like a candle, and serves them with light while they use their fishery in the night. Here also grows *lignum sanctum*, by others called *guaiacum*, the virtues of which are very well known, more especially unto them who observe not the sixth Commandment and are given to all manner of impure copulations, physicians drawing from hence, under several compositions, the greatest antidote for all venereal diseases, as also for cold and vicious humours. The trees likewise that afford *gummi elemi* grow here in great abundance, and in like manner *radix Chinæ*, or China root[1]; yet this is not so good as that which comes from other parts of the Western world. It is very white and soft, and serves for pleasant food unto the wild-boars when they can find nothing else. This island also is not deficient in aloes, nor an infinite number of other medicinal herbs, which may please the curiosity of such as are given to their contemplation. Moreover for the building of ships, or any other sort of architecture, here are found, in this spot of Neptune, several sorts of timber very convenient. The fruits, likewise, which here abundantly grow, are nothing inferior, as to their quantity or quality, unto what the adjacent islands produced. I shall name only some of the most ordinary and common. Such are magniot[2], potatoes, acajou apples[3],

[1] See note 2 on p. 31.

[2] Obsolete form of manioc, the cassava plant (genus Manihot): cf. Brooke's transl. of Le Blanc's *Travels* [1660], p. 399: "Mandioc a root is their chiefest diet, whereof they make flower [flour]."

[3] The cashew-nut tree (*anacardium occidentale*). Cf. J. Van Linschoten, *Voyages* [1598], Bk. ii, p. 251: "There is an other tree in

yannas[1], bacones, paquayes, carosoles, mamayns[2], ananas[3], and diverse other sorts, which, not to be tedious, I omit to specify. Here grow likewise in huge number those trees called palmettos, or palmites[4], whence is drawn a certain juice which serves the inhabitants instead of wine, and whose leaves do cover their houses instead of tiles.

In this island abounds also, with daily increase, the wild-boar. The Governor has prohibited the hunting of them with dogs, fearing lest, the island being but small, the whole race of those animals in short time should be destroyed. The reason why he thought convenient to preserve those wild-beasts was that in case of any invasion of an external enemy the inhabitants might sustain themselves with their food, especially if they were constrained to retire unto the woods and mountains. By this means he judged they were enabled to maintain any sudden assault or long persecution. Yet this sort of game is almost impeded by itself, by reason of the many rocks and precipices, which for the greatest part are covered with little shrubs, very green and thick, whence the huntsmen have ofttimes precipitated themselves, and left us the sad experience and grief of many memorable disasters.

At a certain time of the year there resort unto this island of Tortuga huge flocks of wild-pigeons, at which season the inhabitants feed on them very plentifully, having more than they can consume, and leaving totally to their repose all other sorts of fowl, both wild and tame, to the intent that in absence of the pigeons these may supply their place. But as nothing in the universe, though never so pleasant, can be found but what has something of bitterness joined to it, the

bignesse like a sorben, the fruit whereof is by them called *Aca-iou*, of forme and greatness like a hennes egge, which being ripe is of a golde yellow colour like a quince, very good and savory to eate, having a certayne sharpe taste, and in it a juice that cooleth heate."

[1] Yams. Span. *ñame:* other English forms are (1) *nname*: cf. Mendoza, *Hist. of China*, trans. by Parke [1589], vol. ii, p. 256 of 1854 edn.: "nnames, patatas, fish, rise, ginger, hennes; (2) *jamb:* cf. Bosman, *Guinea*, transl. 1705: "Their common food is a pot full of millet . . . or instead of that jambs and potatoes."

[2] Mammees (*Mammea americana*), a large tree of tropical America, bearing a large fruit with a yellow pulp of pleasant taste.

[3] Pine-apples. Cf. Hakluyt, *Voyages* [1600], vol. iii, p. 319: "a fruite of great excellencie which they call ananas." According to Evelyn's *Diary*, 19 July, 1661, *ananassa sativa* was first seen in England in 1657.

[4] Spanish *palmito*, the dwarf fan-palm.

very symbol of this truth we see in the aforesaid pigeons. For these, the season being past wherein God has appointed them to afford delicious food unto those people, can scarcely be touched with the tongue, they become so extremely lean and bitter even to admiration. The reason of this bitterness is attributed unto a certain seed which they eat about that time, even as bitter as gall. About the sea-shores everywhere are found great multitudes of crabs belonging both to the land and sea, and both sorts very big. These are good to feed servants and slaves[1], who find them very pleasing to the palate, yet withal very hurtful to the sight. Besides which symptom, being eaten too often, they also cause great giddiness in the head, with much weakness of the brain, insomuch that very frequently they are deprived of sight for the space of one quarter of an hour.

The French, having established themselves in the isle of St Christopher, planted there a sort of trees, of which at present there possibly may be greater quantities. With the timber of those trees they made long-boats and hoys[2], which they sent thence westward, being well manned and victualled, to discover other islands. These, setting sail from St Christopher, came within sight of the island of Hispaniola, where at length they arrived with abundance of joy. Having landed, they marched into the country, where they found huge quantities of cattle, such as cows, bulls, horses, and wild-boars. But finding no great profit in those animals unless they could enclose them, and knowing likewise the island to be pretty well peopled by the Spaniards, they thought it convenient to enterprize upon and seize the island of Tortuga. This they performed without any difficulty, there being upon the island no more than ten or twelve Spaniards to guard it. These few men let the French come in peaceably and possess the island for the space of six months, without any trouble. In the meanwhile they passed and repassed with their canoes to Hispaniola, whence they transported many people, and at last began to plant the whole isle of Tortuga. The few

[1] Some of the land-crabs of the West Indies are to-day regarded as delicacies—especially the violet land-crab.

[2] Dutch *heude, heu*, a small, yet heavy, coasting-vessel for goods or passengers, particularly in short distances at the sea-coast. Cf. Hakluyt, *Voyages*, vol. i, p. 160 [1598]: "English pinasses, hoyes, and drumblers."

Spaniards remaining there, perceiving the French to increase their number daily, began at last to repine at their prosperity and grudged them the possession they had freely given. Hence they gave notice to others of their own nation, their neighbours, who sent several great boats, well armed and manned, to dispossess the French of that island. This expedition succeeded according to their desires. For the new possessors, seeing the great number of Spaniards that came against them, fled with all they had unto the woods; and hence by night they wafted over with canoes unto the isle of Hispaniola. This they more easily performed as having no women or children with them, nor any great substance to carry away. Here they also retired into the woods, both to seek themselves food, and thence with secrecy to give intelligence to others of their own faction, as judging for certain that within a little while they should be in a capacity to hinder the Spaniards from fortifying in Tortuga.

Meanwhile the Spaniards of the greater island ceased not to seek after their new guests, the French, with intent to root them out of the woods, if possible, or cause them to perish with hunger. But this their design soon failed, having found that the French were masters both of good guns, powder, and bullets. Here, therefore, the fugitives waited for a certain opportunity, wherein they knew the Spaniards were to come from Tortuga, with arms and great number of men, to join with those of the greater island for their destruction. When this occasion proffered, they in the meanwhile deserting the woods where they were, returned unto Tortuga, and dispossessed the small number of Spaniards that remained at home. Having so done, they fortified themselves as best they could, thereby to prevent the return of the Spaniards, in case they should attempt it. Moreover, they sent immediately unto the Governor of St Christopher, craving his aid and relief, and demanding of him to send them a Governor, the better to be united among themselves and strengthened on all occasions. The Governor of St Christopher received their petition with expressions of much satisfaction and without any delay sent to them Monsieur le Passeur in quality of a Governor, together with a ship full of men and all other things necessary both for their establishment and defence. No sooner had they received this recruit than the Governor commanded a fortress to be built upon the top of a high rock, whence he could hinder the access of any ships or other vessels that should design to enter the port. Unto this fort no other access could be had than by almost climbing through a very narrow passage that was capable only of receiving two persons at once, and those not without difficulty. In the middle of this rock was a great cavity, which now serves for a storehouse; and, besides, here was a great convenience for raising a battery. The fort being finished, the Governor commanded two guns to be mounted, which could not be performed without huge toil and labour, as also a house to be built within the fort; and, afterwards, the narrow way that led unto the said fort to be broken and demolished, leaving no other ascent thereto than by a ladder. Within the fort gushes out a plentiful fountain of fresh water, which perpetually runs with a pure and crystalline stream sufficient to refresh a garrison of a thousand men. Being possessed of these conveniences, and the security these things might promise, the French began to people the island, and each of them to seek his living, some by the exercise of hunting, others by planting tobacco, and others by cruising and robbing upon the coasts of the Spanish islands—which trade is continued by them to this day.

The Spaniards, notwithstanding, could not behold but with jealous eyes the daily increase of the French in Tortuga, fearing lest in time they might by them be dispossessed also of Hispaniola. Thus, taking an opportunity when many of the French were abroad at sea and others employed in hunting, with 800 men in several canoes, they landed again in Tortuga, almost without being perceived by the French. But, finding that the Governor had cut down many trees, for the better discovery of an enemy in case of any assault, as also that nothing of consequence could be done without great guns, they consulted about the fittest place for raising a battery. This place was soon concluded to be the top of a mountain which was in sight, seeing that thence alone they could level their guns at the fort, which now lay open to them since the cutting down of the trees by the new possessors. Hence they resolved to open a way for carriage of some pieces of ordnance to the top. This mountain is somewhat high, and the upper part thereof plain, from whence the whole island may be viewed. The sides thereof are very rugged by reason of an huge number of inaccessible rocks surrounding it everywhere ; so that the ascent was very difficult, and would always have been the same, had not the Spaniards undergone the immense labour and toil of making the way aforementioned, as I shall now relate.

The Spaniards had in their company many slaves and Indians, labouring men, whom they call *matates*, or, in English, half-yellow men. Unto these they gave orders with iron tools to dig a way through the rocks. This they performed with the greatest speed imaginable. And through this way by the help of many ropes and pulleys, they at last made shift to get up two sole cannon-pieces, wherewith they made a battery, and intended next day to batter the fort. Meanwhile the French were not ignorant of these designs, but rather prepared themselves for a defence (while the Spaniards were busied about the battery), sending notice everywhere to their companions and requiring their help. Thus the hunters of the island all joined together, and with them all the pirates who were not already too far from home. These landed by night at Tortuga, lest they should be seen by the Spaniards. And, under the same obscurity of the night, they all together by a back way climbed up the mountain where the Spaniards were posted ; which they more easily could perform as being acquainted with those rocks. They came thither at the very instant that the Spaniards, who were above, were preparing to shoot at the fort, not knowing in the least of their coming. Here they set upon them, at their backs, with such fury as forced the greatest part to precipitate themselves from the top to the bottom, and dash their bodies in pieces. Few or none escaped this attack, for if any remained alive they were all put to the sword, without giving quarter to the meanest. Some Spaniards did still keep the bottom of the mountain, but, hearing the shrieks and cries of them that were killed and believing some tragical revolution to be above, fled immediately towards the sea, despairing, through this accident, to ever regain the isle of Tortuga.

The Governors of this island did always behave themselves as proprietors and absolute lords thereof until the year 1664 ; at which time the West India Company of France took possession thereof, and sent thither for their Governor

Monsieur Ogeron. These planted the colony for themselves, by the means of their factors and servants, thinking to drive some considerable trade thence with the Spaniards, even as the Hollanders do from Curaçoa. But this design did not answer their expectation. For with other nations they could drive no trade, by reason they could not establish any secure commerce from the beginning with their own. Forasmuch as at the first institution of this Company in France, they made an agreement with the pirates, hunters, and planters, first possessors of Tortuga, that these should buy all their necessaries from the said Company, taking them upon trust. And, although this agreement was put in execution, yet the factors of the Company soon after found that they could not recover either moneys or returns from those people. Insomuch as they were constrained to bring some armed men into the island, in behalf of the Company, for to get in some of their payments. But neither this endeavour nor any other could prevail towards settling the secure trade with those of the island. And hereupon the Company recalled their factors, giving them orders to sell all that was their own in the said plantation, both the servants belonging to the Company (which were sold, some for 20, others for 30, pieces-of-eight)[1], as also all other merchandizes and properties which they had there. With this resolution all their designs fell to the ground.

In this occasion I was also sold, as being a servant under the said Company, in whose service I came out of France. But my fortune was very bad, for I fell into the hands of the most cruel tyrant and perfidious man that ever was born of woman, who was then Governor, or rather Lieutenant-General, of that island. This man treated me with all the hard usages imaginable, yea, with that of hunger, with which I thought to have perished inevitably. Withal he was willing to let me buy my freedom and liberty, but not under the rate of 300 pieces-of-eight, I not being master of one, at that time, in the whole world. At last through the manifold miseries I endured, as also affliction of mind, I was thrown into a dangerous fit of sickness. This misfortune, being added to the rest of my calamities, was the cause of my happiness. For my wicked master, seeing my condition, began to fear lest he should lose his moneys with my life.

[1] See note on p. 60.

Hereupon he sold me the second time to a surgeon for the price of 70 pieces-of-eight. Being in the hands of this second master, I began soon after to recover my health through the good usage I had received from him, as being much more humane and civil than that of my first patron. He gave me both clothes and very good food, and after that I had served him but one year he offered me my liberty, with only this condition, that I should pay him 100 pieces-of-eight when I was in a capacity of wealth so to do.. Which kind proposal of his I could not choose but accept with infinite joy and gratitude of mind.

Being now at liberty, though like unto Adam when he was first created by the hands of his Maker—that is, naked and destitute of all human necessaries, nor knowing how to get my living—I determined to enter into the wicked order of the Pirates, or Robbers at Sea. Into this Society I was received with common consent both of the superior and vulgar sort, and among them I continued until the year 1672. Having assisted them in all their designs and attempts, and served them in many notable exploits, of which hereafter I shall give the reader a true account, I returned to my own native country. But, before I begin to relate the things above-mentioned, I shall say something, for the satisfaction of such as are curious, of the island Hispaniola, which lies towards the Western parts of America, as also give my reader a brief description thereof, according to my slender ability and experience.

CHAPTER III

Description of the great and famous island of Hispaniola

THE very large and rich island called Hispaniola lies situate in the latitude of seventeen degrees and a half. The greatest part thereof extends, from East to West, 20 degrees Southern latitude. The circumference is 300 leagues, the length 120, its breadth almost 50, being more or less broad or narrow at certain places. I shall not need here to insert how this island was at first discovered, it being known unto the world that it was performed by the means of Christopher Columbus, in the year 1492, being sent for this purpose by Ferdinand the Catholic, then King of Spain. From which time, to this present, the Spaniards have been continually possessors thereof. There are upon this island many very good and strong cities, towns, and hamlets ; as also it abounds in a great number of pleasant and delicious country-houses and plantations—all which are owing unto the care and industry of the Spaniards, its inhabitants.

The chief city and metropolis of this island is called San Domingo, being dedicated to St Dominic, from whom it derives this name. It is situated towards the South, in a place which affords a most excellent prospect, the country round about being embellished with innumerable rich plantations, as also verdant meadows and fruitful gardens—all which do produce plenty and variety of excellent and pleasant fruits, according to the nature of those countries. The Governor of the island makes his residence in this city, which is, as it were, the storehouse of all the other cities, towns, and villages, which hence export and provide themselves with all necessaries whatsoever for human life. And yet has it this particularity above many other cities in other places, that it entertains no external commerce with any other nation than its own, the Spaniards. The greatest part of the inhabitants are rich and substantial merchants, or such as are shopkeepers and do sell by retail.

Another city of this island is named Santiago, or, in English, St James, as being consecrated to the Apostle of that name. This is an open place, without either walls or castle, situate in the latitude of 19 degrees South. The greatest part of the inhabitants are hunters and planters, the adjacent territory and soil being very proper for the said exercises of its constitution. The city is surrounded with large and delicious fields, as much pleasing to the view as those of San Domingo ; and these abound with all sorts of beasts, both wild and tame, whence are taken a huge number of skins and hides, that afford unto the owners a very considerable traffic.

Towards the Southern parts of this island is seen another city called Nuestra Señora del Alta Gracia. The territory hereof produces great quantities of cacao, which occasions the inhabitants to make great store of the richest sort of chocolate. Here grows also much ginger and tobacco ; and much tallow is prepared of the beasts which hereabouts are hunted.

The inhabitants of this beautiful island of Hispaniola often go and come in their canoes to the Isle of Savona, not far distant thence, where is their chief fishery, expecially of tortoises. Hither those fish constantly resort in huge multitudes at certain seasons of the year, there to lay their eggs, burying them in the sands of the shore. Thus by the heat of the sun, which in those parts is very ardent, they are hatched, and continue the propagation of their species. This island of Savona has little or nothing that is worthy consideration or may merit any particular description, as being so extremely barren by reason of its sandy soil. True it is that here grows some small quantity of *lignum sanctum* or *guaiacum*, of whose use we have said something in another place.

Westwards of the city of San Domingo is also situated another great village, called by the name of El Pueblo del Aso, or the Town of Aso. The inhabitants of this town drive a great commerce and traffic with those of another village, which is placed in the very middle of the island and is called San Juan de Goave, or St John of Goave. This place is environed with a magnificent prospect of gardens, woods, and meadows. Its territory extends above twenty leagues in length, and grazes an huge number of wild bulls and cows. In this village scarce dwell any others than hunters and butchers, who flay the beasts that are killed. These are for the most part a mongrel sort of people of several bloods; some of which are born of white European people and negroes, and these are called *mulattos*. Others are born of Indians and white people, and such are termed *mestizos*[1]. But others are begotten of negroes and Indians, and these also have their peculiar name, being called *alcatraces*[2]. Besides which sorts of people, there are several other species and races, both here and in other places of the West Indies, of whom this account may be given, that the Spaniards love better the negro women, in those Western parts, or the tawny Indian females, than their own white European race, when as peradventure the negroes

[1] Cf. Hakluyt, *Voyages* [1600], vol. iii, p. 482: "Paul Horsewell is married to a *Mestisa*, as they name those whose fathers were Spaniards, and their mothers Indians."

[2] A nickname. "The alcatrace is a sea-fowle different to all that I have seen, either on the land or in the see. His head is like to the head of a gull, but his bill like unto a snytes bill, somewhat shorter and in all places alike. . . . He is all blacke of the colour of a crow."—Hawkins, *Voyage into the South Sea* [1593–1622], § xix (p. 153 of the 1878 edition).

and Indians have greater inclinations to the white women, or those that come near them, the tawny, than their own. From the said village are exported yearly vast quantities of tallow and hides, they exercising no other traffic nor toil. For, as to the lands in this place, they are not cultivated, by reason of the excessive dryness of the soil. These are the chiefest places that the Spaniards possess in this island, from the Cape of Lobos towards St John de Goave unto the Cape of Samana, nigh the sea, on the North side, and from the Eastern part towards the sea, called Punta d'Espada. All the rest of the island is possessed by the French, who are also planters and hunters.

This island has very good ports for ships, from the Cape of Lobos to the Cape of Tiburon, which lies on the Western side thereof. In this space of land there are no less than four ports, which exceed in goodness, largeness, and security even the very best of England. Besides these, from the Cape of Tiburon unto the Cape of Donna Maria, there are two very excellent ports, and from this Cape to the Cape of St Nicholas there are no less than twelve others. Every one of these ports has also the confluence of two or three good rivers, in which are found several sorts of fish, very pleasing to the palate and also in great plenty. The country hereabouts is sufficiently watered with large and profound rivers and brooks so that this part of the land may easily be cultivated without any great fear of droughts, it being certain that better streams are not to be found in any part of the world. The sea-coasts and shores are also very pleasant, unto which the tortoises resort in huge numbers, there to lay their eggs.

This island was formerly very well peopled on the North side thereof with many towns and villages ; but these, being ruined by the Hollanders, were at last for the greatest part deserted by the Spaniards.

CHAPTER IV

Of the Fruits, Trees, and Animals that are found at Hispaniola

THE spacious fields of this island do commonly extend themselves to the length of five or six leagues, the beauty whereof is so pleasing to the eye that, together with the great variety of their natural productions, they infinitely applaud and captivate the senses of the contemplator. For here at once they not only, with diversity of objects, recreate the sight, but, with many of the same, also do please the smell, and, with most, contribute abundance of delights to the taste. With sundry diversities also they flatter and excite the appetite; but more especially with the multitude of oranges and lemons, here growing both sweet and sour, and those that participate of both tastes and are only pleasantly tart. Besides which, here abundantly grow several other sorts of the same fruit, such as are called citrons, toronjas, and limes, in English not improperly called crab-lemons. True it is that, as to the lemons, they exceed not here the bigness of a hen's egg, which smallness distinguishes them from those of Spain most frequently used in these our Northern countries. The date-trees, which here are seen to cover the whole extent of very spacious plains, are exceedingly tall in their proportion, which notwithstanding does not offend but rather delight the view. Their height is observed to be from 150 to 200 feet, being wholly destitute of branches unto the very tops. Here it is there grows a certain pleasant white substance not unlike unto that of white cabbage, whence the branches and leaves do sprout, and in which also the seed or dates are contained. Every month one of those branches falls to the ground, and at the same time another sprouts out. But the seed ripens not but once in the year. The dates are food extremely coveted by the hedgehogs. The white substance growing at the top of the tree is used by the Spaniards after the same manner for common sustenance as cabbage in Europe, they cutting it into slices, and boiling it in their *ollas*[1], with all sorts of meat. The leaves of this sort of date-tree are seven or eight foot in length and three or four in breadth, being very fit to cover houses with. For they defend from rain equally with the best tiles, though never so rudely huddled together. They make use of them also to wrap up smoked flesh with, and to make a certain sort of buckets wherewith to carry water, though no longer durable than the space of six, seven, or eight days. The cabbages of these trees, for so we may call them, are of a greenish colour on the outside, though inwardly very white, whence may be separated a sort of rind, which is very like unto parchment, being fit to write upon as we do upon paper. The bodies of these trees are of an huge bulk or thickness, which two men can hardly compass with their arms. And yet they cannot properly be termed woody, but only three or four inches deep in thickness, all the rest of the internal part being very soft, insomuch that, paring off those three or four inches of woody substance, the remaining part of the body may be sliced like new cheese. They wound them three or four foot above the root, and, making an incision or broach in the body, thence gently distils a sort of liquor, which in short time by fermentation becomes as strong as the richest wine, and which does easily inebriate if not used with moderation. The French call this sort of palm-trees 'frank-palms,' and they only grow, both here and elsewhere, in saltish grounds.

Besides these palm-trees of which we have made mention, there are also in Hispaniola four other species of palms, which are distinguished by the names of *latanier*, *palma espinosa* or prickle-palm, *palma á chapelet* or rosary-palm, *palma vinosa* or wine-palm. The latanier-palm is not so tall as the wine-palm, although it has almost the same shape, only that the leaves are very like unto the fans our women use. They grow mostly in gravelly and sandy ground, their circumference being of seven foot more or less. The body has many prickles or

[1] A Spanish word, meaning a round earthen pot, a dish compounded of various kinds of meat and vegetables. Cf. Howell, *Letters* [1630], V, 38: "He can marinat [marinade = pickle] fish, make gellies . . . besides, he is passing good for an *ollia*."

thorns of the length of half a foot, very sharp and pungent. It produces its seed after the same manner as that abovementioned, which likewise serves for food unto the wild beasts.

Another sort of these palm-trees is called prickle-palm, as we said before, by reason it is infinitely full of prickles, from the root to the very leaves thereof, much more than the precedent. With these prickles some of the barbarous Indians use to torment their prisoners of war whom they take in battle. They tie them to a tree, and then, taking these thorns, they put them into little pellets of cotton, which they dip in oil, and thus stick them in the sides of the miserable prisoners, as thick as the bristles of a hedgehog; which of necessity cause an incredible torment to the patient. Afterwards they set them on fire, and, if the tormented prisoner sings in the midst of his torments and flames, he is esteemed as a valiant and courageous soldier who neither fears his enemies nor their torments. But if, on the contrary he cries out, they esteem him but as a poltroon or coward and unworthy of any memory. This custom was told me by an Indian, who said he had used his enemies thus oftentimes. The like cruelties to these many Christians have seen while they lived among those barbarians. But returning unto the prickle-palm, I shall only tell you that this palm-tree is in this only different from the latanier, that the leaves are like unto those of the frank-palm. Its seed is like unto that of the other palm-trees, being only much bigger and rounder, almost as a farthing, and inwardly full of little kernels, which are as pleasing to the taste as our walnuts in Europe. This tree grows for the most part in the marshes and low grounds of the sea-coast.

The wine-palm is so called from the abundance of wine which is gathered from it. This palm grows in high and rocky mountains, not exceeding in tallness the height of 40 or 50 foot, but yet of an extraordinary shape or form. For, from the root unto the half of its proportion, it is only three or four inches thick. But, upwards, something above the two-thirds of its height, it is as big and as thick as an ordinary bucket or milk-pail. Within, it is full of a certain matter very like unto the tender stalk of a white cabbage, which is very juicy of a liquor that is much pleasing to the palate. This liquor after fermentation and settling of the grounds reduces itself into a very good and clear wine, which is purchased[1] with no great industry. For, having wounded the tree with an ordinary hatchet, they make a square incision or orifice in it, through which they bruise the said matter until it be capable of being squeezed out, or expressed with the hands, they needing no other instrument than this. With the leaves they make certain vessels, not only to settle and purify the aforementioned liquor, but also to drink in. It bears its fruit like other palms, but of a very small shape, being not unlike cherries. The taste hereof is very good, but of dangerous consequence unto the throat, where it causes huge and extreme pains, that produce malignant quinsies in them that eat it.

The *palma à chapelet*, or rosary-palm, was thus called both by the French and Spaniards because its seed is very fit to make rosaries or beads to say prayers upon, the beads being small, hard, and capable of being easily bored for that use. This fourth species grows on the tops of the highest mountains, and is of an excessive tallness, but withal very straight and adorned with very few leaves.

Here grows also in this island a certain sort of apricot-trees, whose fruit equals in bigness that of our ordinary melons. The colour is like unto ashes, and the taste the very same as that of our apricots in Europe, the inward stones of this fruit being of the bigness of a hen's egg. On these the wild-boars feed very deliciously, and fatten even to admiration.

The trees called caremites are very like unto our pear-trees, whose fruits resemble much our Damascene plums or pruants[2] of Europe, being of a very pleasant and agreeable taste and almost as sweet as milk. This fruit is black on the inside, and the kernels thereof, sometimes only two in number, sometimes three, others five, of the bigness of a lupin. This plum affords no less pleasant food to the wild-boars than the apricots above-mentioned, only that it is not so commonly to be found upon the island, nor in such quantity as those are.

The genipa-trees are seen everywhere all over this island, being very like unto our cherry-trees, although its branches are more dilated. The fruit hereof is of an ash-colour, of the bigness of two fists, which interiorly is full of many

[1] See note on p. 67.

[2] Prunes: cf. Elyot, *Castel of Helthe* [1533], Bk. ii, p. 27: "The damask prune rather bindeth than lowseth, and is more commodious vnto the stomake."

prickles or points that are involved under a thin membrane or skin, the which, if not taken away at the time of eating, causes great obstructions and gripings of the belly. Before this fruit grows ripe, if pressed, it affords a juice as black as ink, being fit to write withal upon paper. But the letters disappear within the space of nine days, the paper remaining as white as if it never had been written upon. The wood of this tree is very strong, solid, and hard, good to build ships withal, seeing it is observed to last many years in the water without putrefaction.

Besides these, divers other sorts of trees are natives of this delicious island, that produce very excellent and pleasant fruits. Of these I shall omit to name several, knowing there are entire volumes of learned authors that have both described and searched them with greater attention and curiosity than my own. Notwithstanding, I shall continue to make mention of some few more in particular. Such are the cedars, which trees this part of the world produces in prodigious quantity. The French nation calls them *acajou*[1]; and they find them very useful for the building of ships and canoes. These canoes are like little wherry-boats, being made of one tree only, excavated, and fitted for the sea. They are withal so swift as for that very property they may be called 'Neptune's post-horses'. The Indians make these canoes without the use of any iron instruments, by only burning the trees at the bottom nigh the root, and afterwards governing the fire with such industry as nothing is burnt more than what they would have. Some of them have hatchets made of flint, wherewith they scrape, or pare off, whatsoever was burnt too far. And thus, by the sole instrument of fire, they know how to give them that shape which renders them capable of navigating threescore or fourscore leagues with ordinary security.

As to medicinal productions, here is to be found the tree that affords the *gum elemi* used in our apothecaries' shops. Likewise *guaiacum*, or *lignum sanctum*; *lignum aloes*, or aloe-wood; *cassia lignea*; China-roots[2]; with several others. The

[1] The French *acajou* is mahogany—loosely used here for cedar.

[2] The name of the tuber of various species of smilax, allied to sarsaparilla, at one time used to relieve gout and to purify the blood. Cf. "The tree likewise that affords *Gummi Elemi* grows here in great abundance; as doth *Radix Chinæ*, or China-root."—*Description of the Isthmus of Darien* [1699], p. 4.

tree called *mapou*, besides that it is medicinal, is also used for making of canoes, as being very thick ; yet is it much inferior to the *acajou* or cedar, as being somewhat spongy, whereby it sucks in much water, which renders it dangerous in navigation. The tree called *acoma* has its wood very hard and heavy, of the colour of palm. These qualities render it very fit to make oars for the sugar-mills. Here are also in great quantities *brasilete*, or brazil-wood, and that which the Spaniards call *mançanilla*.

Brazil-wood is now very well known in the provinces of Holland and the Low Countries. By another name it is called by the Spaniards *lenna de peje palo*. It serves only, or chiefly, for dyeing and what belongs to that trade. It grows abundantly along the sea-coasts of this island, especially in two places called Jacmel and Jaquina. These are two commodious ports or bays, capable of receiving ships of the greatest bulk.

The tree called *mançanilla*, or dwarf apple-tree, grows nigh unto the sea-shore, being naturally so low that its branches, though never so short, always touch the water. It bears a fruit something like unto our sweet-scented apples which, notwithstanding, is of a very venomous quality. For, these apples being eaten by any person, he instantly changes colour, and such an huge thirst seizes him as all the water of the Thames cannot extinguish, he dying raving mad within a little while after. But, what is more, the fish that eat, as it often happens, of this fruit are also poisonous. This tree affords also a liquor, both thick and white, like unto the fig-tree, which, if touched by the hand, raises blisters upon the skin, and these are so red in colour as if it had been deeply scalded with hot water. One day being hugely tormented with mosquitos, or gnats, and as yet unacquainted with the nature of this tree, I cut a branch thereof, to serve me instead of a fan, but all my face swelled the next day and filled with blisters, as if it were burnt to such a degree that I was blind for three days.

Ycao is the name of another sort of tree, so called by the Spaniards, which grows by the sides of rivers. This bears a certain fruit, not unlike unto our bullace or damson-plums. And this food is extremely coveted by the wild-boar, when at its perfect maturity ; with which they fatten as much as our hogs with the sweetest acorns of Spain. These trees love sandy ground, yet are so low that, their branches being very large, they take up a great circumference, almost couched upon the ground. The trees named *abelcoses* bear fruit of like colour with the *ycaos* above-mentioned, but of the bigness of melons, the seeds or kernels being as big as eggs. The substance of this fruit is yellow, and of a pleasant taste; which the poorest among the French do eat instead of bread, the wild-boar not caring at all for this fruit. These trees grow very tall and thick, being somewhat like unto our largest sort of pear-trees.

As to the insects which this island produces, I shall only take notice of three sorts of flies, which excessively torment all human bodies, but more especially such as never before, or but a little while, were acquainted with these countries. The first sort of these flies is as big as our common horse-flies in Europe. And these, darting themselves upon men's bodies, there stick and suck their blood till they can no longer fly. Their importunity obliges to make almost continual use of branches of trees wherewith to fan them away. The Spaniards in those parts call them mosquitos[1] or gnats, but the French give them the name of *maranguines*. The second sort of these insects is no bigger than a grain of sand. These make no buzzing noise, as the preceding species does, for which reason it is less avoidable, as being able also through its smallness to penetrate the finest linen or cloth. The hunters are forced to anoint their faces with hog's-grease, thereby to defend themselves from the stings of these little animals. By night, in their huts or cottages, they constantly for the same purpose burn the leaves of tobacco, without which smoke they were not able to rest. True it is that in the daytime they are not very troublesome, in case any wind be stirring, for this, though never so little, causes them to dissipate. The gnats of the third species exceed not the bigness of a grain of mustard. The colour is red[2]. These sting not at all, but do bite so sharply upon the flesh as to create little ulcers therein. Whence it often comes that the face swells and is rendered hideous to the view, through this inconvenience. These are

[1] Bosman, in his *Guinea* [transl. 1705], refers to "the innumerable millions of gnats, which the Portuguese call musquito's"—*Letter* xxi.

[2] The *bête rouge*, to this day a pest in the West Indies.

chiefly troublesome by day, even from the beginning of the morning until sun-setting, after which time they take up their rest, and permit human bodies to do the same. The Spaniards gave these insects the name of *rojados*, and the French that of *calarodes*.

The insects which the Spaniards call *cochinillas*, and the English glow-worms, are also to be found in these parts. These are very like unto such as we have in Europe, unless that they are somewhat bigger and longer than ours. They have two little specks on their heads, which by night give so much light that three or four of those animals, being together upon a tree, it is not discernible at a distance from a bright shining fire. I had on a certain time at once three of these *cochinillas* in my cottage, which there continued until past midnight, shining so brightly that without any other light I could easily read in any book, although of never so small a print. I attempted to bring some of these insects into Europe when I came from those parts, but as soon as they came into a colder climate they died by the way. They lost also their shining upon the change of air, even before their death. This shining is so great, according to what I have related, that the Spaniards with great reason may well call them from their luminous quality *moscas de fuego*, that is to say fire-flies.

There be also in Hispaniola an excessive number of *grillones* or crickets. These are of an extraordinary magnitude, if compared to ours, and so full of noise that they are ready to burst themselves with singing, if any person comes near them. Here is no lesser number of reptiles, such as serpents are and others, but by a particular providence of the Creator these have no poison. Neither do they any other harm than unto what fowl they can catch, but more especially unto pullets, pigeons, and others of this kind. Ofttimes these serpents or snakes are useful in houses to cleanse them of rats and mice. For with great cunning they counterfeit their shrieks, and hereby both deceive and catch them at their pleasure. Having taken them, they in no wise eat the guts of these vermin, but only suck their blood at first. Afterwards throwing away the guts, they swallow almost entire the rest of the body, which, as it should seem, they readily digest into soft excrements, of which they discharge their bellies. Another sort of reptiles belonging to this island is called by the name of *caçadores de moscas*, or fly-catchers. This name was given unto this reptile by the Spaniards, by reason they never could experience it lived upon any other food than flies. Hence it cannot be said this creature causes any harm unto the inhabitants, but rather benefit, seeing it consumes by its continual exercise of hunting the vexatious and troublesome flies.

Land-tortoises here be also in great quantities. They mostly breed in mud and fields that are overflown with water. The inhabitants eat them, and testify they are very good food. But a sort of spider which is here found is very hideous. These are as big as an ordinary egg, and their feet as long as those of the biggest sea-crabs. Withal, they are very hairy, and have four black teeth, like unto those of a rabbit, both in bigness and shape. Notwithstanding, their bitings are not venomous, although they can bite very sharply, and do use it very commonly. They breed for the most part in the roofs of houses. This island also is not free from the insect called in Latin *millepes*, and in Greek *scolopendria*, or 'many-feet': neither is it void of scorpions. Yet, by the providence of nature, neither the one nor the other bears the least suspicion of poison. For, although they cease not to bite, yet their wounds require not the application of any medicament for their cure. And, although their bitings cause some inflammation and swelling at the beginning, however these symptoms disappear of their own accord. Thus in the whole circumference of Hispaniola, no animal is found that produces the least harm with its venom.

After the insects above-mentioned, I shall not omit to say something of that terrible beast called cayman. This is a certain species of crocodile, wherewith this island very plentifully abounds. Among these caymans some are found to be of a corpulency very horrible to the sight. Certain it is, that such have been seen as had no less than three-score-and-ten foot in length and twelve in breadth. Yet more marvellous than their bulk is their cunning and subtlety wherewith they purchase their food. Being hungry, they place themselves nigh the sides of rivers, more especially at the fords, where cattle come to drink or wade over. Here they lie without any motion, nor stirring any part of their body, resembling an old tree fallen into the river, only floating upon the waters, whither these will carry them. Yet they recede not far from the bank-sides, but continually lurk in the same place, waiting till some wild-boar or salvage cow comes to drink or refresh themselves at that place. At which point of time, with huge activity, they assault them, and seizing on them with no less fierceness, they drag the prey into the water and there stifle it. But what is more worthy admiration is, that three or four days before the caymans go upon this design, they eat nothing at all. But, diving into the river, they swallow one or two hundred-weight of stones, such as they can find. With these they render themselves more heavy than before, and make addition to their natural strength (which in this animal is very great), thereby to render their assault the more terrible and secure. The prey being thus stifled, they suffer it to lie four or five days underwater untouched; for they could not eat the least bit thereof, unless half-rotten. But, when it is arrived at such a degree of putrefaction as is most pleasing to their palate, they devour it with great appetite and voracity. If they can lay hold on any hides of beasts, such as the inhabitants ofttimes place in the fields for drying against the sun, they drag them into the water. Here they leave them for some days, well loaden with stones, till the hair falls off. Then they eat them with no less appetite than they would the animals themselves, could they catch them. I have seen myself, many times, like things unto these I have related. But, besides my own experience, many writers of natural things have made entire treatises of these animals, describing not only their shape, magnitude, and other qualities, but also their voracity and brutish inclinations; which, as I have told you, are very strange. A certain person of good reputation and credit told me that one day he was by the river-side washing his *baraca*, or tent, wherein he used to lie in the fields. As soon as he began his work, a cayman fastened upon the tent, and with incredible fury dragged it under water. The man, desirous to see if he could save his tent, pulled on the contrary side with all his strength, having in his mouth a butcher's knife (where-with as it happened he was scraping the canvas) to defend himself in case of urgent necessity. The cayman, being angry at this opposition, vaulted upon his body, out of the river, and drew him with great celerity into the water, endeavouring with the weight of his bulk to stifle him under the banks. Thus finding himself in the greatest extremity, almost crushed to death by that huge and formidable animal, with his knife he gave the cayman several wounds in the belly, wherewith he suddenly expired. Being thus delivered from the hands of imminent fate, he drew the cayman out of the water, and with the same knife opened the body, to satisfy his own curiosity. In his stomach he found nearly one hundred-weight of stones, each of them being almost of the bigness of his fist.

The caymans are ordinarily busied in hunting and catching of flies, which they eagerly devour. The occasion is, because close unto their skin they have certain little scales which smell with a sweet scent, something like unto musk. This aromatic odour is coveted by the flies, and here they come to repose themselves and sting. Thus they both persecute each other continually, with an incredible hatred and antipathy. Their manner of procreating and hatching their young ones is as follows. They approach the sandy banks of some river that lies exposed to the rays of the south sun. Among these sands they lay their eggs, which afterwards they cover with their feet; and here they find them hatched, and with young generation, by only the heat of the sun. These, as soon as they are out of the shell, by natural instinct run unto the water. Many times those eggs are destroyed by birds that find them out, as they scrape among the sands. Hereupon the females of the caymans, at such times as they fear the coming of any flocks of birds, do ofttimes by night swallow these their eggs, and keep them in their stomach till the danger is over. And, from time to time, they bury them again in the sand, as I have told you, bringing them forth again out of their belly till the season is come of being excluded the shell. At this time, if the mother be nigh at hand, they run unto her and play with her as little whelps would do with their dams, sporting themselves according to their own custom. In this sort of sport they will oftentimes run in and out of their mother's belly, even as rabbits into their holes. This I have seen them do many times, as I have spied them at play with their dam over the water upon the contrary banks of some river. At which time I have often disturbed their sport by throwing a stone that way, causing them on a sudden to creep into the mother's bowels, for fear of some imminent danger. The manner of procreating of those animals is always the same as I have related, and at the same time of the year, for they neither meddle nor mate with one another but in the month of May. They give them in this country the name of crocodiles, though in other places of the West Indies they go under the name of caymans.

CHAPTER V

Of all sorts of quadruped animals and birds that are found in this island. As also a relation of the French Buccaneers

BESIDES the fruits which this island produces, whose plenty, as is held for certain, surpasses all the islands of America, it abounds also very plentifully in all sorts of quadruped animals, such as horses, bulls, cows, wild-boars, and others very useful to human kind, not only for common sustenance of life, but also for cultivating the ground and the management of a sufficient commerce.

In this island, therefore, are still remaining an huge number of wild-dogs. These destroy yearly multitudes of all sorts of cattle. For no sooner has a cow brought forth her calf, or a mare foaled, but these wild-mastiffs come to devour the young breed, if they find not some resistance from keepers and other domestic dogs. They run up and down the woods and fields commonly in whole troops of fifty, three-score, or more together, being withal so fierce that they ofttimes will assault an entire herd of wild-boars, not ceasing to persecute them till they have at last overcome and torn in pieces two or three. One day a French Buccaneer caused me to see a strange action of this kind. Being in the fields hunting together, we heard a great noise of dogs, which had surrounded a wild-boar. Having tame dogs with us, we left them to the custody of our servants, desirous to see the sport, if possible. Hence my companion and I, each of us, climbed up into several trees, both for security and prospect. The wild-boar was all alone, and standing against a tree; with his tusks he endeavoured to defend himself from a great number of dogs that had enclosed him, having with his teeth killed and wounded several of them. This bloody fight continued about an hour, the wild-boar meanwhile attempting many times to escape. At last, being upon the flight, one of those dogs, leaping on his back, fastened upon the testicles, which at one pull he tore in pieces. The rest of the dogs, perceiving the courage of their companion, fastened likewise upon the boar, and presently after killed him. This being done, all of them, the first only excepted, laid themselves down upon the ground about the prey, and there peaceably continued till he, the first and most courageous of the troop, had eaten as much as he could devour. When this dog had ended his repast and left the dead beast, all the rest fell in to take their share, till nothing was left that they could devour. What ought we to infer from this notable action, performed by the brutish sense of wild animals? Only this, that even beasts themselves are not destitute of knowledge, and that they give us documents how to honour such as have well deserved, seeing these, being irrational animals as they were, did reverence and respect him that exposed his life to the greatest danger, in vanquishing courageously the common enemy.

The Governor of Tortuga, Monsieur Ogeron, understanding that the wild-dogs killed too many of the wild-boars, and that the hunters of that island had much-a-do to find any, fearing lest that common sustenance of the isle should fail, caused a great quantity of poison to be brought from France, therewith to destroy the wild-mastiffs. This was performed in the year 1668, by commanding certain horses to be killed and envenomed, and laid open in the woods and fields, at certain places where mostly wild-dogs used to resort. This being continued for the space of six months, there were killed an incredible number in the said time. And yet all this industry was not sufficient to exterminate and destroy the race; yea, scarce to make any diminution thereof, their number appearing to be almost as entire as before. These wild-dogs are easily rendered tame among people, even as tame as the ordinary dogs we breed in houses. Moreover, the hunters of those parts, whensoever they find a wild bitch with young whelps, do commonly take away the puppies and bring them to their houses, where they experience them, being grown up, to hunt much better than other dogs.

But here the curious reader may peradventure inquire whence or by what accident came so many wild dogs into those islands. The occasion was that the Spaniards, having possessed themselves of these isles, found them much peopled with Indians. These were a barbarous sort of people totally given to sensuality and a brutish custom of life, hating all manner of labour, and only inclined to run from place to place, killing and making war against their neighbours, not out of any ambition to reign, but only because they agreed not with themselves in some common terms of language. Hence perceiving the dominion of the Spaniards laid a great restriction upon their lazy and brutish customs, they conceived an incredible odium against them, such as never was to be reconciled. But more especially, because they saw them take possession of their kingdoms and dominions. Hereupon they made against them all the resistance they were capable of, opposing everywhere their designs to the utmost of their power, until that the Spaniards, finding themselves to be cruelly hated by those Indians, and nowhere secure from their treacheries, resolved to extirpate and ruin them every one; especially seeing they could neither tame them by the civilities of their customs, nor conquer them by the sword. But the Indians, it being their ancient custom to make their woods their chieftest places of defence, at present made these their refuge whenever they fled from the Spaniards that pursued them. Hereupon those first conquerors of the New World made use of dogs to range and search the intricatest thickets of woods and forests for those their implacable and unconquerable enemies. By these means they forced them to leave their ancient refuge and submit unto the sword, seeing no milder usage would serve turn. Hereupon they killed some of them, and, quartering their bodies, placed them in the highways, to the intent that others might take warning from such a punishment, not to incur the like danger. But this severity proved to be of ill consequence. For, instead of frighting them and reducing their minds to a civil society, they conceived such horror of the Spaniards and their proceedings, that they resolved to detest and fly their sight for ever. And hence the greatest part died in caves and subterraneous places of the woods and mountains; in which places I myself have seen many times great numbers of human bones. The Spaniards afterwards, finding no more Indians to appear about the woods, endeavoured to rid themselves of the great number of dogs they had in their houses, whence these animals, finding no masters to keep them, betook themselves unto the woods and fields, there to hunt for food to preserve their lives. Thus by degrees they became unacquainted with the houses of their ancient masters, and at last grew wild. This is the truest account I can give of the multitudes of wild-dogs which are seen to this day in these parts.

But besides the wild-mastiffs above-mentioned, here are also huge numbers of wild-horses to be seen everywhere. These run up and down in whole herds or flocks all over the island of Hispaniola. They are but low of stature, short-bodied, with great heads, long necks, and big or thick legs. In a word, they have nothing that is handsome in all their shape. They are seen to run up and down commonly in troops of two or three hundred together, one of them going always before, to lead the multitude. When they meet any person that travels through the woods or fields, they stand still, suffering him to approach till he can almost touch them, and then, suddenly starting, they betake themselves to flight, running away disorderly, as fast as they are able. The hunters catch them with industry, only for the benefit of their skins, although sometimes they preserve their flesh likewise, which they harden with smoke, using it for provisions when they go to sea.

Here would be also wild-bulls and cows, in greater number than at present, if by continuation of hunting their race were not much diminished. Yet considerable profit is made even to this day by such as make it their business to kill them. The wild-bulls are of a vast corpulency, or bigness of body; and yet they do no hurt unto any person if they be not exasperated but left to their own repose. The hides which are taken from them are from eleven to thirteen foot long.

The diversity of birds inhabiting the air of this island is so great that I should be troublesome, as well unto the reader as myself, if I should attempt to muster up their species. Hence, leaving aside the prolix catalogue of their multitude, I shall content myself only to mention some few of the chiefest. Here is a certain species of pullets in the woods, which the Spaniards call by the name of *pintadas*, which the inhabitants find without any distinction to be as good as those which are bred in houses. It is already known to everybody that the parrots which we have in Europe are transported to us from these parts of the world. Whence may be inferred that, seeing such a number of these talkative birds are preserved among us, notwithstanding the diversity of climates, much greater multitudes are to be found where the air and temperament is natural to them. The parrots make their nests in holes of palmetto-trees, which holes are before made to their hand by other birds. The reason is, forasmuch as they are not capable of excavating any wood though never so soft, as having their own bills too crooked and blunt. Hence provident nature has supplied them with the labour and industry of another sort of small birds called *carpinteros*, or carpenters. These are no bigger than sparrows, yet notwithstanding of such hard and piercing bills that no iron instrument can be made more apt to excavate any tree, though never so solid and hard. In the holes, therefore, fabricated beforehand by these birds, the parrots get possession, and build their nests, as has been said.

Pigeons of all sorts are also here abundantly provided unto the inhabitants by Him that created in the beginning and provided all things. For eating of them, those of this island observe the same seasons as we said before, speaking of the isle of Tortuga. Betwixt the pigeons of both islands little or no difference is observable, only that these of Hispaniola are something fatter and bigger than those. Another sort of small birds here are called *cabreros*, or goat-keepers. These are very like unto others called *heronsetas*, and do chiefly feed upon crabs of the sea. In these birds are found seven distinct bladders of gall, and hence their flesh is as bitter unto the taste as aloes. Crows or ravens, more troublesome unto the inhabitants than useful, do here make a hideous noise through the whole circumference of the island. Their ordinary food is the flesh of wild-dogs, or the carcases of those beasts the Buccaneers kill and throw away. These clamorous birds do no sooner hear the report of a fowling-piece or musket but they gather from all sides into whole flocks, and fill the air and woods with their unpleasant notes. They are in nothing different from those we see in Europe.

It is now high time to speak of the French nation, who inhabit a great part of this island. We have told, at the beginning of this book, after what manner they came at first into these parts. At present, therefore, we shall only describe their manner of living, customs, and ordinary employments. The different callings or professions they follow are generally but three: either to hunt, or plant, or else to rove on the sea in quality of pirates. It is a general and solemn custom amongst them all to seek out for a comrade or companion, whom we may call partner, in their fortunes; with whom they join the whole stock of what they possess, towards a mutual and reciprocal gain. This is done also by articles drawn and signed on both sides, according to what has been agreed between them. Some of these constitute their surviving companion absolute heir unto what is left by the death of the first of the two. Others, if they be married, leave their estates unto their wives and children; others unto other relations. This being done, every one applies himself unto his calling, which is always one of the three aforementioned.

The hunters are again subdivided into two several sorts. For some of these are given to hunt only wild-bulls and cows; others hunt only wild-boars. The first of these two sorts of hunters are called Buccaneers. These not long ago were about the number of 600 upon this island; but at present there are not reckoned to be above 300 more or less. The cause has been the great decrease of wild-cattle through the dominions of the French in Hispaniola, which has appeared to be so notable that, far from getting any considerable gain, they at present are but poor in this exercise. When the Buccaneers go into the woods to hunt for wild-bulls and cows, they commonly remain there the space of a whole twelvemonth or two years, without returning home. After the hunt is over and the spoil divided among them, they commonly sail to the isle of Tortuga, there to provide themselves with guns, powder, bullets, and small shot, with all other necessaries against another going out or hunting. The rest of their gains they spend with great liberality, giving themselves freely to all manner of vices and debauchery, among which the first is that of drunkenness, which they exercise for the most part with brandy; this they drink as liberally as the Spaniards do clear fountain-water. Sometimes they buy together a pipe of wine: this they stave at the one end, and never cease drinking till they have made an end of it. Thus they celebrate the festivals of Bacchus so long as they have any money left. Neither do they forget at the same time the goddess Venus, for whose beastly delights they find more women than they can make use of. For all the tavern-keepers and strumpets wait for the coming of these lewd Buccaneers, even after the same manner that they do at Amsterdam for the arrival of the East India fleet at the Texel. The said Buccaneers are hugely cruel and tyrannical towards their servants: insomuch that commonly these had rather be galley-slaves in the Straits, or saw brazil-wood in the rasp-houses[1] of Holland, than serve such barbarous masters.

The second sort of hunters hunt nothing else but wild-boars. The flesh of these they salt, and, being thus preserved from corruption, they sell it unto the planters. These hunters have also the same vicious customs of life, and are as much addicted to all manner of debauchery as the former. But their manner of hunting is quite different from what is practised in Europe. For these Buccaneers have certain places, designed for hunting, where they live for the space of three or four months, and sometimes, though not often, a whole year. Such places are called *deza boulan;* and in these, with only the company of five or six friends, who go along with them, they continue all the time above-mentioned in mutual friendship. The first Buccaneers we spoke of many times make an agreement with certain planters to furnish them with meat all the whole year at a certain price. The payment hereof is often made with two or three hundred-weight of tobacco, in the leaf. But the planters commonly into the bargain furnish them likewise with a servant, whom they send to help. Unto the servant they afford a sufficient quantity of all necessaries for that purpose, especially of powder, bullets, and small shot, to hunt withal

The planters began to cultivate and plant the isle of Tortuga in the year 1598. The first plantation was of tobacco, the which grew to admiration, being likewise of very good quality. Notwithstanding, by reason of the small circumference of the island, they were then able to plant but little; especially there being many pieces of land in that isle that were not fit to produce tobacco. They attempted likewise to make sugar, but, by reason of the great expenses necessary to defray the

[1] Houses of correction, at one time in use in Holland and Germany. Prisoners were put to rasping wood. Cf. Evelyn, *Diary*, 19 Aug. 1641: "We went to see the rasp-house, where lusty knaves are compell'd to worke, and the rasping of brasill and logwood is very hard labour."

charges, they could not bring it to any effect. So that the greatest part of the inhabitants, as we said before, betook themselves to the exercise of hunting, and the remaining part to that of piracy. At last the hunters, finding themselves scarce able to subsist by their first profession, began likewise to seek out lands that might be rendered fit for culture; and in these also they planted tobacco. The first land that they chose for this purpose was Cul de Sac, whose territory extends towards the Southern part of the island. This piece of ground they divided into several quarters, which were called the Great Amea, Niep, Rochelois, the Little Grave, the Great Grave, and the Augame. Here, by little and little, they increased so much that at present there are above two thousand planters in those fields. At the beginning they endured very much hardship, seeing that, while they were busied about their husbandry, they could not go out of the island to seek provisions. This hardship was also increased by the necessity of grubbing, cutting down, burning, and digging, whereby to extirpate the innumerable roots of shrubs and trees. For when the French possessed themselves of that island, it was wholly overgrown with woods extremely thick, these being inhabited only by an extraordinary number of wild-boars. The method they took to clear the ground was to divide themselves into small companies of two or three persons together, and these companies to separate far enough from each other, provided with a few hatchets and some quantity of coarse provision. With these things they used to go into the woods, and there to build huts for their habitation, of only a few rafters and boughs of trees. Their first endeavour was to root up the shrubs and little trees; afterwards to cut down the great ones. These they gathered into heaps, with their branches, and then set them on fire, excepting the roots, which, last of all, they were constrained to grub and dig up after the best manner they could. The first seed they committed to the ground was beans. These in those countries both ripen and dry away in the space of six weeks.

The second fruit necessary to human life which here they tried was potatoes. These come not to perfection in lesser time than four or five months. On these they most commonly make their breakfasts every morning. They dress them no otherwise than by boiling them in a kettle with fair water.

Afterwards they cover them with a cloth for the space of half-an-hour, by which manner of dressing they become as soft as boiled chestnuts. Of the said potatoes also they make a drink called *maiz*. They cut them into small slices, and cover them with hot water. When they are well imbibed with water, they press them through a coarse cloth, and the liquor that comes out, although somewhat thick, they keep in vessels made for that purpose. Here, after settling two or three days, it begins to work; and, having thrown off its lees, is fit for drink. They use it with great delight, and although the taste is somewhat sour, yet it is very pleasant, substantial, and wholesome. The industry of this composition is owing unto the Indians, as well as of many others, which the ingenuity of those barbarians caused them to invent both for the preservation and the pleasure of their own life.

The third fruit the newly cultivated land afforded was *mandioca*, which the Indians by another name call *cassava*. This is a certain root which they plant, but comes not to perfection till after eight or nine months, yea, sometimes a whole year. Being thoroughly ripe, it may be left in the ground the space of eleven or twelve months, without the least suspicion of corruption. But, this time being past, the said roots must be converted unto use some way or another, otherwise they conceive a total putrefaction. Of these roots of *cassava*, in those countries, is made a sort of granulous flour, or meal, extremely dry and white, which supplies the want of common bread made of wheat, whereof the fields are altogether barren in that island. For this purpose they have in their houses certain graters made either of copper or tin, wherewith they grate the aforementioned roots, just as they use to do mirick in Holland. By the by, let me tell you, mirick is a certain root of a very biting taste, not unlike unto strong mustard, wherewith they usually make sauces for some sorts of fish. When they have grated as much *cassava* root as will serve turn, they put the gratings into bags, or sacks, made of coarse linen, and press out all the moisture, until they remain very dry. Afterwards they pass the gratings through a sieve, leaving them, after sifting, very like unto sawdust. The meal being thus prepared, they lay it upon planches of iron, which are made very hot, upon which it is converted into a sort of cakes, very thin. These cakes are afterwards placed in the sun, upon the tops of houses, where they are thoroughly and perfectly dried. And lest they should lose any part of their meal, what did not pass the sieve is made into up rolls, 5 or 6 inches thick. These are placed one upon another, and left in this posture until they begin to corrupt. Of this corrupted matter they make a liquor, by them called *veycou*, which they find very excellent, and certainly is not inferior unto our English beer.

Bananas are likewise another sort of fruit, of which is made another excellent liquor, which, both in strength and pleasantness of taste, may be compared unto the best wines of Spain. But this liquor of bananas, as it easily causes drunkenness in such as use it immoderately, so it likewise very frequently inflames the throat, and produces dangerous diseases in that part. *Guines agudos* is also another fruit whereof they make drink. But this sort of liquor is not so strong as the preceding. Howbeit, both the one and the other are frequently mingled with water, thereby to quench thirst.

After they had cultivated these plantations, and filled them with all sorts of roots and fruits necessary for human life, they began to plant tobacco, for trading. The manner of planting this frequent commodity is as follows. They make certain beds of earth in the field, no larger than twelve-foot square. These beds they cover very well with palmetto-leaves, to the intent that the rays of the sun may not touch the earth wherein tobacco is sowed. They water them likewise, when it does not rain, as we do our gardens in Europe. When it is grown about the bigness of young lettuce, they transplant it into straight lines, which they make in other spacious fields, setting every plant at the distance of 3 foot from each other. They observe, likewise, the fittest seasons of the year for these things, which are commonly from January until the end of March, these being the months wherein most rains do fall in those countries. Tobacco ought to be weeded very carefully, seeing the least root of any other herb, coming near it, is sufficient to hinder its growth. When it is grown to the height of one foot and a half or thereabouts, they cut off the tops—thereby to hinder the stalks and leaves from shooting too high upwards, to the intent that the whole plant may receive greater strength from the earth, which affords unto it all its vigour and taste. While it ripens and comes to full perfection, they prepare in their houses certain apartments of fifty or three-score foot in length and thirty or forty in breadth. These they fill with branches of trees and rafters, and upon them lay the green tobacco to dry. When it is thoroughly dried, they strip off the leaf from the stalks, and cause it to be rolled up by certain people who are employed in this work and no other. Unto these they afford for their labour the tenth part of what they make up into rolls. This property is peculiar unto tobacco, which therefore I shall not omit, that if, while it is yet in the ground, the leaf be pulled off from the stalk, it sprouts again, no less than four times in one year. Here I should be glad to give an account also of the manner of making sugar, indigo and gimbes[1]; but, seeing these things are not planted in those parts whereof we now speak, I have thought fit to pass them over in silence.

The French planters of the isle of Hispaniola have always unto this present time been subject unto the Governors of Tortuga. Yet this obedience has not been rendered without much reluctance and grudging on their side. In the year 1664 the West India Company of France laid the foundations of a colony in Tortuga, under which colony the planters of Hispaniola were comprehended and named as subjects thereunto. This decree disgusted the said planters very much, they taking it very ill to be reputed subjects unto a private Company of men who had no authority to make them so; especially being in a country which belonged not unto the dominions of the King of France. Hereupon they resolved to work no longer for the said Company. And this resolution of theirs was sufficient to compel the Company to a total dissolution of the Colony. But at last the Governor of Tortuga, who was pretty well stocked with planters, conceiving he could more easily force them than the West India Company, found an invention whereby to draw them unto his obedience. He promised them he would put off their several sorts of merchandize, and cause such returns to be made, in lieu of their goods from France, as they should best like. Withal, he dealt with the merchants under-hand, that all ships whatsoever should come consigned unto him, and no persons should entertain any correspondence with those planters of

[1] Perhaps *gambier, gambir*, an astringent extract from the leaves of *Uncaria Gambir*.

Hispaniola; thinking thereby to avoid many inconveniences, and compel them through necessity and want of all things to obey. By these means he not only obtained the obedience he designed from those people, but also that some merchants who had promised to deal with them and visit them now and then, no longer did it.

Notwithstanding what has been said, in the year 1669 two ships from Holland happened to arrive at the isle of Hispaniola with all sorts of merchandize necessary in those parts. With these ships presently the planters aforesaid resolved to deal, and with the Dutch nation for the future, thinking hereby to withdraw their obedience from the Governor of Tortuga, and, by frustrating his designs, revenge themselves of what they had endured under his government. Not long after the arrival of the Hollanders, the Governor of Tortuga came to visit the plantation of Hispaniola, in a vessel very well armed. But the planters not only forbade him to come ashore, but with their guns also forced him to weigh anchor, and retire faster than he came. Thus the Hollanders began to trade with these people for all manner of things. But such relations and friends as the Governor had in Hispaniola used all the endeavours they were capable of to impede the commerce. This being understood by the planters, they sent them word that *in case they laid not aside their artifices, for the hinderance of the commerce which was begun with the Hollanders, they should every one assuredly be torn in pieces.* Moreover, to oblige farther the Hollanders and contemn the Governor and his party, they gave greater ladings unto the two ships than they could desire, with many gifts and presents unto the officers and mariners, whereby they sent them very well contented to their own country. The Hollanders came again very punctually, according to their promise, and found the planters under a greater indignation than before against the Governor; either because of the great satisfaction they had already conceived of this commerce with the Dutch, or that by their means they hoped to subsist by themselves without any further dependence upon the French nation. However it was, suddenly after they set up another resolution something more strange than the preceding. The tenour hereof was that they would go unto the island of Tortuga, and cut the Governor in pieces. Hereupon they gathered together as many canoes as they could, and set sail from Hispaniola, with design not only to kill the Governor, but also to possess themselves of the whole island. This they thought they could more easily perform by reason of all necessary assistance which they believed would at any time be sent them from Holland. By which means they were already determined in their minds to erect themselves into a new Commonwealth, independent of the Crown of France. But no sooner had they begun this great revolution of their little State, when they received news of a war declared between the two nations in Europe. This wrought such a consternation in their minds as caused them to give over that enterprize and retire without attempting anything.

In the meanwhile the Governor of Tortuga sent into France for aid towards his own security and the reduction of those people to their former obedience. This was granted him, and two men-of-war were sent unto Tortuga, with orders to be at his commands. Having received such a considerable support, he sent them very well equipped to the isle of Hispaniola. Being arrived at the place, they landed part of their forces, with a design to force the people to the obedience of those whom they much hated in their hearts. But the planters, seeing the arrival of those two frigates and not being ignorant of their design, fled into the woods, abandoning their houses and many of their goods, which they left behind. These were immediately rifled and burnt by the French without any compassion, not sparing the least cottage they found. Afterwards the Governor began to relent in his anger, and let them know by some messengers that *in case they would return unto his obedience, he would give ear unto some accommodation betwixt them*. Hereupon the planters, finding themselves destitute of all human relief and that they could expect no help from any side, surrendered unto the Governor upon articles, which were made and signed on both sides. But these were not too strictly observed, for he commanded two of the chief among them to be hanged. The residue were pardoned, and withal he gave them free leave *to trade with any nation whatsoever they found most fit for their purpose*. With the grant of this liberty they began to recultivate their plantations, which gave them an huge quantity of very good tobacco; they selling yearly to the sum of 20 or 30 thousand rolls.

In this country the planters have but very few slaves, for want of which they themselves, and some servants they have, are constrained to do all the drudgery. These servants commonly oblige and bind themselves unto their masters for the space of three years. But their masters, forsaking all conscience and justice, oftentimes traffic with their bodies as with horses at a fair; selling them unto other masters, even just as they sell negroes brought from the coast of Guinea. Yea, to advance this trade, some persons there are who go purposely into France (the same happens in England and other countries), and, travelling through the cities, towns, and villages, endeavour to pick up young men or boys, whom they transport, by making them great promises. These, being once allured and conveyed into the islands I speak of, they force to work like horses, the toil they impose upon them being much harder than what they usually enjoin unto the negroes, their slaves. For these they endeavour in some manner to preserve, as being their perpetual bond-men; but, as for their white servants, they care not whether they live or die, seeing they are to continue no longer than three years in their service. These miserable kidnapped people are frequently subject unto a certain disease, which in those parts is called *coma*, being a total privation of all their senses. And this distemper is judged to proceed from their hard usage, together with the change of their native climate into that which is directly opposite. Oftentimes it happens that, among these transported people, such are found as are persons of good quality and tender education. And these, being of a softer constitution, are more suddenly surprised with the disease above-mentioned, and with several others belonging to those countries, than those who have harder bodies and have been brought up to all manner of fatigue. Besides the hard usage they endure in their diet, apparel, and repose, many times they beat them so cruelly that some of them fall down dead under the hands of their cruel masters. This I have often seen with my own eyes, not without great grief and regret. Of many instances of this nature I shall give you only the following history, as being something more remarkable in its circumstances.

It happened that a certain planter of those countries exercised such cruelty towards one of his servants as caused him to run away. Having absconded for some days in the woods from the fury of his tyrannical master, at last he was taken, and brought back to the dominion of this wicked Pharaoh. No sooner had he got him into his hands but he commanded him to be tied unto a tree. Here he gave him so many lashes upon his naked back as made his body run an entire stream of gore-blood, embruing therewith the ground about the tree. Afterwards, to make the smart of his wounds the greater, he anointed them with juice of lemon mingled with salt and pepper, being grounded small together. In this miserable posture he left him tied unto the tree for the space of four-and-twenty hours. These being past, he commenced his punishment again, lashing him as before, with so much cruelty that the miserable wretch, under this torture, gave up the ghost, with these dying words in his mouth: *I beseech the Almighty God, Creator of heaven and earth, that he permit the wicked Spirit to make thee feel as many torments before thy death as thou hast caused me to feel before mine.* A strange thing and worthy all astonishment and admiration! Scarce three or four days were past after this horrible fact, when the Almighty Judge, who had heard the clamours of that tormented wretch, gave permission to the Author of Wickedness suddenly to possess the body of that barbarous and inhuman *Amirricide*[1], who tormented him to death. Insomuch that those tyrannical hands, wherewith he had punished to death his innocent servant, were the tormentors of his own body. For with them, after a miserable manner, he did beat himself and lacerated his own flesh, till he lost the very shape of man which nature had given him, not ceasing to howl and cry, without any rest either by day or night. Thus he continued to do until he died, in that condition of raving madness wherein he surrendered his ghost unto the same Spirit of Darkness who had tormented his body. Many other examples of this kind I could rehearse, but these, not belonging unto our present discourse, I shall therefore omit.

The planters that inhabit the Caribbee Islands are rather worse and more cruel unto their servants than the preceding. In the Isle of Saint Christopher dwells one, whose name is Bettesa, very well known among the Dutch merchants, who

[1] The allusion here seems to be irrecoverable. Research in all books of reference likely to yield a result, and inquiries of many classical and literary experts have proved quite futile.

has killed above a hundred of his servants with blows and stripes. The English do the same with their servants. And the mildest cruelty they exercise towards them is that, when they have served six years of their time (the years they are bound for among the English being seven complete), they use them with such cruel hardship as forces them to beg of their masters to sell them unto others, although it be to begin another servitude of seven years, or at least three or four. I have known many who after this manner served fifteen and twenty years before they could obtain their freedom. Another thing very rigorous among that nation is a law in those islands, whereby if any man owes to another above five-and-twenty shillings, English money, in case he cannot pay, he is liable to be sold for the space of six or eight months. I shall not trouble the patience of my reader any longer with relations of this kind, as belonging unto another subject different from what I have proposed to myself in this history. Whereupon I shall take my beginning hence to describe the famous actions and exploits of the greatest Pirates of my time, during my residence in those parts. These I shall endeavour to relate without the least note of passion or partiality; yea, with that candour which is peculiar both to my mind and style: withal certifying my reader I shall give him no stories taken from others upon trust or hearsay, but only those enterprizes unto which I was myself an eye-witness.

CHAPTER VI

Of the origin of the most famous Pirates of the coasts of America. A notable exploit of Pierre le Grand

I HAVE told you in the preceding chapters of this book after what manner I was compelled to adventure my life among the Pirates of America—unto which sort of men I think myself obliged to give this name, for no other reason than that they are not maintained or upheld in their actions by any Sovereign Prince. For this is certain, that the Kings of Spain have upon several occasions sent by their Ambassadors to the Kings of France and England, *complaining of the molestations and troubles those Pirates often caused upon the coasts of America, even in the calm of peace.* Unto whose ambassadors it has always been answered: *That such men did not commit those acts of hostility and piracy as subjects of their Majesties; and therefore his Catholic Majesty might proceed against them according as he should find fit.* The King of France, besides what has been said, added unto this answer: *That he had no fortress nor castle upon the isle of Hispaniola; neither did he receive one farthing of tribute thence.* Moreover, the King of England adjoined: *That he had never given any patents or commissions unto those of Jamaica for committing any hostility against the subjects of his Catholic Majesty.* Neither did he only give this bare answer, but also, out of his Royal desire to pleasure the Court of Spain, recalled the Governor of Jamaica, placing another in his room. All this was not sufficient to prevent the Pirates of those parts from acting what mischief they could to the contrary. But, before I commence the relation of their bold and insolent actions, I shall say something of their origin and most common exercises, as also of the chiefest among them, and their manner of arming before they go out to sea.

The first Pirate that was known upon the island of Tortuga

was named Pierre le Grand, or Peter the Great. He was born at the town of Dieppe, in Normandy. The action which rendered him famous was his taking of the Vice-Admiral of the Spanish *flota*[1], nigh unto the Cape of Tiburon, upon the Western side of the island of Hispaniola. This bold exploit he performed alone with one only boat, wherein he had eight-and-twenty persons, no more, to help him. What gave occasion unto this enterprize was that until that time the Spaniards had passed and repassed with all security, and without finding the least opposition, through the Channel of Bahama. So that Pierre le Grand set out to sea by the Caicos, where he took this great ship with almost all facility imaginable. The Spaniards they found aboard were all set on shore, and the vessel presently sent into France. The manner how this undaunted spirit attempted and took such an huge ship, I shall give you out of the Journal of a true and faithful author in the same words I read them: *The boat*, saith he, *wherein Pierre le Grand was with his companions, had now been at sea a long time, without finding anything, according to his intent of piracy suitable to make a prey. And now, their provisions beginning to fail, they could keep themselves no longer upon the ocean or they must of necessity starve. Being almost reduced to despair, they espied a great ship belonging to the Spanish flota which had separated from the rest. This bulky vessel they resolved to set upon and take, or die in the attempt. Hereupon they made sail towards her, with design to view her strength. And, although they judged the vessel to be far above their forces, yet the covetousness of such a prey and the extremity of fortune they were reduced unto, made them adventure upon such an enterprize. Being now come so near that they could not escape without danger of being all killed, the Pirates jointly made an oath unto their captain, Pierre le Grand, to behave themselves courageously in this attempt without the least fear or fainting. True it is that these rovers had conceived an opinion they should find the ship unprovided to fight, and that through this occasion they should master her by degrees. It was in the dusk of the evening, or soon after, when this great action was performed. But, before it was*

[1] Spanish, a fleet of merchant-ships. "The flota is a fleet of large ships which carry the goods of Europe to the ports of America, and bring back the produce of Mexico, Peru, and other kingdoms of the New World"—Swinburne, *Travels in Spain* [1779], Letter 28.

begun, they gave orders unto the surgeon of the boat to bore a hole in the sides thereof, to the intent that, their own vessel sinking under them, they might be compelled to attack more vigorously and endeavour more hastily to run aboard the great ship. This was performed accordingly; and, without any other arms than a pistol in one of their hands and a sword in the other, they immediately climbed up the sides of the ship, and ran altogether into the great cabin, where they found the Captain, with several of his companions, playing at cards. Here they set a pistol to his breast, commanding him to deliver up the ship unto their obedience. The Spaniards, seeing the Pirates aboard their ship, without scarce having seen them at sea, cried out: "Jesus bless us! Are these devils, or what are they?" *In the meanwhile, some of them took possession of the gun-room, and seized the arms and military affairs they found there, killing as many of the ship as made any opposition. By which means the Spaniards presently were compelled to surrender. That very day the Captain of the ship had been told by some of the seamen that the boat, which was in view cruizing, was a boat of Pirates. Unto whom the Captain, slighting their advice, made answer:* "What then? Must I be afraid of such a pitiful thing as that is? No, nor though she were a ship as big and as strong as mine is." *As soon as Pierre le Grand had taken this magnificent prize, he detained in his service as many of the common seamen as he had need of, and the rest he set on shore. This being done, he immediately set sail for France, carrying with him all the riches he found in that huge vessel: there he continued without ever returning unto the parts of America.*

The planters and hunters of the isle of Tortuga had no sooner understood this happy event, and the rich prize those Pirates had obtained, but they resolved to follow their example. Hereupon many of them left their ordinary exercises and common employments, and used what means they could to get either boats or small vessels wherein to exercise piracy. But, being not able either to purchase or build them at Tortuga, at last they resolved to set forth in their canoes and seek them elsewhere. With these, therefore, they cruized at first upon Cape d'Alvarez, whereabouts the Spaniards used much to trade from one city to another in small boats. In these they carry hides, tobacco, and other commodities unto the port of Havana, which is the metropolis of that island

and unto which the Spaniards from Europe do frequently resort.

Hereabouts it was that those Pirates at the beginning took a great number of boats, laden with the aforesaid commodities. These boats they used to carry to the isle of Tortuga, and there sell the whole purchase unto the ships that waited in the port for their return or accidentally happened to be there. With the gains of these prizes they provided themselves with necessaries wherewithal to undertake other voyages. Some of these voyages were made towards the coast of Campeche, and others towards that of New Spain; in both which places the Spaniards at that time did frequently exercise much commerce and trade. Upon those coasts they commonly found great number of trading vessels and many times ships of great burden. Two of the biggest of these vessels, and two great ships which the Spaniards had laden with plate in the port of Campeche to go unto Caracas, they took in less than a month's time, by cruizing to and fro. Being arrived at Tortuga with these prizes, and the whole people of the island admiring their progresses, especially that within the space of two years the riches of the country were much increased, the number also of Pirates did augment so fast that from these beginnings, within a little space of time, there were to be numbered in that small island and port above twenty ships of this sort of people. Hereupon the Spaniards, not able to bear their robberies any longer, were constrained to put forth to sea two great men-of-war, both for the defence of their own coasts and to cruize upon the enemies.

CHAPTER VII

After what manner the Pirates arm their vessels, and how they regulate their voyages

Before the Pirates go out to sea, they give notice unto every-one that goes upon the voyage, of the day on which they ought precisely to embark, intimating also unto them their obligation of bringing each man in particular so many pounds of powder and bullets as they think necessary for that expedition. Being all come on board, they join together in council, concerning what place they ought first to go unto wherein to get provisions—especially of flesh, seeing they scarce eat anything else. And of this the most common sort among them is pork. The next food is tortoises, which they use to salt a little. Sometimes they resolve to rob such or such hog-yards, wherein the Spaniards often have a thousand head of swine together. They come unto these places in the dark of the night, and, having beset the keeper's lodge, they force him to rise and give them as many heads as they desire, threatening withal to kill him in case he disobeys their commands or makes any noise. Yea, these menaces are oftentimes put in execution, without giving any quarter unto the miserable swine-keepers or any other person that endeavours to hinder their robberies.

Having gotten provisions of flesh sufficient for their voyage, they return unto their ship. Here their allowance, twice a day to every one, is as much as he can eat, without either weight or measure. Neither does the steward of the vessel give any greater proportion of flesh, or anything else, unto the Captain than unto the meanest mariner. The ship being well victualled, they call another council, to deliberate towards what place they shall go to seek their desperate fortunes. In this council, likewise, they agree upon certain articles, which are put in writing, by way of bond or obligation, which every one is bound to observe, and all of them, or the chiefest, do set their hands unto. Herein they specify, and set down very distinctly, what sums of money each particular person ought to have for that voyage, the fund of all the payments being the common stock of what is gotten by the whole expedition ; for otherwise it is the same law, among these people as with other Pirates : *No prey, no pay*. In the first place, therefore, they mention how much the Captain ought to have for his ship. Next the salary of the carpenter, or shipwright, who careened, mended, and rigged the vessel. This commonly amounts unto 100 or 150 pieces-of-eight[1], being, according to the agreement, more or less. Afterwards for provisions and victualling they draw out of the same common stock about 200 pieces-of-eight. Also a competent salary for the surgeon and his chest of medicaments, which usually is rated at 200 or 250 pieces-of-eight. Lastly, they stipulate in writing what recompense or reward each one ought to have that is either wounded or maimed in his body, suffering the loss of any limb, by that voyage. Thus they order for the loss of a right arm 600 pieces-of-eight, or 6 slaves ; for the loss of a left arm 500 pieces-of-eight, or 5 slaves ; for a right leg 500 pieces-of-eight, or 5 slaves ; for a left leg 400 pieces-of-eight, or 4 slaves ; for an eye 100 pieces-of-eight, or one slave ; for a finger of the hand the same reward as for the eye. All which sums of money, as I have said before, are taken out of the capital sum or common stock of what is gotten by their piracy. For a very exact and equal dividend is made of the remainder among them all. Yet herein they have also regard unto qualities and places. Thus the Captain, or chief Commander, is allotted five or six portions to what the ordinary seamen have ; the Master's Mate only two ; and other Officers proportionable to their employment. After whom they draw equal parts from the highest even to the lowest mariner, the boys not being omitted. For even these draw half a share, by reason that, when they happen to take a better vessel than their own, it is the duty of the boys to set fire unto the ship or boat wherein they are, and then retire unto the prize which they have taken.

[1] A piece-of-eight is about five shillings sterling. (Note in original book.) It is a "hard dollar", the Spanish *piaster*, worth about 4s. 2d. (before 1914).

They observe among themselves very good orders. For in the prizes they take, it is severely prohibited unto every one to usurp anything in particular unto themselves. Hence all they take is equally divided, according to what has been said before. Yea, they make a solemn oath to each other not to abscond, or conceal the least thing they find amongst the prey. If afterwards any one is found unfaithful, and has contravened the said oath, immediately he is separated and turned out of the society. Among themselves they are very civil and charitable to each other. Insomuch that, if any wants what another has, with great liberality they give it one to another. As soon as these Pirates have taken any prize of ship or boat, the first thing they endeavour is to set on shore the prisoners, detaining only some few for their own help and service, unto whom also they give their liberty after the space of two or three years. They put in very frequently for refreshment at one island or another, but more especially into those which lie on the Southern side of the isle of Cuba. Here they careen their vessels, and in the meanwhile some of them go to hunt, others to cruize upon the seas in canoes, seeking their fortune. Many times they take the poor fishermen of tortoises, and, carrying them to their habitations, they make them work so long as the Pirates are pleased.

In the several parts of America are found four distinct species of tortoises. The first hereof are so great that every one reaches to the weight of 2 or 3 thousand pounds. The scales of the species are so soft as that easily they may be cut with a knife. Yet these tortoises are not good to be eaten. The second species is of an indifferent bigness, and are green in colour. The scales of these are harder than the first, and this sort is of a very pleasant taste. The third is very little different in size and bigness from the second, unless that it has the head something bigger. This third species is called by the French *cavana*, and is not good for food. The fourth is named *caret*, being very like to the tortoises we have in Europe. This sort keeps most commonly among the rocks, whence they crawl out to seek their food, which is for the greatest part nothing but apples of the sea. Those other species above-mentioned feed upon grass which grows in the water upon the banks of the sand. These banks, or shelves, for their pleasant green do here resemble the delightful meadows of the United

Provinces. Their eggs are almost like unto those of the crocodile, but without any shell, being only covered with a thin membrane or film. They are found in such prodigious quantities along the sandy shores of those countries that, were they not frequently destroyed by birds, the sea would infinitely abound with tortoises.

These creatures have certain customary places whither they repair every year to lay their eggs. The chiefest of these places are the three islands called Caymanes, situated in the latitude of 20 degrees and 15 minutes North, being at the distance of five-and-forty-leagues from the isle of Cuba, on the Northern side thereof.

It is a thing much deserving consideration how the tortoises can find out these islands. For the greatest part of them come from the Gulf of Honduras, distant thence the whole space of 150 leagues. Certain it is, that many times the ships, having lost their latitude through the darkness of the weather, have steered their course only by the noise of tortoises swimming that way, and have arrived unto those isles. When their season of hatching is past, they retire towards the island of Cuba, where are many good places that afford them food. But while they are at the islands of Caymanes, they eat very little or nothing. When they have been about the space of one month in the seas of Cuba, and are grown fat, the Spaniards go out to fish for them, they being then to be taken in such abundance that they provide with them sufficiently their cities, towns, and villages. Their manner of taking them is by making with a great nail a certain kind of dart. This they fix at the end of a long stick or pole, with which they wound the tortoises, as with a dagger, whensoever they appear above water to breathe fresh air.

The inhabitants of New Spain and Campeche lade their principal sorts of merchandizes in ships of great bulk; and with these they exercise their commerce to and fro. The vessels from Campeche in winter-time set out towards Caracas, Trinity Isles, and that of Margarita. For in summer the winds are contrary, though very favourable to return unto Campeche, as they use to do at the beginning of that season. The Pirates are not ignorant of these times, being very dexterous in searching out all places and circumstances most suitable to their designs. Hence in the places and seasons aforementioned, they cruize upon the said ships for some while. But, in case they can perform nothing, and that fortune does not favour them with some prize or other, after holding a council thereupon, they commonly enterprize things very desperate. Of these their resolutions I shall give you one instance very remarkable. One certain Pirate, whose name was Pierre François or Peter Francis, happened to be a long time at sea with his boat and six-and-twenty persons, waiting for the ships that were to return from Maracaibo towards Campeche. Not being able to find anything, nor get any prey, at last he resolved to direct his course to Rancherias, which is nigh unto the river called De la Plata, in the latitude of twelve-degrees-and-a-half North. In this place lies a rich bank of pearl, to the fishery whereof they yearly send from Cartagena a fleet of a dozen vessels, with a man-of-war for their defence. Every vessel has at least a couple of negroes in it, who are very dexterous in diving, even to the depths of six fathoms within the sea, whereabouts they find good store of pearls. Upon this fleet of vessels, though small, called the Pearl Fleet, Pierre François resolved to adventure rather than go home with empty hands. They rode at anchor, at that time, at the mouth of the river De la Hacha, the man-of-war being scarce half-a-league distant from the small ships, and the wind very calm. Having espied them in this posture, he presently pulled down his sails and rowed along the coast, dissembling to be a Spanish vessel that came from Maracaibo and only passed that way. But, no sooner was he come unto the Pearl Bank, when suddenly he assaulted the Vice-Admiral of the said fleet, mounted with 8 guns and three-score men well armed, commanding them to surrender. But the Spaniards, running to their arms, did do what they could to defend themselves, fighting for some while ; till at last they were constrained to submit unto the Pirate. Being thus possessed of the Vice-Admiral, he resolved next to adventure with some other stratagem upon the man-of-war, thinking thereby to get strength sufficient to master the rest of the fleet. With this intent he presently sank his own boat in the river ; and, putting forth the Spanish colours, weighed anchor ; with a little wind they began to stir, having with promises and menaces compelled most of the Spaniards to assist him in his design. But no sooner did the man-of-war perceive one of his fleet to set sail when he did so too, fearing lest the mariners should have any design to run away with the vessel and riches they had on board. This caused the Pirates immediately to give over that dangerous enterprize, as thinking themselves unable to encounter force to force with the said man-of-war that now came against them. Hereupon they attempted to get out of the river and gain the open seas with the riches they had taken, by making as much sail as possibly the vessel would bear. This being perceived by the man-of-war, he presently gave 'um chase. But the Pirates, having laid on too much sail, and a gust of wind suddenly arising, had their main-mast blown down by the board, which disabled 'um from prosecuting their escape.

This unhappy event much encouraged those that were in the man-of-war, they advancing and gaining upon the Pirates every moment; by which means at last they were overtaken. But, these notwithstanding, finding themselves still with two-and-twenty persons sound, the rest being either killed or wounded, resolved to defend themselves so long as it were possible. This they performed very courageously for some while, until thereunto forced by the man-of-war, they were compelled to surrender. Yet was not this done without articles, which the Spaniards were glad to allow them, as follows: That they should not use them as slaves, forcing them to carry or bring stones or employing them in other labours for three or four years, as they commonly employ their negroes. But that they should set them on shore upon free land, without doing them harm in their bodies. Upon these articles they delivered themselves, with all that they had taken, which was worth only in pearls to the value of above 100,000 pieces-of-eight, besides the vessel, provisions, goods, and other things. All which being put together would have made unto this Pirate one of the greatest prizes he could desire; which he had obtained, had it not been for the loss of his main-mast, as was said before.

Another bold attempt, not unlike unto that which I have related nor less remarkable, I shall also give you at present. A certain Pirate, born in Portugal and from the name of his country called Bartholomew Portugues, was cruizing in his boat from Jamaica (wherein he had only thirty men and four small guns) upon the Cape de Corrientes, in the island of Cuba.

F

In this place he met with a great ship that came from Maracaibo and Cartegena, bound for the Havana, well provided with twenty great guns and threescore-and-ten men, between passengers and mariners. This ship he presently assaulted, but found as strongly defended by them that were on board. The Pirate escaped the first encounter, resolving to attack her more vigorously than before, seeing he had sustained no great damage hitherto. This resolution he boldly performed, renewing his assaults so often till that, after a long and dangerous fight, he became master of the great vessel. The Portuguese lost only ten men and had four wounded, so that he had still remaining twenty fighting men, whereas the Spaniards had double the same number. Having possessed themselves of such a ship, and the wind being contrary to return unto Jamaica, they resolved to steer their course towards the Cape of Saint Antony (which lies on the Western side of the isle of Cuba), there to repair themselves and take in fresh water, of which they had great necessity at that time.

Being now very near unto the cape above-mentioned, they unexpectedly met with three great ships that were coming from New Spain and bound for the Havana. By these, as not being able to escape, they were easily retaken, both ship and Pirates. Thus they were all made prisoners through the sudden change of fortune, and found themselves poor, oppressed, and stripped of all the riches they had purchased[1] so little before. The cargo of this ship consisted of 120,000 weight of coco-nuts, the chiefest ingredient of that rich liquor called chocolate, and threescore-and-ten thousand pieces-of-eight. Two days after this misfortune, there happened to arise an huge and dangerous tempest, which largely separated the ships from one another. The great vessel, wherein the Pirates were, arrived at Campeche, where many considerable merchants came to salute and welcome the Captain thereof. These presently knew the Portuguese Pirate, as being him who had committed innumerable excessive insolences upon those coasts, not only infinite murders and robberies but also lamentable

[1] Obsolete use of the word 'purchase' (vb. and noun), originally "the action of hunting; the chase; the catching or seizing of prey" (*N.E.D.*): hence pillage, plunder, booty. Frequently used throughout this book and other early books on the Buccaneers.

incendiums[1], which those of Campeche still preserved very fresh in their memory.

Hereupon, the next day after their arrival, the magistrates of the city sent several of their officers to demand and take into custody the criminal prisoners from on board the ship, with intent to punish them according to their deserts. Yet, fearing lest the Captain of those Pirates should escape out of their hands on shore (as he had formerly done, being once their prisoner in the city before), they judged it more convenient to leave him safely guarded on board the ship for the present. In the meanwhile they caused a gibbet to be erected, whereupon to hang him the very next day, without any other form of process than to lead him from the ship unto the place of punishment. The rumour of this future tragedy was presently brought unto Bartholomew Portugues' ears, whereby he sought all the means he could to escape that night. With this design he took two earthen jars, wherein the Spaniards usually carry wine from Spain unto the West Indies, and stopped them very well, intending to use them for swimming, as those who are unskilful in that art do calabashes, a sort of pumpkins, in Spain, and in other places empty bladders. Having made this necessary preparation, he waited for the night, when all should be asleep, even the sentry that guarded him. But, seeing he could not escape his vigilancy, he secretly purchased a knife, and with the same gave him such a mortal stab as suddenly deprived him of life and the possibility of making any noise. At that instant he committed himself to sea, with those two earthen jars before-mentioned, and by their help and support, though never having learned to swim, he reached the shore. Being arrived upon land, without any delay he took his refuge in the woods, where he hid himself for three days, without daring to appear, nor eating any other food than wild herbs.

Those of the city failed not the next day to make a diligent search for him in the woods, where they concluded him to be. This strict inquiry Portugues had the convenience to espy from the hollow of a tree, wherein he lay absconded. Hence perceiving them to return without finding what they sought for, he adventured to sally forth towards the coasts called Del

[1] Conflagrations. So-used in Howell, *Parthenop.* [1654], Preface.

Golfo Triste, forty leagues distant from the city of Campeche. Hither he arrived within a fortnight after his escape from the ship. In which space of time, as also afterwards, he endured extreme hunger, thirst, and fears of falling again into the hands of the Spaniards. For during all this journey he had no other provision with him than a small calabash, with a little water; neither did he eat anything else than a few shell-fish, which he found among the rocks nigh the sea-shore. Besides that, he was compelled to pass yet some rivers, not knowing well to swim. Being in this distress, he found an old board which the waves had thrown upon the shore, wherein did stick a few great nails. These he took, and with no small labour whetted against a stone, until that he had made them capable of cutting like unto knives, though very imperfectly. With these, and no better instruments, he cut down some branches of trees, the which with twigs and osiers he joined together, and made as well as he could a boat, or rather a raft[1], wherewith he rafted[2] over the rivers. Thus he arrived finally at the Cape of Golfo Triste, as was said before, where he happened to find a certain vessel of Pirates, who were great comrades of his own, and were lately come from Jamaica.

Unto these Pirates he instantly related all his adversities and misfortunes, and withal demanded of them that they would fit him with a boat and 20 men. With which company alone he promised to return to Campeche and assault the ship that was in the river, by which he had been taken, and escaped fourteen days before. They readily granted his request, and equipped him a boat with the said number of men. With this small company he set forth towards the execution of his design, which he bravely performed eight days after he separated from his comrades at the Cape of Golfo Triste. For, being arrived at the river of Campeche, with an undaunted courage and without any rumour of noise he assaulted the ship beforementioned. Those that were on board were persuaded this was a boat from land that came to bring *contra banda* goods; and hereupon were not in any posture of defence. Thus the Pirates, laying hold on this occasion, assaulted them without any fear of ill success, and in short space of time compelled the Spaniards to surrender.

[1] In the original 'wafte.'
[2] In the original 'wafted.' No doubt misprints.

Being now masters of the ship, they immediately weighed anchor and set sail, determining to fly from the port lest they should be pursued by other vessels. This they did with extremity of joy, seeing themselves possessors of such a brave ship. Especially Portugues, their captain, who now by a second turn of fortune's wheel was become rich and powerful again, who had been so lately in that same vessel a poor miserable prisoner and condemned to the gallows. With this great purchase he designed in his mind greater things; which he might well hope to obtain, seeing he had found in the vessel great quantity of rich merchandize still remaining on board, although the plate had been transported into the city. Thus he continued his voyage towards Jamaica for some days. But coming nigh into the isle of Pinos, on the South side of the island of Cuba, fortune suddenly turned her back unto him once more, never to show him her countenance again. For a horrible storm arising at sea occasioned the ship to split against the rocks or banks called Jardines. Insomuch that the vessel was totally lost, and Portugues, with his companions, escaped in a canoe. After this manner he arrived at Jamaica, where he remained no long time, being only there till he could prepare himself to seek his fortune anew, which from that time proved always adverse unto him.

Nothing less rare and admirable than the preceding are the actions of another Pirate, who at present lives at Jamaica, and who has on sundry occasions enterprized and achieved things very strange. The place of his birth was the city of Groningen, in the United Provinces; but his own proper name is not known: the Pirates, his companions, having only given him that of Roche Brasiliano by reason of his long residence in the country of Brazil, whence he was forced to flee, when the Portuguese retook those countries from the West India Company of Amsterdam, several nations then inhabiting at Brazil (as English, French, Dutch, and others) being constrained to seek new fortunes.

This fellow at that conjuncture of time retired unto Jamaica, where, being at a stand how to get a livelihood, he entered himself into the society of Pirates. Under these he served in quality of a private mariner for some while, in which degree he behaved himself so well as made him both beloved and respected by all, as one that deserved to be their

ROCK. BRASILIANO

Commander for the future. One day certain mariners happened to engage in a dissension with their Captain ; the effect whereof was that they left the boat. Brasiliano followed the rest, and by these was chosen for their conductor and leader, who also fitted him out a boat or small vessel, wherein he received the title of Captain.

Few days were past from his being chosen Captain, when he took a great ship that was coming from New Spain, on board of which he found great quantity of plate, and both one and the other he carried to Jamaica. This action gave him renown, and caused him to be both esteemed and feared, every one apprehending him much aboard. Howbeit, in his domestic and private affairs he had no good behaviour nor government over himself ; for in these he would oftentimes shew himself either brutish or foolish. Many times being in drink, he would run up and down the streets, beating or wounding whom he met, no person daring to oppose him or make any resistance.

Unto the Spaniards he always showed himself very barbarous and cruel, only out of an inveterate hatred he had against that nation. Of these he commanded several to be roasted alive upon wooden spits, for no other crime than that they would not shew him the places, or hog-yards, where he might steal swine. After many of these cruelties, it happened, as he was cruizing upon the coasts of Campeche, that a dismal tempest suddenly surprised him. This proved to be so violent that at last his ship was wrecked upon the coasts, the mariners only escaping with their muskets and some few bullets and powder, which were the only things they could save of all that was in the vessel. The place where the ship was lost was precisely between Campeche and the Golfo Triste. Here they got on shore in a canoe, and, marching along the coast with all the speed they could, they directed their course towards Golfo Triste, as being a place where the Pirates commonly used to repair and refresh themselves. Being upon this journey and all very hungry and thirsty, as is usual in desert places, they were pursued by some Spaniards, being a whole troop of a hundred horsemen. Brasiliano no sooner perceived this imminent danger than he animated his companions, telling them : *We had better, fellow soldiers, choose to die under our arms fighting, as it becomes men of courage, than surrender unto the Spaniards, who, in case they overcome us, will take away our lives with cruel torments.* The Pirates were no more than 30 in number, who, notwithstanding, seeing their brave Commander oppose himself with courage unto the enemy, resolved to do the like. Hereupon they faced the troop of Spaniards, and discharged their muskets against them with such dexterity that they killed one horsemen with almost every shot. The fight continued for the space of an hour, till at last the Spaniards were put to flight by the Pirates. They stripped the dead, and took from them what they thought most convenient for their use. But such as were not already dead, they helped to quit the miseries of life with the ends of their muskets.

Having vanquished the enemy, they all mounted on several horses they found in the field, and continued the journey aforementioned, Brasiliano having lost but two of his companions in this bloody fight, and had two others wounded. As they prosecuted their way, before they came unto the port they espied a boat from Campeche, well manned, that rode at anchor, protecting a small number of canoes that were lading wood. Hereupon they sent a detachment of six of their men to watch them; and these the next morning by a wild [assault] possessed themselves of the canoes. Having given notice unto their companions, they went all on board, and with no great difficulty took also the boat, or little man-of-war, their convoy. Thus having rendered themselves masters of the whole fleet, they wanted only provisions, which they found but very small aboard those vessels. But this defect was supplied by the horses, which they instantly killed and salted with salt, which by good fortune the woodcutters had brought with them. Upon which victuals they made shift to keep themselves until such time as they could purchase better.

These very same Pirates, I mean Brasiliano and his companions, took also another ship that was going from New Spain unto Maracaibo, laden with divers sorts of merchandize, and a very considerable number of pieces-of-eight, which were designed to buy coco-nuts for their lading home. All these prizes they carried into Jamaica, where they safely arrived, and, according to their custom, wasted in a few days in taverns and stews all they had gotten, by giving themselves to all manner of debauchery with strumpets and wine. Such of these Pirates are found who will spend 2 or 3 thousand pieces-of-eight in one night, not leaving themselves peradventure a good shirt to wear on their backs in the morning. Thus upon a certain time I saw one of them give unto a common strumpet five hundred pieces-of-eight only that he might see her naked. My own master would buy, on like occasions, a whole pipe of wine, and, placing it in the street, would force every one that passed by to drink with him; threatening also to pistol them, in case they would not do it. At other times he would do the same with barrels of ale or beer. And, very often, with both his hands, he would throw these liquors about the streets, and wet the clothes of such as walked by, without regarding whether he spoiled their apparel or not, were they men or women.

Among themselves, and to each other, these Pirates are extremely liberal and free. If any one of them has lost all his goods, which often happens in their manner of life, they freely give him, and make him partaker of what they have. In taverns and ale-houses they always have great credit; but in such houses at Jamaica they ought not to run very deep in debt, seeing the inhabitants of that island do easily sell one another for debt. Thus it happened unto my patron, or master, to be sold for a debt of a tavern, wherein he had spent the greatest part of his money. This man had, within the space of three months before, 3000 pieces-of-eight in ready cash, all which he wasted in that short space of time, and became so poor as I have told you.

But now to return to our discourse: I must let my reader know that Brasiliano, after having spent all that he had robbed, was constrained to go to sea again, to seek his fortune once more. Thus he set forth towards the coast of Campeche, his common place of rendezvous. Fifteen days after his arrival there, he put himself into a canoe, with intent to espy the port of that city, and see if he could rob any Spanish vessel. But his fortune was so bad that both he and all his men were taken prisoners, and carried into the presence of the Governor. This man immediately cast them into a dungeon, with full intention to hang them every person. And doubtless he had performed his intent, were it not for a stratagem that Brasiliano used, which proved sufficient to save their lives. He wrote therefore a letter unto the Governor, making him believe it came from other Pirates that were abroad at sea, and withal telling him: *He should have a care how he used those persons he had in his custody. For in case he caused them any harm, they did swear unto him they would never give quarter to any person of the Spanish nation that should fall into their hands.*

Because these Pirates had been many times at Campeche, and in many other towns and villages of the West Indies belonging to the Spanish dominions, the Governor began to fear what mischief they might cause by means of their companions abroad, in case he should punish them. Hereupon he released them out of prison, exacting only an oath of them beforehand that they would leave their exercise of piracy for ever. And withal he sent them as common mariners, or passengers in the galleons, to Spain. They got in this voyage altogether 500 pieces-of-eight, whereby they tarried not long there after their arrival. But, providing themselves with some few necessaries, they all returned unto Jamaica within a little while; whence they set forth again to sea, committing greater robberies and cruelties than ever they had done before; but more especially abusing the poor Spaniards that happened to fall into their hands, with all sorts of cruelty imaginable.

The Spaniards perceiving they could gain nothing upon this sort of people, nor diminish their number, which rather increased daily, resolved to diminish the number of their ships wherein they exercised trading to and fro. But neither was this resolution of any effect, or did them any good service. For the Pirates, finding not so many ships at sea as before, began to gather into greater companies and land upon the Spanish dominions, ruining whole cities, towns, and villages; and withal pillaging, burning, and carrying away as much as they could [find] possible.

The first Pirate who gave a beginning unto these invasions by land was named Lewis Scot, who sacked and pillaged the City of Campeche. He almost ruined the town, robbing and destroying all he could; and, after he had put it to the ransom of an excessive sum of money, he left it. After Scot came another named Mansvelt, who enterprized to set footing in Granada, and penetrate with his piracies even unto the South Sea. Both which things he effected, till that at last, for want of provision, he was constrained to go back. He assaulted the isle of Saint Catharine, which was the first land he took, and upon it some few prisoners. These showed him the way towards Cartagena, which is a principal city situate in the kingdom of New Granada. But the bold attempts and actions of John Davis, born at Jamaica, ought not to be forgotten in this history, as being some of the most remarkable thereof: especially his rare prudence and valour, wherewith he behaved himself in the aforementioned kingdom of Granada. This Pirate, having cruized a long time in the Gulf of Pocatauro upon the ships that were expected from Cartagena bound for Nicaragua, and not being able to meet any of the said ships, resolved at last to land in Nicaragua, leaving his ship concealed about the coast.

This design he presently put in execution. For taking four-score men, out of four-score-and-ten which he had in all (the rest being left to keep the ship), he divided them equally into three canoes. His intent was to rob the churches, and rifle the houses of the chief citizens of the aforesaid town of Nicaragua. Thus, in the obscurity of the night, they mounted the river which leads to that city, rowing with oars in their canoes. By day they concealed themselves and boats under the branches of trees that were upon the banks. These grow very thick and intricate along the sides of the rivers in those countries, as also along the sea-coast. Under which, likewise, those who remained behind absconded their vessel, lest they should be seen either by fishermen or Indians. After this manner they arrived at the city the third night, where the sentry who kept the post of the river thought them to be fishermen that had been fishing in the lake. And as the greatest part of the Pirates are skilful in the Spanish tongue, so he never doubted thereof as soon as he heard them speak. They had in their company an Indian, who had run away from his master because he would make him a slave after having served him a long time. This Indian went first on shore, and, rushing at the sentry, he instantly killed him. Being animated with this success, they entered into the city, and went directly to three or four houses of the chiefest citizens, where they knocked with dissimulation. These, believing them to be friends, opened the doors, and the Pirates, suddenly possessing themselves of the houses, robbed all the money and plate they could find. Neither did they spare the churches and most sacred things, all which were pillaged and profaned without any respect or veneration.

In the meanwhile great cries and lamentation were heard about the town, of some who had escaped their hands; by which means the whole city was brought into an uproar and alarm. Hence the whole number of citizens rallied together, intending to put themselves in defence. This being perceived by the Pirates, they instantly put themselves to flight, carrying with them all that they had robbed, and likewise some prisoners. These they led away, to the intent that, if any of them should happen to be taken by the Spaniards, they might make use of them for ransom. Thus they got unto their ship, and with all speed imaginable put out to sea, forcing the prisoners, before they would let them go, to procure them as much flesh as they thought necessary for their voyage to Jamaica. But, no sooner had they weighed anchor, when they saw on shore a troop of about five hundred Spaniards, all being very well armed, at the sea-side. Against these they let fly several guns, wherewith they forced them to quit the sands and retire towards home, with no small regret to see those Pirates carry away so much plate of their churches and houses, though distant at least 40 leagues from the sea.

These Pirates robbed on this occasion above 4000 pieces-of-eight in ready money, besides great quantities of plate uncoined and many jewels. All which was computed to be worth the sum of 50,000 pieces-of-eight or more. With this great purchase they arrived at Jamaica soon after the exploit. But, as this sort of people are never masters of their money but a very little while, so were they soon constrained to seek more, by the same means they had used before. This adventure caused Captain John Davis, presently after his return, to be chosen Admiral of seven or eight boats of Pirates, he being now esteemed by common consent an able conductor for such enterprizes as these were. He began the exercise of this new command by directing his fleet towards the coasts of the north of Cuba, there to wait for the fleet which was to pass from New Spain. But, not being able to find anything by this design, they determined to go towards the coasts of Florida. Being arrived there, they landed part of their men, and sacked a small city named Saint Augustine of Florida, the castle of which place had a garrison of 200 men, the which, notwithstanding, could not prevent the pillage of the city, they effecting it without receiving the least damage from either soldiers or townsmen.

Hitherto we have spoken in the First Part of this book of the constitution of the islands of Hispaniola and Tortuga, their peculiarities and inhabitants ; as also of the fruits to be found in those countries. In the Second Part of this work we shall bend our discourse to describe the actions of two of the most famous Pirates, who committed many horrible crimes and inhuman cruelties against the Spanish nation.

The End of the First Part

PART II

CHAPTER I

Origin of Francis L'Ollonais, and beginning of his robberies

FRANCIS L'OLLONAIS was native of that territory in France which is called Les Sables d'Ollone, or the Sands of Ollone. In his youth he was transported to the Caribbee Islands, in quality of a servant or slave, according to the custom of France and other countries; of which we have already spoken in the First Part of this book. Being out of his time, when he had obtained his freedom, he came into the isle of Hispaniola. Here he placed himself for some while among the hunters, before he began his robberies against the Spaniards, whereof I shall make mention at present, until his unfortunate death.

At first he made two or three voyages in quality of a common mariner, wherein he behaved himself so courageously as to deserve the favour and esteem of the Governor of Tortuga, who was then Monsieur de la Place. Insomuch that this gentleman gave him a ship, and made him captain thereof, to the intent he might seek his fortune. This Dame shewed herself very favourable to him at the beginning, for in a short while he purchased great riches. But, withal, his cruelties against the Spaniards were such as that the very fame of them made him known through the whole Indies. For which reason the Spaniards, in his time, whensoever they were attacked by sea, would choose rather to die or sink fighting than surrender, as knowing they should have no mercy nor quarter at his hands. But as Fortune is seldom constant, so after some time she turned her back unto him. The beginning of whose disasters was, that in a huge storm he lost his ship upon the coasts of Campeche. The men were all saved; but, coming upon dry land, the Spaniards pursued them, and killed the greatest part, wounding also L'Ollonais, their captain. Not knowing how to escape, he thought to save his life by a stratagem. Hereupon he took several handfuls of sand and mingled them with the blood of his own wounds, with which he besmeared his face and other parts of his body. Then, hiding himself dexterously among the dead, he continued there till the Spaniards had quitted the field.

After they were gone, he retired into the woods, and bound up his wounds as well as he could. These being by the help of nature pretty well healed, he took his way to the city of Campeche, having perfectly disguised himself in Spanish habit. Here he spoke with certain slaves, unto whom he promised their liberty in case they would obey him and trust in his conduct. They accepted his promises, and, stealing one night a canoe from one of their masters, they went to sea with the Pirate. The Spaniards in the meanwhile had made prisoner several of his companions, whom they kept in close dungeons in the city, while L'Ollonais went about the town and saw all that passed. These were often asked by the Spaniards: *What is become of your Captain ?*, unto whom they constantly answered: *He is dead.* With which news the Spaniards were hugely gladded, and made great demonstrations of joy, kindling bonfires, and, [like] as them that knew nothing to the contrary, giving thanks to God Almighty for their deliverance from such a cruel Pirate. L'Ollonais, having seen these joys for his death, made haste to escape with the slaves above-mentioned, and came safe to Tortuga, the common place of refuge of all sorts of wickedness, and the seminary, as it were, of all manner of Pirates and thieves. Though now his fortune was but low, yet he failed not of means to get another ship, which with craft and subtlety he obtained, and in it one-and-twenty persons. Being well provided with arms and other necessaries, he set forth towards the isle of Cuba, on the South side whereof lies a small village, which is called De los Cayos. The inhabitants of this town drive a great trade in tobacco, sugar, and hides—and all in boats, as not being able to make use of ships by reason of the little depth of that sea.

L'Ollonais was greatly persuaded he should get here some considerable prey; but, by the good fortune of some fishermen who saw him and the mercy of the Almighty, they escaped his tyrannical hands. For the inhabitants of the town of Cayos despatched immediately a messenger overland unto

FRANCIS LOLONOIS.

Havana, complaining unto the Governor that L'Ollonais was come to destroy them, with two canoes. The Governor could very hardly be persuaded unto the truth of this story, seeing he had received letters from Campeche that he was dead. Notwithstanding, at the importunity of the petitioners he sent a ship to their relief, with 10 guns and fourscore-and-ten persons, well armed; giving them withal this express command: *They should not return unto his presence without having totally destroyed those Pirates.* Unto this effect he gave them also a negro, who might serve them for a hangman; his orders being that *They should immediately hang every one of the said Pirates excepting L'Ollonais their Captain, whom they should bring alive unto Havana.* This ship arrived at Cayos; of whose coming the Pirates were advertised beforehand; and, instead of flying, went to seek the said vessel in the river Estera, where she rode at anchor. The Pirates apprehended some fishermen, and forced them by night to shew the entry of the port, hoping soon to obtain a greater vessel than their two canoes, and thereby to mend their fortune. They arrived, after two o'clock in the morning, very nigh unto the ship. And the watch on board the ship asking them: *Whence they came, and if they had seen any Pirates abroad,* they caused one of the prisoners to answer: *They had seen no Pirates, nor anything else.* Which answer brought them into persuasion that they were fled away, having heard of their coming.

But they experienced very soon the contrary; for about break of day the Pirates began to assault the vessel on both sides with their two canoes. This attack they performed with such vigour that, although the Spaniards behaved themselves as they ought and made as good defence as they could, shooting against them likewise some great guns, yet they were forced to surrender, after being beaten by the Pirates, with swords in hand, down under the hatches. Hence L'Ollonais, commanded them to be brought up one by one, and in this order caused their heads to be struck off. Among the rest came up the negro, designed to be the Pirates' executioner by the Governor of Havana. This fellow implored mercy at his hands very dolefully, desiring not to be killed, and telling L'Ollonais he was constituted hangman of that ship; and that, in case he would spare him, he would tell him faithfully all that he should desire to know. L'Ollonais made him confess as many things as he thought fit to ask him; and, having done, commanded him to be murdered with the rest. Thus he cruelly and barbarously put them all to death, reserving of the whole number only one alive, whom he sent back to the Governor of Havana, with this message given him in writing: *I shall never henceforward give quarter to any Spaniard whatsoever; and I have great hopes I shall execute on your own person the very same punishment I have done upon them you sent against me. Thus I have retaliated the kindness you designed unto me and my companions.* The Governor was much troubled to understand these sad and withal insolent news; which occasioned him to swear, in the presence of many, he would never grant quarter unto any Pirate that should fall into his hands. But the citizens of Havana desired him not to persist in the execution of that rash and rigorous oath, *seeing the Pirates would certainly take occasion thence to do the same; and they had an hundred times more opportunity of revenge than he: that, being necessitated to get their livelihood by fishery, they should hereafter always be in danger of losing their lives.* By these reasons he was persuaded to bridle his anger, and remit the severity of his oath aforementioned.

Now L'Ollonais had got himself a good ship, but withal very few provisions and people in it. Hereupon, to purchase both the one and the other, he resolved to use his customary means of cruizing from one port to another. Thus he did for some while, till at last, not being able to purchase anything, he determined to go unto the port of Maracaibo. Here he took by surprize a ship that was laden with plate and other merchandize, being outward bound to buy cacao-nuts. With these prizes he returned unto Tortuga, where he was received with no small joy by the inhabitants, they congratulating his happy success and their own private interest. He continued not long there, but pitched upon new designs of equipping a whole fleet, sufficient to transport 500 men, with all other necessaries. With these preparations he resolved to go unto the Spanish dominions, and pillage both cities, towns, and villages, and finally take Maracaibo itself. For this purpose, he knew the island of Tortuga would afford him many resolute and courageous men, very fit for such enterprizes. Besides that, he had in his service several prisoners, who were exactly acquainted with the ways and places he designed upon.

CHAPTER II

L'Ollonais equips a fleet to land upon the Spanish islands of America, with intent to rob, sack, and burn whatever he meets

Of this his design L'Ollonais gave notice unto all the Pirates who at that conjuncture of time were either at home or abroad; by which means he got together in a little while above 400 men. Besides which, there was at that present in the isle of Tortuga another Pirate, whose name was Michael de Basco. This man by his piracy had gotten riches sufficient to live at ease and go no more abroad to sea; having withal the office of Major of the island. Yet, seeing the great preparations that L'Ollonais made for this expedition, he entered into a straight league of friendship with him, and proffered unto him that, in case he would make him his chief Captain by land (seeing he knew the country very well and all its avenues), he would take part in his fortunes, and go along with him. They both agreed upon articles, with great joy of L'Ollonais, as knowing that Basco had performed great actions in Europe, and had gained the repute of a good soldier. He gave him, therefore, the command he desired, and the conduct of all his people by land. Thus they all embarked in eight vessels, that of L'Ollonais being the greatest, as having ten guns of indifferent[1] carriage.

All things being in readiness, and the whole company on board, they set sail together about the end of April, having a considerable number of men for those parts, that is in all six-hundred and-threescore persons. They directed their course towards that part which is called Bayala, situated on the North side of the island of Hispaniola. Here they also took into their company a certain number of French hunters, who voluntarily offered themselves to go along with them. And here likewise they provided themselves with victuals and other necessaries for that voyage.

[1] Here in the sense of 'unimportant', 'ordinary'; cf. Shakespeare, *Taming of the Shrew*, I, ii, 181: 'Their garters of an indifferent knit.'

Hence they set sail again the last day of July, and steered directly towards the Eastern Cape of the isle called Punta d'Espada. Hereabouts they suddenly espied a ship that was coming from Porto Rico and bound for New Spain, being laden with coco-nuts. L'Ollonais, the Admiral, presently commanded the rest of the fleet they should wait for him nigh unto the isle of Savona, situate on the Eastern side of Cape Punta d'Espada, forasmuch as he alone intended to go and take the said vessel. The Spaniards, although they had been in sight now full two hours, and knew them to be Pirates, yet they would not flee, but rather prepared to fight, as being well armed, and provided of all things necessary thereunto. Thus the combat began between L'Ollonais and the Spanish vessel, which lasted three hours; and, these being past, they surrendered unto him. This ship was mounted with 16 guns, and had 50 fighting men on board. They found in her 120,000 weight of cacao, 40,000 pieces-of-eight, and the value of 10,000 more in jewels. L'Ollonais sent the vessel presently unto Tortuga to be unladed, with orders to return with the said ship as soon as possible to the isle of Savona, where he would wait for their coming. In the meanwhile the rest of the fleet, being arrived at the said island of Savona, met with another Spanish vessel that was coming from Comana with military provisions unto the isle of Hispaniola, and also with money to pay the garrisons of the said island. This vessel also they took without any resistance, although mounted with eight guns. Here were found seven thousand-weight of powder, great number of muskets and other things of this kind together, with 12,000 pieces-of-eight in ready money.

These forementioned events gave good encouragement unto the Pirates, as judging them very good beginnings unto the business they had in hand, especially finding their fleet pretty well recruited within a little while. For, the first ship that was taken being arrived at Tortuga, the Governor ordered to be instantly unladen, and soon after sent her back with fresh provisions and other necessaries unto L'Ollonais. This ship he chose for his own, and gave that which he commanded unto his comrade Antony du Puis. Thus having received new recruits of men, in lieu of them he had lost in taking the prizes above-mentioned and by sickness, he found himself in a good condition to prosecute his voyage. All being well animated and full of courage, they set sail for Maracaibo, which port is situated in the province of New Venezuela, in the latitude of twelve degrees and some minutes North. This island is in length twenty leagues, and twelve in breadth. Unto this port also belong the islands of Onega and Monges. The East side thereof is called Cape St Roman, and the Western side Cape of Caquibacoa. The gulf is called by some the Gulf of Venezuela, but the Pirates usually call it the Bay of Maracaibo.

At the beginning of this gulf are two islands, which extend for the greatest part from East to West. That [which] lies towards the East is called Isla de las Vigilias, or the Watch Isle, because in the middle thereof is to be seen a high hill, upon which stands a house wherein dwells perpetually a watchman. The other is called Isla de las Palomas, or the Isle of Pigeons. Between these two islands runs a little sea, or rather a lake, of fresh water, being three-score leagues in length and 30 in breadth ; which disgorges into the ocean, and dilates itself about the two islands aforementioned. Between them is found the best passage for ships, the channel of this passage being no broader than the flight of a great gun of eight pound carriage, more or less. Upon the Isle of Pigeons stands a castle to impede the entry of any vessels ; all such as will come in being necessitated to approach very nigh unto the castle, by reason of two banks of sand that lie on the other side, with only 14 foot water. Many other banks of sand are also found in this lake, as that which is called El Tablazo, or The Great Table, which is no deeper than ten foot ; but this lies forty leagues within the lake. Others there are that are no more than 6, 7, or 8 foot in depth. All of them are very dangerous, especially unto such mariners as are little acquainted with this lake. On the West side hereof is situated the city of Maracaibo, being very pleasant to the view, by reason its houses are built along the shore, having delicate prospects everywhere round about. The city may possibly contain three or four thousand persons, the slaves being included in this number ; all which do make a town of a reasonable bigness. Among these are judged to be eight hundred persons, more or less, able to bear arms, all of them Spaniards. Here are also one Parish Church, of very good fabric and well adorned, four monasteries, and one hospital.

The city is governed by a Deputy-Governor, who is substituted here by the Governor of Caracas, as being his dependency. The commerce or trading here exercised consists for the greatest part in hides and tobacco. The inhabitants possess great numbers of cattle and many plantations, which extend for the space of thirty leagues within the country, especially on that side that looks towards the great and populous town of Gibraltar. At which place are gathered huge quantities of cacao-nuts, and all other sorts of garden-fruits, which greatly serve for the regalement and sustenance of the inhabitants of Maracaibo, whose territories are much drier than those of Gibraltar. Unto this place those of Maracaibo send great quantities of flesh ; they making returns in oranges, lemons, and several other fruits. For the inhabitants of Gibraltar have great scarcity of provisions of flesh, their fields being not capable of feeding cows or sheep.

Before the city of Maracaibo lies a very spacious and secure port, wherein may be built all sort of vessels ; as having great convenience of timber, which may be transported thither at very little charge. Nigh unto the town lies also a small island called Borrica, which serves them to feed great numbers of goats, of which cattle the inhabitants of Maracaibo make greater use of their skins than their flesh or milk ; they making no great account of these two, unless while they are as yet but tender and young kids. In the fields about the town are fed some numbers of sheep, but of a very small size. In some of the islands that belong unto the lake, and in other places hereabouts, do inhabit many savage Indians, whom the Spaniards call *bravos*, or Wild. These Indians could never agree as yet, nor be reduced to any accord with the Spaniards, by reason of their brutish and untamable nature. They dwell for the most part towards the Western side of the lake, in little huts that are built upon trees which grow in the water, the cause hereof being only to exempt themselves as much as possible from the innumerable quantity of mosquitos or gnats that infest those parts, and by which they are tormented night and day. Towards the East side of the said lake are also to be seen whole towns of fishermen, who likewise are constrained to live in huts, built upon trees, like unto the former. Another reason of thus dwelling is the frequent inundations of waters ; for, after great rains, the land is often overflowed for the space of 2 or 3 leagues, there being no less than five-and-twenty great rivers that feed this lake. The town of Gibraltar is also frequently drowned by these inundations, insomuch that the inhabitants are constrained to leave their houses and retire unto their plantations.

Gibraltar is situated at the side of the lake, forty leagues or thereabouts within it, and receives its necessary provisions of flesh, as has been said, from Maracaibo. The town is inhabited by 1500 persons, more or less, whereof 400 may be capable of bearing arms. The greatest part of the inhabitants keep open shops, wherein they exercise one mechanic trade or other. All the adjacent fields about this town are cultivated with numerous plantations of sugar and cacao, in which are many tall and beautiful trees, of whose timber houses may be built, and also ships. Among these trees are found great store of handsome and proportionable cedars, being seven or eight foot in circumference, which serve there very commonly to build boats and ships. These they build after such manner as to bear one only great sail; and such vessels are called *piraguas*. The whole country round about is sufficiently furnished with rivers and brooks, which are very useful to the inhabitants in time of droughts, they opening in that occasion many little channels, through which they lead the rivulets to water their fields and plantations. They plant in like manner great quantity of tobacco, which is much esteemed in Europe; and for its goodness is called there *Tabaco de Sacerdotes*, or Priests' Tobacco. They enjoy nigh twenty leagues of jurisdiction, which is bounded and defended by very high mountains that are perpetually covered with snow. On the other side of these mountains is situated a great city called Merida, unto which the town of Gibraltar is subject. All sort of merchandize is carried from this town unto the aforesaid city upon mules; and that but at one season of the year, by reason of the excessive cold endured in those high mountains. Upon the said mules great returns are made in flour of meal, which comes from towards Peru by the way of Estaffe.

Thus far I thought it convenient to make a short description of the aforesaid lake of Maracaibo, and its situation; to the intent my reader might the better be enabled to comprehend what I shall say concerning what was acted by the

Pirates in this place, the history whereof I shall presently begin.

As soon as L'Ollonais arrived at the Gulf of Venezuela, he cast anchor with his whole fleet, out of sight of the watch-tower of the island of Vigilias, or Watch Isle. The next day, very early, he set sail hence, with all his ships, for the lake of Maracaibo; where, being arrived, they cast anchor the second time. Soon after, they landed all their men, with design to attack in the first place the castle or fortress that commanded the bar, and is therefore called De la Barra. This fort consists only of several great baskets of earth, placed upon a rising ground, upon which are planted sixteen great guns, with several other heaps of earth round about, for covering the men within. The Pirates, having landed at a distance of a league from this fort, began to advance by degrees towards it. But the Governor thereof, having espied their landing, had placed an ambuscade of some of his men, with design to cut them off behind, while he meant to attack them in the front. This ambuscade was found out by the Pirates; and, hereupon getting before, they assaulted and defeated it so entirely that not one man could retreat unto the castle. This obstacle being removed, L'Ollonais with all his companions advanced in great haste towards the fort. And after a fight of almost three hours, wherein they behaved themselves with desperate courage, such as this sort of people are used to show, they became masters thereof, having made use of no other arms than their swords and pistols. And, while they were fighting, those who were routed in the ambuscade, not being able to get into the castle, retired towards the city of Maracaibo in great confusion and disorder, crying: *The Pirates will presently be here with two-thousand men and more.* This city, having formerly been taken by such kind of people as these were, and sacked even to the remotest corners thereof, preserved still in its memory a fresh *idea* of that misery. Hereupon, as soon as they heard this dismal news, they endeavoured to escape as fast as they could towards Gibraltar in their boats and canoes, carrying with them all the goods and money they could. Being come to Gibraltar, they dispersed the rumours that the fortress was taken, and that nothing had been saved, nor any person able to escape the fury of the Pirates.

The castle being taken by the Pirates, as was said before,

they presently made sign unto the ships of the victory they had obtained, to the end they should come farther in, without apprehension of any danger. The rest of that day was spent in ruining and demolishing the said castle. They nailed the guns, and burnt as much as they could not carry away; burying also the dead, and sending on board the fleet such as were wounded. The next day very early in the morning they weighed anchor, and directed their course all together towards the city of Maracaibo, distant only 6 leagues more or less from the fort. But the wind being very scarce, that day they could advance but little, as being forced to expect the flowing of the tide. The next morning they came within sight of the town, and began to make preparations for landing under the protection of their own guns, being persuaded the Spaniards might have laid an ambuscade among the trees and woods. Thus they put their men into canoes, which for that purpose they brought with them, and landed where they thought most convenient, shooting in the meanwhile very furiously with their great guns. Of the people that were in the canoes, half only went on shore; the other half remained on board the said canoes. They fired with their guns from the ships as fast as was possible towards the woody part of the shore; but could see, and were answered by, nobody. Thus they marched in good order into the town, whose inhabitants, as I told you before, were all retired into the woods, and towards Gibraltar, with their wives, children, and families. Their houses they left well provided with all sort of victuals, such as flour, bread, pork, brandy, wines, and good store of poultry. With these things the Pirates fell to banqueting and making good cheer; for in four weeks before they had had no opportunity of filling their stomachs with such plenty.

They instantly possessed themselves of the best houses in the town, and placed sentries everywhere they thought convenient. The great church served them for their main *corps du garde*. The next day they sent a body of 160 men to find out some of the inhabitants of the town, whom they understood were hidden in the woods not far thence. These returned that very night, bringing with them 20,000 pieces-of-eight, several mules laden with household goods and merchandize, and 20 prisoners, between men, women, and children.

Some of these prisoners were put to the rack, only to make them confess where they had hidden the rest of their goods; but they could extort very little from them. L'Ollonais, who never used to make any great account of murdering, though in cold blood, ten or twelve Spaniards, drew his cutlass and hacked one to pieces in the presence of all the rest, saying: *If you do not confess and declare where you have hidden the rest of your goods, I will do the like to all your companions.* At last, amongst these horrible cruelties and inhuman threats, one was found who promised to conduct him and show the place where the rest of the Spaniards were hidden. But those that were fled, having intelligence that one had discovered their lurking holes unto the Pirates, changed place, and buried all the remnant of their riches underground, insomuch that the Pirates could not find them out, unless some other person of their own party should reveal them. Besides that, the Spaniards, flying from one place to another every day and often changing woods, were jealous even of each other, insomuch as the father scarce presumed to trust his own son.

Finally, after that the Pirates had been fifteen days in Maracaibo, they resolved to go towards Gibraltar. But the inhabitants of this place, having received intelligence thereof beforehand, as also that they intended afterwards to go to Merida, gave notice of this design to the Governor thereof, who was a valiant soldier and had served his king in Flanders in many military offices. His answer was: *He would have them take no care; for he hoped in a little while to exterminate the said Pirates.* Whereupon he transferred himself immediately unto Gibraltar, with 400 men well armed, ordering at the same time the inhabitants of the said town to put themselves in arms; so that in all he made a body of 800 fighting men. With the same speed he commanded a battery to be raised towards the sea, whereon he mounted 20 guns, covering them all with great baskets of earth. Another battery likewise he placed in another place, mounted with 8 guns. After this was done, he barricaded a highway or narrow passage into the town, through which the Pirates of necessity ought to pass; opening at the same time another, through much dirt and mud, in the wood, which was totally unknown to the Pirates.

The Pirates, not knowing anything of these preparations, having embarked all their prisoners and what they had robbed, took their way towards Gibraltar. Being come within sight of the place, they perceived the Royal standard hanging forth, and that those of the town had a mind to fight and defend their houses. L'Ollonais, seeing this resolution, called a council of war, to deliberate what he ought to do in such case ; propounding withal unto his officers and marines, that the difficulty of such an enterprize was very great, seeing the Spaniards had had so much time to put themselves in a posture of defence, and had gotten a good body of men together, with many martial provisions. *But notwithstanding*, said he, *have a good courage. We must either defend ourselves like good soldiers, or lose our lives with all the riches we have gotten. Do as I shall do, who am your Captain. At other times we have fought with fewer men than we have in our company at present, and yet we have overcome greater numbers than there possibly can be in this town. The more they are, the more glory we shall attribute unto our fortune, and the greater riches we shall increase unto it.* The Pirates were under this suspicion, that all those riches which the inhabitants of Maracaibo had absconded, were transported unto Gibraltar, or at least the greatest part thereof. After this speech, they all promised to follow him and obey very exactly his commands. Unto whom L'Ollonais made answer : *'Tis well ; but know ye withal that the first man who shall show any fear, or the least apprehension thereof, I will pistol him with my own hands.*

With this resolution they cast anchor nigh the shore, at the distance of one quarter of a league from the town. The next day, before sunrising, they were all landed, being to the number of three-hundred-and-four-score men, well provided, and armed every one with a cutlass and one or two pistols ; and withal sufficient powder and bullet for 30 charges. Here, upon the shore, they all shook hands with one another in testimony of good courage, and began their march, L'Ollonais speaking these words to them : *Come, my brothers, follow me, and have a good courage.* They followed their way with a guide they had provided. But he, believing he led them well, brought them to the way which the Governor had obstructed with barricades. Through this not being able to pass, they went unto the other which was newly made in the wood among the mire, unto which the Spaniards could shoot at pleasure. Notwithstanding, the Pirates, being full of courage, cut down multitude of branches of trees, and threw them in the dirt upon the way, to the end they might not stick so fast in it. In the meanwhile, those of Gibraltar fired at them with their great guns so furiously that they could scarce hear or see one another through the noise and smoke. Being now past the wood, they came upon firm ground, where they met with a battery of 6 guns, which immediately the Spaniards discharged against them, all being loaded with small bullets and pieces of iron. After this, the Spaniards, sallying forth, set upon them with such fury as caused the Pirates to give way and retire, very few of them daring to advance towards the fort. They continued still firing against the Pirates, of whom they had already killed and wounded many. This made them go back to seek some other way through the middle of the wood ; but, the Spaniards having cut down many trees to hinder the passage, they could find none, and thus were forced to return unto that they had left. Here the Spaniards continued to fire as before ; neither would they sally out of their batteries to attack the Pirates any more. Hereby L'Ollonais and his companions, not being able to grimp[1] up the baskets of earth, were compelled to make use of an old stratagem—wherewith at last they deceived and overcame the Spaniards.

L'Ollonais retired suddenly with all his men, making show as if he fled. Hereupon the Spaniards, crying out : *They flee, they flee ; let us follow them*, sallied forth with great disorder, to pursue the fugitive Pirates. After they had drawn them some distance from their batteries, which was their only design, they turned upon them, unexpectedly with swords in hand, and killed above two hundred men. And thus fighting their way through those who remained alive, they possessed themselves of the batteries. The Spaniards that remained abroad gave themselves up for lost, and consequently took their flight unto the woods. The other part that was in the battery of eight guns surrendered themselves upon conditions

[1] French *grimper*, to climb, cause to mount, raise. *Grymp* is used in *St Brandan*, p. 20, in the sense of to 'grip' : Halliwell (*Dict. of Archaic Words*) suggests a possible misprint. Mr. Grant Allen uses the word in his *Scallywag* [1893], i, 44 : "How the little beasts grimp . . . such plucky little beggars, and so strong for their size !"

of obtaining quarter for their lives. The Pirates, being now become masters of the whole town, pulled down the Spanish colours, and set up their own, taking prisoners at the same time as many as they could find. These they carried unto the great church, whither also they transferred many great guns, wherewith they raised a battery to defend themselves, fearing lest the Spaniards that were fled should rally more of their own party and come upon them again. But the next day, after they were all fortified, all their fears disappeared. They gathered all the dead, with intent to allow them burial, finding the number of above 500 Spaniards killed, besides those that were wounded within the town and those that died of their wounds in the woods, where they sought for refuge. Besides which, the Pirates had in their custody above 150 prisoners, and nigh 500 slaves, many women and children.

Of their own companions the Pirates found only forty dead, and almost as many more wounded. Whereof the greatest part died afterwards, through the constitution of the air, which brought fevers and other accidents upon them. They put all the Spaniards that were slain into two great boats, and carrying them one-quarter-of-a-league within the sea, they sank the boats. These things being done, they gathered all the plate, household stuff, and merchandize they could rob or thought convenient to carry away. But the Spaniards who had anything as yet left unto them, hid it very carefully. Soon after, the Pirates, as if they were unsatisfied with the great riches they had gotten, began to seek for more goods and merchandize, not sparing those who lived in the fields, such as hunters and planters. They had scarce been eighteen days upon the place, when the greatest part of the prisoners they had taken died of hunger. For in the town very few provisions, especially of flesh, were to be found. Howbeit, they had some quantity of flour of meal, although perhaps something less than what was sufficient. But this the Pirates had taken into their custody to make bread for themselves. As to the swine, cows, sheep, and poultry that were found upon the place, they took them likewise for their own sustenance, without allowing any share thereof unto the poor prisoners. For these they only provided some small quantity of mules' and asses' flesh, which they killed for that purpose. And such as could not eat of that loathsome provision were constrained to die of hunger, as many did, their stomachs not being accustomed to such unusual sustenance. Only some women were found, who were allowed better cheer by the Pirates, because they served them in their sensual delights, unto which those robbers are hugely given. Among those women, some had been forced, others were volunteers; though almost all had rather taken up that vice through poverty and hunger more than any other cause. Of the prisoners many also died under the torments they sustained, to make them confess where they had hidden their money or jewels. And of these, some, because they had none nor knew of none, and others for denying what they knew, endured such horrible deaths.

Finally, after having been in possession of the town four entire weeks, they sent four of the prisoners remaining alive unto the Spaniards that were fled into the woods, demanding of them a ransom for not burning the town. The sum hereof they constituted 10,000 pieces-of-eight, which, unless it were sent unto them, they threatened to fire and reduce into ashes the whole village. For bringing in of this money they allowed them only the space of two days. These being past, and the Spaniards not having been able to gather so punctually such a sum, the Pirates began to set fire to many places of the town. Thus the inhabitants, perceiving the Pirates to be in earnest, begged of them to help to extinguish the fire; and withal promised the ransom should be readily paid. The Pirates condescended to their petition, helping as much as they could to stop the progress of the fire. Yet, though they used the best endeavours they possibly could, one part of the town was ruined, especially the church belonging to the monastery, which was burnt even to dust. After they had received the sum above-mentioned, they carried on board their ships all the riches they had robbed, together with a great number of slaves which had not as yet paid their ransom. For all the prisoners had sums of money set upon them, and the slaves were also commanded to be redeemed. Hence they returned to Maracaibo, where being arrived they found a general consternation in the whole city. Unto which they sent three or four prisoners to tell the governor and inhabitants: *They should bring them* 30,000 *pieces-of-eight on board their ships, for a ransom of their houses; otherwise they should be entirely sacked anew and burnt.*

Among these debates a certain party of Pirates came on

shore to rob, and these carried away the images, the pictures, and bells of the great church, on board the fleet. The Spaniards, who were sent to demand of those who were fled the sum aforementioned, returned with orders to make some agreement with the Pirates. This they performed, and concluded with the Pirates they would give for their ransom and liberty the sum of 20,000 pieces-of-eight and 500 cows. The condition hereof being that they should commit no farther acts of hostility against any person, but should depart thence presently after payment of the money and cattle. The one and the other being delivered, they set sail with the whole fleet, causing great joy unto the inhabitants of Maracaibo to see themselves quit of this sort of people. Notwithstanding, three days after they resumed their fears and admiration, seeing the Pirates to appear again and re-enter the port they had left with all their ships. But these apprehensions soon vanished, by only hearing one of the Pirates' errand, who came on shore to tell them from L'Ollonais : *They should send him a skilful Pilot to conduct one of his greatest ships over the dangerous bank that lies at the entry of the lake.* Which petition, or rather command, was instantly granted.

The Pirates had now been full two months in those towns, wherein they committed those cruel and insolent actions we have told you of. Departing therefore thence, they took their course towards the island Hispaniola, and arrived thither in eight days, casting anchor in a port called Isla de la Vaca, or Cow Island. This isle is inhabited by French Buccaneers, who most commonly sell the flesh they hunt unto Pirates and others who now and then put in there with intent of victualling or trading with them. Here they unladed the whole cargazons[1] of riches they had robbed—the usual storehouse of the Pirates being commonly under the shelter of the Buccaneers. Here also they made a dividend amongst them of all their prizes and gains, according to that order and degree which belonged unto every one, as hath been mentioned above. Having cast up the account and made exact calculation of all they had purchased, they found in ready money 260,000 pieces-of-eight. Whereupon, this being divided, every one received

[1] Spanish for cargo : cf. "There should come in euery ship the fourth part of her cargason in money"—Hakluyt, *Voyages* [1583], vol. II, i, p. 246. (Arber's *English Garner*, vol. iii, p. 172.)

to his share in money, and also in pieces of silk, linen, and other commodities, the value of above 100 pieces-of-eight. Those who had been wounded in this expedition received their part before all the rest ; I mean, such recompenses as I spoke of in the First Book, for the loss of their limbs which many sustained. Afterwards they weighed all the plate that was uncoined, reckoning after the rate of 10 pieces-of-eight for every pound. The jewels were prized with much variety, either at too high or too low rates ; being thus occasioned by their own ignorance. This being done, every one was put to his oath again that he had not concealed anything nor substracted from the common stock. Hence they proceeded to the dividend of what shares belonged to such as were dead amongst them, either in battle or otherwise. These shares were given to their friends to be kept entire for them, and to be delivered in due time unto their nearest relations, or whomsoever should appear to be their lawful heirs.

The whole dividend being entirely finished, they set sail thence for the isle of Tortuga. Here they arrived one month after, to the great joy of most that were upon the island. For, as to the common Pirates, in three weeks they had scarce any money left them, having spent it all in things of little value, or at play either of cards or dice. Here also arrived, not long before them, two French ships laden with wine and brandy and other things of this kind ; whereby these liquors, at the arrival of the Pirates, were sold indifferent cheap. But this lasted not long ; for soon after they were enhanced extremely, a gallon of brandy being sold for 4 pieces-of-eight. The Governor of the island bought of the Pirates the whole cargo of the ship laden with cacao, giving them for that rich commodity scarce the twentieth part of what it was worth. Thus they made shift to lose and spend the riches they had got in much less time than they were purchased by robbing. The taverns and stews, according to the custom of Pirates, got the greatest part thereof, insomuch that soon after they were constrained to seek more by the same unlawful means they had obtained the preceding.

CHAPTER III

L'Ollonais makes new preparations to take the city of St James de Leon; as also that of Nicaragua, where he miserably perishes

L'OLLONAIS had got himself very great esteem and repute at Tortuga by this last voyage, by reason he brought them home such considerable profit. And now he needed take no great care how to gather men to serve under his colours, seeing more came in voluntarily to proffer their service unto him than he could employ, every one reposing such great confidence in his conduct for seeking their fortunes that they judged it a matter of the greatest security imaginable to expose themselves in his company to the hugest dangers that might possibly occur. He resolved, therefore, for a second voyage, to go with his officers and soldiers towards the parts of Nicaragua, and pillage there as many towns as he could meet.

Having published his new preparations, he had all his men together at the time appointed, being about the number of 700, more or less. Of these he put 300 on board the ship he took at Maracaibo, and the rest in other vessels of lesser burden, which were five more; so that the whole number were in all six ships. The first port they went unto was in the island of Hispaniola, to a place called Bayala, where they determined to victual the fleet and take in provisions. This being done, they set sail thence, and steered their course to a port called Matamana, lying on the South side of the isle of Cuba. Their intent was to take here all the canoes they could meet, these coasts being frequented by a huge number of fishermen of tortoises, who carry them thence unto Havana. They took as many of the said canoes, to the great grief of those miserable people, as they thought necessary for their designs. For they had great necessity of these small bottoms, by reason the port whither they designed to go was not of depth sufficient to bear ships of any burden. Hence they took their course towards the cape called Gracias à Dios, situate upon the continent in latitude fifteen degrees North, at the distance of one hundred leagues from the island De los Pinos. But, being out at sea, they were taken with a sad and tedious calm, and by the agitation of the waves alone were thrown into the Gulf of Honduras. Here they laboured very much to regain what they had lost, but all in vain; both the waters in their course and the winds being contrary to their endeavours. Besides that, the ship wherein L'Ollonais was embarked could not follow the rest; and, what was worse, they wanted already provisions. Hereupon they were forced to put into the first port or bay they could reach, to revictual their fleet. Thus they entered with their canoes into a river called Xagua, inhabited by Indians, whom they totally robbed and destroyed; they finding amongst their goods great quantity of millet, many hogs and hens. Not contented with what they had done, they determined to remain there until the bad weather was over, and to pillage all the towns and villages lying along the coast of the gulf. Thus they passed from one place to another, seeking as yet more provisions, by reason they had not what they wanted for the accomplishment of their designs. Having searched and rifled many vilages, where they found no great matter, they came at last to Puerto Cavallo. In this port the Spaniards have two several storehouses, which serve to keep the merchandize that are brought from the inner parts of the country until the arrival of the ships. There was in the port at that occasion a Spanish ship mounted with four-and-twenty guns and sixteen *pedreros*[1] or mortar-pieces. This ship was immediately seized by the Pirates; and then, drawing nigh the shore, they landed and burnt the two storehouses, with all the rest of the houses belonging to the place. Many inhabitants likewise they took prisoners and committed upon them the most insolent and inhuman cruelties that ever heathens invented, putting them to the cruellest tortures they could imagine or devise. It was the custom of L'Ollonais

[1] *Pedrero* (Spanish), a swivel-gun, used for firing off stones, scraps of iron, etc. Cf. Barret, *Theorie of Warres* [1598]: 'the cannon and double cannon; the Pedrera, Basilisco, and such like.' Anglicized as *patarero*. Cf. Angelo and Carli, *Congo* [1700; in Pinkerton's *Voyages*, XVI, p. 180]: 'The ship carried fifty guns, four-and-twenty patareroes, and other necessaries.'

that, having tormented any persons and they not confessing, he would instantly cut them in pieces with his anger, and pull out their tongues; desiring to do the same, if possible, to every Spaniard in the world. Oftentimes it happened that some of these miserable prisoners, being forced thereunto by the rack, would promise to discover the places where the fugitive Spaniards lay hidden; which being not able afterwards to perform, they were put to more enormous and cruel deaths than they who were dead before.

The prisoners being all dead and annihilated (excepting only two, whom they reserved to show them what they desired), they marched hence to the town of San Pedro, or St Peter, distant 10 or 12 leagues from Puerto Cavallo, having in their company 300 men, whom L'Ollonais led, and leaving behind him Moses van Vin for his lieutenant to govern the rest in his absence. Being come 3 leagues upon their way, they met with a troop of Spaniards, who lay in ambuscade for their coming. These they set upon with all the courage imaginable, and at last totally defeated, howbeit they behaved themselves very manfully at the beginning of the fight. But, not being able to resist the fury of the Pirates, they were forced to give way and save themselves by flight, leaving many Pirates dead upon the place and wounded, as also some of their own party maimed by the way. These L'Ollonais put to death without mercy, having asked them what questions he thought fit for his purpose.

There were still remaining some few prisoners who were not wounded. These were asked by L'Ollonais if any more Spaniards did lie farther on in ambuscade: unto whom they answered, there were. Then he commanded them to be brought before him, one by one, and asked if there was no other way to be found to the town but that. This he did out of a design to excuse, if possible, those ambuscades. But they all constantly answered him, they knew none. Having asked them all, and finding they could show him no other way, L'Ollonais grew outrageously passionate; insomuch that he drew his cutlass, and with it cut open the breast of one of those poor Spaniards, and, pulling out his heart with his sacrilegious hands, began to bite and gnaw it with his teeth like a ravenous wolf, saying to the rest: *I will serve you all alike if you show me not another way.*

Hereupon those miserable wretches promised to show him another way; but withal they told him it was extremely difficult and laborious. Thus, to satisfy that cruel tyrant, they began to lead him and his army. But finding it not for his purpose, even as they told him, he was constrained unto return to the former way, swearing with great choler and indignation: *Mort Dieu, les Espagnols me le payeront!* (*By God's death, the Spaniards shall pay me for this!*).

The next day he fell into another ambuscade, the which he assaulted with such horrible fury that in less than an hour's time he routed the Spaniards, and killed the greatest part of them. The Spaniards were persuaded that by these ambuscades they should better be able to destroy the Pirates, assaulting them by degrees; and for this reason had posted themselves in several places. At last he met with a third ambuscade, where was placed a party of Spaniards both stronger and to greater advantage than the former. Yet, notwithstanding, the Pirates, by throwing with their hands little fireballs in great number, and continuing to do so for some time, forced this party, as well as the preceding, to flee; and this with such great loss of men as that, before they could reach the town, the greatest part of the Spaniards were either killed or wounded. There was but one path which led to the town. This path was very well barricaded with good defences; and the rest of the town round about was planted with certain shrubs or trees named *raquelles*, very full of thorns and these very sharp-pointed. This sort of fortification seemed stronger than the triangles which are used in Europe, when an army is of necessity to pass by the place of an enemy, it being almost impossible for the Pirates to traverse those shrubs. The Spaniards that were posted behind the said defences, seeing the Pirates come, began to shoot at them with their great guns. But these, perceiving them ready to fire, used to stoop down, and, when the shot was made, fall upon the defendants with fireballs in hands and naked swords, killing with these weapons many of the town. Yet, notwithstanding, not being able to advance any farther, they were constrained to retire for the first time. Afterwards they returned to the attack again, with fewer men than before; and, observing not to shoot till they were very near, they gave the Spaniards a charge so dexterously that with every shot they killed an enemy.

"L'Ollonais . . . drew his cutlass, and with it cut open the breast of one of those poor Spaniards, and, pulling out his heart with his sacrilegious hands, began to bite and gnaw it with his teeth" (p. 103).

The attack continuing thus eager on both sides till night, the Spaniards were compelled to hang forth a white flag, in token of truce and that they desired to come to a parley. The only conditions they required for delivering the town were: *That the Pirates should give the inhabitants quarter for two hours.* This short space of time they demanded, with intent to carry away and abscond as much of their goods and riches as they could, as also to flee to some other neighbouring town. Upon the agreement of this article they entered the town, and continued there the two hours above-mentioned, without committing the least act of hostility or causing any trouble to the inhabitants. But no sooner that time was passed than L'Ollonais ordered the inhabitants should be followed and robbed of all they had carried away; and not only goods, but their persons, likewise, to be made all prisoners. Notwithstanding, the greatest part of their merchandize and goods were in such manner absconded as the Pirates could not find them; they meeting only a few leathern sacks that were filled with anil, or indigo[1].

Having stayed at this town some few days, and according to their usual customs committed there most horrid insolences, they at last quitted the place, carrying away with them all that they possibly could, and reducing the town totally into ashes. Being come to the seaside, where they left a party of their own comrades, they found these had busied themselves in cruizing upon the fishermen that lived thereabouts or came that way from the river of Guatemala. In this river also was expected a ship that was to come from Spain. Finally they resolved to go towards the islands that lie on the other side of the gulf, there to cleanse and careen their vessels. But in the meanwhile they left two canoes before the coast, or rather the mouth of the river of Guatemala, to the intent they should take the ship which, as I said before, was expected from Spain.

But their chief intention of going to those islands was to seek provisions, as knowing the tortoises of those places are very excellent and pleasant food. As soon as they arrived there, they divided into troops, each party choosing a fit post for that fishery. Every one of them undertook to knit a net

[1] The West Indian indigo plant, *Indigofera anil*. Cf. Linschoten, *Voyages*, Bk. i, vol. i, p. 61 (ed. 1885): 'annell or indigo groweth onely in Cambaia.'

with the rinds of certain trees called in those parts *macoa*. Of these rinds they make also ropes and cables for the service of ships; insomuch that no vessel can be in need of such things whensoever they can but find the said trees. There are also in those parts many places where they find pitch[1], which is gathered thereabouts in great abundance. The quantity hereof is so great that, running down the sea-coasts being melted by the heat of the sun, it congeals in the water into great heaps, and represents the shape of small islands. This pitch is not like unto that we have in the countries of Europe, but is hugely like, both in colour and shape, that froth of the sea which is called by the naturalists bitumen. But in my judgment this matter is nothing else but wax, which stormy weather has cast into the sea, being part of that huge quantity which in the neighbouring territories is made by the bees. Thus from places far distant from the sea it is also brought to the sea-coast by the winds and rolling waves of great rivers; being likewise mingled with sand, and having the smell of black amber, such as is sent us from the Orient. In those parts are found great quantities of the said bees, who make their honey in trees; whence it happens that the honey-combs being fixed unto the bodies of the trees, when tempests arise they are torn away, and by the fury of the winds carried into the sea, as has been said before. Some naturalists are willing to say that between the honey and the wax is made a separation by means of the salt water, whence proceeds also the good amber. This opinion is rendered the more probable because the said amber, being found and tasted, it affords the like taste as wax does.

But now, returning to my discourse, I shall let you know that the Pirates made in those islands all the haste to equip their vessels they could possibly, by reason they had news the Spanish ship which they expected was come. They spent some time in cruizing upon the coasts of Yucatan, whereabouts inhabit many Indians, who seek for the amber above-mentioned in those seas. But seeing we are come to this place, I shall here, by the by, make some short remarks on the manner of living of these Indians, and the divine worship which they practice.

[1] The pitch lake of La Brea, Trinidad, is celebrated. Asphalt is an important article of export from Trinidad at the present day.

The Indians of the coasts of Yucatan have now been above one hundred years under the dominion of the Spaniards. Unto this nation they performed all manner of service; for, whensoever any of them had need of a slave or servant, they sent to seek one of these Indians to serve them as long as they pleased. By the Spaniards they were initiated at first in the principles of Christian faith and religion. Being thus made a part of Christianity, they used to send them every Sunday and holiday through the whole year a priest to perform divine service among them. Afterwards, for what reasons are not known, but certainly through evil temptations of the Father of Idolatry, the Devil, they suddenly cast off Christian religion again, and abandoned the true divine worship, beating withal and abusing the priest that was sent them. This provoked the Spaniards to punish them according to their deserts, which they did by casting many of the chiefest of these Indians into prison. Every one of those barbarians had, and has still, a god to himself whom he serves and worships. It is a thing that deserves all admiration, to consider how they use in this particular a child that is newly born into the world. As soon as this is issued from the womb of the mother, they carry it to the temple. Here they make a circle or hole, which they fill with ashes, without mingling anything else with them. Upon this heap of ashes they place the child naked, leaving it there a whole night alone, not without great danger; nobody daring to come near it. In the meanwhile the temple is open on all sides, to the intent all sorts of beasts may freely come in and out. The next day the father and relations of the infant return thither, to see if the track or step of any animal appears to be printed in the ashes. Not finding any, they leave the child there until some beast has approached the infant and left behind him the mark of his feet. Unto this animal, whatsoever it be, they consecrate the creature newly born as unto its god, which he is bound to worship and serve all his life, esteeming the said beast as his patron and protector in all cases of danger or necessity. They offer unto their gods sacrifices of fire, wherein they burn a certain gum called by them *copal*[1], whose smoke affords a very delicious smell. When the infant is grown up, the parents thereof tell him and show him

[1] Spanish *copal:* a resin. Cf. Frampton, *Joyfull Newes* [1577]: 'The copal is a rosine very white.'

whom he ought to worship, serve, and honour as his own proper god. This being known, he goes to the temple, where he makes offerings unto the said beast. Afterwards, if in the course of his life any one has injured him or any evil happens to him, he complains thereof to that beast, and sacrifices unto it for revenge. Whence many times comes that those who have done the injury of which he complains are found to be bitten, killed, or otherwise hurt by such animals.

After this superstitious and idolatrous manner do live those miserable and ignorant Indians that inhabit all the islands of the Gulf of Honduras, as also many of them that dwell upon the continent of Yucatan. In the territories of which country are found most excellent ports for the safety of ships, where those Indians most commonly love to build their houses. These people are not very faithful one to another, and likewise use strange ceremonies at their marriages. Whensoever any one pretends to marry a young damsel, he first applies himself to her father or nearest relation. He then examines him very exactly concerning the manner of cultivating their plantations and other things at his pleasure. Having satisfied the questions that were put to him by the father-in-law, he gives the young man a bow and arrow. With these things he repairs to the young maid, and presents her with a garland of green leaves, interweaved with sweet-smelling flowers. This she is obliged to put upon her head, and lay aside that which she wore before that time; it being the custom of the country that all virgins go perpetually crowned with flowers. This garland being received and put upon the head, every one of the relations and friends go to advise with others among themselves, whether that marriage will be useful and of likely happiness or not. Afterwards the aforesaid relations and friends meet together at the house of the damsel's father, and they drink of a certain liquor made of maize, or Indian wheat. And here before the whole company the father gives his daughter in marriage unto the bridegroom. The next day the newly-married bride comes to her mother, and in her presence pulls off the garland and tears it in pieces, with great cries and bitter lamentations, according to the custom of the country. Many other things I could relate at large of the manner of living and customs of those Indians; but these I shall omit, thereby to follow my discourse.

Our Pirates, therefore, had many canoes of the Indians in the isle of Sambale, five leagues distant from the coasts of Yucatan. In the aforesaid island is found great quantity of amber, but more especially when any storm arises from towards the East, whence the waves bring many things and very different. Through this sea no vessels can pass, unless very small, the waters being too shallow. In the lands that are surrounded by this sea is found huge quantity of Campeche wood[1] and other things of this kind, that serve for the art of dyeing, which occasions them to be much esteemed in Europe, and doubtless would be much more, in case we had the skill and science of the Indians, who are so industrious as to make a dye or tincture that never changes its colour nor fades away.

After that the Pirates had been in that gulf three entire months, they received advice that the Spanish ship was come. Hereupon they hastened unto the port, where the ship lay at anchor unlading the merchandize it brought, with design to assault her as soon as it was possible. But, before this attempt, they thought it convenient to send away some of their boats from the mouth of the river, to seek for a small vessel which was expected, having notice that she was very richly laden, the greatest part of the cargo being plate, indigo, and cochineal. In the meanwhile the people of the ship that was in the port had notice given that the Pirates designed upon them. Hereupon they prepared all things very well for the defence of the said vessel, which was mounted with 42 guns, had many arms on board and other necessaries, together with 130 fighting men. Unto L'Ollonias all this seemed but little; and thus he assaulted her with great courage, his own ship carrying only 22 guns, and having no more than a small *saëtia*, or flyboat, for help. But the Spaniards defended themselves after such manner as they forced the Pirates to retire. Notwithstanding, while the smoke of the powder continued very thick, as amidst a dark fog or mist, they sent four canoes very well manned, and boarded the ship with great agility, whereby they compelled the Spaniards to surrender.

The ship being taken, they found not in her what they thought, as being already almost wholly unladed. All the

[1] Logwood, named from Campeachy on the West coast of Yucatan. Cf. "The chiefest merchandize which they lade there in small frigats is a certeine wood called *campeche* (wherewith they vse to die)."—Hakluyt, *Voyages* [1600], vol. iii, p. 461.

treasure they here got consisted only in fifty bars of iron, a small parcel of paper, some earthen jars full of wine, and other things of this kind: all of small importance.

Presently after, L'Ollonais called a council of the whole fleet, wherein he told them he intended to go to Guatemala. Upon this point they divided into several sentiments; some of them liking the proposal very well, and others disliking it as much—especially a certain party of them, who were but new in those exercises of piracy, and who had imagined at their setting forth from Tortuga that pieces-of-eight were gathered as easily as pears from a tree. But, having found at last most things contrary to their expectation, they quitted the fleet, and returned whence they set out. Others, on the contrary, affirmed they had rather die of hunger than return home without a great deal of money.

But the major part of the company, judging the propounded voyage little fit for their purpose, separated from L'Ollonais and the rest. Among these was ringleader one Moses Vanclein, who was captain of the ship taken at Puerto Cavallo. This fellow took his course towards Tortuga, designing to cruize to and fro in those seas. With him also joined another comrade of his own, by name Pierre le Picard, who, seeing the rest to leave L'Ollonais, thought fit to do the same. These runaways having thus parted company, steered their course homewards, coasting along the continent till they came at last unto Costa Rica. Here they landed a strong party of men nigh unto the river of Veraguas, and marched in good order unto the town of the same name. This place they took and totally pillaged, notwithstanding that the Spaniards made a strong and warlike resistance. They brought away some of the inhabitants as prisoners, with all that they had robbed, which was of no great importance, the reason hereof being the poverty of the place, which exercises no manner of trade than only working in the mines, where some of the inhabitants do constantly attend. Yet no other persons seek for the gold than only slaves. These they compel to dig, whether they live or die, and wash the earth that is taken out in the neighbouring rivers; where oftentimes they find pieces of gold as big as peas. Finally, the pirates found in this robbery no greater value than 7 or 8 pounds weight of gold. Hereupon they returned back, giving over the design they had to go farther on to the town of

Nata, situated upon the coasts of the South Sea. Hitherto they designed to march, knowing the inhabitants to be rich merchants, who had their slaves at work in the mines of Veraguas. But from this enterprize they were deterred by the multitude of Spaniards whom they saw gather on all sides to fall upon them; whereof they had timely advice beforehand.

L'Ollonais, thus abandoned by his companions, remained alone in the Gulf of Honduras, by reason his ship was too great to get out at the time of the reflux of those seas, which the smaller vessels could do more easily. There he sustained great want of all sorts of provisions, insomuch as they were constrained to go ashore every day to seek wherewithal to maintain themselves. And, not finding anything else, they were forced to kill monkeys and other animals such as they could find, for their sustenance.

At last having found, in the latitude of the Cape of Gracias à Dios, certain little islands called De las Pertas, here, nigh unto these isles, his ship fell upon a bank of sand, where it stuck so fast as no art could be found to get her off into deep water again, notwithstanding they unladed all the guns, iron, and other weighty things as much as possibly they could: but all they could do was to little or no effect. Hereupon they were necessitated to break the ship in pieces, and with some of the planks and nails build themselves a boat, wherewith to get away from those islands. Thus they began their work; and, while they are employed about it, I shall pass to describe succinctly the isles aforementioned and their inhabitants.

The islands called De las Pertas are inhabited by Indians, who are properly savages, as not having at any time known or conversed with any civil people. They are tall in stature and very nimble in running, which they perform almost as fast as horses. At diving also in the sea they are very dexterous and hardy. From the bottom of the sea I saw them take up an anchor that weighed 600 pound, by tying a cable unto it with great dexterity and pulling it from a rock. They use no other arms than such as are made of wood, without any iron, unless that some instead therefore do fix a crocodile-tooth, which serves for a point. They have neither bows nor arrows among them, as other Indians have; but their common weapon is a sort of lances, that are long a fathom and a half.

In these islands there are many plantations surrounded with woods, whence they gather great abundance of fruits. Such are potatoes, bananas, racoven, ananas, and many others, which the constitution of the soil affords. Nigh unto these plantations they have no houses to dwell in, as in other places of the Indies. Some are of opinion that these Indians eat human flesh, which seems to be confirmed by what happened when L'Ollonais was there. Two of his companions, the one being a Frenchman and the other a Spaniard, went into the woods, where, having straggled up and down some while, they met with a troop of Indians that began to pursue them. They defended themselves as well as they could with their swords, but at last were forced to flee. This the Frenchman performed with great agility: but the Spaniard, being not so swift as his companion, was taken by those barbarians, and heard of no more. Some days after, they attempted to go into the woods to see what was become of their companion. Unto this effect twelve Pirates set forth very well armed, amongst whom was the Frenchman, who conducted them, and shewed them the place where he left his companion. Here they found, nigh unto the place, that the Indians had kindled fire; and, at a small distance thence, they found the bones of the said Spaniard very well roasted. Hence they inferred that they had roasted the miserable Spaniard, of whom they found more, some pieces of flesh ill scraped off from the bones and one hand, which had only two fingers remaining.

They marched farther on, seeking for Indians. Of these they found a great number together, who endeavoured to escape, seeing the Pirates so strong and well armed. But they overtook some of them, and brought on board their ships five men and four women. With these they used all the means they could invent to make themselves to be understood and gain their affections, giving them certain small trifles, as knives, beads, and the like things. They gave them also victuals and drink, but nothing of either would they taste. It was also observable that all the while they were prisoners on board the ships, they spoke not one word to each other among themselves. Thus the Pirates, seeing these poor Indians were much afraid of them, presented them again with some small things, and let them go. When they departed, they made signs, giving them to understand they would come again. But they soon forgot their benefactors, and were never heard nor seen more. Neither could any notice afterwards be had of these Indians or any others in the whole island after that time; which occasioned the Pirates to suspect that both those that were taken, and all the rest of the island, did all swim away by night to some other little neighbouring islands, especially considering they could never set eyes on any Indian more; neither was there ever seen any boat or other vessel in the whole circumference of the island.

In the meanwhile the Pirates were very desirous to see their long-boat finished, which they were building with the timber of the ship that stuck upon the sands. Yet, considering their work would be long, they began to cultivate some pieces of ground. Here they sowed French beans, which came to maturity in six weeks time, and many other fruits. They had good provision of Spanish wheat, bananas, racoven, and other things. With the wheat they made bread, and baked it in portable ovens which they had brought with them to this effect. Thus they feared not hunger in those desert places. After this manner they employed themselves for the space of five or six months. Which time being passed, and the long-boat finished, they determined to go unto the river of Nicaragua, to see if they could take some few canoes, and herewith return unto the said islands and fetch away their companions that remained behind, by reason the boat they had built was not capable of transporting so many men together. Hereupon, to avoid any disputes that might arise, they cast lots among themselves, determining thereby who should go, or stay, in the island.

The lot fell only upon one half of the people of the lost vessel, who embarked upon the long-boat they had built, and also the skiff which they had before, the other half remaining on shore. L'Ollonais, having set sail, arrived in a few days at the mouth of the river of Nicaragua. Here suddenly his ill-fortune assailed him, which of long time had been reserved for him as a punishment due unto the multitude of horrible crimes which in his licentious and wicked life he had committed. Here he met with both Spaniards and Indians, who jointly together set upon him and his companions, and used them so roughly that the greatest part of the Pirates were killed upon the place. L'Ollonais, with those that remained alive, had much ado to escape on board their boats aforementioned. Yet, notwithstanding this great loss of men, he resolved not to return to seek those he had left at the Isle of Pertas without taking some boats, such as he looked for. Unto this effect he determined to go farther on to the coasts of Cartagena, with design to seek for canoes. But God Almighty, the time of His Divine justice being now already come, had appointed the Indians of Darien to be the instruments and executioners thereof. The Indians of Darien are esteemed as *bravos*, or wild savage Indians, by the neighbouring Spaniards, who never could reduce them to civility. Hither L'Ollonais came (being rather brought by his evil conscience that cried for punishment of his crimes), thinking to act in that country his former cruelties. But the Indians within a few days after his arrival took him prisoner and tore him in pieces alive, throwing his body limb by limb into the fire, and his ashes into the air, to the intent no trace or memory might remain of such an infamous, inhuman creature. One of his companions gave me an exact account of the aforesaid tragedy, affirming withal that he himself had escaped the same punishment, not without the greatest of difficulties. He believed also that many of his comrades who were taken prisoners in that encounter by the Indians of Darien were after the same manner as their cruel captain torn in pieces and burned alive. Thus ends the history of the life and miserable death of that infernal wretch L'Ollonias, who, full of horrid, execrable, and enormous deeds, and also debtor to so much innocent blood, died by cruel and butcherly hands, such as his own were in the course of his life.

Those that remained in the island De las Pertas, waiting for the return of them who got away only to their great misfortune, hearing no news of their captain nor companions, at last embarked themselves upon the ship of a certain Pirate who happened to pass that way. This fellow was come from Jamaica with intent to land at the Cape of Gracias à Dios, and hence to mount the river with his canoes and take the city of Cartagena. These two parcels of Pirates being now joined together were infinitely gladded at the presence and society of one another. Those because they found themselves delivered from their miseries, poverty, and necessities, wherein now they had lived the space of ten entire months—these, because they were now considerably strengthened, whereby to effect with greater satisfaction their intended designs. Hereupon, as soon as they were arrived unto the aforesaid Cape of Gracias à Dios, they all put themselves into canoes, and with these vessels mounted the river, being in number 500 men ; leaving only 5 or 6 persons in every ship to keep them. They took no provisions with them, as being persuaded they should find everywhere sufficient. But these their own hopes were found totally vain, as not being grounded in God Almighty. For He ordained it so that the Indians, having perceived their coming, were all fled before them, not leaving in their houses nor plantations, which for the most part do border upon the sides of rivers, anything of necessary provisions or victuals. Hereby in few days after they had quitted their ships, they were reduced to such necessity and hunger as nothing could be more extreme. Notwithstanding, the hopes they had conceived of making their fortunes very soon did animate them for the present, being contented in this affliction with a few green herbs, such as they could gather as they went upon the banks of the river.

Yet all this courage and vigour of mind could not last above a fortnight. After which, their hearts, as well as their bodies, began to fail for hunger ; insomuch as they found themselves constrained to quit the river and betake themselves unto the woods, seeking out some small villages where they might find relief for their necessity. But all was in vain ; for, having ranged up and down the woods for some days without finding the least comfort to their hungry desires, they were forced to return again unto the river. Where being come, they thought it convenient to descend unto the sea-coasts where they had left their ships, not being able to find in the present enterprize what they sought for. In this laborious journey they were reduced to such extremity that many of them devoured their own shoes, the sheaths of their swords, knives, and other things of this kind, being almost ravenous, and fully desirous to meet some Indians, intending to sacrifice them unto their teeth. At last they arrived at the coast of the sea, where they found some comfort and relief to their former miseries, and also means to seek more. Yet, notwithstanding, the greatest part of them perished through faintness and other diseases contracted by hunger ; which occasioned also the remaining part to disperse—till at last by degrees many or most of them fell into the same pit that L'Ollonais did. Of him and of his companions I have hitherto given my reader a compendious narrative, which now I shall continue with the actions and exploits of Captain Henry Morgan, who may not undeservedly be called the second L'Ollonais, as not being unlike or inferior unto him either in achievements against the Spaniards or in robberies of many innocent people.

CHAPTER IV

Of the origin and descent of Captain Henry Morgan--his exploits and a continuation of the most remarkable actions of his life

CAPTAIN HENRY MORGAN was born in the kingdom of England, and there in the principality of Wales. His father was a rich yeoman, or farmer, and of good quality in that country, even as most who bear that name in Wales are known to be Morgan, being as yet young, had no inclinations to follow the calling of his father; and therefore left his country and came towards the sea-coasts to seek some other employ more suitable to his humour, that aspired to something else. There he found entertainment in a certain port where several ships lay at anchor, that were bound for the isle of Barbados. With these ships he resolved to go in the service of one who, according to what is commonly practised in those parts by the English and other nations, sold him as soon as he came on shore. He served his time at Barbados, and when he had obtained his liberty, thence transferred himself unto the island of Jamaica, there to seek new fortunes. Here he found two vessels of Pirates that were ready to go to sea. Being destitute of employ, he put himself into one of these ships, with intent to follow the exercises of that sort of people. He learned in a little while their manner of living; and so exactly that, having performed three or four voyages with some profit and good success, he agreed with some of his comrades, who had gotten by the same voyages a small parcel of money, to join stocks and buy a ship. The vessel being bought, they unanimously chose him to be the Captain and Commander thereof.

With this ship, soon after, he set forth from Jamaica to cruize upon the coasts of Campeche, in which voyage he had the fortune to take several ships, with which he returned triumphant to the same island. Here he found at the same time an old Pirate named Mansvelt (of whom we have already made mention in the First Part of this book), who was then busied in equipping a considerable fleet of ships, with design to land upon the Continent and pillage whatever came in his way. Mansvelt, seeing Captain Morgan return with so many prizes, judged him from his actions to be of undaunted courage, and hereupon was moved to choose him for his Vice-Admiral in that expedition. Thus, having fitted out fifteen ships between great and small, they set sail from Jamaica with 500 men, both Walloons and French. With this fleet they arrived not long after at the isle of St Catharine, situated nigh unto the continent of Costa Rica, in the latitude of twelve-degrees-and-a-half North, and distant thirty-five leagues from the river of Chagre, between North and South. Here they made their first descent, landing most of their men presently after.

Being now come to try their arms and fortune, they in a short while forced the garrison that kept the island to surrender and deliver into their hands all the forts and castles belonging thereunto. All these they instantly demolished, reserving only one, wherein they placed one hundred men of their own party and all the slaves they had taken from the Spaniards. With the rest of their men they marched unto another small island nigh unto that of St Catharine, and adjoining so near unto it that with a bridge they could get over. In few days they made a bridge, and passed thither, conveying also over it all the pieces of ordnance which they had taken upon the great island. Having ruined and destroyed, with sword and fire, both the islands, leaving what orders were necessary at the castle above-mentioned, they put forth to sea again with the Spaniards they had taken prisoners. Yet these they set on shore, not long after, upon the firm land nigh unto a place called Porto Bello. After this they began to cruize upon the coasts of Costa Rica, till that finally they came unto the river of Colla, designing to rob and pillage all the towns they could find in those parts, and afterwards to pass unto the village of Nata, to do the same.

The President, or Governor, of Panama, having had advice of the arrival of these Pirates and the hostilities they committed everywhere, thought it his duty to set forth to their encounter with a body of men. His coming caused the Pirates to retire suddenly with all speed and care, especially seeing the whole country alarmed at their arrival, and that their designs were known and consequently could be of no great effect at that present. Hereupon they returned unto the isle of St Catharine, to visit the hundred men they had left in garrison there. The Governor of these men was a certain Frenchman named Le Sieur Simon, who behaved himself very well in that charge, while Mansvelt was absent; insomuch that he had put the great island in a very good posture of defence, and the little one he had caused to be cultivated with many fertile plantations, which were sufficient to revictual the whole fleet with provisions and fruits, not only for present refreshment but also in case of a new voyage. Mansvelt's inclinations were very much bent to keep these two islands in perpetual possession, as being very commodious and profitably situated for the use of the Pirates, chiefly because they were so near unto the Spanish dominions and easily to be defended against them; as I shall represent in the Third Part of this history more at large, in a copper plate delineated for this purpose.

Hereupon Mansvelt determined to return unto Jamaica, with design to send some recruit to the isle of St Catharine, that, in case of any invasion of the Spaniards, the Pirates might be provided for a defence. As soon as he arrived, he propounded his mind and intentions unto the Governor of that island; but he liked not the propositions of Mansvelt, fearing lest by granting such things he should displease his master, the King of England, besides that, giving him the men he desired, and other necessaries for that purpose, he must of necessity diminish and weaken the forces of that island whereof he was Governor. Mansvelt seeing the unwillingness of the Governor of Jamaica, and that of his own accord he could not compass what he desired, with the same intent and designs went to the isle of Tortuga. But there, before he could accomplish his desires or put in execution what was intended, death suddenly surprised him and put a period to his wicked life; all things hereby remaining in suspense, until the occasion which I shall hereafter relate.

Le Sieur Simon, who remained at the isle of St Catharine in quality of Governor thereof, receiving no news from Mansvelt, his admiral, was greatly impatient and desirous to know what might be the cause thereof. In the meanwhile Don John Perez de Guzman, being newly come to the government of Costa Rica, thought it no ways convenient for the interest of the King of Spain that that island should remain in the hands of the Pirates. And hereupon he equipped a considerable fleet, which he sent unto the said island to retake it. But, before he came to use any great violence, he wrote a letter to Le Sieur Simon, wherein he gave him to understand, if he would surrender the island unto his Catholic Majesty, he should be very well rewarded; but, in case of refusal, severely punished when he had forced him to do it. Le Sieur Simon, seeing no appearance or probability of being able to defend it alone, nor any emolument that by so doing could accrue either unto him or his people, after some small resistance delivered up the island into the hands of its true lord and master, under the same articles they had obtained it from the Spaniards. Few days after the surrender of the island there arrived from Jamaica an English ship which the Governor of the said island had sent underhand, wherein was a good supply of people, both men and women. The Spaniards from the castle, having espied this ship, put forth the English colours, and persuaded Le Sieur Simon to go on board and conduct the said ship into a port they assigned him. This he performed immediately with dissimulation, whereby they were all made prisoners. A certain Spanish engineer has published, before me, an exact account and relation of the retaking of the isle of St Catharine by the Spaniards; which printed paper being fallen into my hands, I have thought it fit to be inserted here.

A true Relation and particular Account of the Victory obtained by the Arms of his Catholic Majesty against the English Pirates, by the direction and valour of Don John Perez de Guzman, *Knight of the Order of St James, Governor and Captain-General of Terra Firma and the Province of Veraguas*

THE kingdom of Terra Firma, which of itself is sufficiently strong to repulse and extirpate great fleets but more especially the Pirates of Jamaica, had several ways notice under several hands imparted to the Governor thereof, that fourteen English vessels did cruize upon the coasts belonging to his Catholic Majesty. The 14th day of July 1665 news came unto Panama that the English Pirates of the said fleet were arrived at Puerto de Naos, and had forced the Spanish garrison of the isle of St Catharine, whose Governor was Don Estevan del Campo, and that they had possessed themselves of the said island, taking prisoners the inhabitants and destroying all that ever they met. Moreover, about the same time Don John Perez de Guzman received particular information of these robberies from the relation of some Spaniards who escaped out of the island (and whom he ordered to be conveyed unto Porto Bello), who more distinctly told him that the aforementioned Pirates came into the Island the 2nd day of May by night, without being perceived by anybody; and that the next day, after some disputes by arms, they had taken the fortresses and made prisoners all the inhabitants and soldiers, not one excepted unless those that by good fortune had escaped their hands. This being heard by Don John, he called a council of war, wherein he declared the great progress the said Pirates had made in the dominions of his Catholic Majesty. Here likewise he propounded: *That it was absolutely necessary to send some forces unto the isle of St Catharine, sufficient to retake it from the Pirates, the honour and interest of his Majesty of Spain being very narrowly concerned herein. Otherwise the Pirates by such conquests might easily in course of time possess themselves of all the countries thereabouts.* Unto these reasons some were found who made answer: *That the Pirates, as not being able to subsist in the said island, would of necessity consume and waste themselves, and be forced to quit it without any necessity of retaking it. That consequently it was not worth the while to engage in so many expenses and troubles as might be foreseen this would cost.* Notwithstanding these reasons to the contrary, Don John, as one who was an expert and valiant soldier, gave order that a quantity of provisions should be conveyed to Porto Bello, for the use and service of the militia. And, neither to be idle nor negligent in his master's affairs, he transported himself thither, with no small danger of his life. Here he arrived the 7th day of July, with most things necessary to the expedition in hand; where he found in the port a good ship, called *St Vincent*, that belonged unto the Company of the Negroes. This ship being of itself a strong vessel and well mounted with guns, he manned and victualled very well, and sent unto the isle of St Catharine, constituting Captain Joseph Sanchez Ximenez, Mayor of the city of Porto Bello, Commander thereof. The people he carried with him were, 270 soldiers, and 37 prisoners of the same island, besides 34 Spaniards belonging to the garrison of Porto

Bello, 29 mulattos of Panama, 12 Indians very dexterous at shooting with bows and arrows, 7 expert and able gunners, 2 lieutenants, 2 pilots, one surgeon, and one religious man of the Order of St Francis for their chaplain.

Don John soon after gave his orders to every one of the officers, instructing them how they ought to behave themselves, telling them withal that the Governor of Cartagena would assist and supply them with more men, boats, and all things else they should find necessary for that enterprize ; to which effect he had already written unto the said Governor. On the 24th day of the said month Don John commanded the ship to weigh anchor and sail out of the port. Then, seeing a fair wind to blow, he called before him all the people designed for that expedition, and made them a speech, encouraging them to fight against the enemies of their country and religion, but more especially against those inhuman Pirates who had heretofore committed so many horrid and cruel actions against the subjects of his Catholic Majesty—withal promising to every one of them most liberal rewards, but especially unto such as should behave themselves as they ought in the service of their king and country. Thus Don John bid them farewell, and immediately the ship weighed anchor, and set sail under a favourable gale of wind. The 22nd of the said month they arrived at Cartagena, and presented a letter unto the Governor of the said city from the noble and valiant Don John, who received it with testimonies of great affection unto the person of Don John and his Majesty's service. And, seeing their resolute courage to be conformable to his desires and expectation, he promised them his assistance, which should be with one frigate, one galleon, one boat, and 126 men, the one half out of his own garrison, and the other half mulattos. Thus, all of them being well provided with necessaries, they set forth from the port of Cartagena the 2nd day of August, and the 10th of the said month they arrived within sight of the isle of St Catharine, towards the Western point thereof. And, although the wind was contrary, yet they reached the port, and came to an anchor within it, having lost one of their boats, by foul weather, at the rock called Quita Signos.

The Pirates, seeing our ships come to an anchor, gave them presently three guns with bullets, the which were soon answered in the same coin. Hereupon the Mayor Joseph Sanchez Ximenez sent on shore unto the Pirates one of his officers, to require them in the name of the Catholic King, his Master, to surrender the island, seeing they had taken it in the midst of peace between the two crowns of Spain and England, and that, in case they would be obstinate, he would certainly put them all to the sword. The Pirates made answer; *That island had once before belonged unto the Government and dominions of the King of England; and that, instead of surrendering it, they preferred to lose their lives.*

On Friday, the 13th of the said month, three negroes, from the enemy, came swimming aboard our Admiral. These brought intelligence that all the Pirates that were upon the island were only threescore-and-twelve in number, and that they were under a great consternation, seeing such considerable forces come against them. With this intelligence the Spaniards resolved to land and advance towards the fortresses, the which ceased not to fire as many great guns against them as they possibly could, which were corresponded in the same manner on our side till dark night. On Sunday, the 15th of the said month, which was the day of the Assumption of Our Lady, the weather being very calm and clear, the Spaniards began to advance thus. The ship named *St Vincent*, which rode Admiral, discharged two whole broadsides upon the battery called the Conception. The ship called *St Peter*, that was Vice-Admiral, discharged likewise her guns against the other battery named St James. In the meanwhile our people were landed in small boats, directing their course towards the point of the battery last mentioned, and thence they marched towards the gate called Cortadura. The lieutenant Frances de Cazeres, being desirous to view the strength of the enemy, with only 15 men, was compelled to retreat in all haste by reason of the great guns which played so furiously upon the place where he stood, they shooting not only pieces of iron and small bullets, but also the organs of the church, discharging in every shot threescore pipes at a time.

Notwithstanding this heat of the enemy, Captain Don Joseph Ramirez de Leyva, with threescore men, made a strong attack, wherein they fought on both sides very desperately, till that at last he overcame and forced the Pirates to surrender the fort he had taken in hand.

On the other side, Captain John Galeno, with fourscore-and-ten men, passed over the hills, to advance that way towards the castle of St Teresa. In the meanwhile the Mayor Don Joseph Sanchez Ximenez, as commander-in-chief, with the rest of his men set forth from the battery of St James, passing the fort with four boats, and landing in despite of the enemy. About this same time Captain John Galeno began to advance with the men he led unto the forementioned fortress. So that our men made three attacks upon the enemy, on three several sides, at one and the same time, with great courage and valour. Thus the Pirates, seeing many of their men already killed and that they could in no manner subsist any longer, retreated towards Cortadura, where they surrendered themselves and likewise the whole island into our hands. Our people possessed themselves of all, and set up the Spanish colours, as soon as they had rendered thanks to God Almighty for the victory obtained on such a signalized day. The number of dead were six men of the enemy's with many wounded, and threescore-and-ten prisoners. On our side was found only one man killed, and four wounded.

There was found upon the island 800 pound of powder, 250 pound of small bullets, with many other military provisions. Among the prisoners were taken also two Spaniards who had borne arms under the English against his Catholic Majesty. These were commanded to be shot to death the next day by order of the Mayor. The 10th day of September arrived at the isle an English vessel, which being seen at a great distance by the Mayor, he gave order unto Le Sieur Simon, who was a Frenchman, to go and visit the said ship, and tell them that were on board the island belonged still unto the English. He performed the commands, and found in the said ship only 14 men, one woman and her daughter, who were all instantly made prisoners.

The English Pirates were all transported to Porto Bello, excepting only three, who by order of the Governor were carried to Panama, there to work in the castle of St Jerome. This fortification is an excellent piece of workmanship, and very strong, being raised in the middle of the port, of quadrangular form, and of very hard stone. Its elevation or height is 88 geometrical feet, the walls being 14 and the curtains 75 feet diameter. It was built at the expense of several private persons, the Governor of the city furnishing the greatest part of the money; so that it did not cost his Majesty any sum at all.

CHAPTER V

Some account of the island of Cuba. Capt. Morgan attempts to preserve the isle of St Catharine as a refuge and nest unto Pirates; but fails of his designs. He arrives at and takes the village of El Puerto del Principe

CAPTAIN MORGAN, seeing his predecessor and Admiral Mansvelt was dead, endeavoured as much as he could, and used all the means that were possible, to preserve and keep in perpetual possession the Isle of St Catharine, seated nigh unto that of Cuba. His principal intent was to consecrate it as a refuge and sanctuary unto the Pirates of those parts, putting it in a sufficient condition of being a convenient receptacle or storehouse of their preys and robberies. Unto this effect he left no stone unmoved whereby to compass his designs, writing for the same purpose unto several merchants that lived in Virginia and New England, and persuading them to send him provisions and other necessary things towards the putting the said island in such a posture of defence as it might neither fear any external dangers nor be moved at any suspicions of invasion from any side that might attempt to disquiet it. At last all his thoughts and cares proved ineffectual by the Spaniards retaking the said island. Yet, notwithstanding, Captain Morgan retained his ancient courage, which instantly put him upon new designs. Thus he equipped at first a ship, with intention to gather an entire fleet, both as great and as strong as he could compass. By degrees he put the whole matter in execution, and gave order unto every member of this fleet, they should meet at a certain port of Cuba. Here he determined to call a council, and deliberate concerning what were best to be done, and what place first hey should fall upon. Leaving these new preparations in this condition, I shall here give my reader some small account of the aforementioned isle of Cuba, in whose ports this expedition was hatched, seeing I omitted to do it in its proper place.

The island of Cuba lies from East to West, in the latitude and situation of twenty unto 23 degrees North, being in length 150 German leagues and about 40 in breadth. Its fertility is equal unto that of the island of Hispaniola. Besides which, it affords many things proper for trading and commerce, such as are hides of several beasts, particularly those that in Europe are called Hides of Havana. On all sides it is surrounded with a great number of small islands, which go altogether under the name of Cayos. Of these little islands the Pirates make great use, as of their own proper ports of refuge. Here most commonly they make their meetings and hold their councils, how to assault more easily the Spaniards. It is thoroughly irrigated on all sides with the streams of plentiful and pleasant rivers, whose entries do form both secure and spacious ports, besides many other harbours for ships, which along the calm shores and coasts do adorn many parts of this rich and beautiful island; all which contribute very much unto its happiness, by facilitating the exercise of trade, whereunto they invite both natives and aliens. The chiefest of these ports are Santiago, Bayame, Santa Maria, Espiritu Santo, Trinidad, Xagoa, Cabo de Corrientes, and others, all which are seated on the south side of the island. On the northern side hereof are found the following: La Havana, Puerto Mariano, Santa Cruz, Mata Ricos, and Barracoa.

This island has two principal cities, by which the whole country is governed, and unto which all the towns and villages thereof do give obedience. The first of these is named Santiago, or St James, being seated on the South side, and having under its jurisdiction one half of the island. The chief magistrates hereof are a Bishop and a Governor, who command over the villages and towns belonging to the half above-mentioned. The chiefest of these are, on the Southern side Espiritu Santo, Puerto del Principe, and Bayame; on the North side it has Barracoa and the town called De los Cayos. The greatest part of the commerce driven at the aforementioned city of Santiago comes from the Canary Islands, whither they transport great quantity of tobacco, sugar, and hides: which sorts of merchandize are drawn to the head city from the subordinate towns and villages. In former times this city of Santiago was miserably sacked by the Pirates of Jamaica and Tortuga, notwithstanding that it is defended by a considerable castle.

The city and port De la Havana lies between the North and West side of the island. This is one of the renownedest and strongest places of all the West Indies. Its jurisdiction extends over the other half of the island, the chiefest places under it being Santa Cruz on the Northern side and La Trinidad on the South. Hence is transported huge quantities of tobacco, which is sent in great plenty unto New Spain and Costa Rica, even as far as the South Sea; besides many ships laden with this commodity that are consigned to Spain and other parts of Europe, not only in the leaf but also in rolls. This city is defended by three castles, very great and strong, two of which lie towards the port, and the other is seated upon a hill that commands the town. 'Tis esteemed to contain 10,000 families, more or less; among which number of people the merchants of this place trade in New Spain, Campeche, Honduras, and Florida. All the ships that come from the parts aforementioned, as also from Caracas, Cartagena, and Costa Rica, are necessitated to take their provisions in at Havana, wherewith to make their voyage for Spain; this being the necessary and straight course they ought to steer for the South of Europe and other parts. The plate-fleet of Spain, which the Spaniards call *flota*, being homeward bound, touches here yearly, to take in the rest of their full cargo, as hides, tobacco, and Campeche wood.

Captain Morgan had been no longer than two months in the above-mentioned ports of the South of Cuba, when he had got together a fleet of twelve sail, between ships and great boats; wherein he had 700 fighting men, part of which were English and part French. They called a council, and some were of opinion 'twere convenient to assault the city of Havana under the obscurity of the night; which enterprize, they said, might easily be performed, especially if they could but take any few of the ecclesiastics and make them prisoners—yea, that the city might be sacked, before the castles could put themselves in a posture of defence. Others propounded, according to their several opinions, other attempts. Notwithstanding, the former proposal was rejected, because many of the Pirates had been prisoners at other times in the said city; and these affirmed nothing of consequence could be done unless with 1500 men. Moreover, that with all this number of people they ought first to go unto the island De los Pinos, and land them in small boats about Matamana, 14 leagues distant from the aforesaid city, whereby to accomplish by these means and order their designs.

Finally, they saw no possibility of gathering so great a fleet; and hereupon with that they had they concluded to attempt some other place. Among the rest was found, at last, one who propounded they should go and assault the town of El Puerto del Principe. This proposition he endeavoured to persuade, by saying he knew that place very well, and that, being at a distance from the sea, it never was sacked by any Pirates, whereby the inhabitants were rich, as exercising their trade for ready money with those of Havana, who kept here an established commerce which consisted chiefly in hides. This proposal was presently admitted by Captain Morgan and the chiefest of his companions. And hereupon they gave order to every Captain to weigh anchor and set sail, steering their course towards that coast that lies nearest unto El Puerto del Principe. Hereabouts is to be seen a bay named by the Spaniards El Puerto de Santa Maria. Being arrived at this bay, a certain Spaniard, who was prisoner on board the fleet, swam ashore by night, and came unto the town of Puerto del Principe, giving account to the inhabitants of the design the Pirates had against them. This he affirmed to have overheard in their discourse, while they thought he did not understand the English tongue. The Spaniards, as soon as they received this fortunate advice, began instantly to hide their riches, and carry away what movables they could. The Governor also immediately raised all the people of the town, both freeman and slaves; and with part of them took a post by which of necessity the Pirates were to pass. He commanded likewise many trees to be cut down and laid amidst the ways to hinder their passage. In like manner he placed several ambuscades, which were strengthened with some pieces of cannon, to play upon them on their march. He gathered in all about 800 men, of which he distributed several into the aforementioned ambuscades, and with the rest he begirt the town, displaying them upon the plain of a spacious field, whence they could see the coming of the Pirates at length.

Captain Morgan, with his men, being now upon the march, found the avenues and passages unto the town impenetrable. Hereupon they took the way through the wood, traversing it with great difficulty, whereby they escaped divers ambuscades. Thus at last they came into the plain aforementioned, which, from its figure, is called by the Spaniards La Savana, or The Sheet. The Governor, seeing them come, made a detachment of a troop of horse, which he sent to charge them in the front, thinking to disperse them, and, by putting them to flight, pursue them with his main body. But this design succeeded not as it was intended. For the Pirates marched in very good rank and file, at the sound of their drums and with flying colours. When they came nigh unto the horse, they drew into the form of a semicircle, and thus advanced towards the Spaniards, who charged them like valiant and courageous soldiers for some while. But, seeing that the Pirates were very dexterous at their arms, and their Governor with many of their companions killed, they began to retreat towards the wood. Here they designed to save themselves with more advantage ; but, before they could reach it, the greatest part of them were unfortunately killed by the hands of the Pirates. Thus they left the victory unto these new-come enemies, who had no considerable loss of men in this battle, and but very few wounded, howbeit the skirmish continued for the space of four hours. They entered the town, though not without great resistance of such as were within, who defended themselves as long as was possible, thinking by their defence to hinder the pillage. Hereupon many, seeing the enemy within the town, shut themselves up in their own houses, and thence made several shot against the Pirates, who perceiving the mischief of this disadvantage, presently began to threaten them saying: *If you surrender not voluntarily, you shall soon see the town in a flame, and your wives and children torn in pieces before your faces.* With these menaces the Spaniards submitted entirely to the discretion of the Pirates, believing they could not continue there long and would soon be forced to dislodge.

As soon as the Pirates had possessed themselves of the town, they enclosed all the Spaniards, both men, women, and children, and slaves, in several churches; and gathered all the goods they could find by way of pillage. Afterwards they searched the whole country round about the town, bringing [in] day by day many goods and prisoners, with much provision. With this they fell to banqueting among themselves and making great cheer after their customary way, without remembering the poor prisoners, whom they permitted to starve in the churches for hunger. In the meanwhile they ceased not to torment them daily after an inhuman manner, thereby to make them confess where they hid their goods, moneys, and other things, though little or nothing was left them. Unto this effect they punished also the women and little children, giving them nothing to eat; whereby the greatest part perished.

When they could find no more to rob, and that provisions began to grow scarce, they thought it convenient to depart and seek new fortunes in other places. Hence they intimated to the prisoners: *They should find moneys to ransom themselves, else they should be all transported to Jamaica. Which being done, if they did not pay a second ransom for the town, they would turn every house into ashes.* The Spaniards, hearing these severe menaces, nominated among themselves four fellow-prisoners to go and seek for the above-mentioned contributions. But the Pirates, to the intent they should return speedily with the ransoms prescribed, tormented several in their presence, before they departed, with all the rigour imaginable. After few days, the Spaniards returned from the fatigue of their unreasonable commissions, telling Captain Morgan: *We have run up and down, and searched all the neighbouring woods and places we most suspected, and yet have not been able to find any of our own party, nor consequently any fruit of our embassy. But if you are pleased to have a little longer patience with us, we shall certainly cause all that you demand to be paid within the space of fifteen days.* Captain Morgan was contented, as it should seem, to grant them this petition. But, not long after, there came into the town seven or eight Pirates, who had been ranging the woods and fields, and got thereabouts some considerable booty. These brought among other prisoners a certain negro, whom they had taken with letters about him. Captain Morgan having perused them, found they were from the Governor of Santiago, being written to some of the prisoners ; wherein he told them : *They should not make too much haste to pay any ransom for their town or persons or any other pretext. But, on the contrary, they should put off the Pirates as well as they could with excuses and delays, expecting to be relieved by him within a short while, when he would certainly come to their aid.* This intelligence being heard by Captain Morgan, he immediately gave orders that all they had robbed should be carried on board the ships. And, withal, he intimated to the Spaniards that the very next day they should pay their ransoms forasmuch as he would not wait one moment longer but reduce the whole town to ashes in case they failed to perform the sum demanded.

With this intimation Captain Morgan made no mention unto the Spaniards of the letters he had intercepted. Whereupon they made him answer that it was totally impossible for them to give such a sum of money in so short a space of time, seeing their fellow-townsmen were not to be found in all the country thereabouts. Captain Morgan knew full well their intentions, and, withal, thought it not convenient to remain there any longer time. Hence he demanded of them only 500 oxen or cows, together with sufficient salt wherewith to salt them. Hereunto he added only this condition, that they should carry them on board his ships, which they promised to do. Thus he departed with all his men, taking with him only six of the principal prisoners, as pledges of what he intended. The next day the Spaniards brought the cattle and salt to the ships, and required the prisoners. But Captain Morgan refused to deliver them till such time as they helped his men to kill and salt the beeves. This was likewise performed in great haste, he not caring to stay there any longer, lest he should be surprised by the forces that were gathering against him. Having received all on board his vessels, he set at liberty the prisoners he had kept as hostages of his demands. While these things were in agitation, there happened to arise some dissensions between the Englishmen and the French. The occasion of their discord was as follows : A certain Frenchman being employed in killing and salting one of the beeves, an English Pirate came to him and took away the marrow-bones he had taken out of the ox ; which sort of meat these people esteem very much. Hereupon they challenged one another. Being come unto the place of duel, the Englishman drew his sword treacherously against the Frenchman, wounding him in the back, before he had put himself into a just posture of defence; whereby he suddenly fell dead upon the place. The other Frenchmen, desirous to revenge this base action, made an insurrection against the English. But Captain Morgan soon extinguished this flame, by commanding the criminal to be bound in chains, and thus carried to Jamaica, promising to them all he would see justice done upon him. For, although it were permitted unto him to challenge his adversary, yet it was not lawful to kill him treacherously, as he did.

As soon as all things were in readiness and on board the ships, and likewise the prisoners set at liberty, they sailed thence, directing their course to a certain island, where Captain Morgan intended to make a dividend of what they had purchased in that voyage. Being arrived at the place assigned, they found nigh the value of 50,000 pieces-of-eight, both in money and goods. The sum being known, it caused a general resentment and grief, to see such a small purchase, which was not sufficient to pay their debts at Jamaica. Hereupon Captain Morgan propounded to them they should think upon some other enterprize and pillage before they returned home. But the Frenchmen, not being able to agree with the English, separated from their company, leaving Captain Morgan alone with those of his own nation, notwithstanding all the persuasions he used to induce them to continue in his company. Thus they parted with all external signs of friendship, Captain Morgan reiterating his promises unto them that he would see justice done upon that criminal. This he performed; for, being arrived at Jamaica, he caused him to be hanged, which was all the satisfaction the French Pirates could expect.

CHAPTER VI

Captain Morgan resolves to attack and plunder the city of Porto Bello. Unto this effect he equips a fleet, and with little expense and small forces takes the said place

Some nations may think that, the French having deserted Captain Morgan, the English alone could not have sufficient courage to attempt such great actions as before. But Captain Morgan, who always communicated vigour with his words, infused such spirits into his men as were able to put every one of them instantly upon new designs, they being all persuaded by his reasons that the sole execution of his orders would be a certain means of obtaining great riches. This persuasion had such influence upon their minds that with inimitable courage they all resolved to follow him. The same likewise did a certain Pirate of Campeche, who in this occasion joined with Captain Morgan to seek new fortunes under his conduct, and greater advantages than he had found before. Thus Captain Morgan in a few days gathered a fleet of nine sail, between ships and great boats, wherein he had four-hundred-and-threescore military men.

After that all things were in good posture of readiness, they put forth to sea, Captain Morgan imparting the design he had in his mind unto nobody for that present. He only told them on several occasions that he held as indubitable he should make a good fortune by that voyage, if strange occurrences altered not the course of his designs. They directed their course towards the continent, where they arrived in few days upon the coast of Costa Rica, with all their fleet entire. No sooner had they discovered land than Captain Morgan declared his intentions to the Captains, and presently after unto all the rest of the company. He told them he intended in that expedition to plunder Porto Bello, and that he would perform it by night, being resolved to put the whole city to the sack, not the least corner escaping his diligence. Moreover, to encourage them, he added: *This enterprize could not fail to succeed well, seeing he had kept it secret in his mind without revealing it to anybody; whereby they could not have notice of his coming.* Unto this proposition some made answer: *They had not a sufficient number of men wherewith to assault so strong and great a city.* But Captain Morgan replied: *If our number is small, our hearts are great. And the fewer persons we are, the more union and better shares we shall have in the spoil.* Hereupon, being stimulated with the ambition of those vast riches they promised themselves from their good success, they unanimously concluded to venture upon that design. But now, to the intent my reader may better comprehend the incomparable boldness of this exploit, it may be necessary to say something beforehand of the city of Porto Bello.

The city which bears this name in America is seated in the Province of Costa Rica, under the latitude of 10 degrees North, at the distance of 14 leagues from the Gulf of Darien, and 8 Westwards from the port called Nombre de Dios. It is judged to be the strongest place that the King of Spain possesses in all the West Indies, excepting two, that is to say Havana and Cartagena. Here are two castles, almost inexpugnable, that defend the city, being situated at the entry of the port, so that no ship or boat can pass without permission. The garrison consists of three hundred soldiers, and the town constantly inhabited by four hundred families, more or less. The merchants dwell not here, but only reside for awhile, when the galleons come or go from Spain, by reason of the unhealthiness of the air, occasioned by certain vapours that exhale from the mountains. Notwithstanding, their chief warehouses are at Porto Bello, howbeit their habitations are all the year long at Panama, whence they bring the plate upon mules at such times as the fair begins, and when the ships belonging to the Company of Negroes arrive here to sell slaves.

Captain Morgan, who knew very well all the avenues of this city, as also all the neighbouring coasts, arrived in the dusk of the evening at the place called Puerto de Naos, distant ten leagues towards the West of Porto Bello. Being come unto this place, they mounted the river in their ships, as far as another harbour called Puerto Pontin, where they came to an anchor. Here they put themselves immediately into boats and canoes, leaving in the ships only a few men to keep them and conduct them the next day unto the port. About midnight they came to a certain place called Estera Longa Lemos, where they all went on shore, and marched by land to the first posts of the city. They had in their company a certain Englishman who had been formerly a prisoner in those parts and who now served them for a guide. Unto him, and three or four more, they gave commission to take the sentry, if possible, or kill him upon the place. But they laid hands on him and apprehended him with such cunning that he had no time to give warning with his musket or make any other noise. Thus they brought him, with his hands bound, unto Captain Morgan, who asked him : *How things went in the city, and what forces they had ;* with many other circumstances, which he was desirous to know. After every question, they made him a thousand menaces to kill him, in case he declared not the truth. Thus they began to advance towards the city, carrying always the said sentry bound before them. Having marched about one quarter of a league, they came unto the castle that is nigh unto the city, which presently they closely surrounded, so that no person could get either in or out of the said fortress.

Being thus posted under the walls of the castle, Captain Morgan commanded the sentry whom they had taken prisoner to speak unto those that were within, charging them to surrender and deliver themselves up to his discretion—otherwise they should be all cut to pieces, without giving quarter to any one. But they would hearken to none of these threats, beginning instantly to fire ; which gave notice unto the city, and this was suddenly alarmed. Yet, notwithstanding, although the Governor and soldiers of the said castle made as great resistance as could be performed, they were constrained to surrender unto the Pirates. These no sooner had taken the castle but they resolved to be as good as their words, in putting the Spaniards to the sword, thereby to strike a terror into the rest of the city. Hereupon, having shut up all the soldiers and officers as prisoners into one room, they instantly set fire to the powder (whereof they found great quantity), and blew up the whole castle into the air, with all the Spaniards that were within. This being done, they pursued the course of their victory, falling upon the city, which as yet was not in order to receive them. Many of the inhabitants cast their precious jewels and moneys into wells and cisterns, or hid them in other places underground, to excuse, as much as were possible, their being totally robbed. One party of the Pirates, being assigned to this purpose, ran immediately to the cloisters, and took as many religious men and women as they could find. The Governor of the city not being able to rally the citizens through the huge confusion of the town, retired unto one of the castles remaining, and thence began to fire incessantly at the Pirates. But these were not in the least negligent either to assault him or defend themselves with all the courage imaginable. Thus it was observable that, amidst the horror of the assault, they made very few shot in vain. For, aiming with great dexterity at the mouths of the guns, the Spaniards were certain to lose one or two men every time they charged each gun anew.

The assault of this castle where the Governor was continued very furious on both sides, from break of day until noon. Yea, about this time of the day the case was very dubious which party should conquer or be conquered. At last the Pirates, perceiving they had lost many men and as yet advanced but little towards the gaining either this or the other castles remaining, thought to make use of fireballs, which they threw with their hands, designing if possible to burn the doors of the castle. But, going about to put this into execution, the Spaniards from the wall let fall great quantities of stones and earthen pots full of powder and other combustible matter, which forced them to desist from that attempt. Captain Morgan, seeing this generous defence made by the Spaniards, began to despair of the whole success of the enterprize. Hereupon many faint and calm meditations came into his mind ; neither could he determine which way to turn himself in that straitness of affairs. Being involved in these thoughts, he was suddenly animated to continue the assault by seeing the English colours put forth at one of the lesser castles, then entered by his men, of whom he presently after spied a troop that came to meet him, proclaiming victory with loud shouts of joy. This instantly put him upon new resolutions of making new efforts to take the rest of the castles that stood out against him, especially seeing the chiefest citizens were fled unto them and had conveyed thither great part of their riches, with all the plate belonging to the churches and other things dedicated to divine service.

Unto this effect, therefore, he ordered ten or twelve ladders to be made, in all possible haste, so broad that three or four men at once might ascend by them. These being finished, he commanded all the religious men and women whom he had taken prisoners to fix them against the walls of the castle. Thus much he had beforehand threatened the Governor to perform, in case he delivered not the castle. But his answer was: *He would never surrender himself alive.* Captain Morgan was much persuaded that the Governor would not employ his utmost forces, seeing religious women and ecclesiastical persons exposed in the front of the soldiers to the greatest dangers. Thus the ladders, as I have said, were put into the hands of religious persons of both sexes; and these were forced, at the head of the companies, to raise and apply them to the walls. But Captain Morgan was fully deceived in his judgment of this design. For the Governor who acted like a brave and courageous soldier, refused not, in performance of his duty, to use his utmost endeavours to destroy whosoever came near the walls. The religious men and women ceased not to cry unto him and beg of him by all the Saints of Heaven he would deliver the castle, and hereby spare both his and their own lives. But nothing could prevail with the obstinacy and fierceness that had possessed the Governor's mind. Thus many of the religious men and nuns were killed before they could fix the ladders—which at last being done, though with great loss of the said religious people, the Pirates mounted them in great numbers, and with no less valour, having fireballs in their hands, and earthen pots full of powder—all which things, being now at the top of the walls, they kindled and cast in among the Spaniards.

This effort of the Pirates was very great, insomuch as the Spaniards could no longer resist nor defend the castle, which was now entered. Hereupon they all threw down their arms, and craved quarter for their lives. Only the Governor of the city would admit or crave no mercy, but rather killed many of the Pirates with his own hands, and not a few of his own soldiers, because they did not stand to their arms. And, although the Pirates asked him if he would have quarter, yet he constantly answered: *By no means: I had rather die as a valiant soldier than be hanged as a coward.* They endeavoured, as much as they could, to take him prisoner. But he defended himself so obstinately that they were forced to kill him, notwithstanding all the cries and tears of his own wife and daughter, who begged of him upon their knees he would demand quarter and save his life. When the Pirates had possessed themselves of the castle, which was about night, they enclosed therein all the prisoners they had taken, placing the women and men by themselves with some guards upon them. All the wounded were put into a certain apartment by itself, to the intent their own complaints might be the cure of their diseases, for no other was afforded them.

This being done, they fell to eating and drinking after their usual manner—that is to say, committing in both these things all manner of debauchery and excess. These two vices were immediately followed by many insolent actions of rape and adultery committed upon very honest women, as well married as virgins, who being threatened with the sword were constrained to submit their bodies to the violence of these lewd and wicked men. After such manner they delivered themselves up to all sort of debauchery of this kind, that if there had been found only fifty courageous men, they might easily have retaken the city, and killed all the Pirates. The next day, having plundered all they could find, they began to examine some of the prisoners (who had been persuaded by their companions to say they were the richest of the town), charging them severely to discover where they had hidden their riches and goods. But, not being able to extort anything out of them, as they were not the right persons who possessed any wealth, they at last resolved to torture them. This they performed with such cruelty that many of them died upon the rack, or presently after. Soon after, the President of Panama had news brought him of the pillage and ruin of Porto Bello. This intelligence caused him to employ all his care and industry to raise forces, with design to pursue and cast out the Pirates thence. But these cared little for what extraordinary means the President used, as having their ships nigh at hand and being determined to set fire unto the city and retreat. They had now been at Porto Bello fifteen days, in which space of time they had lost many of their men, both by the unhealthiness of the country and the extravagant debaucheries they had committed.

Hereupon they prepared for a departure, carrying on board their ships all the pillage they had gotten. But, before all, they provided the fleet with sufficient victuals for the voyage. While these things were getting ready, Captain Morgan sent an injunction unto the prisoners, that they should pay him a ransom for the city, or else he would by fire consume it to ashes and blow up all the castles into the air. Withal he commanded them to send speedily two persons to seek and procure the sum he demanded, which amounted to 100,000 pieces-of-eight. Unto this effect two men were sent to the President of Panama, who gave him an account of all these tragedies. The President, having now a body of men in a readiness, set forth immediately towards Porto Bello, to encounter the Pirates before their retreat. But these people, hearing of his coming, instead of flying away went out to meet him at a narrow passage through which of necessity he ought to pass. Here they placed an hundred men very well armed, the which at the first encounter put to flight a good party of those of Panama. This accident obliged the President to retire for that time, as not being yet in a posture of strength to proceed any farther. Presently after this encounter, he sent a message unto Captain Morgan, to tell him: *That, in case he departed not suddenly with all his forces from Porto Bello, he ought to expect no quarter for himself nor his companions, when he should take them, as he hoped soon to do.* Captain Morgan, who feared not his threats, as knowing he had a secure retreat in his ships which were nigh at hand, made him answer: *He would not deliver the castles before he had received the contribution-money he had demanded. Which in case it were not paid down, he would certainly burn the whole city, and then leave it, demolishing beforehand the castles and killing the prisoners.*

The Governor of Panama perceived by this answer no means would serve to mollify the hearts of the Pirates, nor reduce them to reason. Hereupon he determined to leave them, as also those of the city, whom he came to relieve, involved in the difficulties of making the best agreement they could with their enemies. Thus in few days more the miserable citizens gathered the contribution wherein they were fined, and brought the entire sum of 100,000 pieces-of-eight unto the Pirates for a ransom of the cruel captivity they were fallen into. But the President of Panama, by these transactions, was brought into an extreme admiration, considering that four-hundred men had been able to take such a great city with so many strong castles, especially seeing they had no pieces of cannon nor other great guns wherewith to raise batteries against them. And, what was more, knowing that the citizens of Porto Bello had always great repute of being good soldiers themselves, and who had never wanted courage in their own defence. This astonishment was so great that it occasioned him, for to be satisfied herein, to send a messenger unto Captain Morgan, desiring him to send him some small pattern of those arms wherewith he had taken with such violence so great a city. Captain Morgan received this messenger very kindly, and treated him with great civility. Which being done, he gave him a pistol and a few small bullets of lead, to carry back unto the President, his master, telling him withal: *He desired him to accept that slender pattern of the arms wherewith he had taken Porto Bello, and keep them for a twelvemonth; after which time he promised to come to Panama and fetch them away.* The Governor of Panama returned the present very soon to Captain Morgan, giving him thanks for the favour of lending him such weapons as he needed not, and withal sent him a ring of gold, with this message: *That he desired him not to give himself the labour of coming to Panama, as he had done to Porto Bello, for he did certify to him, he should not speed so well here as he had done there.*

After these transactions, Captain Morgan (having provided his fleet with all necessaries, and taken with him the best guns of the castles, nailing the rest which he could not carry away) set sail from Porto Bello with all his ships. With these he arrived in few days unto the island of Cuba, where he sought out a place wherein with all quiet and repose he might make the dividend of the spoil they had gotten. They found in ready money 250,000 pieces-of-eight, besides all other merchandizes, as cloth, linen, silks, and other goods. With this rich purchase they sailed again thence unto their common place of rendezvous, Jamaica. Being arrived, they passed here some time in all sorts of vices and debauchery, according to their common manner of doing, spending with huge prodigality what others had gained with no small labour and toil.

CHAPTER VII

Captain Morgan takes the city of Maracaibo, on the coast of New Venezuela. Piracies committed in those seas. Ruin of three Spanish ships that were set forth to hinder the robberies of the Pirates

Not long after the arrival of the Pirates at Jamaica, being precisely that short time they needed to lavish away all the riches above-mentioned, they concluded upon another enterprize whereby to seek new fortunes. Unto this effect Captain Morgan gave orders to all the Commanders of his ships to meet together at the island called De la Vaca, or Cow Isle, seated on the South side of the isle of Hispaniola, as has been mentioned above. As soon as they came to this place, there flocked unto them great numbers of other Pirates, both French and English, by reason the name of Captain Morgan was now rendered famous in all the neighbouring countries for the great enterprizes he had performed. There was at that present at Jamaica an English ship newly come from New England, well mounted with thirty-six guns. This vessel likewise, by order of the Governor of Jamaica, came to join with Captain Morgan to strengthen his fleet and give him greater courage to attempt things of huge consequence. With this supply Captain Morgan judged himself sufficiently strong, as having a ship of such port being the greatest of his fleet, in his company. Notwithstanding, there being in the same place another great vessel that carried 24 iron guns and twelve of brass, belonging to the French, Captain Morgan endeavoured as much as he could to join this ship in like manner unto his own. But the French, not daring to repose any trust in the English, of whose actions were not a little jealous, denied absolutely to consent unto any such thing.

The French Pirates belonging to this great ship had accidentally met at sea an English vessel; and, being then under an extreme necessity of victuals, they had taken some provisions out of the English ship without paying for them, as having peradventure no ready money on board. Only they had given them bills-of-exchange, for Jamaica and Tortuga, to receive money there for what they had taken. Captain Morgan, having notice of this accident and perceiving he could not prevail with the French Captain to follow him in that expedition, resolved to lay hold on this occasion as a pretext to ruin the French and seek his own revenge. Hereupon he invited, with dissimulation, the French commander and several of his men to dine with him on board the great ship that was come from Jamaica, as was said before. Being come thither, he made them all prisoners, pretending the injury aforementioned done to the English vessel in taking away some few provisions without pay.

This unjust action of Captain Morgan was soon followed by divine punishment, as we may very rationally conceive. The manner I shall instantly relate. Captain Morgan, presently after he had taken the French prisoners abovesaid, called a council to deliberate what place they should first pitch upon, in the course of this new expedition. At this council it was determined to go to the isle of Savona, there to wait for the *flota* which was then expected from Spain, and take any of the Spanish vessels that might chance to straggle from the rest. This resolution being taken, they began on board the great ship to feast one another for joy of their new voyage and happy council, as they hoped it would prove. In testimony hereof, they drank many healths, and discharged many guns, as the common sign of mirth among seamen used to be. Most of the men being drunk, by what accident is not known the ship suddenly was blown up into the air, with 350 Englishmen, besides the French prisoners above-mentioned that were in the hold. Of all which number there escaped only thirty men, who were in the great cabin at some distance from the main force of the powder. Many more 'tis thought might have escaped, had they not been so much overtaken with wine.

The loss of such a great ship brought much consternation and conflict of mind upon the English. They knew not whom to blame; but at last the accusation was laid upon the French prisoners, whom they suspected to have fired the powder of the ship wherein they were, out of design to revenge themselves, though with the loss of their own lives. Hereupon they sought to be revenged on the French anew, and accumulate new accusations unto the former, whereby to seize the ship and all that was in it. With this design they forged another pretext against the said ship, by saying the French designed to commit piracy upon the English. The grounds of this accusation were given them by a commission from the Governor of Barracoa, found on board the French vessel, wherein were these words: *That the said Governor did permit the French to trade in all Spanish ports, etc. . . . as also to cruize upon the English Pirates in what place soever they could find them, because of the multitude of hostilities which they had committed against the subjects of his Catholic Majesty in time of peace betwixt the two Crowns.* This Commission for trade was interpreted by the English as an express order to exercise piracy and war against them, notwithstanding it was only a bare licence for coming into the Spanish ports; the cloak of which permission were those words inserted: *That they should cruize upon the English.* And, although the French did sufficiently expound the true sense of the said Commission, yet they could not clear themselves unto Captain Morgan nor his council. But, in lieu hereof, the ship and men were seized and sent unto Jamaica. Here they also endeavoured to obtain justice and the restitution of their ship, by all the means possible. But all was in vain; for, instead of justice, they were long time detained in prison and threatened with hanging.

Eight days after the loss of the said ship, Captain Morgan commanded the bodies of the miserable wretches who were blown up to be searched for, as they floated upon the waters of the sea. This he did, not out of any design of affording them Christian burial, but only to obtain the spoil of their clothes and other attire. And, if any had golden rings on their fingers, these were cut off for purchase, leaving them in that condition exposed to the voracity of the monsters of the sea. At last they set sail for the isle of Savona, being the place of their assignation. They were in all 15 vessels, Captain Morgan commanding the biggest, which carried only 14 small guns. The number of men belonging to this fleet were nine-hundred-and-threescore. In few days after, they arrived at the Cape called Cabo de Lobos, on the South side of the isle of Hispaniola, between Cape Tiburon and Cape Punta d'Espada. Hence they could not pass, by reason of contrary winds that continued the space of three weeks, notwithstanding all the endeavours Captain Morgan used to get forth, leaving no means unattempted thereunto. At the end of this time they doubled the cape, and presently after spied an English vessel at a distance. Having spoken with her, they found she came from England, and bought of her for ready money some provisions they stood in need of.

Captain Morgan proceeded in the course of his voyage, till he came unto the port of Ocoa. Here he landed some of his men, sending them into the woods to seek water and what provisions they could find, the better to spare such as he had already on board his fleet. They killed many beasts, and among other animals some horses. But the Spaniards, being not well satisfied at their hunting, attempted to lay a stratagem for the Pirates. Unto this purpose they ordered three or four hundred men to come from the city of San Domingo, not far distant from this port, and desired them to hunt in all the parts thereabouts adjoining the sea, to the intent that, if any Pirates should return, they might find no subsistence. Within a few days the same Pirates returned, with design to hunt. But, finding nothing to kill, a party of them, being about fifty in number, straggled farther on into the woods. The Spaniards, who watched all their motions, gathered a great herd of cows, and set two or three men to keep them. The Pirates having spied this herd, killed a sufficient number thereof; and, although the Spaniards could see them at a distance, yet they would not hinder their work for the present. But, as soon as they attempted to carry them away, they set upon them with all fury imaginable, crying: *Mata, mata!* that is, *Kill, kill!* Thus the Pirates were soon compelled to quit the prey, and retreat towards their ships as well as they could. This they performed, notwithstanding, in good order, retiring from time to time by degrees; and, when they had any good opportunity, discharging full volleys of shot upon the Spaniards. By this means the Pirates killed many of the enemies, though with some loss on their own side.

The rest of the Spaniards, seeing what damage they had sustained, endeavoured to save themselves by flight, and carry off the dead bodies and wounded of their companions.

The Pirates, perceiving them to flee, could not content themselves with what hurt they had already done, but pursued them speedily into the woods, and killed the greatest part of those that were remaining. The next day Captain Morgan, being extremely offended at what had passed, went himself with 200 men into the woods, to seek for the rest of the Spaniards. But, finding nobody there, he revenged his wrath upon the houses of the poor and miserable rustics that inhabit scatteringly those fields and woods: of which he burnt a great number. With this he returned unto his ships, something more satisfied in his mind, for having done some considerable damage unto the enemy, which was always his most ardent desire.

The huge impatience wherewith Captain Morgan had waited now this long while for some of his ships, which were not yet arrived, made him resolve to set sail without them, and steer his course for the isle of Savona, the place he had always designed. Being arrived there, and not finding any of his ships as yet come, he was more impatient and concerned than before, as fearing their loss, or that he must proceed without them. Nothwithstanding, he waited for their arrival some few days longer. In the meanwhile, having no great plenty of provisions, he sent a crew of 150 men to the isle of Hispaniola, to pillage some towns that were nigh unto the city of San Domingo. But the Spaniards, having had intelligence of their coming, were now so vigilant and in such good posture of defence that the Pirates thought it not convenient to assault them, choosing rather to return empty-handed unto Captain Morgan's presence than to perish in that desperate enterprize.

At last Captain Morgan, seeing the other ships did not come, made a review of his people, and found only five-hundred men, more or less. The ships that were wanting were seven, he having only eight in his company, of which the greatest part were very small. Thus, having hitherto resolved to cruize upon the coasts of Caracas, and plunder all the towns and villages he could meet, finding himself at present with such small forces, he changed his resolution, by the advice of a French Captain that belonged to his fleet. This Frenchman had served L'Ollonais in like enterprizes, and was at the taking of Maracaibo, whereby he knew all the entries, passages, forces, and means how to put in execution the same again in the company of Captain Morgan, unto whom, having made a full relation of all, he concluded to sack it again the second time, as being himself persuaded, with all his men, of the facility the Frenchman propounded. Hereupon they weighed anchor, and steered their course towards Curaçao. Being come within sight of that island, they landed at another, which is nigh unto it, and is called Ruba, seated about twelve leagues from Curaçao, towards the West. This island is defended but by a slender garrison, and is inhabited by Indians, who are subject to the Crown of Spain, and speak Spanish by reason of the Roman Catholic religion, which is here cultivated by some few priests that are sent from time to time from the neighbouring continent.

The inhabitants of this isle exercise a certain commerce or trade with the Pirates that go and come this way. These buy of the islanders sheep, lambs, and kids, which they exchange unto them for linen, thread, and other things of this kind. The country is very dry and barren, the whole substance thereof consisting in those three things above-mentioned, and in a small quantity of wheat, which is of no bad quality, This isle produces a great number of venomous insects, as vipers, spiders, and others. These last are so pernicious here that, if any man is bitten by them, he dies mad. And the manner of recovering such persons is to tie them very fast both hands and feet, and in this condition to leave them for the space of four-and-twenty hours without eating or drinking the least thing imaginable. Captain Morgan, as was said, having cast anchor before this island, bought of the inhabitants many sheep, lambs, and also wood, which he needed for all his fleet. Having been there two days he set sail again, in the time of the night, to the intent they might not see what course he steered.

The next day they arrived at the sea of Maracaibo, having always great care of not being seen from Vigilias, for which reason they anchored out of the sight of the watch-tower. Night being come, they set sail again towards the land, and the next morning by break of day found themselves directly over against the bar of the lake above-mentioned. The Spaniards had built another fort since the action of L'Ollonais, whence they did now fire continually against the Pirates, while they were

PUERTO DEL PRINCIPE TAKEN AND SACKED

putting their men into boats for to land. The dispute continued very hot on both sides, being managed with huge courage and valour from morning till dark night. This being come, Captain Morgan, in the obscurity thereof, drew nigh unto the fort; which having examined, he found nobody in it, the Spaniards having deserted it not long before. They left behind them a match kindled nigh unto a train of powder, wherewith they designed to blow up the Pirates and the whole fortress, as soon as they were in it. This design had taken effect, had the Pirates failed to discover it the space of one quarter of an hour. But Captain Morgan prevented the mischief by snatching away the match with all speed, whereby he saved both his own and his companions' lives. They found here great quantity of powder, whereof he provided his fleet; and afterwards demolished part of the walls, nailing sixteen pieces of ordnance, which carried from 12 to 24 pound of bullet. Here they found also great number of muskets and military provisions.

The next day they commanded the ships to enter the bar; among which, they divided the powder, muskets, and other things they found in the fort. These things being done, they embarked again, to continue their course towards Maracaibo. But the waters were very low, whereby they could not pass a certain bank that lies at the entry of the lake. Hereupon they were compelled to put themselves into canoes and small boats, with which they arrived the next day before Maracaibo, having no other defence but some small pieces which they could carry in the said boats. Being landed, they ran immediately to the fort called De la Barra, which they found in like manner as the preceding, without any person in it; for all were fled before them into the woods, leaving also the town without any people, unless a few miserable poor folk who had nothing to lose.

As soon as they had entered the town, the Pirates searched every corner thereof, to see if they could find any people that were hidden who might offend them at unawares. Not finding anybody, every party, according as they came out of their several ships, chose what houses they pleased to themselves, the best they could find. The church was deputed for the common *corps de garde*, where they lived after their military manner, committing many insolent actions. The next day after their arrival, they sent a troop of 100 men to seek for the inhabitants and their goods. These returned the next day following, bringing with them to the number of thirty persons, between men, women, and children, and fifty mules laden with several good merchandize. All these miserable prisoners were put to the rack, to make them confess where the rest of the inhabitants were and their goods. Amongst other tortures then used, one was to stretch their limbs with cords, and at the same time beat them with sticks and other instruments. Others had burning matches placed betwixt their fingers, which were thus burnt alive. Others had slender cords or matches twisted about their heads, till their eyes burst out of the skull. Thus all sort of inhuman cruelties were executed upon those innocent people. Those who would not confess, or who had nothing to declare, died under the hands of those tyrannical men. These tortures and racks continued for the space of three whole weeks, in which time they ceased not to send out, daily, parties of men to seek for more people to torment and rob; they never returning home without booty and new riches.

Captain Morgan, having now gotten by degrees into his hands about one hundred of the chiefest families, with all their goods, at last resolved to go to Gibraltar, even as L'Ollonais had done before. With this design he equipped his fleet, providing it very sufficiently with all necessary things. He put likewise on board all the prisoners; and thus, weighing anchor, set sail for the said place, with resolution to hazard the battle. They had sent before them some prisoners unto Gibraltar, to denounce unto the inhabitants they should surrender: otherwise Captain Morgan would certainly put them all to the sword, without giving quarter to any person he should find alive. Not long after, he arrived with his fleet before Gibraltar, whose inhabitants received him with continual shooting of great cannon-bullets. But the Pirates, instead of fainting hereat, ceased not to encourage one another, saying: *We must make one meal upon bitter things before we come to taste the sweetness of the sugar this place affords.*

The next day, very early in the morning, they landed all their men. And, being guided by the Frenchman abovementioned, they marched towards the town, not by the common way but crossing through the woods; which way the

Spaniards scarce thought they would have come. For, at the beginning of their march, they made appearance as if they intended to come the next and open way that led unto the town, hereby the better to deceive the Spaniards. But these, remembering as yet full well what hostilities L'Ollonais had committed upon them but two years before, thought it not safe to expect the second brunt, and hereupon were all fled out of the town as fast as they could, carrying with them all their goods and riches as also all the powder, and having nailed all the great guns: insomuch as the Pirates found not one person in the whole city, excepting one only poor and innocent man who was born a fool. This man they asked whither the inhabitants were fled, and where they had absconded their goods. Unto all which questions and the like he constantly made answer: *I know nothing, I know nothing.* But they presently put him to the rack, and tortured him with cords; which torments forced him to cry out: *Do not torture me any more, but come with me and I will show you my goods and my riches.* They were persuaded, as it should seem, he was some rich person who had disguised himself under those clothes so poor as also that innocent tongue. Hereupon they went along with him; and he conducted them to a poor and miserable cottage, wherein he had a few earthen dishes and other things of little or no value; and amongst these, three pieces-of-eight, which he had concealed with other trumpery underground. After this, they asked him his name, and he readily made answer: *My name is Don Sebastian Sanchez, and I am brother unto the Governor of Maracaibo.* This foolish answer, it must be conceived, these men, though never so inhuman, took for a certain truth. For no sooner had they heard it, but they put him again upon the rack, lifting him up on high with cords, and tying huge weights unto his feet and neck; besides which cruel and stretching torment, they burnt him alive, applying palm-leaves burning unto his face, under which miseries he died in half-an-hour. After his death they cut the cords wherewith they had stretched him, and dragged him forth into the adjoining woods, where they left him without burial.

The same day they sent out a party of Pirates to seek for the inhabitants, upon whom they might employ their inhuman cruelties. These brought back with them an honest peasant with two daughters of his, whom they had taken prisoners, and whom they intended to torture as they used to do with others, in case they showed not the places where the inhabitants had absconded themselves. The peasant knew some of the said places, and hereupon, seeing himself threatened with the rack, went with the Pirates to show them. But the Spaniards, perceiving their enemies to range everywhere up and down the woods, were already fled thence much farther off into the thickest parts of the said woods, where they built themselves huts, to preserve from the violence of the weather those few goods they had carried with them. The Pirates judged themselves to be deceived by the said peasant; and hereupon, to revenge their wrath upon him, notwithstanding all the excuses he could make and his humble supplications for his life, they hanged him upon a tree.

After this, they divided into several parties, and went to search the plantations. For they knew the Spaniards that were absconded could not live upon what they found in the woods, without coming now and then to seek provisions at their own country-houses. Here they found a certain slave, unto whom they promised mountains of gold and that they would give him his liberty by transporting him unto Jamaica, in case he would show them the places where the inhabitants of Gibraltar lay hidden. This fellow conducted them unto a party of Spaniards, whom they instantly made all prisoners, commanding the said slave to kill some of them before the eyes of the rest; to the intent that by this perpetrated crime he might never be able to leave their wicked company. The negro, according to their orders, committed many murders and insolent actions upon the Spaniards, and followed the unfortunate traces of the Pirates, who, after the space of eight days, returned unto Gibraltar with many prisoners and some mules laden with riches. They examined every prisoner by himself (who were in all about 250 persons) where they had absconded the rest of their goods, and if they knew of their fellow-townsmen. Such as would not confess were tormented after a most cruel and inhuman manner. Among the rest, there happened to be a certain Portuguese, who by the information of a negro was reported, though falsely, to be very rich. This man was commanded to produce his riches. But his answer was, he had no more than 100 pieces-of-eight in the whole world, and that these had been stolen from him two days before by a servant of his. Which words, although he sealed with many oaths and protestations, yet they would not believe. But dragging him unto the rack, without any regard unto his age, as being three-score years old, they stretched him with cords, breaking both his arms behind his shoulders.

This cruelty went not alone. For he not being able or willing to make any other declaration than the above said, they put him to another sort of torment that was worse and more barbarous than the preceding. They tied him with small cords by his two thumbs and great-toes unto four stakes that were fixed in the ground at a convenient distance, the whole weight of his body being pendent in the air upon those cords. Then they thrashed upon the cords with great sticks and all their strength, so that the body of this miserable man was ready to perish at every stroke, under the severity of those horrible pains. Not satisfied as yet with this cruel torture, they took a stone which weighed above 200 pound, and laid it upon his belly, as if they intended to press him to death. At which time they also kindled palm-leaves, and applied the flame unto the face of this unfortunate Portuguese, burning with them the whole skin, beard, and hair. At last these cruel tyrants, seeing that neither with these tortures nor others they could get anything out of him, they untied the cords, and carried him, being almost half-dead, unto the church, where was their *corps du garde*. Here they tied him anew to one of the pillars thereof, leaving him in that condition, without giving him either to eat or drink unless very sparingly and so little as would scarce sustain life, for some days. Four or five being past, he desired that one of the prisoners might have the liberty to come to him, by whose means he promised he would endeavour to raise some money to satisfy their demands. The prisoner whom he required was brought unto him, and he ordered him to promise the Pirates 500 pieces-of-eight for his ransom. But they were both deaf and obstinate at such a small sum, and, instead of accepting it, did beat him cruelly with cudgels, saying unto him: *Old fellow, instead of* 500 *you must say* 500,000 *pieces-of-eight; otherwise you shall here end your life.* Finally, after a thousand protestations that he was but a miserable man and kept a poor tavern for his living, he agreed with them for the sum of 1000 pieces-of-eight. These he raised in few days, and, having paid them unto the Pirates, got his liberty, although so horribly maimed in his body that 'tis scarce to be believed he could supervive many weeks after.

Several other tortures besides these were exercised upon others, which this Portuguese endured not. Some were hanged up by the testicles or by their privy members and left in that condition till they fell unto the ground, those private parts being torn from their bodies. If with this they were minded to show themselves merciful to those wretches, thus lacerated in the most tender parts of their bodies, their mercy was to run them through and through with their swords, and by this means rid them soon of their pains and lives. Otherwise, if this were not done, they used to lie four or five days under the agonies of death, before dying. Others were crucified by these tyrants, and with kindled matches were burnt between the joints of their fingers and toes. Others had their feet put into the fire, and thus were left to be roasted alive. At last, having used both these and other cruelties with the white men, they began to practice the same over again with the negroes, their slaves, who were treated with no less inhumanity than their masters.

Among these slaves was found one who promised Captain Morgan to conduct him unto a certain river belonging to the lake, where he should find a ship and four boats richly laden with goods that belonged unto the inhabitants of Maracaibo. The same slave discovered likewise the place where the Governor of Gibraltar lay hidden, together with the greatest part of the women of the town. But all this he revealed, through great menaces wherewith they threatened to hang him in case he told not what he knew. Captain Morgan sent away presently 200 men in two *saëties*, or great boats, towards the river above-mentioned, to seek for what the slave had discovered. But he himself, with two-hundred-and-fifty more, undertook to go and take the Governor. This gentleman was retired unto a small island seated in the middle of the river, where he had built a little fort, after the best manner he could, for his defence. But hearing that Captain Morgan came in person with great forces to seek him, he retired farther off unto the top of a mountain not much distant from that place; unto which there was no ascent but by a very narrow passage—yea, this was so straight that whosoever did pretend to gain the ascent must of necessity cause his men to pass one by one. Captain Morgan spent two days before he could arrive at the little island above-mentioned. Thence he designed to proceed unto the mountain where the Governor was posted, had he not been told of the impossibility he should find in the ascent, not only of the narrowness of the path that led to the top, but also because the Governor was very well provided with all sorts of ammunition above. Besides that, there was fallen an huge rain, whereby all the baggage belonging to the Pirates, and their powder, was wet. By this rain also they had lost many of their men at the passage over a river that was overflown. Here perished likewise some women and children, and many mules laden with plate and other goods; all which they had taken in the fields from the fugitive inhabitants. So that all things were in a very bad condition with Captain Morgan, and the bodies of his men as much harassed, as ought to be inferred from this relation. Whereby, if the Spaniards in that juncture of time had had but a troop of fifty men well armed with pikes or spears, they might have entirely destroyed the Pirates, without any possible resistance on their side. But the fears which the Spaniards had conceived from the beginning were so great, that, only hearing the leaves on the trees to stir, they often fancied them to be Pirates. Finally, Captain Morgan and his people, having upon this march sometimes waded up to their middles in water for the space of half or whole miles together, they at last escaped for the greatest part. But of the women and children they brought home prisoners, the major part died.

Thus twelve days after they set forth to seek the Governor, they returned unto Gibraltar with a great number of prisoners. Two days after, arrived also the two *saëties* that went unto the river, bringing with them four boats and some prisoners. But, as to the greatest part of the merchandize that were in the said boats, they found them not, the Spaniards having unladed and secured them, as having intelligence beforehand of the coming of the Pirates. Whereupon they designed also, when the merchandize were all taken out, to burn the boats. Yet the Spaniards made not so much haste as was requisite to unlade the said vessels, but that they left both in the ship and boats great parcels of goods, which, they being fled from thence, the Pirates seized, and brought thereof a considerable booty unto Gibraltar. Thus, after they had been in possession of the place five entire weeks, and committed there infinite number of murders, robberies, rapes, and suchlike insolences, they concluded upon their departure. But, before this could be performed, for the last proof of their tyranny they gave orders unto some prisoners to go forth into the woods and fields, and collect a ransom for the town; otherwise they would certainly burn every house down to the ground. Those poor afflicted men went forth as they were sent. And, after they had searched every corner of the adjoining fields and woods, they returned to Captain Morgan, telling him they had scarce been able to find anybody. But that unto such as they had found, they had proposed his demands, to which had they made answer that the Governor had prohibited them to give any ransom for not burning the town. But, notwithstanding any prohibition to the contrary, they beseeched him to have a little patience, and among themselves they would collect to the sum of 5000 pieces-of-eight; and, for the rest, they would give him some of their own townsmen as hostages, whom he might carry with him to Maracaibo, till such time as he had received full satisfaction.

Captain Morgan, having now been long time absent from Maracaibo and knowing the Spaniards had had sufficient time wherein to fortify themselves and hinder his departure out of the lake, granted them their proposition above-mentioned; and withal made as much haste as he could to set things in order for his departure. He gave liberty to all the prisoners, having beforehand put them every one to the ransom; yet he detained all the slaves with him. They delivered unto him four persons that were agreed upon for hostages of what sums of money more he was to receive from them; and they desired to have the slave of whom we made mention above, intending to punish him according to his deserts. But Captain Morgan would not deliver him, being persuaded they would burn him alive. At last they weighed anchor, and set sail with all the haste they could, directing their course towards Maracaibo. Here they arrived in four days, and found all things in the same posture they had left them when they departed. Yet here they received news, from the information of a poor distressed old man, who was sick and whom alone they found in the town, that three Spanish men-of-war were arrived at the entry of the lake, and there waited for the return of the Pirates out of those parts. Moreover, that the castle at the entry thereof was again put into a good posture of defence, being well provided with guns and men and all sorts of ammunition.

This relation of the old man could not choose but cause some disturbance in the mind of Captain Morgan, who now was careful how to get away through those narrow passages of the entry of the lake. Hereupon he sent one of his boats, the swiftest he had, to view the entry and see if things were as they had been related. The next day the boat came back, confirming what was said, and assuring they had viewed the ships so nigh that they had been in great danger of the shot they made at them. Hereunto they added that the biggest ship was mounted with 40 guns, the second with 30, and the smallest with four-and-twenty. These forces were much beyond those of Captain Morgan ; and hence they caused a general consternation in all the Pirates, whose biggest vessel had not above 14 small guns. Every one judged Captain Morgan to despond in his mind and be destitute of all manner of hopes, considering the difficulty either of passing safely with his little fleet amidst those great ships and the fort, or that he must perish. How to escape any other way by sea or land, they saw no opportunity nor convenience. Only they could have wished that those three ships had rather come over the lake to seek them at Maracaibo than to remain at the mouth of the strait where they were. For at that passage they must of necessity fear the ruin of their fleet, which consisted only for the greatest part of boats.

Hereupon, being necessitated to act as well as he could, Captain Morgan resumed new courage, and resolved to show himself as yet undaunted with these terrors. To this intent he boldly sent a Spaniard unto the Admiral of those three ships, demanding of him a considerable tribute or ransom for not putting the city of Maracaibo to the flame. This man (who doubtless was received by the Spaniards with great admiration of the confidence and boldness of those Pirates) returned two days after, bringing unto Captain Morgan a letter from the said Admiral, whose contents were as follows :—

Letter of Don Alonso del Campo y Espinosa, Admiral of the Spanish Fleet, unto Captain Morgan, commander of the pirates.

Having understood by all our friends and neighbours the unexpected news that you have dared to attempt and commit hostilities in the countries, cities, towns, and villages belonging unto the dominions of his Catholic Majesty, my Sovereign Lord and Master, I let you understand by these lines that I am come unto this place, according to my obligation, nigh unto that castle which you took out of the hands of a parcel of cowards; where I have put things into a very good posture of defence, and mounted again the artillery which you had nailed and dismounted. My intent is to dispute with you your passage out of the lake, and follow and pursue you everywhere, to the end you may see the performance of my duty. Notwithstanding, if you be contented to surrender with humility all that you have taken, together with the slaves and all other prisoners, I will let you freely pass, without trouble or molestation; upon condition that you retire home presently unto your own country. But, in case that you make any resistance or opposition unto these things that I proffer unto you, I do assure you I will command boats to come from Caracas, wherein I will put my troops, and, coming to Maracaibo, will cause you utterly to perish, by putting you every man to the sword. This is my last and absolute resolution. Be prudent, therefore, and do not abuse my bounty with ingratitude. I have with me very good soldiers, who desire nothing more ardently than to revenge on you and your people all the cruelties and base infamous actions you have committed upon the Spanish nation in America. Dated on board the Royal Ship named the Magdalen, *lying at anchor at the entry of the Lake of Maracaibo, this 24th day of April, 1669.*

Don Alonso del Campo y Espinosa

As soon as Captain Morgan had received this letter, he called all his men together in the market-place of Maracaibo; and, after reading the contents thereof, both in French and English, he asked their advice and resolutions upon the whole matter, and whether they had rather surrender all they had purchased, to obtain their liberty, than fight for it.

They answered all unanimously: *They had rather fight, and spill the very last drop of blood they had in their veins, than surrender so easily the booty they had gotten with so much danger of their lives.* Among the rest, one was found who said unto

Captain Morgan: *Take you care for the rest, and I will undertake to destroy the biggest of those ships with only twelve men. The manner shall be by making a brûlot, or fire-ship, of that vessel we took in the river of Gibraltar—which, to the intent she may not be known for a fire-ship, we will fill her decks with logs of wood, standing with hats and montera caps*[1], *to deceive their sight with the representation of men. The same we will do at the port-holes that serve for guns, which shall be filled with counterfeit cannon. At the stern we will hang out the English colours, and persuade the enemy she is one of our best men-of-war that goes to fight them.* This proposition, being heard by the *Junta*[2], was admitted and approved of by every one, howbeit their fears were not quite dispersed.

For, notwithstanding what had been concluded there, they endeavoured the next day to see if they could come to an accommodation with Don Alonso. Unto this effect Captain Morgan sent him two persons, with these following propositions. First: *That he would quit Maracaibo, without doing any damage to the town, nor exacting any ransom for the firing thereof.* Secondly: *That he would set at liberty one half of the slaves, and likewise all other prisoners, without ransom.* Thirdly: *That he would send home freely the four chief inhabitants of Gibraltar which he had in his custody as hostages for the contributions those people had promised to pay.* These propositions from the Pirates, being understood by Don Alonso, were instantly rejected by every one, as being dishonourable for him to grant. Neither would he hear any word more of any other accommodation, but sent back this message: *That in case they surrendered not themselves voluntarily into his hands within the space of two days, under the conditions which he had offered them by his letter, he would immediately come and force them to do it.*

No sooner had Captain Morgan received this message from Don Alonso than he put all things in order to fight, resolving to get out of the lake by main force, and without surrendering anything. In the first place, he commanded all the slaves and

[1] *Montera*, a Spanish hunting-cap: cf. Hawkins, *Voyage to the South Seas* [1593–1622], § xiii: ". . . upon their heads they weare a night-capp, upon it a montero, and a hat over that."

[2] *Junta*, Spanish, a meeting, council: cf. Howell, *Letters* [1622], iii, x: "a particular *Junta* of some of the Counsell of State and War might be appointed to determine the businesse."

prisoners to be tied and guarded very well. After this, they gathered all the pitch, tar, and brimstone they could find in the whole town, wherewith to prepare the fire-ship abovementioned. Likewise they made several inventions of powder and brimstone, with great quantities of palm-leaves, very well ointed with tar. They covered very well their counterfeit cannon, laying under every piece thereof many pounds of powder. Besides which, they cut down many outworks belonging to the ship, to the end the powder might exert its strength the better. Thus they broke open also new portholes, where, instead of guns they placed little drums, of which the negroes make use. Finally, the decks were handsomely beset with many pieces of wood dressed up in the shape of men with hats, as monteras, and likewise armed with swords, muskets, and bandoliers.

The *brûlot*, or fire-ship, being thus fitted to their purpose, they prepared themselves to go to the entry of the port. All the prisoners were put into one great boat, and in another of the biggest they placed all the women, plate, jewels, and other rich things which they had. Into others, they put all the bales of goods and merchandize, and other things of greatest bulk. Each of these boats had twelve men on board, very well armed. The *brûlot* had orders to go before the rest of the vessels, and presently to fall foul with the great ship. All things being in readiness, Captain Morgan exacted an oath of all his comrades, whereby they protested to defend themselves against the Spaniards even to the last drop of blood, without demanding quarter at any rate: promising them withal that whosoever thus behaved himself should be very well rewarded.

With this disposition of mind and courageous resolution, they set sail to seek the Spaniards on the 30th day of April, 1669. They found the Spanish fleet riding at anchor in the middle of the entry of the lake. Captain Morgan, it being now late and almost dark, commanded all his vessels to come to an anchor, with design to fight thence even all night, if they should provoke him thereunto. He gave orders that a careful and vigilant watch should be kept on board every vessel till the morning, they being almost within shot, as well as within fight, of the enemy. The dawning of the day being come, they weighed anchors, and set sail again, steering their

The Spanish Armada destroyed by Captaine Morgan

course directly towards the Spaniards, who, observing them to move, did instantly the same. The fire-ship, sailing before the rest, fell presently upon the great ship, and grappled to her sides in a short while. Which, by the Spaniards being perceived to be a fire-ship, they attempted to escape the danger by putting her off ; but in vain, and too late. For the flame suddenly seized her timber and tackling, and in a short space consumed all the stern, the forepart sinking into the sea, whereby she perished. The second Spanish ship, perceiving the Admiral to burn, not by accident but by industry of the enemy, escaped towards the castle, where the Spaniards themselves caused her to sink, choosing this way of losing their ship, rather than to fall into the hands of those Pirates, which they held for inevitable. The third, as having no opportunity nor time to escape, was taken by the Pirates. The seamen that sank the second ship nigh unto the castle, perceiving the Pirates to come towards them to take what remains they could find of their ship-wreck (for some part of the bulk was extant above water), set fire in like manner unto this vessel, to the end the Pirates might enjoy nothing of that spoil. The first ship being set on fire, some of the persons that were in her swam towards the shore. These the Pirates would have taken up in their boats, but they would neither ask nor admit of any quarter, choosing rather to lose their lives than receive them from the hands of their persecutors, for such reasons as I shall relate hereafter.

The Pirates were extremely gladded at this signal victory, obtained in so short a time and with so great inequality of forces ; whereby they conceived greater pride in their minds than they had before. Hereupon they all presently ran ashore, intending to take the castle. This they found very well provided both with men, great cannon, and ammunition—they having no other arms than muskets and a few fire-balls in their hands. Their own artillery they thought incapable, for its smallness, of making any considerable breach in the walls. Thus they spent the rest of that day firing at the garrison with their muskets till the dusk of the evening, at which time they attempted to advance nigh unto the walls, with intent to throw in the fire-balls. But the Spaniards, resolving to sell their lives as dear as they could, continued firing so furiously at them that they thought it not convenient to approach any nearer nor persist any longer in that dispute. Thus, having experienced the obstinacy of the enemy, and seeing thirty of their own men already dead and as many more wounded, they retired unto their ships.

The Spaniards, believing the Pirates would return the next day to renew the attack, as also make use of their own cannon against the castle, laboured very hard all night to put things in order for their coming. But more particularly they employed themselves that night in digging down and making plain some little hills and eminent places whence possibly the castle might be offended.

But Captain Morgan intended not to come ashore again, busying himself the next day in taking prisoners some of the men who still swam alive upon the waters, and hoping to get part of the riches that were lost in the two ships that perished. Among the rest he took a certain pilot, who was a stranger and who belonged to the lesser ship of the two, with whom he held much discourse, inquiring of him several things. Such questions were: *What number of people those three ships had had in them? Whether they expected any more ships to come? From what port they set forth the last time, when they came to seek them out?* His answer unto all these questions was as follows, which he delivered in the Spanish tongue:

Noble Sir, be pleased to pardon and spare me, that no evil be done unto me, as being a stranger unto this nation I have served, and shall sincerely inform you of all [that] passed till our arrival at this lake. We were sent by orders from the Supreme Council of State in Spain, being 6 men-of-war well equipped into these seas, with instructions to cruize upon the English pirates, and root them out from these parts by destroying as many of them as we could. These orders were given by reason of the news brought unto the Court of Spain of the loss and ruin of Porto Bello and other places. Of all which damages and hostilities committed here by the English very dismal lamentations have oftentimes penetrated the ears of both the Catholic King and Council, unto whom belongs the care and preservation of this New World. And, although the Spanish Court has many times by their ambassadors sent complaints hereof unto the King of England, yet it has been the constant answer of his Majesty of Great Britain: That he never gave any letters-patent nor commissions for the acting any hostility whatsoever against the subjects of the King of Spain. Hereupon the Catholic

King, being resolved to revenge his subjects and punish these proceedings, commanded six men-of-war to be equipped, which he sent into these parts under the command of Don Augustin de Bustos, who was constituted Admiral of the said fleet. He commmanded the biggest ship thereof, named Na Sa[1] de la Soledad, *mounted with eight-and-forty great guns and eight small ones. The Vice-Admiral was Don Alonso del Campo y Espinosa, who commanded the second ship, called* La Concepcion, *which carried forty-four great guns and eight small ones. Besides which vessels, there were also four more, whereof the first was named the* Magdalen, *and was mounted with* 36 *great guns and* 12 *small ones, having on board* 250 *men. The second was called* St Lewis, *with* 26 *great guns,* 12 *small ones and* 200 *men. The third was called* La Marquesa, *which carried* 16 *great guns,* 8 *small ones and* 150 *men. The fourth and last,* Na Sa[1] del Carmen, *with* 18 *great guns,* 8 *small ones, and likewise* 150 *men.*

We were now arrived at Cartagena, when the two greatest ships received orders to return into Spain, as being judged too big for cruizing upon these coasts. With the four ships remaining, Don Alonso del Campo y Espinosa departed thence towards Campeche, to seek out the English. We arrived at the port of the said city, where, being surprised by a huge storm that blew from the north we lost one of our four ships, being that which I named in the last place among the rest. Hence we set sail for the isle of Hispaniola, in sight of which we came within few days, and directed our course unto the port of San Domingo. Here we received intelligence there had passed that way a fleet from Jamaica, and that some men thereof having landed at a place called Alta Gracia, the inhabitants had taken one of them prisoner, who confessed their whole design was to go and pillage the city of Caracas. With these news Don Alonso instantly weighed anchor, and set sail thence, crossing over unto the continent, till we came in sight of Caracas. Here we found not the English, but happened to meet with a boat which certified us they were in the Lake of Maracaibo, and that the fleet consisted of 7 *small ships and one boat.*

Upon this intelligence we arrived here; and, coming nigh unto the entry of the lake, we shot off a gun to demand a pilot from the shore. Those on land, perceiving that we were Spaniards, came willingly to us with a pilot, and told us that the English had taken the city of Maracaibo, and that they were at present at the pillage of Gibraltar. Don Alonso, having understood this news, made a handsome speech to all his soldiers and mariners, encouraging them to perform their duty, and withal promising

[1] *Nuestra Señora*, Our Lady.

to divide among them all they should take from the English. After this, he gave order that the guns which we had taken out of the ship that was lost should be put into the castle, and there mounted for its defence, with 2 pieces more out of his own ship, of 18 pounds port each. The pilots conducted us into the port, and Don Alonso commanded the people that were on shore to come unto his presence, unto whom he gave orders to repossess the castle, and reinforce it with 100 men more than it had before its being taken by the English. Not long after, we received news that you were returned from Gibraltar unto Maracaibo, unto which place Don Alonso wrote you a letter, giving you account of his arrival and design, and withal exhorting you to restore all that you had taken. This you refused to do; whereupon he renewed his promises and intentions to his soldiers and seamen. And, having given a very good supper unto all his people, he persuaded them neither to take nor give any quarter unto the English that should fall into their hands. This was the occasion of so many being drowned, who dared not to crave any quarter for their lives, as knowing their own intentions of giving none. Two days before you came against us, a certain negro came on board Don Alonso's ship, telling him: Sir, be pleased to have great care of yourself, for the English have prepared a fire-ship with desire to burn your fleet. But Don Alonso would not believe this intelligence, his answer being: How can that be? Have they, peradventure, wit enough to build a fireship? or what instruments have they [to] do it withal?

The pilot above-mentioned, having related so distinctly all the aforesaid things unto Captain Morgan, was very well used by him, and, after some kind proffers made unto him, remained in his service. He discovered, moreover, unto Captain Morgan, that in the ship which was sunk there was a great quantity of plate, even to the value of 40,000 pieces-of-eight; and that this was certainly the occasion they had oftentimes seen the Spaniards in boats about the said ship. Hereupon Captain Morgan ordered that one of his ships should remain there to watch all occasions of getting out of the said vessel what plate they could. In the meanwhile he himself, with all his fleet, returned unto Maracaibo, where he refitted the great ship he had taken of the three afore-mentioned. And, now being well accommodated, he chose it for himself, giving his own bottom to one of his Captains.

After this he sent again a messenger unto the Admiral, who

was escaped on shore and got into the castle, demanding of him a tribute or ransom of fire for the town of Maracaibo ; which being denied, he threatened he would entirely consume and destroy it. The Spaniards, considering how unfortunate they had been all along with those Pirates, and not knowing after what manner to get rid of them, concluded among themselves to pay the said ransom, although Don Alonso would not consent unto it.

Hereupon they sent unto Captain Morgan to ask what sum he demanded. He answered them he would have 30,000 pieces-of-eight, and 500 beeves, to the intent his fleet might be well victualled with flesh. This ransom being paid, he promised in such case he would give no farther trouble unto the prisoners, nor cause any ruin or damage unto the town. Finally they agreed with him upon the sum of 20,000 pieces-of-eight, besides the 500 beeves. The cattle the Spaniards brought in the next day, together with one part of the money. And, while the pirates were busied in salting the flesh, they returned with the rest of the whole sum of 20,000 pieces-of-eight, for which they had agreed.

But Captain Morgan would not deliver for that present the prisoners, as he had promised to do, by reason he feared the shot of the artillery of the castle at his going forth of the lake. Hereupon he told them he intended not to deliver them till such time as he was out of that danger, hoping by this means to obtain a free passage. Thus he set sail with all his fleet in quest of that ship which he had left behind, to seek for the plate of the vessel that was burnt. He found her upon the place, with the sum of 15,000 pieces-of-eight, which they had purchased out of the wreck, besides many other pieces of plate, as hilts of swords and other things of this kind ; also great quantity of pieces-of-eight that were melted and run together by the force of the fire of the said ship.

Captain Morgan scarce thought himself secure, neither could he contrive how to evade the damages the said castle might cause unto his fleet. Hereupon he told the prisoners it was necessary they should agree with the Governor to open the passage with security for his fleet ; unto which point, if he should not consent, he would certainly hang them all up in his ships. After this warning the prisoners met together to confer upon the persons they should depute unto the said Governor

Don Alonso ; and they assigned some few among them for that embassy. These went unto him, beseeching and supplicating the Admiral he would have compassion and pity on those afflicted prisoners who were as yet, together with their wives and children, in the hands of Captain Morgan, and that unto this effect he would be pleased to give his word to let the whole fleet of Pirates freely pass, without any molestation, forasmuch as this would be the only remedy of saving both the lives of them that came with this petition as also of those who remained behind in captivity—all being equally menaced with the sword and gallows, in case he granted not this humble request. But Don Alonso gave them for answer a sharp reprehension of their cowardice, telling them : *If you had been as loyal unto your King in hindering the entry of these Pirates as I shall do their going out, you had never caused these troubles, neither unto yourselves nor unto our whole nation, which have suffered so much through your pusillanimity. In a word, I shall never grant your request, but shall endeavour to maintain that respect which is due unto my King, according to my duty.*

Thus the Spaniards returned to their fellow-prisoners with much consternation of mind and no hopes of obtaining their requests, telling unto Captain Morgan what answer they had received. His reply was : *If Don Alonso will not let me pass, I will find means how to do it without him.* Hereupon he began presently to make a dividend of all the booty they had taken in that voyage, fearing lest he might not have an opportunity of doing it in another place, if any tempest should arise and separate the ships, as also being jealous that any of the Commanders might run away with the best part of the spoil which then did lie much more in one vessel than another. Thus they all brought in, according to their laws, and declared what they had ; having beforehand made an oath not to conceal the least thing from the public. The accounts being cast up, they found to the value of 250,000 pieces-of-eight in money and jewels, besides the huge quantity of merchandize and slaves : all which purchase was divided into every ship or boat, according to its share.

The dividend being made, the question still remained on foot how they should pass the castle and get out of the lake. Unto this effect they made use of a stratagem, of no ill invention, which was as follows. On the day that preceded the night wherein they determined to get forth, they embarked many of their men in canoes, and rowed towards the shore, as if they designed to land them. Here they concealed themselves under the branches of trees that hang over the coast for a while till they had laid themselves down along in the boats. Then the canoes returned unto the ships, with the appearance only of two or three men rowing them back, all the rest being concealed at the bottom of the canoes. Thus much only could be perceived from the castle; and this action of false landing of men, for so we may call it, was repeated that day several times. Hereby the Spaniards were brought into persuasion the Pirates intended to force the castle by scaling it, as soon as night should come. This fear caused them to place most of their great guns on that side which looks towards the land, together with the main force of their arms, leaving the contrary side belonging to the sea almost destitute of strength and defence.

Night being come, they weighed anchor, and by the light of the moon, without setting sail, committed themselves to the ebbing tide, which gently brought them down the river, till they were nigh unto the castle. Being now almost over against it, they spread their sails with all the haste they could possibly make. The Spaniards, perceiving them to escape, transported with all speed their guns from the other side of the castle, and began to fire very furiously at the Pirates. But these, having a favourable wind, were almost past the danger before those of the castle could put things into convenient order of offence. So that the Pirates lost not many of their men, nor received any considerable damage in their ships. Being now out of the reach of the guns, Captain Morgan sent a canoe unto the castle with some of the prisoners; and the Governor thereof gave them a boat that every one might return to his own home. Notwithstanding, he detained the hostages he had from Gibraltar, by reason those of that town were not as yet come to pay the rest of the ransom for not firing the place. Just as he departed, Captain Morgan ordered seven great guns with bullets to be fired against the castle, as it were to take his leave of them. But they answered not so much as with a musket-shot.

The next day after their departure, they were surprised with a great tempest, which forced them to cast anchor in the depth of 5 or 6 fathom water. But the storm increased so much that they were compelled to weigh again and put out to sea, where they were in great danger of being lost. For if on either side they should have been cast on shore, either to fall into the hands of the Spaniards or of the Indians, they would certainly have obtained no mercy. At last the tempest being spent, the wind ceased, which caused much content and joy in the whole fleet.

While Captain Morgan made his fortune by pillaging the towns above-mentioned, the rest of his companions, who separated from his fleet at the Cape de Lobos for to take the ship of which was spoken before, endured much misery, and were very unfortunate in all their attempts. For, being arrived at the isle of Savona, they found not Captain Morgan there, nor any of their companions. Neither had they the good fortune to find a letter which Captain Morgan at his departure left behind him in a certain place where in all probability they would meet with it. Thus, not knowing what course to steer, they at last concluded to pillage some town or other, whereby to seek their fortune. They were in all 400 men, more or less, who were divided into ships and one boat. Being ready to set forth, they constituted an Admiral among themselves, by whom they might be directed in the whole affair. Unto this effect they chose a certain person who had behaved himself very courageously at the taking of Porto Bello, and whose name was Captain Hansel. This Commander resolved to attempt the taking of the town of Comana, seated nigh upon the continent of Caracas, nigh threescore leagues from the West side of the isle of Trinidad. Being arrived there, they landed their men, and killed some few Indians that were near the coast. But approaching unto the town, the Spaniards, having in their company many Indians, disputed them the entry so briskly that with great loss and in great confusion they were forced to retire towards their ships. At last they arrived at Jamaica, where the rest of their companions who came with Captain Morgan ceased not to mock and jeer them for their ill success at Comana, often telling them : *Let us see what money you brought from Comana, and if it be as good silver as that which we bring from Maracaibo.*

The end of the Second Part

PART III

CHAPTER I

Captain Morgan goes to the isle of Hispaniola to equip a new fleet, with intent to pillage again upon the coasts of the West Indies

CAPTAIN MORGAN perceived now that fortune favoured his arms by giving good success to all his enterprizes, which occasioned him, as it is usual in human affairs, to aspire to greater things, trusting she would always be constant unto him. Such was the burning of Panama, wherein fortune failed not to assist him, in like manner as she had done before, crowning the event of his actions with victory, howbeit she had led him thereunto through thousands of difficulties. The history hereof I shall now begin to relate, as being so much remarkable in all its circumstances as peradventure nothing more deserving memory may occur to be read by future ages.

Not long after Captain Morgan arrived at Jamaica, he found many of his chief officers and soldiers reduced to their former state of indigence through their immoderate vices and debauchery. Hence they ceased not to importune him for new invasions and exploits, thereby to get something to expend anew in wine and strumpets, as they had already wasted what was purchased so little before. Captain Morgan, being willing to follow fortune while she called him, hereupon stopped the mouths of many of the inhabitants of Jamaica, who were creditors to his men for large sums of money, with the hopes and promises he gave them of greater achievements than ever by a new expedition he was going about. This being done, he needed not give himself much trouble to levy men for this or any other enterprize, his name being now so famous through all those islands as that alone would readily bring him in more men than he could well employ. He undertook, therefore, to equip a new fleet of ships; for which purpose he assigned the South side of the isle of Tortuga as a place of rendezvous. With this resolution, he wrote divers letters to all the ancient and expert Pirates there inhabiting, as also to the Governor of the said isle, and to the planters and hunters of Hispaniola, giving them to understand his intentions, and desiring their appearance at the said place, in case they intended to go with him. All these people had no sooner understood his designs but they flocked unto the place assigned in huge numbers, with ships, canoes, and boats, being desirous to obey his commands. Many who had not the convenience of coming unto him by sea traversed the woods of Hispaniola, and with no small difficulties arrived there by land. Thus all were present at the place assigned, and in readiness, against the 24th day of October, 1670.

Captain Morgan was not wanting to be there according to his punctual custom, who came in his ship unto the same side of the island, to a port called by the French Port Couillon, over against the island De la Vaca, this being the place which he had assigned unto others. Having now gathered the greatest part of his fleet, he called a council, to deliberate about the means of finding provisions sufficient for so many people. Here they concluded to send four ships and one boat, manned with 400 men, over to the continent, to the intent they should rifle some country-towns and villages, and in these get all the corn or maize they could gather. They set sail for the continent, towards the river De la Hacha, with design to assault a small village called La Rancheria, where is usually to be found the greatest quantity of maize of all those parts thereabouts. In the meanwhile Captain Morgan sent another party of his men to hunt in the woods, who killed there an huge number of beasts, and salted them. The rest of his companions remained in the ships, to clean, fit, and rig them out to sea, so, at the return of those who were sent abroad, all things might be in readiness to weigh anchor and follow the course of their designs.

CHAPTER II

What happened in the river De la Hacha

THE four ships above-mentioned, after they had set sail from Hispaniola, steered their course till they came within sight of the river De la Hacha, where they were suddenly overtaken with a tedious calm. Being thus within sight of land becalmed for some days, the Spaniards inhabiting along the coasts, who had perceived them to be enemies, had sufficient time to prepare themselves for the assault, at least to hide the best part of their goods, to the end that, without any care of preserving them, they might be in readiness to retire when they found themselves unable to resist the force of the Pirates, by whose frequent attempts upon those coasts they had already learnt what they had to do in such cases. There was in the river at that present a good ship, which was come from Cartagena to lade maize, and was now when the Pirates came almost ready to depart. The men belonging to this ship endeavoured to escape, but, not being able to do it, both they and the vessel fell into their hands. This was a fit purchase for their mind, as being good part of what they came to seek for with so much care and toil. The next morning about break of day they came with their ships towards the shore, and landed their men, although the Spaniards made huge resistance from a battery which they had raised on that side where of necessity they were to land; but, notwithstanding what defence they could make, they were forced to retire towards a village, unto which the Pirates followed them. Here the Spaniards, rallying again, fell upon them with great fury, and maintained a strong combat, which lasted till night was come; but then, perceiving they had lost great number of men, which was no smaller on the Pirates' side, they retired unto places more occult in the woods.

The next day when the Pirates saw they were all fled, and the town left totally empty of people, they pursued them as far as they could possibly. In this pursuit they overtook a party of Spaniards, whom they made all prisoners and exercised the most cruel torments, to discover where they had hidden their goods: some were found who by the force of intolerable tortures confessed, but others who would not do the same were used more barbarously than the former. Thus, in the space of fifteen days that they remained there, they took many prisoners, much plate and movable goods, with all other things they could rob, with which booty they resolved to return unto Hispaniola. Yet, not contented with what they had already got, they dispatched some prisoners into the woods to seek for the rest of the inhabitants, and to demand of them a ransom for not burning the town. Unto this they answered, they had no money nor plate; but, in case they would be satisfied with a certain quantity of maize, they would give as much as they could afford. The Pirates accepted this proffer, as being more useful to them at that occasion than ready money, and agreed they should pay 4000 hanegs[1] (or bushels) of maize. These were brought in three days after, the Spaniards being desirous to rid themselves as soon as possible of that inhuman sort of people. Having laded them on board their ships, together with all the rest of their purchase, they returned unto the island of Hispaniola, to give account unto their leader, Captain Morgan, of all they had performed.

They had now been absent five entire weeks, about the commission aforementioned, which long delay occasioned Captain Morgan almost to despair of their return, as fearing lest they were fallen into the hands of the Spaniards, especially considering that the place whereunto they went could easily be relieved from Cartagena and Santa Maria, if the inhabitants were anything careful to alarm the country: on the other side he feared lest they should have made some great fortune in that voyage, and with it escaped to some other place. But at last seeing his ships return, and in greater number than they had departed, he resumed new courage, this sight causing both him and his companions infinite joy. This was much

[1] *hanega*, Portug. *fanega*, a dry measure of capacity, about a bushel to a bushel and a half English.

increased when, being arrived, they found them full laden with maize, whereof they stood in great need for the maintenance of so many people, by whose help they expected great matters through the conduct of their Commander.

After Captain Morgan had divided the said maize, as also the flesh which the hunters brought in, among all the ships according to the number of men that were in every vessel, he concluded upon the departure, having viewed beforehand every ship, and observed their being well equipped and clean. Thus he set sail, and directed his course towards Cape Tiburon, where he determined to take his measures and resolution of what enterprize he should take in hand. No sooner were they arrived there but they met with some other ships that came newly to join them from Jamaica. So that now the whole fleet consisted of 37 ships, wherein were 2000 fighting men, besides mariners and boys ; the Admiral hereof was mounted with 22 great guns and 6 small ones, of brass ; the rest carried some 20, some 16, some 18, and the smallest vessel at least 4, besides which they had great quantity of ammunition and fire balls, with other inventions of powder.

Captain Morgan finding himself with such a great number of ships, divided the whole fleet into two squadrons, constituting a Vice-Admiral, and other officers and Commanders of the second squadron, distinct from the former. Unto every one of these he gave letters patent, or commissions, to act all manner of hostility against the Spanish nation, and take of them what ships they could, either abroad at sea or in the harbours, in like manner as if they were open and declared enemies (as he termed it) of the King of England, his pretended master. This being done, he called all his Captains and other officers together, and caused them to sign some articles of common agreement betwixt them, and in the name of all. Herein it was stipulated that he should have the hundredth part of all that was gotten to himself alone : That every captain should draw the shares of eight men, for the expenses of his ship, besides his own : That the surgeon, besides his ordinary pay, should have 200 pieces-of-eight, for his chest of medicaments : And every carpenter, above his common salary, should draw 100 pieces-of-eight. As to recompenses and rewards, they were regulated in this voyage much higher than was expressed in the First Part of this book. Thus, for the loss of both legs, they assigned 1500 pieces-of-eight or 15 slaves, the choice being left to the election of the party; for the loss of both hands, 1800 pieces-of-eight or 18 slaves; for one leg, whether the right or the left, 600 pieces-of-eight or 6 slaves; for a hand, as much as for a leg; and for the loss of an eye, 100 pieces-of-eight or 1 slave. Lastly, unto him that in any battle should signalize himself, either by entering the first any castle, or taking down the Spanish colours and setting up the English, they constituted 50 pieces-of-eight for a reward. In the head of these articles it was stipulated that all these extraordinary salaries, recompenses, and rewards should be paid out of the first spoil or purchase they should take, according as every one should then occur to be either rewarded or paid.

This contract being signed, Captain Morgan commanded his Vice-Admirals and Captains to put all things in order, every one in his ship, for to go and attempt one of three places, either Cartagena, Panama, or Vera Cruz; but the lot fell upon Panama as being believed to be the richest of all three: notwithstanding this city being situated at such distance from the Northern sea, as they knew not well the avenues and entries necessary to approach unto it, they judged it necessary to go beforehand to the isle of St Catharine, there to find and provide themselves with some persons who might serve them for guides in this enterprize; for in the garrison of that island are commonly employed many banditti and outlaws belonging to Panama and the neighbouring places, who are very expert in the knowledge of all that country. But, before they proceeded any farther, they caused an act to be published through the whole fleet, containing that, in case they met with any Spanish vessel, the first Captain who with his men should enter and take the said ship should have for his reward the tenth part of whatsoever should be found within her.

CHAPTER III

Captain Morgan leaves the island of Hispaniola, and goes to that of St Catharine, which he takes

CAPTAIN MORGAN and his companions weighed anchor from the Cape of Tiburon, the 16th day of December in the year 1670. Four days after they arrived within sight of the isle of St Catharine, which was now in possession of the Spaniards again, as was said in the Second Part of this history, and unto which they commonl banish all the malefactors of the Spanish dominions in the West Indies. In this island are found huge quantities of pigeons at certain seasons of the year; it is watered continually by four rivulets or brooks, whereof two are always dry in the summer season. Here is no manner of trade nor commerce exercised by the inhabitants, neither do they give themselves the trouble to plant more fruits than what are necessary for the sustentation of human life; howbeit the country would be sufficient to make very good plantations of tobacco, which might render considerable profit, were it cultivated for that use.

As soon as Captain Morgan came nigh unto the island with his fleet, he sent before one of his best sailing vessels to view the entry of the river and see if any other ships were there who might hinder him from landing; as also fearing lest they should give intelligence of his arrival to the inhabitants of the island, and they by this means prevent his designs.

The next day before sunrise, all the fleet came to anchor nigh unto the island, in a certain bay called Aguada Grande: upon this bay the Spaniards had lately built a battery, mounted with four pieces of cannon. Captain Morgan landed with 1000 men, more or less, and disposed them into squadrons, beginning his march through the woods, although they had no other guides than some few of his own men who had been there before when Mansvelt took and ransacked the island. The same day they came unto a certain place where the Governor at other times did keep his ordinary residence: here they found a battery called *The Platform*, but nobody in it, the Spaniards having retired unto the lesser island, which, as was said before, is so nigh unto the great one that a short bridge only may conjoin them.

This lesser island aforesaid was so well fortified with forts and batteries round about it as might seem impregnable. Hereupon, as soon as the Spaniards perceived the pirates to approach, they began to fire upon them so furiously that they could advance nothing that day, but were contented to retreat a little, and take up their rest upon the grass in the open fields, which afforded no strange beds to these people, as being sufficiently used to such kind of repose: what most afflicted them was hunger, having not eaten the least thing that whole day. About midnight it began to rain so hard that those miserable people had much ado to resist so much hardship, the greatest part of them having no other clothes than a pair of seaman's trousers or breeches and a shirt, without either shoes or stockings. Thus finding themselves in great extremity, they began to pull down a few thatched houses to make fires withal: in a word, they were in such condition that one hundred men, indifferently well armed, might easily that night have torn them all in pieces. The next morning about break of day the rain ceased, at which time they began to dry their arms, which were entirely wet, and proceed on their march. But not long after, the rain recommenced anew, rather harder than before, as if the skies were melted into waters, which caused them to cease from advancing towards the forts, whence the Spaniards did continually fire at the Pirates, seeing them to approach.

The Pirates were now reduced unto great affliction and danger of their lives through the hardness of the weather, their own nakedness, and the great hunger they sustained. For a small relief hereof, they happened to find in the fields an old horse, which was both lean and full of scabs and blotches, with galled back and sides. This horrid animal they instantly killed and flayed, and divided into small pieces among themselves as far as it would reach, for many could not obtain one morsel, which they roasted and devoured without either salt or bread, more like unto ravenous wolves than men. The rain as yet ceased not to fall, and Captain Morgan perceived their minds to relent, hearing many of them say they would return on board the ships. Amongst these fatigues both of mind and body, he thought it convenient to use some sudden and almost unexpected remedy: unto this effect he commanded a canoe to be rigged in all haste, and colours of truce to be hanged out of it. This canoe he sent to the Spanish Governor of the island with this message: *That if within a few hours he delivered not himself and all his men into his hands, he did by that messenger swear unto him and all those that were in his company, he would most certainly put them all to the sword, without granting quarter to any.*

After noon the canoe returned with this answer: *That the Governor desired two hours' time to deliberate with his officers in a full council about that affair; which being past, he would give his positive answer to the message.* The time now being elapsed the said Governor sent two canoes with white colours, and two persons, to treat with Captain Morgan; but before they landed, they demanded of the Pirates two persons as hostages of their security. These were readily granted by Captain Morgan, who delivered unto them two of his Captains, for a mutual pledge of the security required. With this the Spaniards propounded unto Captain Morgan that their Governor in a full assembly had resolved to deliver up the island, as not being provided with sufficient forces to defend it against such an armada or fleet. But withal he desired that Captain Morgan would be pleased to use a certain stratagem of war, for the better saving of his own credit and the reputation of his officers both abroad and at home, which should be as follows: *That Captain Morgan would come with his troops by night, nigh unto the bridge that joined the lesser island unto the great one, and there attack the fort of St Jerome: that at the same time all the ships of his fleet would draw nigh unto the castle of Santa Teresa, and attack it by sea, landing in the meanwhile some more troops near the battery called St Matthew: that these troops which were newly landed should by this means intercept the Governor by the way, as he endeavoured to pass unto St Jerome's fort, and then take him prisoner, using the formality, as if they forced him to deliver the said castle; and that he would lead the English into it, under the fraud of being his own troops; that on one side and t'other there should be continual firing at one another, but without bullets, or at least into the air, so that no side might receive any harm by this device ; that thus having obtained two such considerable forts, the chiefest of the isle, he needed not take care for the rest, which of necessity must fall by course into his hands.*

These propositions, every one, were granted by Captain Morgan, upon condition they should see them faithfully observed, for otherwise they should be used with all rigour imaginable : this they promised to do, and hereupon took their leaves, and returned to give account of their negotiation to the Governor. Presently after, Captain Morgan commanded the whole fleet to enter the port, and his men to be in readiness for to assault that night the castle of St Jerome. Thus the false alarm or battle began with incessant firing of great guns from both the castles against the ships, but without bullets, as was said before. Then the Pirates landed, and assaulted by night the lesser island, which they took, as also possession of both the fortresses, forcing all the Spaniards, in appearance, to fly unto the church. Before this assault Captain Morgan had sent word to the Governor he should keep all his men together in a body, otherwise, if the Pirates met any straggling Spaniards in the streets, they should certainly shoot them.

The island being taken by this unusual stratagem, and all things put in due order, the Pirates began to make a new war against the poultry, cattle, and all sorts of victuals they could find. This was their whole employ for some days, scarce thinking of anything else than to kill those animals, roast, and eat, and make good cheer, as much as they could possibly attain unto. If wood was wanting, they presently fell upon the houses, and, pulling them down, made fires with the timber as had been done before in the field. The next day they numbered all the prisoners they had taken upon the whole island, which were found to be in all 450 persons, between men, women, and children, viz. 190 soldiers belonging to the garrison, 40 inhabitants who were married, 43 children, 34 slaves belonging to the King, with 8 children, 8 banditti ; 39 negroes belonging to private persons, with 27 female blacks and 34 children. The Pirates disarmed all the Spaniards, and sent them out immediately unto the plantations to seek for provisions, leaving the women in the church, there to exercise their devotions.

Soon after, they took a review of the whole island and all the fortresses belonging thereunto, which they found to be nine in all, as follows: the fort of St Jerome, nighest unto the bridge, had 8 great guns, of twelve, six, and eight pound carriage, together with 6 pipes of muskets, every pipe containing 10 muskets. Here they found still 60 muskets, with sufficient quantity of powder and all other sorts of ammunition. The second fortress, called St Matthew, had 3 guns, of 8 pound carriage each. The third and chiefest among all the rest, named Santa Teresa, had 20 great guns, of 18, 12, 8, and 6 pound carriage, with 10 pipes of muskets, like those we said before, and 90 muskets remaining, besides all other warlike ammunition. This castle was built with stone and mortar, with very thick walls on all sides, and a large ditch round about it of 20-foot depth, the which although it was dry was very hard to get over. Here was no entry but through one door, which corresponded to the middle of the castle. Within it was a mount or hill, almost inaccessible, with four pieces of cannon at the top, whence they could shoot directly into the port. On the sea side this castle was impregnable, by reason of the rocks which surrounded it and the sea beating furiously upon them. In like manner, on the side of the land, it was so commodiously seated on a mountain that there was no access to it but by a path of three or four foot broad. The fourth fortress was named St Augustine, having 3 guns, of eight and six pound carriage. The fifth, named La Plattaforma de la Concepcion, had only 2 guns, of eight pound carriage. The sixth, by name San Salvador, had likewise no more than 2 guns. The seventh, being called Plattaforma de los Artilleros, had also 2 guns. The eight, called Santa Cruz, had 3 guns. The ninth, which was called St Joseph's Fort, had 6 guns, of twelve and eight pound carriage, besides two pipes of muskets and sufficient ammunition.

In the storehouse were found above thirty-thousand pound of powder, with all other sorts of ammunition, which were transported by the Pirates on board the ships. All the guns were stopped and nailed, and the fortresses demolished, excepting that of St Jerome, where the Pirates kept their guard and residence. Captain Morgan inquired if any banditti were there from Panama or Porto Bello; and hereupon three were brought before him, who pretended to be very expert in all the avenues of those parts. He asked them if they would be his guides and show him the securest ways and passages unto Panama ; which if they performed, he promised them equal shares in all they should pillage and rob in that expedition, and that afterwards he would set them at liberty by transporting them unto Jamaica. These propositions pleased the banditti very well, and they readily accepted his proffers, promising to serve him very faithfully in all he should desire ; especially one of these three, who was the greatest rogue, thief, and assassin among them, and who had deserved for his crimes rather to be broken alive upon the wheel than punished with serving in a garrison. This wicked fellow had a great ascendancy over the other two banditti, and could domineer and command over them as he pleased, they not daring to refuse obedience to his orders.

Hereupon Captain Morgan commanded four ships and one boat to be equipped and provided with all things necessary, for to go and take the castle of Chagre, seated upon the river of that name. Neither would he go himself with his whole fleet, fearing lest the Spaniards should be jealous of his farther designs upon Panama. In these vessels he caused to embark 400 men, who went to put in execution the orders of their chief Commander Captain Morgan, while he himself remained behind in the island of St Catharine, with the rest of the fleet, expecting to hear the success of their arms.

CHAPTER IV

Captain Morgan takes the castle of Chagre with four hundred men sent unto this purpose from the Isle of St Catharine

CAPTAIN MORGAN, sending these four ships and a boat to the river of Chagre, chose for Vice-Admiral thereof a certain person named Captain Brodely. This man had been a long time in those quarters, and committed many robberies upon the Spaniards when Mansvelt took the isle of St Catharine, as was related in the Second Part of the history. He, being thereof well acquainted with those coasts, was thought a fit person for this exploit, his actions likewise having rendered him famous among the Pirates and their enemies the Spaniards. Captain Brodely being chosen Chief Commander of these forces, in three days after he departed from the presence of Captain Morgan arrived within sight of the said castle of Chagre, which by the Spaniards is called St Lawrence. This castle is built upon a high mountain, at the entry of the river, and surrounded on all sides with strong palisades, or wooden walls, being very well terre-pleined[1], and filled with earth, which renders them as secure as the best walls made of stone or brick. The top of this mountain is in a manner divided into two parts, between which lies a ditch of the depth of thirty-foot. The castle itself has but one entry, and that by a draw-bridge which passes over the ditch aforementioned. On the land-side it had four bastions, that of the sea containing only two more. That part thereof which looks towards the South is totally inaccessible and impossible to be climbed, through the infinite asperity of the mountain. The North side is

[1] A French fortification term—the platform on top of a rampart: cf. "If it fall so out that you cannot make trauerses vppon the terre-plaine, for that the enemy doth hinder it . . ."—Garrard, *Art of Warre* [1591], p. 317.

surrounded by the river, which hereabouts runs very broad. At the foot of the said castle, or rather mountain, is seated a strong fort, with eight great guns; which commands and impedes the entry of the river. Not much lower are to be seen two other batteries, whereof each has 6 pieces of cannon, to defend likewise the mouth of the said river. At one side of the castle are built two great storehouses, in which are deposited all sorts of warlike ammunition and merchandize, which are brought thither from the inner parts of the country. Nigh unto these houses is a high pair of stairs, hewed out of the rock, which serves to mount unto the top of the castle. On the West side of the said fortress lies a small port, which is not above seven or eight fathom deep, being very fit for small vessels, and of very good anchorage. Besides this, there lies before the castle, at the entry of the river, a great rock, scarce to be perceived above water, unless at low tides.

No sooner had the Spaniards perceived the Pirates to come but they began to fire incessantly at them with the biggest of their guns. They came to an anchor in a small port, at the distance of a league more or less from the castle. The next morning very early they went on shore, and marched through the woods, to attack the castle on that side. This march continued until two of the clock of the afternoon before they could reach the castle, by reason of the difficulties of the way, and its mire and dirt. And, although their guides served them exactly, notwithstanding they came so nigh the castle at first that they lost many of their men with the shot from the guns, they being in an open place where nothing could cover nor defend them. This much perplexed the Pirates in their minds, they not knowing what to do, nor what course to take, for on that side of necessity they must make the assault, and, being uncovered from head to foot, they could not advance one step without great danger. Besides that, the castle, both for its situation and strength, did cause them much to fear the success of that enterprize. But to give it over they dared not, lest they should be reproached and scorned by their companions.

At last, after many doubts and disputes among themselves, they resolved to hazard the assault and their lives after a most desperate manner. Thus they advanced towards the castle, with their swords in one hand and fire-balls in the other. The Spaniards defended themselves very briskly, ceasing not to fire at them with their great guns and muskets continually, crying withal: *Come on, ye English dogs, enemies to God and our King; let your other companions that are behind come on too; ye shall not go to Panama this bout.* After the Pirates had made some trial to climb up the walls, they were forced to retreat, which they accordingly did, resting themselves until night. This being come, they returned to the assault, to try if by the help of their fire-balls they could overcome and pull down the pales before the wall. This they attempted to do, and while they were about it there happened a very remarkable accident, which gave them the opportunity of the victory. One of the Pirates was wounded with an arrow in his back, which pierced his body to the other side. This instantly he pulled out with great valour at the side of his breast: then, taking a little cotton that he had about him, he wound it about the said arrow, and putting it into his musket, he shot it back into the castle. But the cotton, being kindled by the powder, occasioned two or three houses that were within the castle, as being thatched with palm-leaves, to take fire, which the Spaniards perceived not so soon as was necessary. For this fire, meeting with a parcel of powder, blew it up, and thereby caused great ruin, and no less consternation, to the Spaniards, who were not able to occur unto [1] this accident, not having seen the beginning thereof.

Thus the Pirates, perceiving the good effect of the arrow and the beginning of the misfortune of the Spaniards, were infinitely gladded thereat. And, while they were busied in extinguishing the fire, which caused great confusion in the whole castle, having not sufficient water wherewithal to do it, the Pirates made use of this opportunity, setting fire likewise unto the palisades. Thus the fire was seen at the same time in several parts about the castle, which gave them huge advantage against the Spaniards. For many breaches were made at once by the fire among the pales, great heaps of earth falling down into the ditch. Upon these the Pirates climbed up, and got over into the castle, notwithstanding that some Spaniards who were not busied about the fire cast down upon them many flaming pots, full of combustible matter

[1] Latin *occurrere*, to meet, prevent, counteract.

and odious smells, which occasioned the loss of many of the English.

The Spaniards, notwithstanding the great resistance they made, could not hinder the palisades from being entirely burnt before midnight. Meanwhile the Pirates ceased not to persist in their intention of taking the castle. Unto which effect, although the fire was great, they would creep upon the ground as nigh unto it as they could, and shoot amidst the flames against the Spaniards they could perceive on the other side, and thus cause many to fall dead from the walls. When day was come, they observed all the movable earth that lay betwixt the pales to be fallen into the ditch in huge quantity. So that now those within the castle did in a manner lie equally exposed to them without, as had been on the contrary before. Whereupon the Pirates continued shooting very furiously against them, and killed great numbers of Spaniards. For the Governor had given them orders not to retire from those posts which corresponded to the heaps of earth fallen into the ditch, and caused the artillery to be transported unto the breeches.

Notwithstanding, the fire within the castle still continued, and now the Pirates from abroad used what means they could to hinder its progress, by shooting incessantly against it. One party of the Pirates was employed only to this purpose, and another commanded to watch all the motions of the Spaniards, and take all opportunities against them. About noon the English happened to gain a breach, which the Governor himself defended with twenty-five soldiers. Here was performed a very courageous and warlike resistance by the Spaniards, both with muskets, pikes, stones, and swords. Yet, notwithstanding, through all these arms the Pirates forced and fought their way, till at last they gained the castle. The Spaniards who remained alive cast themselves down from the castle into the sea, choosing rather to die precipitated by their own selves (few or none surviving the fall) than to ask any quarter for their lives. The Governor himself retreated unto the *corps du garde*, before which were placed two pieces of cannon. Here he intended still to defend himself; neither would he demand any quarter. But at last he was killed with a musket-shot, which pierced his skull into the brain.

The Governor being dead, and the *corps du garde* surrendered, they found still remaining in it alive to the number of thirty men, whereof scarce ten were not wounded. These informed the Pirates that eight or nine of their soldiers had deserted their colours, and were gone to Panama to carry news of their arrival and invasion. These thirty men alone were remaining of 314 wherewith the castle was garrisoned, among which number not one officer was found alive. These were all made prisoners, and compelled to tell whatsoever they knew of their designs and enterprizes. Among other things they declared that the Governor of Panama had notice sent him three weeks ago from Cartagena, how that the English were equipping a fleet at Hispaniola, with design to came to take the said city of Panama. Moreover, that this their intention had been known by a person who was run away from the Pirates, at the river De la Hacha, where they provided their fleet with corn. That, upon this news, the said Governor had sent 164 men to strengthen the garrison of that castle, together with much provision and warlike ammunition; the ordinary garrison whereof did only consist of 150 men; so that in all they made the number aforementioned of 314 men, being all very well armed. Besides this they declared that the Governor of Panama had placed several ambuscades all along the river of Chagre; and that he waited for their coming in the open fields of Panama, with 3600 men.

The taking of this castle of Chagre cost the Pirates excessively dear in comparison to the small numbers they used to lose at other times and places: yea, their toil and labour here did far exceed what they sustained at the conquest of the isle of St Catharine and its adjacent. For, coming to number their men, they found they had lost above 100, besides those that were wounded, whose number exceeded 70. They commanded the Spaniards that were prisoners to cast all the dead bodies of their own men down from the top of the mountain to the seaside, and afterwards to bury them. Such as were wounded were carried unto the church belonging to the castle, of which they made an hospital, and where also they shut up the women. Thus it was likewise turned into a place of prostitution, the Pirates ceasing not to defile the bodies of those afflicted widows with all manner of insolent actions and threats.

Captain Morgan remained not long time behind at the isle of St Catharine, after taking the castle of Chagre; of which he had noticed presently sent him. Yet notwithstanding, before he departed thence, he caused to be embarked all the provisions [that] could be found, together with great quantities of maize, or Indian wheat, and cassava, whereof in like manner is made bread in those parts. He commanded likewise great store of provisions should be transported unto the garrison of the aforesaid castle of Chagre, from what parts soever they could be gotten. At a certain place of the island they cast into the sea all guns belonging thereto, with a design to return and leave that island well garrisoned, unto the perpetual possession of Pirates. Notwithstanding, he ordered all the houses and forts to be set on fire, excepting only the castle of St Teresa, which he judged to be the strongest and securest wherein to fortify himself at his return from Panama. He carried with him all the prisoners of the island, and thus set sail for the river of Chagre, where he arrived in the space of eight days. Here the joy of the whole fleet was so great, when they spied the English colours upon the castle, that they minded not their way into the river, which occasioned them to lose four of their ships at the entry thereof, that wherein Captain Morgan went being one of the four. Yet their fortune was so good as to be able to save all the men and goods that were in the said vessels—yea, the ships likewise had been preserved, if a strong northerly wind had not risen on that occasion, which cast the ships upon the rock above-mentioned that lies at the entry of the said river.

Captain Morgan was brought into the castle with great acclamations of triumph and joy of all the Pirates, both of those who were within and also them that were but newly come. Having understood the whole transactions of the conquest, he commanded all the prisoners to begin to work and repair what was necessary—especially in setting up new palisades, or pales, round about the forts depending on the castle. There were still in the river some Spanish vessels, called by them *chatten*, which serve for the transportation of merchandize up and down the said river, as also for to go to Porto Bello and Nicaragua. These are commonly mounted with 2 great guns of iron and 4 other small ones of brass. All these vessels they seized on, together with 4 little ships they found there, and all the canoes. In the castle they left a garrison of 500 men, and in the ships within the river one-hundred-and-fifty more. These things being done, Captain Morgan departed towards Panama, at the head of twelve hundred men. He carried very small provisions with him, being in good hopes he should provide himself sufficiently among the Spaniards, whom he knew to lie in ambuscade at several places by the way.

CHAPTER V

Captain Morgan departs from the Castle of Chagre, at the head of twelve hundred men, with design to take the city of Panama

CAPTAIN MORGAN set forth from the castle of Chagre, towards Panama, the 18th day of August in the year 1670. He had under his conduct 1200 men, 5 boats with artillery and 32 canoes, all which were filled with the said people. Thus he steered his course up the river towards Panama. That day they sailed only six leagues, and came to a place called De los Bracos. Here a party of his men went on shore, only to sleep some few hours and stretch their limbs, they being almost crippled with lying too much crowded in the boats. After they had rested a while, they went abroad to see if any victuals could be found in the neighbouring plantations. But they could find none, the Spaniards being fled and carrying with them all the provisions they had. This day, being the first of their journey, there was amongst them such scarcity of victuals that the greatest part were forced to pass with only a pipe of tobacco, without any other refreshment.

The next day, very early in the morning, they continued their journey, and came about evening to a place called Cruz de Juan Gallego. Here they were compelled to leave their boats and canoes, by reason the river was very dry for want of rain and the many obstacles of trees that were fallen into it.

The guides told them that about two leagues farther on the country would be very good to continue the journey by land. Hereupon they left some companies, being in all 160 men, on board the boats to defend them, with intent they might serve for a place of refuge in case of necessity.

The next morning, being the third day of their journey, they all went ashore, excepting those above-mentioned who were to keep the boats. Unto these Captain Morgan gave very strict orders, under great penalties, that no man, upon

A Map of the Countrey and City of PANAMA. Part. 3. Chap. 5.

any pretext whatsoever should dare to leave the boats and go ashore. This he did, fearing lest they should be surprised and cut off by an ambuscade of Spaniards that might chance to lie thereabouts in the neighbouring woods, which appeared so thick as to seem almost impenetrable. Having this morning begun their march, they found the ways so dirty and irksome that Captain Morgan thought it more convenient to transport some of the men in canoes (though it could not be done without great labour) to a place farther up the river called Cedro Bueno. Thus they re-embarked, and the canoes returned for the rest that were left behind. So that about night they found themselves altogether at the said place. The Pirates were extremely desirous to meet any Spaniards or Indians, hoping to fill their bellies with what provisions they should take from them; for now they were reduced almost to the very extremity of hunger.

On the fourth day, the greatest part of the Pirates marched by land, being led by one of the guides. The rest went by water, farther up with the canoes, being conducted by another guide, who always went before them with two of the said canoes, to discover on both sides the river the ambuscades of the Spaniards. These had also spies, who were very dexterous, and could at any time give notice of all accidents or of the arrival of the Pirates six hours at least before they came to any place. This day about noon they found themselves nigh unto a post called Torna Cavallos. Here the guide of the canoes began to cry aloud he perceived an ambuscade. His voice caused infinite joy unto all the Pirates, as persuading themselves they should find some provisions wherewith to satiate their hunger, which was very great. Being come unto the place, they found nobody in it, the Spaniards who were there not long before being every one fled, and leaving nothing behind unless it were a small number of leather bags, all empty, and a few crumbs of bread scattered upon the ground where they had eaten. Being angry at this misfortune, they pulled down a few little huts which the Spaniards had made, and afterwards fell to eating the leathern bags, as being desirous to afford something to the ferment of their stomachs, which now was grown so sharp that it did gnaw their very bowels, having nothing else to prey upon. Thus they made a huge banquet upon those bags of leather, which doubtless had been more grateful unto them if divers quarrels had not risen concerning who should have the greatest share. By the circumference of the place, they conjectured 500 Spaniards, more or less, had been there. And these, finding no victuals, they were now infinitely desirous to meet, intending to devour some of them rather than perish: whom they would certainly in that occasion have roasted or boiled, to satisfy their famine, had they been able to take them.

After they had feasted themselves with those pieces of leather, they quitted the place, and marched farther on till they came about night to another post called Torna Munni. Here they found another ambuscade, but as barren and desert as the former. They searched the neighbouring woods, but could not find the least thing to eat, the Spaniards having been so provident as not to leave behind them anywhere the least crumb of sustenance, whereby the Pirates were now brought to the extremity aforementioned. Here again he was happy that had reserved since noon any small piece of leather whereof to make his supper, drinking after it a good draught of water for his greatest comfort. Some persons who never were out of their mothers' kitchens may ask how these Pirates could eat, swallow, and digest those pieces of leather, so hard and dry: unto whom I only answer: That could they once experiment what hunger, or rather famine, is, they would certainly find the manner, by their own necessity, as the Pirates did. For these first took the leather, and sliced it in pieces. Then did they beat it between two stones, and rub it, often dipping it in the water of the river to render it by these means supple and tender. Lastly, they scraped off the hair, and roasted or broiled it upon the fire. And, being thus cooked, they cut it into small morsels, and eat it, helping it down with frequent gulps of water, which by good fortune they had nigh at hand.

They continued their march the fifth day, and about noon came unto a place called Barbacoa. Here likewise they found traces of another ambuscade, but the place totally as unprovided as the two preceding were. At a small distance were to be seen several plantations, which they searched very narrowly, but could not find any person, animal, or other thing that was capable of relieving their extreme and ravenous hunger. Finally, having ranged up and down and searched a long time, they found a certain grotto which seemed to be but lately hewn out of a rock, in the which they found two sacks of meal, wheat, and like things, with two great jars of wine, and certain fruits called *plantanos*[1]. Captain Morgan, knowing that some of his men were now through the extremity of hunger reduced almost to the extremity of their lives, and fearing lest the major part should be brought into the same condition, caused all that was found to be distributed amongst them who were in greatest necessity. Having refreshed themselves with these victuals, they began to march anew with greater courage than ever. Such as could not well go for weakness were put into the canoes, and those commanded to land that were in them before. Thus they prosecuted their journey till late at night, at which time they came unto a plantation where they took up their rest; but without eating anything at all, for the Spaniards, as before, had swept away all manner of provisions, leaving not behind them the least signs of victuals.

On the sixth day they continued their march, part of them by land through the woods, and part by water in the canoes: howbeit they were constrained to rest themselves very frequently by the way, both for the ruggedness thereof and the extreme weakness they were under. Unto this they endeavoured to occur[2], by eating some leaves of trees and green herbs or grass such as they could pick, for such was the miserable condition they were in. This day, at noon, they arrived at a plantation, where they found a barn full of maize. Immediately they beat down the doors, and fell to eating of it dry, as much as they could devour. Afterwards they distributed great quantity, giving unto every man a good allowance thereof. Being thus provided, they prosecuted their journey, which having continued for the space of an hour or thereabouts, they met with an ambuscade of Indians. This they no sooner had discovered but they threw away their maize, with the sudden hopes they conceived of finding all things in abundance. But, after all this haste, they found themselves much deceived, they meeting neither Indians, nor victuals, nor anything else

[1] Spanish, plantain, used for the tree or the fruit: cf. ". . . siders, limas, plantanos, and palmas"—Mendoza, *History of China*, transl. by Parke [1589], vol. ii, p. 330 (Hakluyt Soc. 1853–4).

[2] Equivalent to 'this they endeavoured to counter'—see note on p. 187.

of what they had imagined. They saw notwithstanding on the other side of the river a troop of 100 Indians, more or less, who all escaped away through the agility of their feet. Some few Pirates there were who leapt into the river, the sooner to reach the shore, to see if they could take any of the said Indians prisoners. But all was in vain; for, being much more nimble at their feet than the Pirates, they easily baffled their endeavours. Neither did they only baffle them, but killed also two or three of the Pirates with their arrows, howting[1] at them at a distance, and crying: *Ha! perros, á la savana, á la savana! Ha, ye dogs! go to the plain; go to the plain!*

This day they could advance no farther, by reason they were necessitated to pass the river hereabouts to continue their march on the other side. Hereupon they took up their repose for that night: howbeit their sleep was not heavy nor profound, for great murmurings were heard that night in the camp, many complaining of Captain Morgan and his conduct in that enterprize, and being desirous to return home. On the contrary, others would rather die there than go back one step from what they had undertaken. But others who had greater courage than any of these two parties did laugh and joke at all their discourses. In the meanwhile they had a guide who much comforted them, saying: *It would not be long before they met with people from whom they should reap some considerable advantage.*

The seventh day in the morning they all made clean their arms, and every one discharged his pistol or musket, without bullet, to examine the security of their firelocks. This being done, they passed to the other side of the river in the canoes, leaving the post where they had rested the night before, called Santa Cruz. Thus they proceeded on their journey till noon, at which time they arrived at a village called Cruz. Being at a great distance as yet from the place, they perceived much smoke to arise out of the chimneys. The sight hereof afforded them great joy and hopes of finding people in the town, and afterwards what they most desired, which was plenty of good cheer. Thus they went on with as much haste as they could, making several arguments to one another upon

[1] hooting: cf. Nash, *Pierce Penilesse* [1592]: "The people poynted at her for a murtherer, yonge children howted at her as a strumpet." An onomatopœic word.

those external signs, though all like castles built in the air. *For* (said they) *there is smoke coming out of every house—therefore they are making good fires, for to roast and boil what we are to eat.* With other things to this purpose.

At length they arrived there in great haste, all sweating and panting, but found no person in the town, nor anything that was eatable wherewith to refresh themselves, unless it were good fires to warm themselves, which they wanted not. For the Spaniards before their departure had every one set fire to his own house, excepting only the storehouses and stables belonging to the King.

They had not left behind them any beast whatsoever, either alive or dead. This occasioned much confusion in their minds, they not finding the least thing to lay hold on, unless it were some few cats and dogs, which they immediately killed and devoured with great appetite. At last in the King's stables they found by good fortune fifteen or sixteen jars of Peru wine, and a leather sack full of bread. But no sooner had they begun to drink of the said wine when they fell sick, almost every man. This sudden disaster made them think that the wine was poisoned, which caused a new consternation in the whole camp, as judging themselves now to be irrecoverably lost. But the true reason was their huge want of sustenance in that whole voyage, and the manifold sorts of trash which they had eaten upon that occasion. Their sickness was so great that day as caused them to remain there till the next morning, without being able to prosecute their journey, as they used to do, in the afternoon. This village is seated in the latitude of 9 degrees and 2 minutes North, being distant from the river of Chagre 26 Spanish leagues, and 8 from Panama. Moreover, this is the last place unto which boats or canoes can come; for which reason they built here storehouses, wherein to keep all sorts of merchandize, which hence to and from Panama are transported upon the backs of mules.

Here, therefore, Captain Morgan was constrained to leave his canoes and land all his men, though never so weak in their bodies. But, lest the canoes should be surprized or take up too many men for their defence, he resolved to send them all back to the place where the boats were, excepting one, which he caused to be hidden, to the intent it might serve to carry intelligence according to the exigence of affairs. Many of the Spaniards and Indians belonging to this village were fled unto the plantations thereabouts. Hereupon Captain Morgan gave express orders that none should dare to go out of the village except in whole companies of 100 together. The occasion hereof was his fear lest the enemies should take an advantage upon his men by any sudden assault. Notwithstanding, one party of English soldiers stickled not to contravene these commands, being thereunto tempted with the desire of finding victuals. But these were soon glad to fly into the town again, being assaulted with great fury by some Spaniards and Indians, who snatched up one of the Pirates, and carried him away prisoner. Thus the vigilance and care of Captain Morgan was not sufficient to prevent every accident that might happen.

On the eighth day in the morning Captain Morgan sent 200 men before the body of his army, to discover the way to Panama, and see if they had laid any ambuscades therein. Especially considering that the places by which they were to pass were very fit for that purpose, the paths being so narrow that only ten or twelve persons could march in a file, and oftentimes not so many. Having marched about the space of ten hours, they came unto a place called Quebrada Obscura. Here, all on a sudden, three or four thousand arrows were shot at them, without being able to perceive whence they came or who shot them. The place whence it was presumed they were shot was a high rocky mountain, excavated from one side to the other, wherein was a grotto that went through it, only capable of admitting one horse or other beast laded. This multitude of arrows caused a huge alarm among the Pirates, especially because they could not discover the place whence they were discharged. At last, seeing no more arrows to appear, they marched a little farther, and entered into a wood. Here they perceived some Indians to fly as fast as they could possibly before them, to take the advantage of another post, and thence observe the march of the Pirates. There remained notwithstanding one troop of Indians upon the place, with full design to fight and defend themselves. This combat they performed with huge courage, till such time as their Captain fell to the ground wounded, who, although he was now in despair of life, yet his valour being greater than his strength, would demand no quarter, but, endeavouring to raise himself, with undaunted mind laid hold of his *azagaya*[1], or javelin, and struck at one of the Pirates. But, before he could second the blow, he was shot to death with a pistol. This was also the fate of many of his companions, who like good and courageous soldiers lost their lives with their Captain, for the defence of their country.

The Pirates endeavoured, as much as was possible, to lay hold on some of the Indians and take them prisoners. But, they being infinitely swifter than the Pirates, everyone escaped, leaving eight Pirates dead upon the place and ten wounded: yea, had the Indians been more dexterous in military affairs, they might have defended that passage and not let one sole man to pass. Within a little while after they came to a large campaign-field open and full of variegated meadows. Hence they could perceive at a distance before them a parcel of Indians who stood on the top of a mountain, very nigh unto the way by which the Pirates were to pass. They sent a troop of fifty men, the nimblest they could pick out, to see if they could catch any of them and afterwards force them to declare whereabouts their companions had their mansions. But all their industry was in vain, for they escaped through their nimbleness, and presently after showed themselves in another place, hallooing unto the English, and crying: *Á la savana, á la savana, cornudos, perros Ingleses!*—that is, *To the plain, to the plain, ye cuckolds, ye English dogs!* While these things passed, the ten Pirates that were wounded a little before were dressed and plastered up.

At this place there was a wood, and on each side thereof a mountain. The Indians had possessed themselves of the one, and the Pirates took possession of the other that was opposite unto it. Captain Morgan was persuaded that in the wood the Spaniards had placed an ambuscade, as lying so conveniently for that purpose. Hereupon he sent before 200 men to search it. The Spaniards and Indians perceiving the Pirates to decend the mountain, did so too, as if they designed to attack them. But, being got into the wood out of sight of the Pirates, they disappeared, and were seen no more, leaving the passage open to them.

[1] The Spanish form of *assegai*, a dart or light spear used by the Moors. The French form was also in use in England in the sixteenth century: cf. " . . . fought with speares, iauelyns, archegayes, and swerdes"—Froissart, *Chronicles*, transl. by Berners [1523], i, 237, p. 340 (1812 edn.).

About night there fell a great rain, which caused the Pirates to march the faster and seek everywhere for houses wherein to preserve their arms from being wet. But the Indians had set fire to every one thereabouts, and transported all their cattle unto remote places, to the end that the Pirates, finding neither houses nor victuals, might be constrained to return homewards. Notwithstanding, after diligent search they found a few little huts belonging to shepherds, but in them nothing to eat. These not being capable of holding many men, they placed in them out of every company a small number, who kept the arms of all the rest of the army. Those who remained in the open field endured much hardship that night, the rain not ceasing to fall until the morning.

The next morning, about break of day, being the ninth of this tedious journey, Captain Morgan continued his march while the fresh air of the morning lasted. For the clouds then hanging as yet over their heads were much more favourable unto them than the scorching rays of the sun, by reason the way was now more difficult and laborious than all the preceding. After two hours' march they discovered a troop of about 20 Spaniards, who observed the motions of the Pirates. They endeavoured to catch some of them, but could lay hold on none, they suddenly disappearing, and absconding themselves in caves among the rocks totally unknown to the Pirates. At last they came to a high mountain, which, when they had ascended, they discovered from the top thereof the South Sea. This happy sight, as if it were the end of their labours, caused infinite joy among all the Pirates. Hence they could descry also one ship and six boats, which were set forth from Panama and sailed towards the islands of Tavogo and Tavogilla. Having descended this mountain, they came unto a vale, in which they found great quantity of cattle, whereof they killed good store. Here, while some were employed in killing and flaying of cows, horses, bulls, and chiefly asses, of which there was greatest number, others busied themselves in kindling of fires and getting wood wherewith to roast them. Thus cutting the flesh of these animals into convenient pieces, or goblets[1], they threw them into the fire, and, half-carbonadoed[2] or roasted,

[1] Morsels, something you can swallow. Later, 'gobbet,' a 'chunck.' A large block of stone is still called a 'gobbet' by stonemasons.

[2] Span., a piece of meat sliced and broiled, a rasher: cf. ". . . if I

they devoured them with incredible haste and appetite. For such was their hunger that they more resembled cannibals than Europeans at this banquet, the blood many times running down from their beards unto the middle of their bodies.

Having satisfied their hunger with these delicious meats, Captain Morgan ordered them to continue the march. Here again he sent before the main body 50 men, with intent to take some prisoners, if possibly they could. For he seemed now to be much concerned that in nine days' time he could not meet one person who might inform him of the condition and forces of the Spaniards. About evening they discovered a troop of 200 Spaniards, more or less, who hallooed unto the Pirates, but these could not understand what they said. A little while after they came the first time within sight of the highest steeple of Panama. This steeple they no sooner had discovered but they began to show signs of extreme joy, casting up their hats into the air, leaping for mirth, and shouting, even just as if they had already obtained the victory and entire accomplishment of their designs. All their trumpets were sounded and every drum beaten, in token of this universal acclamation and huge alacrity of their minds. Thus they pitched their camp for that night with general content of the whole army, waiting with impatience for the morning, at which time they intended to attack the city. This evening there appeared 50 horse, who came out of the city, hearing the noise of the drums and trumpets of the Pirates, to observe, as it was thought, their motions. They came almost within musket-shot of the army, being preceded by a trumpet that sounded marvellously well. Those on horseback halloed aloud to the Pirates, and threatened them, saying: *Perros! nos veremos!*—that is, *Ye dogs! we shall meet ye!* Having made this menace, they returned into the city, excepting only seven or eight horsemen who remained hovering thereabouts, to watch what motions the Pirates made. Immediately after, the city began to fire, and ceased not to play with their biggest guns all night long against the camp, but with little or no harm unto the Pirates, whom they could not conveniently reach. About this time also the 200 Spaniards whom the pirates had seen in the afternoon appeared again within sight, making resemblance as if they would block

come in his [way] willingly, let him make a carbonado of me"—Shakespeare, *I Henry IV*, V, iii, 61.

up the passages, to the intent no Pirates might escape the hands of their forces. But the Pirates, who were now in a manner besieged, instead of conceiving any fear of their blockades, as soon as they had placed sentries about their camp, began every one to open their satchels, and, without any preparation of napkins or plates, fell to eating very heartily the remaining pieces of bulls' and horses' flesh which they had reserved since noon. This being done, they laid themselves down to sleep upon the grass with great repose and huge satisfaction, expecting only with impatience the dawning of the next day.

On the tenth day, betimes in the morning, they put all their men into convenient order, and with drums and trumpets sounding, continued their march directly towards the city. But one of the guides desired Captain Morgan not to take the common highway that led thither, fearing lest they should find in it much resistance and many ambuscades. He presently took his advice, and chose another way that went through the wood, although very irksome and difficult. Thus the Spaniards, perceiving the Pirates had taken another way, which they scarce had thought on or believed, were compelled to leave their stops and batteries, and come out to meet them. The Governor of Panama put his forces in order, consisting of 2 squadrons, 4 regiments of foot, and a huge number of wild-bulls, which were driven by a great number of Indians, with some negroes and others, to help them.

The Pirates, being now upon their march, came unto the top of a little hill, whence they had a little prospect of the city and campaign country underneath. Here they discovered the forces of the people of Panama extended in battle array, which, when they perceived to be so numerous, they were suddenly surprised with great fear, much doubting the fortune of the day. Yea, few or none there were but wished themselves at home, or at least free from the obligation of that engagement, wherein they perceived their lives must be so narrowly concerned. Having been some time at a stand, in a wavering condition of mind, they at last reflected upon the straits they had brought themselves into, and that now they ought of necessity either to fight resolutely or die, for no quarter could be expected from an enemy against whom they had committed so many cruelties on all occasions.

Hereupon they encouraged one another, and resolved either to conquer, or spend the very last drop of blood in their bodies. Afterwards they divided themselves into three battalions, or troops, sending before them one of 200 Buccaneers, which sort of people are infinitely dexterous at shooting with guns. Thus the Pirates left the hill and descended, marching directly towards the Spaniards, who were posted in a spacious field waiting for their coming. As soon as they drew nigh unto them the Spaniards began to shout, and cry: *Viva el Rey!—God save the King!*—and immediately their horse began to move against the Pirates. But the field being full of quags and very soft underfoot, they could not ply to and fro and wheel about, as they desired. The 200 Buccaneers who went before, every one putting one knee to the ground, gave them a full volley of shot, wherewith the battle was instantly kindled very hot. The Spaniards defended themselves very courageously, acting all they could possibly perform to disorder the Pirates. Their foot, in like manner, endeavoured to second the horse, but were constrained by the Pirates to separate from them. Thus, finding themselves frustrated of their designs, they attempted to drive the bulls against them at their backs and by this means put them into disorder. But the greatest part of that wild cattle ran away, being frightened with the noise of the battle. And some few that broke through the English companies did no other harm than to tear the colours in pieces; whereas the Buccaneers, shooting them dead, left not one to trouble them thereabouts.

The battle, having now continued for the space of two hours, at the end thereof the greatest part of the Spanish horse was ruined and almost all killed. The rest fled away. Which being perceived by the foot, and that they could not possibly prevail, they discharged the shot they had in their muskets, and, throwing them on the ground, betook themselves to flight, every one which way he could run. The Pirates could not possibly follow them, as being too much harassed and wearied with the long journey they had lately made. Many of them, not being able to fly whither they desired, hid themselves for that present among the shrubs of the sea-side. But very unfortunately: for most of them being found out by the Pirates were instantly killed without giving quarter to any. Some religious men were brought prisoners before Captain

Morgan; but he, being deaf to their cries and lamentations, commanded them all to be immediately pistoled, which was accordingly done. Soon after they brought a Captain to his presence, whom he examined very strictly about several things, particularly, wherein consisted the forces of those of Panama. Unto which he answered: Their whole strength did consist in 400 horse, 24 companies of foot, each being of 100 men complete, 60 Indians, and some negroes, who were to drive 2000 wild-bulls and cause them to run over the English camp, and thus by breaking their files put them into a total disorder and confusion. He discovered more, that in the city they had made trenches and raised batteries in several places, in all which they had placed many guns, and that at the entry of the highway which led to the city they had built a fort, which was mounted with 8 great guns of brass, and defended by 50 men.

Captain Morgan, having heard this information, gave orders instantly they should march another way. But, before setting forth, he made a review of all his men, whereof he found both killed and wounded a considerable number, and much greater than had been believed. Of the Spaniards were found 600 dead upon the place, besides the wounded and prisoners. The Pirates were nothing discouraged seeing their number so much diminished, but rather filled with greater pride than before, perceiving what huge advantage they had obtained against their enemies. Thus having rested themselves some while, they prepared to march courageously towards the city, plighting their oaths to one another in general they would fight till never a man was left alive. With this courage they recommenced their march, either to conquer or be conquered, carrying with them all the prisoners.

They found much difficulty in their approach unto the city. For within the town the Spaniards had placed many great guns, at several quarters thereof, some of which were charged with small pieces of iron and others with musket-bullets. With all these they saluted the Pirates, at their drawing nigh unto the place, and gave them full and frequent broadsides, firing at them incessantly. Whence it came to pass that unavoidably they lost, at every step they advanced, great numbers of men. But neither these manifest dangers of their lives, nor the sight of so many of their own as dropped down continually at their sides, could deter them from advancing farther, and gaining ground every moment upon the enemy. Thus, although the Spaniards never ceased to fire and act the best they could for their defence, yet notwithstanding they were forced to deliver the city after the space of three hours' combat. And the Pirates, having now possessed themselves thereof, both killed and destroyed as many as attempted to make the least opposition against them. The inhabitants had caused the best of their goods to be transported unto more remote and occult places. Howbeit they found within the city as yet several warehouses, very well stocked with all sorts of merchandize, as well silks and cloths as linen, and other things of considerable value. As soon as the first fury of their entrance into the city was over, Captain Morgan assembled all his men at a certain place which he assigned, and there commanded them under very great penalties that none of them should dare to drink or taste any wine. The reason he gave for this injunction was because he had received private intelligence that it had been all poisoned by the Spaniards. Howbeit it was the opinion of many [that] he gave these prudent orders to prevent the debauchery of his people, which he foresaw would be very great at the beginning, after so much hunger sustained by the way: fearing withal lest the Spaniards, seeing them in wine, should rally their forces and fall upon the city, and use them as inhumanly as they had used the inhabitants before.

CHAPTER VI

Captain Morgan sends several canoes and boats unto the South Sea. He sets fire to the city of Panama. Robberies and cruelties committed there by the Pirates till their return to the Castle of Chagre

CAPTAIN MORGAN, as soon as he had placed guards at several quarters where he thought necessary, both within and without the city of Panama, immediately commanded twenty-five men to seize a great boat which had stuck in the mud of the port for want of water at a low tide, so that she could not put out to sea. The same day, about noon, he caused certain men privately to set fire unto several great edifices of the city, nobody knowing whence the fire proceeded nor who were the authors thereof, much less what motives persuaded Captain Morgan thereunto, which are as yet unknown to this day. The fire increased so fast that before night the greatest part of the city was in flame. Captain Morgan endeavoured to make the public believe the Spaniards had been the cause thereof, which suspicions he surmised among his own people, perceiving they reflected upon him for that action. Many of the Spaniards, as also some of the Pirates, used all means possible either to extinguish the flame or, by blowing up houses with gunpowder and pulling down others, to stop its progress. But all was in vain; for in less than half-an-hour it consumed a whole street. All the houses of this city were built with cedar, being of very curious and magnificent structure, and richly adorned within, especially with hangings and paintings, whereof part was already transported out of the Pirates' way, and another great part was consumed by the voracity of the fire.

There belonged unto this city (which is also the head of a bishopric) eight monasteries, whereof seven were for men and one for women, two stately churches, and one hospital.

The Battel Between the
Spaniards and the pyrats or
Buccaniers before the City of
PANAMA. part.3 Chap:6:

The churches and monasteries were all richly adorned with altar-pieces and paintings, huge quantity of gods and silver, with other precious things; all which the ecclesiastics had hidden and concealed. Besides which ornaments, here were to be seen 2000 houses of magnificent and prodigious building, as being all, or the greatest part, inhabited by merchants of that country, who are vastly rich. For the rest of the inhabitants of lesser quality and tradesmen, this city contained 5000 houses more. Here were also great number of stables, which served for the horses and mules that carry all the plate, belonging as well to the King of Spain as to private men, towards the coast of the North Sea. The neighbouring fields belonging to this city are all cultivated with fertile plantations and pleasant gardens, which afford delicious prospects unto the inhabitants the whole year long.

The Genoese had in this city of Panama a stately and magnificent house, belonging to their trade and commerce of negroes. This building likewise was commanded by Captain Morgan to be set on fire; whereby it was burnt to the very ground. Besides which pile of building there were consumed to the number of 200 warehouses and great number of slaves who had hid themselves therein, together with an infinite multitude of sacks of meal. The fire of all which houses and buildings was seen to continue four weeks after the day it began. The Pirates in the meanwhile, at least the greatest part of them, encamped some time without the city, fearing and expecting that the Spaniards would come and fight them anew. For it was known they had an incomparable number of men more than the Pirates were. This occasioned them to keep the field, thereby to preserve their forces united, which now were very much diminished by the losses of the preceding battles, as also because they had a great many wounded, all which they had put into one of the churches which alone remained standing, the rest being consumed by the fire. Moreover, beside these decreases of their men, Captain Morgan had sent a convoy of 150 men to the Castle of Chagre, to carry the news of his victory obtained against Panama.

They saw many times whole troops of Spaniards cruize to and fro in the campaign-fields, which gave them occasion to suspect their rallying anew. Yet they never had the courage to attempt anything against the Pirates. In the afternoon of this fatal day Captain Morgan re-entered again the city with his troops, to the intent every one might take up his lodgings, which now they could hardly find, very few houses having escaped the desolation of the fire. Soon after, they fell to seeking very carefully among the ruins and ashes for utensils of plate or gold which peradventure were not quite wasted by the flames. And of such things they found no small number in several places, especially in wells and cisterns, where the Spaniards had hid them from the covetous search of the Pirates.

The next day Captain Morgan dispatched away two troops of Pirates, of 150 men each, being all very stout soldiers and well armed, with orders to seek for the inhabitants of Panama who were escaped from the hands of their enemies. These men, having made several excursions up and down the campaign-fields, woods, and mountains adjoining to Panama, returned after two days' time, bringing with them above 200 prisoners, between men, women, and slaves. The same day returned also the boat above-mentioned, which Captain Morgan had sent into the South Sea, bringing with her three other boats, which they had taken in a little while. But all these prizes they could willingly have given, yea, although they had employed greater labour into the bargain, for one certain galleon, which miraculously escaped their industry, being very richly laden with all the King's plate and great quantity of riches of gold, pearl, jewels, and other most precious goods, of all the best and richest merchants of Panama. On board of this galleon were also the religious women belonging to the nunnery of the said city, who had embarked with them all the ornaments of their church, consisting in great quantity of gold, plate, and other things of great value.

The strength of this galleon was nothing considerable, as having only 7 guns, and 10 or 12 muskets for its whole defence, being on the other side very ill provided of victuals and other necessaries, with great want of fresh water, and having no more sails than the uppermost sails of the main mast. This description of the said ship the Pirates received from certain persons, who had spoken with seven mariners belonging to the galleon, at such time as they came ashore in the cock-boat to take in fresh water. Hence they concluded for certain they might easily have taken the said vessel, had they given her chase and pursued her, as they ought to do, especially considering the said galleon could not long subsist abroad at sea. But they were impeded from following this vastly rich prize by the lascivious exercises wherein they were totally at that present involved with women, which unto this effect they had carried with them and forced on board their boat. Unto this vice was also joined that of gluttony and drunkenness, having plentifully debauched themselves with several sorts of rich wines they found there ready to their hands. So that they chose rather to satiate their lust and appetite with the things above-mentioned than to lay hold on the occasion of such an huge advantage, although this only prize would certainly have been of far greater value and consequence unto them than all they purchased at Panama and other places thereabouts. The next day, repenting of their negligence and being totally wearied of the vices and debaucheries aforesaid, they sent forth to sea another boat well armed, to pursue with all speed imaginable the said galleon. But their present care and diligence was in vain, the Spaniards who were on board the said ship having received intelligence of the danger they were in one or two days before, while the Pirates were cruizing so nigh unto them, whereupon they fled unto places more remote and unknown to their enemies.

Notwithstanding, the Pirates found in the ports of the islands of Tavoga and Tavogilla several boats that were laden with many sorts of very good merchandize—all which they took and brought unto Panama, where, being arrived, they made an exact relation of all that had passed while they were abroad unto Captain Morgan. The prisoners confirmed what the Pirates had said, adding thereunto that they undoubtedly knew whereabouts the said galleon might be at the present, but that it was very probable they had been relieved before now from other places. These relations stirred up Captain Morgan anew to send forth all the boats that were in the port of Panama, with design to seek and pursue the said galleon till they could find her. The boats aforesaid, being in all four, set sail from Panama, and, having spent eight days in cruizing to and fro and searching several ports and creeks, they lost all their hopes of finding what they so earnestly sought for. Hereupon they resolved to return unto the isles of Tavoga and Tavogilla. Here they found a reasonable good ship that was newly come from Payta, being laden with cloth, soap, sugar, and biscuit, with 20,000 pieces-of-eight in ready money. This vessel they instantly seized, not finding the least resistance from any person within her. Nigh unto the said ship was also a boat, whereof in like manner they possessed themselves. Upon the boat they laded great part of the merchandize they had found in the ship, together with some slaves they had taken in the said islands. With this purchase they returned unto Panama, something better satisfied of their voyage, yet withal much discontented they could not meet with the galleon.

The convoy which Captain Morgan had sent unto the Castle of Chagre returned much about the same time, bringing with them very good news. For while Captain Morgan was upon his journey to Panama, those he had left in the Castle of Chagre had sent forth to sea two boats to exercize piracy. These happened to meet with a Spanish ship, which they began to chase within sight of the Castle. This being perceived by the Pirates that were in the Castle, they put forth Spanish colours, thereby to allure and deceive the ship that fled before the boats. Thus the poor Spaniards, thinking to refuge themselves under the Castle and the guns thereof, by flying into the port were caught in a snare and made prisoners, where they thought to find defence. The cargo which was found on board the said vessel consisted in victuals and provisions, that were all eatable things. Nothing could be more opportune than this prize for the Castle, where they had begun already to experiment[1] great scarcity of things of this kind.

This good fortune of the garrison of Chagre gave occasion unto Captain Morgan to remain longer time than he had determined at Panama. And hereupon he ordered several new excursions to be made into the whole country round about the city. So that, while the Pirates at Panama were employed in these expeditions, those at Chagre were busied in exercizing piracy upon the North Sea. Captain Morgan used to send forth daily parties of 200 men, to make inroads into all the fields and country thereabouts; and, when one party came back, another consisting of 200 more was ready to

[1] Experience. Cf. Day, *English Secretary* [1586], i: "Of his . . . good behaviour [I] have had sound and large experiment"; Howell, *Letters* [1645], ii, 113: "I know by experiments I have had of you . . ."

go forth. By this means they gathered in a short time huge quantity of riches and no lesser number of prisoners. These, being brought into the city, were presently put unto the most exquisite tortures imaginable, to make them confess both other people's goods and their own. Here it happened that one poor and miserable wretch was found in the house of a gentleman of great quality, who had put on, amidst that confusion of things, a pair of taffety breeches belonging to his master with a little silver key hanging at the strings thereof. This being perceived by the Pirates, they immediately asked him where was the cabinet of the said key. His answer was: *He knew not what was become of it, but only that, finding those breeches in his master's house, he had made bold to wear them.* Not being able to extort any other confession out of him, they first put him upon the rack, wherewith they inhumanly disjointed his arms. After this, they twisted a cord about his forehead, which they wrung so hard that his eyes appeared as big as eggs and were ready to fall out of his skull. But neither with these torments could they obtain any positive answer to their demands. Whereupon they soon after hung him up by the testicles, giving him infinite blows and stripes while he was under that intolerable pain and posture of body. Afterwards they cut off his nose and ears, and singed his face with burning straw, till he could speak nor lament his misery no longer. Then, losing all hopes of hearing any confession from his mouth, they commanded a negro to run him through with a lance, which put an end to his life and a period to their cruel and inhuman tortures. After this execrable manner did many others of those miserable prisoners finish their days, the common sport and recreation of these Pirates being these and other tragedies not inferior to these.

They spared, in these their cruelties, no sex nor condition whatsoever. For, as to religious persons and priests, they granted them less quarter than unto others, unless they could produce a considerable sum of money, capable of being a sufficient ransom. Women themselves were no better used, except they would condescend unto the libidinous demands and concupiscency of the Pirates. For such as would not consent unto their lust were treated with all the rigour and cruelty imaginable. Captain Morgan, their leader and Commander, gave them no good example in this point. For, as soon as any beautiful woman was brought as a prisoner to his presence, he used all the means he could, both of rigour and mildness, to bend her to his lascivious will and pleasure: for a confirmation of which assertion, I shall here give my reader a short history of a lady whose virtue and constancy ought to be transmitted unto posterity, as a memorable example of her sex.

Among the prisoners that were brought by the Pirates from the islands of Tavoga and Tavogilla, there was found a gentlewoman of good quality, as also no less virtue and chastity, who was wife unto one of the richest merchants of all those countries. Her years were but few, and her beauty so great as peradventure I may doubt whether in all Europe any could be found to surpass her perfections either of comeliness or honesty. Her husband, at that present, was absent from home, being gone as far as the kingdom of Peru, about great concerns of commerce and trade, wherein his employments did lie. This virtuous lady, likewise, hearing that Pirates were coming to assault the city of Panama, had absented herself thence in the company of other friends and relations, thereby to preserve her life amidst the dangers which the cruelties and tyrannies of those hard-hearted enemies did seem to menace unto every citizen. But no sooner had she appeared in the presence of Captain Morgan instantly she was designed for his voluptuous pleasures and concupiscence. Hereupon he commanded they should lodge her in a certain apartment by herself, giving her a negress, or black woman, to wait upon her, and that she should be treated with all the respect and regale[ment] due unto her quality. The poor afflicted lady did beg, with multitude of sobs and tears, she might be suffered to lodge among the other prisoners, her relations, fearing lest that unexpected kindness of the Commander might prove to be a design upon her chastity. But Captain Morgan would by no means hearken to her petition, and all he commanded, in answer thereunto, was she should be treated with more particular care than before, and have her victuals carried from his own table.

This lady had formerly heard very strange reports concerning the Pirates, before their arrival at Panama, intimating unto her, as if they were not men, but, as they said, heretics, who did neither invoke the Blessed Trinity nor believe in Jesus Christ. But now she began to have better thoughts of them than ever before, having experimented the manifold civilities of Captain Morgan, especially hearing him many times to swear by the name of God and of Jesus Christ, in whom, she was persuaded, they did not believe. Neither did she now think them to be so bad, or to have the shapes of beasts, as from the relations of several people she had oftentimes heard. For, as to the name of 'robbers' or 'thieves', which was commonly given them by others, she wondered not much at it, seeing, as she said, that among all nations of the universe there were to be found some wicked men who naturally coveted to possess the goods of others. Conformable to the persuasion of this lady was the opinion of another woman, of weak understanding, at Panama, who used to say, before the Pirates came thither, she desired very much and had a great curiosity to see one of those men called Pirates, for as much as her husband had often told her that they were not men, like others, but rather irrational beasts. This silly woman, at last happening to see the first of them, cried out aloud, saying : *Jesus bless me ! these thieves are like unto us Spaniards.*

This false civility of Captain Morgan, wherewith he used this lady, as a thing very common unto such persons as pretend and cannot obtain, was soon after changed into barbarous cruelty. For, three or four days being past, he came to see her, and entertained her with dishonest and lascivious discourses, opening unto her his ardent desires of enjoying the accomplishment of his lust. The virtuous lady constantly repulsed him, with all the civility imaginable and many humble and modest expressions of her mind. But Captain Morgan still persisted in his disorderly request, presenting her withal with much pearl, gold, and all that he had got that was precious and valuable in that voyage. But the lady, being in no manner willing to consent thereunto, nor accept his presents, and showing herself in all respects like unto Susannah for constancy, he presently changed note, and began to speak unto her in another tone, threatening her with a thousand cruelties and hard usages at his hands. Unto all these things she gave this resolute and positive answer, than which no other could be extorted from her ; *Sir, my life is in your hands ; but, as to my body, in relation to that which you would persuade me unto, my soul shall sooner be separated from it, through the violence of your arms, than I shall condescend to your request.* No sooner had

Captain Morgan understood this heroic resolution of her mind than he commanded her to be stripped of the best of her apparel, and imprisoned in a darksome and stinking cellar. Here she had allowed her an extremely small quantity of meat and drink, wherewith she had much ado to sustain her life for a few days.

Under this hardship the constant and virtuous lady ceased not to pray daily unto God Almighty for constancy and patience against the cruelties of Captain Morgan. But he, being now thoroughly convinced of her chaste resolutions, as also desirous to conceal the cause of her confinement and hard usage, since many of the Pirates, his companions, did compassionate her condition, laid many false accusations to her charge, giving to understand she held intelligence with the Spaniards, and corresponded with them by letters, abusing thereby his former lenity and kindness. I myself was an eye-witness unto these things here related, and could never have judged such constancy of mind and virtuous chastity to be found in the world, if my own eyes and ears had not informed me thereof. But of this incomparable lady I shall say something more hereafter in its proper place; whereupon I shall leave her at present, to continue my history.

Captain Morgan, having now been at Panama the full space of three weeks, commanded all things to be put in order for his departure. Unto this effect, he gave orders to every company of his men to seek out for so many beasts of carriage as might suffice to convey the whole spoil of the city to the river where his canoes lay. About this time a great rumour was spread in the city of a considerable number of Pirates who intended to leave Captain Morgan; and that, by taking a ship which was in the port, they determined to go and rob upon the South Sea till they had got as much as they thought fit, and then return homewards by the way of the East Indies into Europe. For which purpose they had already gathered great quantity of provisions, which they had hidden in private places, with sufficient store of powder, bullets, and all other sorts of ammunition; likewise some great guns belonging to the town, muskets, and other things, wherewith they designed not only to equip the said vessel but also to fortify themselves and raise batteries in some island or other, which might serve them for a place of refuge.

This design had certainly taken effect as they intended, had not Captain Morgan had timely advice thereof given him by one of their comrades. Hereupon he instantly commanded the main-mast of the said ship should be cut down and burnt, together with all the other boats that were in the port. Hereby the intentions of all or most of his companions were totally frustrated. After this, Captain Morgan sent forth many of the Spaniards into the adjoining fields and country, to seek for money wherewith to ransom not only themselves but also all the rest of the prisoners, as likewise the ecclesiastics, both secular and regular. Moreover, he commanded all the artillery of the town to be spoiled, that is to say, nailed and stopped up. At the same time he sent out a strong company of men to seek for the Governor of Panama, of whom intelligence was brought that he had laid several ambuscades in the way by which he ought to pass at his return. But those who were sent upon this design returned soon after, saying they had not found any sign or appearance of any such ambuscades; for a confirmation whereof, they brought with them some prisoners they had taken, who declared how that the said Governor had had an intention of making some opposition by the way, but that the men whom he had designed to effect it were unwilling to undertake any such enterprize, so that, for want of means, he could not put his design in execution.

On the 24th of February of the year 1671 Captain Morgan departed from the city of Panama, or rather from the place where the said city of Panama did stand ; of the spoils whereof he carried with him 175 beasts of carriage, laden with silver, gold, and other precious things, besides 600 prisoners, more or less, between men, women, children, and slaves. That day they came unto a river that passes through a delicious campaign-field, at the distance of a league from Panama. Here Captain Morgan put all his forces into good order of martial array, in such manner as that the prisoners were in the middle of the camp, surrounded on all sides with Pirates. At which present conjuncture nothing else was to be heard but lamentations, cries, shrieks, and doleful sighs, of so many women and children, who were persuaded Captain Morgan designed to transport them all and carry them into his own country for slaves. Besides that, among all those miserable prisoners, there was extreme hunger and thirst endured at that time; which hardship and misery Captain Morgan designedly caused them to sustain, with intent to excite them more earnestly to seek for moneys wherewith to ransom themselves, according to the tax he had set upon every one. Many of the women begged of Captain Morgan upon their knees, with infinite sighs and tears, he would permit to return unto Panama; there to live in company of their dear husbands and children, in little huts of straw which they would erect, seeing they had no houses until the rebuilding of the city. But his answer was: he came not thither to hear lamentations and cries, but rather to seek moneys. Therefore they ought to seek out for that in the first place, wherever it were to be had, and bring it to him, otherwise he would assuredly transport them all unto such places whither they cared not to go.

The next day, when the march began, those lamentable cries and shrieks were renewed, in so much as it would have caused compassion in the hardest heart to hear them. But Captain Morgan, as a man little given to mercy, was not moved therewith in the least. They marched in the same order as was said before, one party of the Pirates preceding in the van, the prisoners in the middle, and the rest of the Pirates in the rear-guard, by whom the miserable Spaniards were, at every step, punched and thrust in their backs and sides with the blunt end of their arms, to make them march the faster. That beautiful and virtuous lady, of whom we made mention heretofore, for her unparalleled constancy and chastity, was led prisoner by herself, between two Pirates who guarded her. Her lamentations now did pierce the skies, seeing herself carried away into foreign captivity, often crying unto the Pirates, and telling them: *That she had given order unto two religious persons, in whom she had relied, to go unto a certain place and fetch so much money as her ransom did amount unto. That they had promised faithfully to do it, but, having obtained the said money, instead of bringing it unto her they had employed it another way, to ransom some of their own and particular friends.* This ill-action of theirs was discovered by a slave, who brought a letter unto the said lady. Her complaints, and the cause thereof, being brought unto the ears of Captain Morgan, he thought fit to inquire thereinto. Having found the thing to be true, especially hearing it confirmed by the confession of the said religious men, though under some frivolous excuses, of having diverted the money but for a day or two within which time they expected more sums to repay it, he gave liberty unto the said lady, whom otherwise he designed to transport unto Jamaica. But in the meanwhile he detained the said religious men as prisoners in her place, using them according to the deserts of their incompassionate intrigues.

As soon as Captain Morgan arrived, upon his march, at the town called Cruz, seated on the banks of the river Chagre as was mentioned before, he commanded an order to be published among the prisoners that within the space of three days every one of them should bring in his ransom, under the penalty aforementioned of being transported unto Jamaica. In the meanwhile he gave orders for so much rice and maize to be collected thereabouts as was necessary for the victualling all his ships. At this place some of the prisoners were ransomed, but many others could not bring in their moneys in so short time. Hereupon he continued his voyage, leaving the village on the 5th day of March next following, and carrying with him all the spoil that ever he could transport. From this village he likewise led away some new prisoners who were inhabitants of the said place. So that these prisoners were added unto those of Panama who had not as yet paid their ransoms, and all transported. But the two religious men who had diverted the money belonging to the lady were ransomed three days after their imprisonment, by other persons who had more compassion for their condition than they had showed for hers. About the middle of the way unto the Castle of Chagre Captain Morgan commanded them to be placed in due order, according to their custom, and caused every one to be sworn that they had reserved nor concealed nothing privately to themselves, even not so much as the value of sixpence. This being done, Captain Morgan having had some experience that those lewd fellows would not much stickle to swear falsely in points of interest, he commanded every one to be searched very strictly, both in their clothes and satchels and everywhere it might be presumed they had reserved anything. Yea, to the intent this order might not be ill taken by his companions, he permitted himself to be searched, even to the very soles of his shoes. Unto this effect, by common consent, there was assigned one out of every company to be the searchers of all the rest. The French Pirates that went on this expedition with Captain Morgan were not well satisfied with this new custom of searching, Yet their number being less than that of the English, they were forced to submit unto it, as well as the others had done before them. The search being over, they re-embarked in their canoes and boats, which attended them on the river, and arrived at the Castle of Chagre on the 9th day of the said month of March. Here they found all things in good order, excepting the wounded men whom they had left there at the time of their departure. Foı of these the greatest number were dead, through the wounds they had received.

From Chagre Captain Morgan sent presently after his arrival a great boat to Porto Bello, wherein were all the prisoners he had taken at the isle of St Catharine, demanding by them a considerable ransom for the Castle of Chagre, where he then was, threatening otherwise to ruin and demolish it even to the ground. Unto this message those of Porto Bello made answer: *They would not give one farthing towards the ransom of the said castle, and that the English might do with it as they pleased.* This answer being come, the dividend was made of all the spoil they had purchased in that voyage. Thus every company and every particular person therein included received their portion of what was gotten, or, rather, what part thereof Captain Morgan was pleased to give them. For so it was, that the rest of his companions, even of his own nation, complained of his proceedings in this particular, and feared not to tell him openly to his face that he had reserved the best jewels to himself. For they judged it impossible that no greater share should belong to them than 200 pieces-of-eight *per capita*, of so many valuable purchases and robberies as they had obtained—which small sum they thought too little reward for so much labour and such huge and manifest dangers as they had so often exposed their lives unto. But Captain Morgan was deaf unto all these and many other complaints of this kind, as having designed in his mind to cheat them of as much as he could.

At last Captain Morgan, finding himself obnoxious to many obloquies and detractions among his people, began to fear the consequence thereof, and hereupon, thinking it unsafe to remain any longer time at Chagre, he commanded the ordnance of the said Castle to be carried on board his ship. Afterwards he caused the greatest part of the walls to be demolished, and the edifices to be burnt, and as many other things spoiled and ruined as could conveniently be done in a short while. These orders being performed, he went secretly on board his own ship, without giving any notice of his departure unto his companions, nor calling any council, as he used to do. Thus he set sail and put out to sea, not bidding anybody adieu, being only followed by three or four vessels of the whole fleet. These were such (as the French Pirates believed) as went shares with Captain Morgan towards the best and greatest part of the spoil which had been concealed from them in the dividend. The Frenchmen could very willingly have revenged this affront upon Captain Morgan and those that followed him, had they found themselves with sufficient means to encounter him at sea. But they were destitute of most things necessary thereunto—yea, they had much ado to find sufficient victuals and provisions for their voyage to Jamaica, he having left them totally unprovided of all things.

CHAPTER VII

Of a voyage made by the author along the coasts of Costa Rica, at his return towards Jamaica. What happened most remarkable in the said voyage. Some observations made by him at that time

CAPTAIN MORGAN left us all in such a miserable condition as might serve for a lively representation of what reward attends wickedness at the latter end of life—whence we ought to have learned how to regulate and amend our actions for the future. However it was, our affairs being reduced to such a posture, every company that was left behind, whether English or French, were compelled to seek what means they could to help themselves. Thus most of them separated from each other, and several companies took several courses at their return homewards. As for that party to which I belonged, we steered our voyage along the coast of Costa Rica, where we intended to purchase some provisions and careen our vessel in some secure place or other. For the boat wherein we were was now grown so foul as to be rendered totally unfit for sailing. In few days we arrived at a great port, called Boca del Toro, where are always to be found an huge quantity of good and eatable tortoises. The circumference hereof is 10 leagues, more or less, being surrounded with little islands, under which vessels may ride very secure from the violence of the winds.

The said islands are inhabited by Indians, who never could be subjugated by the Spaniards, and hence they give them the name of *Indios bravos*, or Wild Indians. They are divided, according to the variety of idioms of their language, into several customs and fashions of people, whence arises that they have perpetual wars against one another. Towards the east side of this port are found some of them who formerly did much trade with the Pirates, selling unto them the flesh of divers animals which they hunt in their countries, as also all sorts of fruits that the land produces. The exchange of which commodities was iron instruments that the Pirates brought [with] them, beads, and other toys, whereof they made great account for wearing, more than of precious jewels, which they knew not nor esteemed in the least. This commerce afterwards failed, because the Pirates committed many barbarous inhumanities against them, killing many of their men on a certain occasion, and taking away their women to serve their disordinate lust. These abuses gave sufficient cause for a perpetual cessation of all friendship and commerce between them and the Pirates.

We went ashore with design to seek provisions, our necessity being now almost extreme. But our fortune was so bad that we could find nothing else than a few eggs of crocodiles, wherewith we were forced to content ourselves for that present. Hereupon we left those quarters, and steered our course eastwards. Being upon this tack, we met with three boats more of our own companions, who had been left behind by Captain Morgan. These told us they had been able to find no relief for the extreme hunger they sustained; moreover, that Captain Morgan himself and all his people were already reduced to such misery that he could afford them no more allowance than once a day, and that very short too.

We, therefore, hearing from these boats that little or no good was like to be done by sailing farther eastwards, changed our course, and steered towards the west. Here we found an excessive quantity of tortoises, more than we needed for the victualling our boats, should we be never so long without any other flesh or fish. Having provided ourselves with this sort of victuals, the next thing we wanted was fresh water. There was enough to be had in the neighbouring islands, but we scarce dared to land on them, by reason of the enmity above mentioned between us and the Pirates and those Indians. Notwithstanding, necessity having no law, we were forced to do as we could, rather than as we desired to do. And hereupon we resolved to go all of us together unto one of the said islands. Being landed, one party of our men went to range in the woods, while another filled the barrels with water. Scarce one whole hour was past, after our people were got ashore, when suddenly the Indians came upon us, and we heard one of our men cry: *Arm! arm!* We presently took up our arms, and began to fire at them as hot as we could. This caused them to advance no farther, and in a short while put them to flight, sheltering themselves in the woods. We pursued them some part of the way, but not far, by reason we then esteemed rather to get in our water than any other advantages upon the enemy. Coming back, we found two Indians dead upon the shore, whereof the habiliments of one gave us to understand he was a person of quality amongst them. For he had about his body a girdle, or sash, very richly woven; and on his face he wore a beard of massive gold—I mean, a small planch[1] of gold hung down at his lips by two strings (which penetrated two little holes, made there on purpose) that covered his beard, or served instead thereof. His arms were made of sticks of palmetto-trees, being very curiously wrought, at one end whereof was a kind of hook, which seemed to be hardened with fire. We could willingly have had opportunity to speak with some of these Indians, to see if we could reconcile their minds unto us, and by this means renew the former trade with them, and obtain provisions. But this was a thing impossible, through the wildness of their persons and savageness of their minds. Notwithstanding, this encounter hindered us not from filling our barrels with water, and carrying them aboard.

The night following we heard from the shore huge cries and shrieks among the Indians. These lamentations caused us to believe, because they were heard so far, they had called in much more people to aid them against us; as, also, that they lamented the death of those two men who were killed the day before. These Indians never come upon the waters of the sea, neither have they ever given themselves to build canoes or any other sort of vessels for navigation—not so much as fisher-boats, of which art of fishery they are totally ignorant. At last, having nothing else to hope for in these parts, we resolved to depart thence for Jamaica, whither we designed to go. Being set forth, we met with contrary winds, which caused us to make use of our oars, and row as far as the river of Chagre. When we came nigh unto it, we perceived

[1] (plank), slab. Cf. transl. of *The Conquest of West India* [1578], 233: ". . . there sawe golde in planches like bricke battes."

a ship that made towards us, and began to give us chase. Our apprehensions were that it was a ship from Cartagena, which might be sent to rebuild and retake possession of the Castle of Chagre, now all the Pirates were departed thence. Hereupon we set all our sail and ran before the wind, to see if we could escape or refuge ourselves in any place. But the vessel, being much swifter and cleaner than ours, easily got the wind of us, and stopped our course. Then approaching nigh unto us, we discovered that they were, and knew them to be our former comrades, in the same expedition of Panama, who were but lately set out from Chagre. Their design was to go unto Nombre de Dios, and thence to Cartagena, to seek some purchase or other in or about that frequented port. But, the wind at that present being contrary to their intention, they concluded to go in our company towards the same place where we were before, called Boca del Toro.

This accident and encounter retarded our journey, in the space of two days, more than we could regain in a whole fortnight. This was the occasion that obliged us to return to our former station, where we remained for a few days. Thence we directed our course for a place called Boca del Dragon, there to make provisions of flesh, especially of a certain animal which the Spaniards call *manentines*[1], and the Dutch 'sea-cows', because the head, nose, and teeth of this beast are very like unto those of a cow. They are found commonly in such places as under the depth of the waters are very full of grass, on which, it is thought, they do pasture. These animals have no ears, and only in place of them are to be seen two little holes, scarce capable of receiving the little finger of a man. Nigh unto the neck they have two wings, under which are seated two udders or breasts, much like unto the breasts of a woman. The skin is very close and united together, resembling the skin of a Barbary (or Guinea) dog. This skin upon the back is of the thickness of two fingers, which, being dried, is as hard as any whalebone, and may serve to make walking-staffs withal. The belly is in all things like unto that of a cow, as far as the kidneys, or reins. Their manner of

[1] Manatee, Span. *manati*, an aquatic mammal, at one time supposed to have originated the legends of the mermaids. Cf. Eden, *Decades*, section ii (1555): ". . . also manates, and murene, and manye other fysshes which haue no names in oure language."

engendering, likewise, is the same with the usual manner of a land-cow, the male of this kind being in similitude almost one and the same thing with a bull. Yet, notwithstanding, they conceive and breed but once. But the space of time that they go with calf, I could not as yet learn. These fishes have the sense of hearing extremely acute, in so much that in taking them the fisherman ought not to make the least noise, nor row, unless it be very slightly. For this reason they make use of certain instruments for rowing which the Indians call *pagayos*[1], and the Spaniards name *canaletas*, with which although they row, yet it is performed without any noise that can fright the fish. While they are busied in this fishery, they use not speak to one another, but all is transacted by signs. He that darts them with the javelin uses it after the same manner as when they kill tortoises. Howbeit, the point of the said javelin is somewhat different, as having two hooks at the extremity, and these longer than that of the other fishery. Of these fishes some are found to be of the length of twenty unto twenty-four foot. Their flesh is very good to eat, being very like in colour unto that of a land-cow, but in taste unto that of pork. It contains much fat, or grease, which the Pirates use to melt and keep in earthen pots, to make use thereof instead of oil.

On a certain day, wherein we were not able to do any good at this sort of fishery, some of our men went into the woods to hunt, and others to catch other fish. Soon after we espied a canoe, wherein were two Indians. These no sooner had discovered our vessels but they rowed back with all the speed they could towards the land, being unwilling to trade or have anything to do with us Pirates. We followed them to the shore, but through their natural nimbleness, being much greater than ours, they retired into the woods before we could overtake them. Yea, what was more admirable, they drew on shore and carried with them their canoe into the wood as easily as if it were made of straw, although it weighed above 2000 pounds. This we knew by the canoe itself, which we found afterwards and had much ado to get it into the water again, although we were in all eleven persons to pull at it.

[1] Cf. " . . . for this reason they use certain instruments for rowing by the Indians called *pagayos*, with which they row without any noise to fright the fish."—*Description of the Isthmus of Darien* [1699], p. 9—evidently derived from this book.

We had at that time in our company a certain pilot who had been divers times in those quarters. This man, seeing this action of the Indians, told us that some few years before a squadron of Pirates happened to arrive at that place. Being there, they went in canoes to catch a certain sort of little birds, which inhabits the sea-coast under the shade of very beautiful trees, which here are to be seen. While they were busied at that work, certain Indians who had climbed up into the trees to view their actions, seeing now the canoes underneath, leaped down into the sea, and with huge celerity seized some of the canoes and Pirates that kept them, both which they transported so nimbly into the remotest parts of the woods as that the prisoners could not be relieved by their companions. Hereupon the Admiral of the said squadron landed presently after with 500 men, to seek and rescue the men he had lost. But they saw such an excessive number of Indians flock together to oppose them as obliged them to retreat with all possible diligence unto their ships, concluding among themselves that, if such forces as those could not perform anything towards the recovery of their companions, they ought to stay no longer time there. Having heard this history, we came away thence, fearing some mischief might befall us, and bringing with us the canoe aforementioned. In this we found nothing else but a fishing-net, though not very large, and four arrows made of palm-tree, of the length of seven-foot each and of the figure, or shape, as follows.

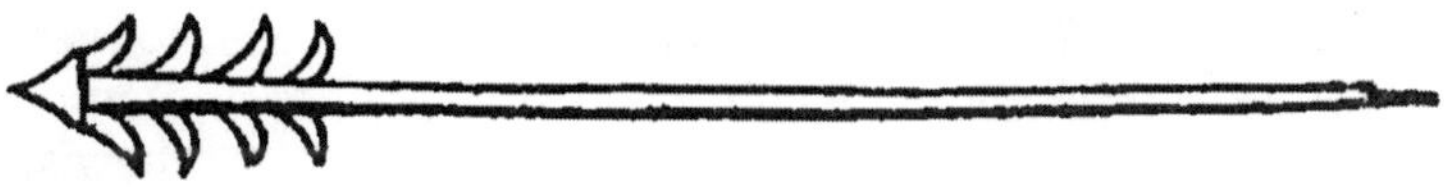

These arrows we believed to be their arms. The canoe we brought away was made of cedar, but very roughly hewn and polished, which caused us to think that those people have no instruments of iron.

We left that place, and arrived in twenty-four hours at another called Rio de Zeura, where we found some few houses belonging to the city of Cartagena. These houses are inhabited by Spaniards, whom we resolved to visit, not being able to find any tortoises nor yet any of their eggs. The inhabitants were all fled from the said houses, having left no victuals nor provisions behind them, in so much that we were forced to content ourselves with a certain fruit, which there is called *plantano*. Of these *plantanos* we filled our boats, and continued our voyage, coasting along the shore. Our design was to find out some creek or bay wherein to careen our vessel, which now was very leaky on all sides—yea, in such a dangerous condition that both night and day we were constrained to employ several men at the pump, unto which purpose we made use of all our slaves. This voyage lasted a whole fortnight, all which time we lay under the continual frights of perishing every moment. At last we arrived at a certain port called the Bay of Bleevelt, being so named from a pirate who used to resort thither with the same design that we did. Here one party of our men went into the woods to hunt, while another undertook to refit and careen our vessel.

Our companions who went abroad to hunt found hereabouts porcupines of a huge and monstrous bigness. But their chief exercise was killing of monkeys, and certain birds called by the Spaniards *faisanes*, or pheasants. The toil and labour we had in this employment of shooting did seem, at least unto me, to be sufficiently compensated with the pleasure of killing the said monkeys. For at these we usually made fifteen to sixteen shots before we could kill three or four of them, so nimbly would they escape our hands and aim, even after being desperately wounded. On the other side, it was delightful to see the female monkeys carry their little ones upon their backs, even just as the negresses do their children. When any person passes under the trees where these monkeys are sitting, they will commonly open their bellies and squirt their excrement upon their heads and clothes. Likewise, if shooting at a parcel of them, any monkey happens to be wounded, the rest of the company will flock about him, and lay their hands upon the wound, to hinder the blood from issuing forth. Others will gather moss that grows upon the trees, and thrust it into the wound, and thereby stop the blood. At other times they will gather such or such herbs, and, chewing them in their mouth, apply them after the manner of a poultice, or cataplasm. All which things did cause in me great admiration, seeing such strange actions in those irrational creatures, which testified the fidelity and love they had for one another.

On the 9th day after our arrival at that place, our women-slaves being busied in their ordinary employments of washing dishes, sewing, drawing water out of wells, which we had made on the shore, and the like things, we heard great cries of one of them, who said she had seen a troop of Indians appear towards the woods, whereby she began immediately to cry out: *Indians! Indians!* We, hearing this rumour, ran presently to our arms, and their relief. But, coming unto the wood, we found no person there excepting two of our women-slaves killed upon the place, with the shot of arrows. In their bodies we saw so many arrows sticking as might seem they had been fixed there with particular care and leisure, for otherwise we knew that one of them alone was sufficient to bereave any human body of life. These arrows were all

A. *A marcasite*[1], *which was tied unto the extremity of the arrow*
B. *A hook, tied to the same extremity*
C. *The arrow*
D. *The case, at the other end*

of a rare fashion and shape, their length being eight feet, and their thickness of a man's thumb. At one of the extremities hereof was to be seen a hook made of wood and tied to the body of the arrow with a string. At the other end was a certain case, or box, like the case of a pair of tweezers, in the which we found certain little pebbles, or stones. The colour thereof was red, and very shining, as if they had been locked up some considerable time. All which, we believed were arms belonging to their captains and leaders.

These arrows were all made without instruments of iron. For, whatsoever the Indians make, they harden it first very artificially with fire, and afterwards polish it with flints.

As to the nature of these Indians, they are extremely

[1] An obsolete name for certain crystalized forms of iron pyrites' Cf. Hakluyt, *Voyages* [1600], vol. iii, p. 575: "We found a mine of marcazites, which glister like golde (but all is not gold that glistereth).' Sometimes called the "fire-stone" (v. Cotgrave, *Dictionary* [1611]).

robust of constitution, strong and nimble at their feet. We sought them carefully up and down the woods, but could not find the least trace of them, neither any of their canoes, nor floats, whereof they make use to go out to fish. Hereupon we retired unto our vessels, where, having embarked all our goods, we put off from the shore, fearing lest finding us there they should return in any considerable number, and over-powering our forces tear us all in pieces.

CHAPTER VIII

The author departs towards the Cape of Gracias á Dios. Of the commerce which here the Pirates exercise with the Indians. His arrival at the island De los Pinos; and, finally, his return unto Jamaica

THE fear we had, more than usual, of those Indians abovementioned, by reason of the death of our two women-slaves, of which we told you in the former chapter, occasioned us to depart as fast as we could from that place. We directed our course thence towards the Cape of Gracias á Dios, where we had fixed our last hopes of finding provisions. For thither do usually resort many Pirates, who entertain a friendly correspondence and trade with the Indians of those parts. Being arrived at the said cape, we hugely rejoiced, and gave thanks unto God Almighty, for having delivered us out of so many dangers and brought us unto this place of refuge, where we found people who showed us most cordial friendship, and provided us with all necessaries whatsoever.

The custom of this island is such that, when any Pirates arrive there, every one has the liberty to buy for himself an Indian woman, at the price of a knife or any old axe, wood-bill, or hatchet. By this contract the woman is obliged to remain in the custody of the Pirate all the time he stays there. She serves him in the meanwhile, and brings him victuals of all sorts that the country affords. The Pirate, moreover, has liberty to go when he pleases, either to hunt, or fish, or about any other divertisements of his pleasure; but withal is not to commit any hostility, or depredation upon the inhabitants, seeing the Indians bring him in all that he stands in need of, or that he desires.

Through the frequent converse and familiarity these Indians have with the Pirates, they sometimes use to go to sea with them, and remain among them for whole years, without returning home. Whence it comes that many of them can speak English and French, and some of the Pirates their Indian language. They are very dexterous at darting with the javelin, whereby they are very useful to the Pirates towards the victualling their ships, by the fishery of tortoises, and *manitas*, a sort of fish so called by the Spaniards. For one of these Indians is alone sufficient to victual a vessel of an hundred persons. We had among our crew two Pirates who could speak very well the Indian language. By the help of these men I was so curious [as] to inquire into their customs, lives, and policy, whereof I shall give you here a brief account.

This island contains about thirty leagues in circumference, more or less. It is governed after the form of a little commonwealth, they having no king nor sovereign-prince among them. Neither do they entertain any friendship or correspondence with other neighbouring islands, much less with the Spaniards. They are in all but a small nation, whose number does not exceed sixteen or seventeen hundred persons. They have among them some few negroes, who serve them in quality of slaves. These happened to arrive there, swimming, after shipwreck made upon that coast. For, being bound for Terra Firma in a ship that carried them to be sold in those parts, they killed the Captain and mariners, with design to return unto their country. But, through their ignorance in marinery, they stranded their vessel hereabouts. Although, as I said before, they make but a small nation, yet they live divided, as it were, into two several provinces. Of these, the one sort employ themselves in cultivating the ground and making several plantations; but the others are so lazy that they have not courage to build themselves huts, much less houses, to dwell in. They frequent chiefly the sea-coast, wandering disorderly up and down, without knowing or caring so much as to cover their bodies from the rains, which are very frequent in those parts, unless it be with a few palm-leaves. These they put upon their heads, and keep their backs always turned to the wind that blows. They use no other clothes than an apron, which being tied to their middle, cometh down so far as to hide the shameful parts of their bodies. Such aprons are made of the rinds of trees, which they strongly beat upon stones till they are softened. Of these same they make use for bed-clothes, to cover themselves when they sleep. Some make to themselves bed-clothes of cotton, but these are but few in number. Their usual arms are nothing but *azagayas*, or spears, which they make fit for their use with points of iron or teeth of crocodiles.

They know, after some manner, that there is a God, yet they live without any religion or divine worship. Yea, as far as I can learn, they believe not in nor serve the devil, as many other nations of America do both believe, invoke, and worship him. Hereby they are not so much tormented by him as other nations are. Their ordinary food, for the greatest part, consists in several fruits, such as are called bananas, racoven, ananas, potatoes, cassava; as also crabs, and some few fish of other sorts, which they kill in the sea with darts. As to their drink, they are something expert in making certain pleasant and delicate liquors. The commonest among them is called *achioc*. This is made of a certain seed of palm-tree, which they bruise and afterwards steep or infuse in hot water, till it be settled at the bottom. This liquor, being strained off, has a very pleasant taste, and is very nourishing. Many other sorts of liquors they prepare, which I shall omit for brevity. Only I shall say something, in short, of that which is made of *plantanos*. These they knead betwixt their hands with hot water, and afterwards put into great calabashes, which they fill up with cold water, and leave in repose for the space of eight days, during which time it ferments as well as the best sort of wine. This liquor they drink for pleasure, and as a great regale[ment], in so much that, when these Indians invite their friends or relations, they cannot treat them better than to give them some of this pleasant drink.

They are very unskilful in dressing of victuals; and hence it is that they very seldom treat one another with banquets. For this purpose, when they go or send to any house to invite others, they desire them to come and drink of their liquors. Before the invited persons come to their house, those that expect them comb their hair very well, and anoint their faces with oil of palm mingled with a certain black tincture, which renders them very hideous. The women, in like manner, daub their faces with another sort of stuff, which causes them to look as red as crimson. And such are the greatest civilities they use in their ornaments and attire. Afterwards, he that invites the other takes his arms, which are three or four *azagayas*, and goes out of his cottage the space of three or four hundred steps, to wait for and receive the persons that are to come to visit him. As soon as they draw nigh unto him, he falls down upon the ground, lying flat on his face, in which posture he remains without any motion, as if he were dead. Being thus prostrate before them, the invited friends take him up and set him on his feet, and thus they go altogether unto the hut. Here the persons who are invited use the same ceremony, falling down on the ground, as the inviter did before. But he lifts them up one by one, and, giving them his hand, conducts them into his cottage, where he causes them to sit. The women on these occasions perform few or no ceremonies.

Being thus brought into the house, they are presented every one with a calabash full of the liquor above-mentioned, made of *plantanos*, which is very thick, almost like unto water-gruel, or children's pap, wherein is contained four quarts, more or less, of the said liquor. These they are to drink off as well as they can, and get down at any rate. The calabashes being emptied into their stomachs, the master of the house, with many ceremonies, goes about the room, and gathers his calabashes. And this drinking hitherto is reckoned but for one welcome, whereas every invitation ought to contain several welcomes. Afterwards, they begin to drink of the clear liquor above-mentioned, for which they were called to this treat. Hereunto follow many songs and dances and a thousand caresses to the women that are present: in so much that oftentimes, for a testimony of their great love unto them, they take their darts and with the points thereof pierce and wound their genital parts. This relation I confess I could not believe, though oftentimes it had been certified unto me, until such time as my own eyes were witnesses unto these and the like actions. Neither only on this occasion do they perform this ceremony of piercing their genitals, but also when they make love unto any woman, intending thereby to let them understand the greatness of their affection and constancy.

They use not to marry any young maid without the consent of her parents. Hereupon, if any one desires to take a wife, he is first examined by the damsel's father concerning several points relating to good husbandry. These are most commonly:

whether he can make *azagayas*, darts for fishing, or spin a certain thread which they use about their arrows. Having answered to satisfaction, the examiner calls to his daughter, for a little calabash full of the liquor above-mentioned. Of this he drinks first; then gives the cup unto the young man; and he finally unto the bride, who drinks it up; and with this only ceremony the marriage is made. When any one drinks to the health of another, the second person ought to drink up the liquor which the other person has left in the calabash. But, in case of marriage, as was said before, it is consumed alone among those three, the bride obtaining the greatest part to her share.

When the woman lies in, neither she nor her husband observe the time, as is customary among the Caribbees. But, as soon as the woman is delivered, she goes instantly unto the next river, brook, or fountain, and washes the new-born creature, swaddling it up afterwards in certain rollers, or swaddling bands, which there are called *cabalas*. This being done, she goes about her ordinary labour, as before. At their entertainments it is usual that, when the man dies, his wife buries him with all his *azagayas*, aprons, and jewels that he used to wear at his ears. Her next obligation is to come every day to her husband's grave, bringing him meat and drink for a whole year together. Their years they reckon by the moons, allowing fifteen to every year, which make their entire circle, as our twelve months make ours.

Some historians writing of the Caribbee Islands do affirm that this ceremony of carrying victuals to the dead is generally observed among them. Moreover, that the devil comes unto the sepulchres, and carries away all the meat and drink which is placed there. But I myself am not of this opinion, seeing I have oftentimes with my own hands taken away these offerings, and eaten them instead of other victuals. Unto this I was moved, because I knew that the fruits used on these occasions were the choicest and ripest of all others, as also the liquors of the best sort they made use of for their greatest regale[ment] and pleasure. When the widow has thus completed her year, she opens the grave, and takes out all her husband's bones. These she scrapes and washes very well, and afterwards dries against the beams of the sun. When they are sufficiently dried, she ties them all together, and puts them into a *cabala*, being a certain pouch or satchel, and is obliged for another year to carry them upon her back in the daytime, and to sleep upon them in the night, until the year be completely expired. This ceremony being finished, she hangs up the bag and bones against the post of her own door, in case she be mistress of any house. But, having no house of her own, she hangs them at the door of her next neighbour or relation.

The widows cannot marry a second time, according to the laws or customs of this nation, until the whole space of the two years above-mentioned be completed. The men are bound to perform no such ceremonies towards their wives. But, if any Pirate marries an Indian Woman, she is bound to do with him in all things as if he were an Indian man born. Then negroes that are upon this island live here in all respects according to the customs of their own country. All these things I have thought fit to take notice of in this place, though briefly, as judging them worthy the curiosity of some judicious and inquisitive persons. Now I shall continue the account of our voyage.

After that we had refreshed and provided ourselves, as well as we could, at the island aforesaid, we departed thence, and steered our course towards the island De los Pinos. Here we arrived in fifteen days, and were constrained to refit again our vessel, which now the second time was very leaky and not fit for sailing any farther. Hereupon we divided ourselves, as before, and some went about that work of careening the ship, while others betook themselves to fishing. In this last we were so successful as to take in six or seven hours as much fish as would abundantly suffice to feed a thousand persons. We had in our company some Indians from the cape of Gracias á Dios, who were very dexterous both in hunting and fishing. With the help of these men we killed likewise in a short while and salted a huge number of wild-cows, sufficient both to satiate our hungry appetites and to victual our vessel for the sea. These cows were formerly brought into this island by the Spaniards, with design they should here multiply and stock the country with cattle of this kind. We salted in like manner a vast number of tortoises, whereof in this island huge quantities are to be found. With these things our former cares and troubles began to dissipate, and our minds to be so far recreated as to forget the miseries we had lately endured. Hereupon we began to call one another again by the name of brothers, which was customary amongst us, but had been disused in our miseries and scarce remembered without regret.

All the time we continued here, we feasted ourselves very plentifully, without the least fear of enemies. For as to the Spaniards that were upon the island, they were here in mutual league and friendship with us. Thus we were only constrained to keep watch and ward every night, for fear of the crocodiles, which are here in great plenty all over the island. For these, when they are hungry, will assault any man whatsoever and devour him, as it happened in this conjuncture to one of our companions. This man being gone into the wood in company with a negro, they fell into a place where a crocodile lay concealed. The furious animal with incredible agility assaulted the Pirate, and, fastening upon his leg, cast him upon the ground, the negro being fled who should assist him. Yet he, notwithstanding, being a robust and courageous man, drew forth a knife he had then about him, and with the same, after a dangerous combat, overcame and killed the crocodile. Which having done, he himself, both tired with the battle and weakened with the loss of blood that ran from his wounds, lay for dead upon the place, or at least beside his senses. Being found in this posture some while after by the negro, who returned to see what was become of his master, he took him upon his back and brought him to the sea-side, distant thence the space of a whole league. Here we received him into a canoe, and conveyed him on board our ship.

After this misfortune none of our men dared be so bold as to enter the woods without good company. Yea, we ourselves, desirous to revenge the disaster of our companion, went in troops the next day to the woods, with design to find out crocodiles to kill. These animals would usually come every night to the sides of our ship and make resemblance of climbing up into the vessel. One of these, on a certain night, we seized with an iron hook, but he, instead of flying to the bottom, began to mount the ladder of the ship, till we killed him with other instruments. Thus, after we had remained there some considerable time and refitted ourselves with all things necessary, we set sail thence for Jamaica. Here we arrived within few days, after a prosperous voyage, and found Captain

Morgan, who was got home before us, but had seen as yet none of his companions whom he left behind, we being the first that arrived there after him.

The said Captain at that present was very busy, endeavouring to persuade and levy people to transport unto the isle of St Catharine, which he designed to fortify and hold as his own, thinking to make it a common refuge unto all sorts of Pirates, or at least of his own nation, as was said before. But he was soon hindered in the prosecution of this design by the arrival of a man-of-war from England. For this vessel brought orders from his Majesty of Great Britain, to recall the Governor of Jamaica from his charge over that island, unto the Court of England, there to give an account of his proceedings and behaviour in relation to the Pirates whom he had maintained in those parts, to the huge detriment of the subjects of the King of Spain. Unto this purpose the said man-of-war brought over also a new Governor of Jamaica, to supply the place of the preceding. This gentleman, being possessed of the government of the island, presently after gave notice unto all the ports thereof, by several boats which he sent forth to that intent, of the good and entire correspondence which his master the King of England designed henceforwards to maintain in those Western parts of the world towards his Catholic Majesty and all his subjects and dominions. And that unto this effect, for the time to come, he had received from his Sacred Majesty and Privy Council strict and severe orders not to permit any Pirate whatsoever to set forth from Jamaica, to commit any hostility or depredation upon the Spanish nation or dominions, or any other people of those neighbouring islands.

No sooner these orders were sufficiently divulged but the Pirates, who as yet were abroad at sea, began to fear them, insomuch that they dared not return home unto the said island. Hereupon they kept the seas as long as they could, and continued to act as many hostilities as came in their way. Not long after, the same Pirates took and ransacked a considerable town, seated in the isle of Cuba, called La Villa de los Cayos, of which we made mention in the description of the said island. Here they committed again all sorts of hostility and inhuman and barbarous cruelties. But the new Governor of Jamaica behaved himself so constant to his duty, and the orders he had brought from England, that he apprehended several of the chief actors herein, and condemned them to be hanged, which was accordingly done. From this severity many others still remaining abroad took warning, and retired to the isle of Tortuga, lest they should fall into his hands. Here they joined in society with the French Pirates, inhabitants of the said island, in whose company they continue to this day.

CHAPTER IX

The relation of the shipwreck which Monsieur Bertram Ogeron, Governor of the isle of Tortuga, suffered near the Isles of Guadanillas. How both he and his companions fell into the hands of the Spaniards. By what arts he escaped their hands, and preserved his life. The enterprise which he undertook against Porto Rico to deliver his people. The unfortunate success of that design

AFTER the expedition of Panama above-mentioned, the inhabitants of the French islands in America, in the year 1673 (while the war was so fierce in Europe between France and Holland), gathered a considerable fleet, for to go and possess themselves of the islands belonging to the States-General of the United Provinces in the West Indies. Unto this effect their admiral called together and levied all the Pirates and volunteers that would, by any inductions whatsoever, sit down under his colours. With the same design the Governor of Tortuga caused to be built in that island a good strong man-of-war, unto which vessel he gave the name of *Ogeron*. This ship he provided very well with all sorts of ammunition, and manned with five-hundred buccaneers, all resolute and courageous men, as being the vessel he de signed for his own safety. Their first intention was to go and take the isle of Curaçao, belonging to the said States of Holland. But this design met with very ill success, by reason of a shipwreck, which impeded the course of their voyage.

Monsieur Ogeron set sail from the port of Tortuga as soon as all things were in readiness, with intent to join the rest of the said fleet and pursue the enterprize aforementioned. Being arrived on the West side of the Island of St John de Puerto Rico, he was suddenly surprized with a violent storm. This increased to that a degree as caused his new frigate to strike against the rocks that neighbour upon the islands, called Guadanillas, where the vessel broke into a thousand pieces. Yet, being nigh unto the land of Porto Rico, all his men escaped, by saving their lives in boats, which they had at hand.

The next day, all being now got on shore, they were discovered by the Spaniards who inhabit the island. These instantly took them to be French Pirates, whose intent was to take the said island anew, as they had done several times before. Hereupon they alarmed the whole country, and, gathering their forces together, marched out to their encounter. But they found them unprovided of all manner of arms, and consequently not able to make any defence, craving for mercy at their hands, and begging quarter for their lives, as the custom is. Yet notwithstanding, the Spaniards, remembering the horrible and cruel actions those Pirates had many times committed against them, would have no compassion on their condition. But, answering them: *Ha! ye thievish dogs, here's no quarter for you!* they assaulted them with all fury imaginable, and killed the greatest part of the company. At last, perceiving they made no resistance nor had any arms to defend themselves, they began to relent in their cruelty, and stay their blows, taking prisoners as many as remained alive. Yet still they would not be persuaded but that those unfortunate people were come thither with design to take again and ruin the island.

Hereupon they bound them with cords, by two and two or three and three together, and drove them through the woods into the campaign, or open fields. Being come thus far with them, they asked them: *What was become of their captain and leader?* Unto these questions they constantly made answer: *He was drowned in the shipwreck at sea;* although they knew full well it was false. For Monsieur Ogeron, being unknown unto the Spaniards, behaved himself among them as if he were a fool and had no common use of reason. Notwithstanding, the Spaniards, scarce believing what the prisoners had answered, used all the means they could possibly to find him, but could not compass their desires. For Monsieur Ogeron kept himself very close to all the features and mimical actions that might become any innocent fool. Upon this account he was not tied as the rest of his companions, but let loose, to serve the divertisement and laughter of the common soldiers. These now and then would give him scraps of bread and other victuals, whereas the rest of the prisoners had never sufficient wherewith to satisfy their hungry stomachs. For, as to the allowance they had from the Spaniards, their enemies, it was scarce enough to preserve them alive.

It happened there was found among the French Pirates a certain surgeon, who had done some remarkable services to the Spaniards. In consideration of these merits, he was unbound and set at liberty, to go freely up and down, even as Monsieur Ogeron did. Unto this surgeon Monsieur Ogeron, having a fit opportunity thereunto, declared his resolution of hazarding his life to attempt an escape from the cruelty and hard usage of those enemies. After mature deliberation, they both performed it, by flying unto the woods, with design there to make something or other that might be navigable, whereby to transport themselves elsewhere; although unto this effect they had nor could obtain no other thing in the world that could be serviceable in building of vessels but one only hatchet. Thus they joined company, and began their march towards the woods that lay nearest the sea-coast. Having travelled all day long, they came about evening unto the sea-side almost unexpectedly. Here they found themselves without anything to eat, nor any secure place wherein to rest their wearied limbs. At last they perceived nigh the shore an huge quantity of fishes, called by the Spaniards *corlabados*. These frequently approach the sands of the shore in pursuit of other little fishes that serve them for their food. Of these they took as many as they thought necessary, and, by rubbing two sticks tediously together, they kindled fire, wherewith they made coals to roast them. The next day they began to cut down and prepare timber, wherewith to make a kind of small boat, in which they might pass over unto the isle of Santa Cruz, which belongs to the French.

While they were busied about their work, they discovered, at a great distance, a certain canoe, which steered directly towards the place where they were. This occasioned in their minds some fears lest they should be found, and taken again by the Spaniards; and hereupon they retired into the woods till such time as they could see thence and distinguish what people were in the canoe. But at last, as their good fortune would have it, they perceived them to be no more than two men, who in their disposition and apparel seemed to be fishermen. Having made this discovery, they concluded unanimously betwixt themselves to hazard their lives, and overcome them, and afterwards seize the canoe. Soon after they perceived one of them, who was a mulatto, to go with several calabashes hanging at his back towards a spring, not far distant from the shore, to take in fresh water. The other, who was a Spaniard, remained behind, waiting for his return. Seeing them divided, they assaulted the mulatto first, and discharging a great blow on his head with the hatchet, they soon bereaved him of life. The Spaniard, hearing the noise, made instantly towards the canoe, thinking to escape. But this he could not perform so soon, without being overtaken by the two, and there massacred by their hands. Having now compassed their design, they went to seek for the corpse of the mulatto, which they carried on board the canoe. Their intent was to convey them into the middle of the sea, and there cast them overboard, to be consumed by the fish, and by this means conceal this fact from being known unto the Spaniards, either at a short or long distance of time.

These things being done, they took in presently as much fresh water as they could, and set sail to seek thence some place of refuge. That day they steered along the coast of Porto Rico, and came unto the cape called by the Spaniards Cabo Roxo. Hence they traversed directly to the isle of Hispaniola, where so many of their own comrades and companions were to be found. Both the currents of the waters and winds were very favourable unto this voyage, in so much that in a few days they arrived at a place called Samana, belonging to the said island, where they found a party of their own people.

Monsieur Ogeron, being landed at Samana, gave orders unto the surgeon to levy all the people he could possibly in those parts, while he departed to revisit his government of Tortuga. Being arrived at the said port, he used all his endeavours to gather what vessels and men he could to his assistance; so that within a few days he compassed a good number of both, very well equipped and disposed to follow and execute his designs. These were to go unto the island of St John de

Puerto Rico, and deliver his fellow-prisoners whom he had left in the miserable condition as was said before. After having embarked all the people which the surgeon had levied at Samana, he made them a speech, exhorting them to have good courage, and telling them: *You may all expect great spoil and riches from this enterprize, and therefore let all fear and cowardice be set on side. On the contrary, fill your hearts with courage and valour, for thus you will find yourselves soon satisfied of what, at present, bare hopes do promise.* Every one relied much on these promises of Monsieur Ogeron, and, from his words, conceived no small joy in their minds. Thus they set sail from Tortuga, steering their course directly for the coasts of Porto Rico. Being come within sight of land, they made use only of their lower sails, to the intent they might not be discovered at so great a distance by the Spaniards, till they came somewhat near the place where they intended to land.

The Spaniards, notwithstanding this caution, had intelligence beforehand of their coming, and were prepared for a defence, having posted many troops of horse all along the coast, to watch the descent of the French Pirates. Monsieur Ogeron, perceiving their vigilance, gave order to the vessels to draw nigh unto the shore and shoot off many great guns, whereby he forced the cavalry to retire unto places more secure within the woods. Here lay concealed many companies of foot, who had prostrated themselves upon the ground. Meanwhile the Pirates made their descent at leisure, and began to enter among the trees, scarce suspecting any harm to be there, where the horsemen could do no service. But no sooner were they fallen into this ambuscade than the Spaniards arose with great fury, and assaulted the French so courageously that in a short while they destroyed great part of them. And, thus leaving great numbers of dead on the place, the rest with difficulty escaped by retreating in all haste unto their ships.

Monsieur Ogeron, although he escaped this danger, yet could willingly have perished in the fight rather than suffer the shame and confusion the unfortunate success of this enterprize was likely to bring upon his reputation, especially considering that those whom he had attempted to set at liberty were now cast into greater miseries through this misfortune. Hereupon they hastened to set sail, and go back unto Tortuga the same way they came, with great confusion in their minds, much diminished in their number, and nothing laden with those spoils the hopes whereof had possessed their hearts and caused them readily to follow the promises of unfortunate Monsieur Ogeron. The Spaniards were very vigilant, and kept their posts nigh unto the sea-side till such time as the fleet of Pirates was totally out of sight. In the meanwhile they made an end of killing such of their enemies as being desperately wounded could not escape by flight. In like manner they cut off several limbs from the dead bodies, with design to show them to the former prisoners, for whose redemption these others had crossed the seas.

The fleet, being departed, the Spaniards kindled bonfires all over the island, and made great demonstrations of joy for the victory they had obtained. But the French prisoners who were there before had more hardship showed them from that day than ever. Of their misery and misusage was a good eye-witness, Jacob Binkes, Governor at that time in America for the States-General of the United Provinces. For he happened to arrive in that conjuncture at the island of Porto Rico, with some men-of-war, to buy provisions and other necessaries for his fleet. His compassion on their misery was such as caused him to bring away by stealth five or six of the said prisoners, which served only to exasperate the minds of the Spaniards. For soon after they sent the rest of the prisoners to the chief city of the island, there to work and toil about the fortifications which then were making, forcing them to bring and carry stones and all sorts of materials belonging thereunto. These being finished, the Governor transported them unto Havana, where they employed them in like manner, in fortifying that city. Here they caused them to work in the day-time, and by night they shut them up as close prisoners, fearing lest they should enterprize upon the city. For of such attempts the Spaniards had had divers proofs on other occasions, which afforded them sufficient cause to use them after that manner.

Afterwards at several times, wherein ships arrived there from New Spain, they transported them by degrees into Europe, and landed them at the city of Cadiz. But notwithstanding this care of the Spaniards to disperse them, they soon after met almost all together in France, and resolved among themselves to return again unto Tortuga with the first opportunity [that] should proffer. To this effect, they assisted one another very lovingly with what necessaries they could spare, according to every one's condition; so that in a short while the greatest part of those Pirates had nested themselves again at Tortuga, their common place of rendezvous. Here, some time after, they equipped again a new fleet, to revenge their former misfortunes on the Spaniards, under the conduct of one Le Sieur Maintenon, a Frenchman by nation. With this fleet he arrived at the island of Trinidad, situated between the isle of Tobago and the neighbouring coasts of Paria. This island they sacked, and afterwards put to the ransom of 10,000 pieces-of-eight. Hence they departed, with design to take and pillage the city of Caracas, seated over against the island of Curaçao, belonging to the Hollanders.

CHAPTER X

A relation of what encounters lately happened at the islands of Cayana and Tobago between the Count de Estres, Admiral of France, in America, and the Heer Jacob Binkes, Vice-Admiral of the United Provinces, in the same parts

It is a thing already known unto the greatest part of Europe that the Prince of Courland began to establish a colony in the island of Tobago; as, also, that, somewhile after, his people, for want of timely recruits from their own country, abandoned the said island, leaving it to the first that should come and possess it. Thus it fell into the hands of the Heers Adrian and Cornelius Lampsius, natives of the city of Flushing, in the province of Zeeland. For, being arrived at the said island of Tobago, in the year 1654, they undertook to fortify it by command of their sovereigns, the States-General. Hereupon they built a goodly castle, in a convenient situation, capable of hindering the assaults of any enemies that might enterprize upon the island.

The strength of this castle was afterwards sufficiently tried by Monsieur de Estres, as I shall presently relate, after I have first told you what happened before at Cayana in the year 1676. This year the States-General of the United Provinces sent their Vice-Admiral, Jacob Binkes, unto the island of Cayana, then in possession of the French, for to retake the said island, and hereby restore it unto the dominions of the United Provinces aforementioned. With these orders he set forth from Holland on the 16th day of March in the said year, his fleet consisting of seven men-of-war, one fireship, and five other small vessels of less account. This fleet arrived at Cayana the 4th day of the month of May next following. Immediately after their arrival, the Heer Binkes landed nine-hundred men, who, approaching the castle, summoned the Governor to surrender at their discretion. His answer was: *He thought of nothing less than surrendering, but that he and his people were resolved to defend themselves, even to the utmost of their endeavours.* The Heer Binkes, having received this answer, presently commanded his troops to attack the castle on both sides at once. The assault was very furious. But at length the French, being few in number and overwhelmed with the multitude of their enemies, surrendered both their arms and the castle. In it were found thirty-seven pieces of cannon. The Governor, who was named Monsieur Lesi, together with two priests were sent into Holland. The Heer Binkes lost in the combat 14 men only, and had 72 wounded.

The King of France no sooner understood this success but he sent in the month of October following the Count de Estres, for to retake the said island again from the Hollanders. He arrived there in the month of December with a squadron of men-of-war, all very well equipped and provided. Being come on his voyage as far as the river called Aperovaco, he met there with a small vessel of Nantes, which had set forth from the said island of Cayana but a fortnight before. This ship gave him intelligence of the present state and condition wherein he might be certain to find the Hollanders at Cayana. They told him there were 300 men in the castle; that all about it they had fixed strong palisades, or empalements; and that within the castle were mounted 26 pieces of cannon.

Monsieur de Estres, being enabled with this intelligence to take his own measures, proceeded on his voyage, and arrived at a port of the said island 3 leagues distant from the castle. Here he landed 800 men, whom he divided into two several parties. The one he placed under the conduct of the Count de Blinac, and the other he gave unto Monsieur de St Faucher. On board the fleet he left Monsieur Gabaret, with divers other principal troops which he thought not fit or necessary to be landed. As soon as the men were set on shore, the fleet weighed anchor, and sailed very slowly towards the castle, while the soldiers marched by land. These could not travel otherwise than by night by reason of the excessive heat of the sun and intolerable exhalations of the earth, which here is very sulphurous, and consequently no better than a smoky and stinking oven.

On the 19th day of the said month the Count de Estres

sent Monsieur de Lesi (who had been Governor of the island, as was said before), demanding of them, to deliver the castle unto the obedience of the King, his master, and to him in his sovereign's name. But those who were within resolved not to deliver themselves up but at the expense of their lives and blood, which answer they sent unto Monsieur de Estres. Hereupon the French, the following night, assaulted and stormed the castle on seven several sides thereof all at once. The defendants, having performed their obligation very stoutly, and fought with as much valour as was possible, were at last forced to surrender. Within the castle were found 38 persons dead, besides many others that were wounded. All the prisoners were transported into France, where they were used with great hardship.

Monsieur de Estres, having put all things in good order at the isle of Cayana, departed thence for that of Martinique. Being arrived at the said island, he was told that the Heer Binkes was at that present at the island of Tobago and his fleet lay at anchor in the bay. Having received this intelligence, Monsieur de Estres made no long stay there, but set sail again, steering his course directly for Tobago. No sooner was he come nigh unto the island but Vice-Admiral Binkes sent his land-forces, together with a good number of mariners, on shore, to manage and defend the artillery that was there. These forces were commanded by the Captains Van der Graef, Van Dongen and Ciavone, who laboured very hard all that night in raising certain batteries and filling up the palisades, or empalements, of the fortress called Sterreschans.

Two days after, the French fleet came to an anchor in the Bay of Palmit, and immediately, with the help of eighteen boats, they landed all their men. The Heer Binkes, perceiving the French to appear upon the hills, gave orders to burn all the houses that were nigh unto the castle, to the intent the French might have no place to shelter themselves thereabouts. On the 23rd day of February Monsieur de Estres sent a drum over to the Hollanders to demand the surrender of the fort, which was absolutely denied. In this posture of affairs things continued until the 3rd of March. On this day the French fleet came with full sail, and engaged the Dutch fleet. The Heer Binkes presently encountered them, and the dispute was very hot on both sides. In the meanwhile the land-forces belonging to the French, being sheltered by the thickness of the woods, advanced towards the castle, and began to storm it very briskly with more than ordinary force, but were repulsed by the Dutch with such vigour as caused them after three distinct attacks to retire with the loss of above 150 men, and 200 wounded. These they carried off, or rather dragged away, with no small difficulty, by reason of their disorderly retreat.

All this while the two fleets continued the combat, and fought very desperately, until that on both sides some ships were consumed between Vulcan and Neptune. Of this number was Monsieur de Estres' own ship, mounted with 27 guns of prodigious bigness, besides other pieces of lesser port. The battle continued from break of day until the evening; a little before which time Monsieur de Estres quitted the bay with the rest of his ships, unto the Hollanders, excepting only two, which were stranded under sail, as having gone too high within the port. Finally the victory remained on the side of the Hollanders, howbeit with the loss of several of their ships that were burnt.

Monsieur de Estres, finding himself under the shame of the loss of this victory, and that he could expect no advantage for that present over the island of Tobago, set sail from those quarters the 18th day of March, and arrived the 21st day of June next following at the port of Brest in France. Having given an account of these transactions to his most Christian Majesty, he was pleased to command him to undertake again the enterprize of Tobago. Unto this effect, he gave orders for eight great men-of-war to be equipped with all speed, together with eight others of smaller account: with all which vessels he sent again Monsieur de Estres into America the same year. He set sail from the said port of Brest on the 3rd day of October following, and arrived the 1st of December at the island of Barbados. Afterwards, having received some recruits from the isle of Martinique, he sent beforehand to review the island of Tobago, and consider the condition thereof. This being done, he weighed anchor and set sail directly for the said island, where he arrived the 7th day of the said month of December with all his fleet.

Immediately after his arrival he landed 500 men, under the conduct of Monsieur de Blinac, Governor of the French islands in America. These were followed soon after by 1000 more.

The 9th day of the said month they approached within 600. paces of a certain post called Le Cort, where they landed all the artillery designed for this enterprize. On the 10th day Monsieur de Estres went in person to take a view of the castle, and demanded of the Heer Binkes, by a messenger, the surrender thereof, which was generously denied. The next day the French began to advance towards the castle, and on the 12th of the said month the Dutch from within began to fire at them with great perseverance. The French made a beginning to their attack by casting fire-balls into the castle with main violence. The very third ball that was cast in happened to fall in the path-way that led to the storehouse where the powder and ammunition was kept belonging to the castle. In this path was much powder scattered up and down, through the negligence of those that carried it to and fro for the necessary supplies of the defendants. By this means the powder took fire in the path, and thence ran in a moment as far as the storehouse above-mentioned; so that suddenly both the storehouse was blown up, and with it Vice-Admiral Binkes himself, then Governor of the island, and all his officers. Only Captain Van Dongen remained alive. This mischance being perceived by the French, they instantly ran with 500 men, and possessed themselves of the castle. Here they found 300 men alive, whom they took prisoners and transported into France. Monsieur de Estres after this commanded the castle to be demolished, together with other posts that might serve for any defence, as also all the houses standing upon the island. This being done, he departed thence the 27th day of the said month of December, and arrived again in France after a prosperous voyage.

CHAPTER XI

Adventures of Captain Cook, in the year 1678. He is taken by the Spaniards. Bold exploits, and revenge of his losses, performed by some few Buccaneers that were on board his ship

IN the year 1678 Captain Cook, who followed the trade of the West Indies and our several plantations there, happened to go into the Bay of Campeche, there to load his vessel with logwood, as many others had done before. The forests about Campeche are a certain place adjoining to the Bay of Mexico, unto which for many years the Buccaneers have usually resorted to cut wood for the art of dyeing, and prepare hides for shoe-leather, and other uses, towards the lading of several ships that from all parts frequent the forementioned Bay, to trade with them. After he had taken in his lading, having also some of the Buccaneers aboard his vessel, he set sail for the island of Tobago, at which place he was to deliver his cargo ; but his fortune was to fall somewhat short, or leeward, in the phrase of the mariners, of his desired and intended port. Hereupon he came to anchor at the West end of a certain island called Rubia, whereof mention has been already made in the preceding history of the Buccaneers.

Here Captain Cook had not lain long at anchor, expecting a wind for the prosecution of his voyage, when he was unexpectedly surprized and taken by three Spanish men-of-war. These, having possessed themselves of his ship and cargo, presently after set both him and his companions ashore upon the aforesaid island. Here therefore being landed, they found a Dutch Governor or officer, with six men in his retinue, who were only settled there to purchase provisions for their vessels that should happen to touch in those parts.

Our English had not been long on this island but there happened to come into the road a Spanish boat, equipped with sixteen or eighteen men and laden with coconuts (whereof chocolate is made) and plate. The Buccaneers immediately put it into the thoughts of Captain Cook to make reprizal upon the countrymen of those who had so lately stripped them of all they had: he approving of their proposals, in order thereunto they acquainted the Governor's man with their intentions, and withal desired him, under promise of a good reward, to lend them a small number of fusees, or guns, wherewith to put these their designs into execution. The Governor and his men, hearing the promise of so great a reward, were easily persuaded to accommodate them with arms at their request: six men, therefore, of the Buccaneers, being thus resolved and fitted with arms, placed themselves in ambuscade about that part of the island where the boat of the Spanish sloop was to come ashore. The boat happening to land thereabouts in a small time after, as they desired, they immediately set upon the men, and took them prisoners. Having bound them fast upon the strand, they seized the boat and embarked therein with resolution to take the vessel it belonged unto, which they performed in this manner: two of them they appointed among themselves to row the boat; two more to charge their guns; and the remaining couple were to fire into the Spanish bark as briskly as they could pour in their shot. In this posture they rowed in the wake, under the stern of the said vessel. The Spaniards on board soon perceived they were not to expect their own men again but enemies in lieu of them. Therewith immediately they put themselves into the posture of defence, and began to handle their arms. But this they performed so unfortunately on their side, or rather fortunately for the English, that the Buccaneers killed the padre, or priest, they had on board, and the Captain or Master of the vessel likewise; whereupon the rest surrendered themselves by throwing their arms overboard and craving quarter for their lives. Thus at the same time they made themselves masters of the vessel and restitution of their former losses.

Here, in the first place, they gave the Dutch Governor out of their gains a considerable present; and his chief man they rewarded very liberally for the loan of the arms aforementioned. In the next, they assigned unto Captain Cook a valuable consideration for his losses, and likewise something unto each, and every one of the mariners that belonged to his ship. After which, the Buccaneers (for these were the chief, or rather only, men concerned in this attempt) divided among themselves nigh four-hundred pound to each, both in goods and plate. Thus they set sail from the isle of Rubia in the same Spanish bark they had taken, and arrived in few days after at Jamaica, where they took out her lading, and afterwards set fire unto the bottom, as being unfit for their purpose. Here they paid the Governor his duties, and embarked themselves with their goods for England, where some of them live in good reputation unto this day. Yet their names are desired to be concealed in this place, this action resenting too much of self-justice, or *petite piracy*, which is a term they themselves have given unto it.

CHAPTER XII

A brief account of Captain Sharp and other his companions; their voyage from Jamaica unto the province of Darien and South Sea; with the robberies and assaults they committed there for the space of three years, till their return for England in the year 1682. Given by one of the Buccaneers who was present at those transactions

WE set sail from Port Royal, upon the island of Jamaica, in the year of our Lord 1679. Our fleet consisted of five sail of ships, whereof the chief Commanders were named Captain Coxon, Cornelius Essex, Robert Allison, John Rose, and Captain Sharp. The first port we went unto was Port Moranto. Hence we steered our course directly for the coast of Cartagena, or rather for the islands of Pines, commonly called De los Pinos, not far distant from that coast. At these islands we victualled our ships, as at other times has been done by other men of the like trade. But in this passage from Port Moranto unto the Pine Islands we had the misfortune to lose, by stress of weather, two of our number of vessels, to wit Captain Sharp and Cornelius Essex, who both separated from us in a storm. However, having taken in what provision of victuals we thought necessary, we steered thence towards the island called Fuerte, or Forta. Being upon this course about the middle of the islands called Zavallos, or Zambullos, we happened to meet with a French man-of-war, who was mounted with eight guns, and who kept in our company for some days. His commission was but for a small space of time—only for three months. We shewed him our commission, which was now for three years to come. This we had purchased at a cheap rate, having given for it only the sum of ten ducats, or pieces-of-eight. But the truth of the thing was that at first our commission was made only for the space of three months, the same date as the Frenchman's was; whereas among ourselves we had contrived to make it last for three years—for with this we were resolved to seek our fortunes.

Having ranged for some while up and down the islands, which in those seas are pretty frequent, and finding nothing that could give us satisfaction, we at last resolved to attempt Porto Bello, which formerly had been taken and sacked by Sir Henry Morgan, and others, both English and French, hoping his fortune would favour our arms, and that we should bring away no less booty than he had done before. Unto this effect we thought it convenient to leave our ships at certain islands not far distant from Porto Bello, and put our men into fourteen or fifteen canoes, which we had taken for that purpose. With these we landed at a considerable distance from the town and port, and were constrained, after landing, to travel three whole nights before we could reach the place. By day we concealed ourselves in the woods and took our rest, for then we dared not to travel, fearing lest we should be discovered by the Spaniards, our mortal enemies, whom we intended to plunder: yet, notwithstanding, all the care we could possibly take, we were at last, before we came to the town, discovered by a negro, who ran before us unto the place and gave intelligence of our coming. Hereupon, perceiving we were descried, we hastened our march after his steps as fast as we could, and got into the town before he could raise the citizens or any considerable body of defence could be formed against us. Thus we possessed ourselves of the city without any considerable loss on our side, and plundered all we could find in the houses and elsewhere. Our stay here was but short, for fear lest the enemy should rally against us or pour in the country upon our small forces and thus intercept our retreat—especially as we had left our ships at the islands above-mentioned and were masters of only a few canoes to convey us over the seas unto them. Having been therefore in possession of the town the space of two days and two nights, we resolved to quit it and return unto our ships. We divided amongst us, out of the booty, about forty pound sterling to each man, beside what extraordinary shares were drawn by our officers, the owners of the vessels, carpenters, surgeons, and those who lost any limbs, or were killed in this expedition, according to the customary laws of the

Buccaneers, which are described in the History of these people but lately printed. In this exploit of taking the town of Porto Bello our number was not above that of 200 men, the residue being left behind to man and defend our ships. Yet, notwithstanding, these who guarded the ships had their shares equally distributed unto them, as well as those who went on shore. In all our whole number might consist of 300 fighting-men, which we brought out from Jamaica with us—not many more, if I well remember: which point I forgot to tell you at the beginning of this relation.

Being returned on board our ships, we cruized to and fro for some days, hoping to find some other purchase by sea, as we had done by land. But nothing could we meet withal that would stay our thirst and hunger after more prey: only, being upon a certain tack, we happened to meet with a Spanish *barco de aviso*, or packet-boat, which was called St Rose, mounted only with six guns, and which was bound for Spain, or from there to the West Indies, with letters and intelligence concerning the galleons, or *flota*, and other State affairs, as they are usually sent every year by the Catholic King unto his Viceroys, or Governors, in those parts, or else by them unto His Majesty, upon the aforesaid account. This little ship, therefore, we immediately set upon and took, but found not so much in her as would answer our expectations. Neither the letters they had on board could we reach, from which we might possibly have learned something which would have pleased our fancies or flattered our hopes for some while; for the Spaniards cast them into the sea, when they saw themselves in danger of being taken, before we could possess ourselves of the vessel; which was done according to the strict and almost inviolable orders the Captains of these packet boats, or *navios de aviso* (for so they are also named), that is packet-ships, do constantly receive from the King of Spain; unto which effect also they take an oath, viz. to cast their letters overboard, and not deliver them up to any enemy whatsoever. Conformable to this point, all the Captains of the galleons belonging likewise are solemnly sworn to sink, burn, or otherwise to destroy their ships rather than permit them to be taken by an enemy, for fear of enriching him not so much with those their great vessels as with the treasure they bring home.

After taking the packet-boat before-mentioned, perceiving our vessels to be foul, we steered our course for Boca del Toro, there to careen our ships. This place is already mentioned in the History of the Buccaneers, and is often frequented by Pirates for the same purpose. Here we met with Captain Peter Harris, in a Dutch ship of thirty-two guns, and also with Captain Richard Sawkins, who was in a small brigantine mounted with only four guns. Both these ships had put in there either to careen or refresh themselves with water and other provisions.

Having cleansed and careened our bottoms to our satisfaction, we afterwards cruized again for some while, in hopes of finding some such purchase as we most desired. But, being frustrated of our expectations, at last we resolved to quit again our ships and land on the coast of Darien, thinking there to find what we so long had sought for—or at least [to] plunder and pillage some towns belonging to that coast. This resolution therefore we presently put in execution; and, standing over towards the land of Darien, we soon after went on shore there, and began to range up and down the woods, designing to take some prisoners who might serve us with intelligence and be our guides, as being totally ignorant of the country. Here we found an Indian that could speak Spanish, whom therefore we examined very strictly, where the gold and silver of that country did lie; for we had heard that both these coveted metals were digged out or found in some parts of that province by the Spaniards. He told us that not far distant from there there was a place called Tocamora (for so it was named), which was the receptacle-town of all the gold that was found in those parts, saying often unto us in the Spanish language, and repeating these words, *mucho oro ay en Tocamora*, that is *a great deal of gold lieth at Tocamora*, and that he would guide us unto it. With these promises we were infinitely encouraged, and resolved not to return unto our ships until such time as we had made some considerable booty, at least sufficient for one voyage, to satisfy our earnest appetite for gold. We landed in Darien, according to what I can best remember, either about the latter end of March or the beginning of April, in the year 1680, when began the chiefest and hardest of our adventures both by land and sea—those I have rehearsed being only the *preludiums* of such as were to follow.

By the way, as we marched towards Tocamora under the conduct of our Indian, we took other prisoners, and learned from them other things. That the Indians of that country hated mortally the Spaniards and were at enmity with them: that they had a chief Captain, or leader, whom they styled Emperor, and who would be glad of our assistance against the Spaniards, by whom he had been much wronged, and was therefore with them in open and continual war. That, in recompense of our service, he would certainly lead us unto those places where most gold and silver was to be had, these being unjustly detailed from him, and where it was but fighting for it, and having more than we should be able to carry away. These allurements put our minds upon new designs, and were sufficient to entice us to present our auxiliary service unto the Emperor of that country, as judging it more convenient to be put in possession, or rather led unto those so vastly rich places, by the Emperor and the Indians themselves than to have both Indians and Spaniards all at once against us; especially in a foreign country where we knew not one step of the way.

Thus, after an intercourse of some few messengers who were sent to and fro, we came at last (not to be too tedious in the narrative) unto a view and amicable parley with the Emperor himself in person, who readily accepted of our service and promised himself great matters from our aid and assistance against the Spaniards. He failed not to promise us great heaps of gold, would we but fight courageously under his conduct, and regain those places from the Spaniards where they were most certainly to be found. These things we easily believed as feasible, and therefore as readily did embrace his propositions; yet, should we fail of our designs, we had still other things under consideration, which might in great probability be as profitable and turn to the same account. The sum of these was to descend by the river of Darien, or any other, into the South Sea, and there to rove up and down until such time as we could meet any rich prize, or galleon coming from Lima to Panama, or else to plunder again either the city of Panama or any other of so many rich towns and villages are known to border upon the coasts of that sea. As for shipping, though we had it not at present, yet we feared not to obtain it by the help of those canoes we should employ to carry us down the river. After which, we considered it would be no great difficulty to return homewards, either round about the Strait of Magellan, which navigation, though difficult, had been performed by others, or through the same country of Darien, where we were at present. Thus we engaged, about the number of 300 men, in the service of this Indian Emperor, whom we took for our leader, in company of many others of his own subjects, who were to back our designs, as we intended to lead the van of most attempts. The name of this Emperor aforementioned was Andræas, from which we guessed that some footsteps of Christianity had been planted in his country by the Spaniards, and that either he or his ancestors had been by them baptized, though at present they seemed to regard but little what belonged unto Christian religion. He had also a son, whose name was Augustin, and unto whom we made bold, among ourselves, to give the name of King Golden-Cap, from a certain cap, or hat, of pure and massive gold which he had then upon his head when first we saw him.

The first enterprize which the said Emperor propounded unto us was to take the town of Santa Maria, situated pretty near unto the Southern Sea and at the distance of several days journey from the place where these things were agreed upon. This town, as it was said, had been taken from the Emperor by the covetous Spaniard, and was reported to be hugely rich in dust of gold, which there was gathered in great quantity out of the river that runs through the country. Here was a fort and a town pretty well garrisoned, as having between both about 400 Spaniards for their defence and to guard the treasure which there was lodged of gold-dust, as has been said. We marched, therefore, in company of the Emperor Andræas (who always went before us, and encouraged our men wherever they fought) the space of three days journey, to meet his son King Golden-Cap at his own habitation, or palace, lying in our way, he being to join with us in this expedition. He entertained us very nobly at this palace for a day or two, and sent us also presents of victuals to meet us by the way, having heard of our coming. Thence we departed with our entire little camp, the Emperor, and his son, in quest of the town of Santa Maria, as yet distant from there no less than four or five days journey. After several fatigues sustained by the way, together with the loss of some of our canoes by the downfalls of the rivers, and trees likewise which the Spaniards had cast therein to hinder our passage, we arrived by night within two or three miles of Santa Maria, and there reposed ourselves in the woods until the next morning.

Day being come, we marched towards the town, and gave the assault unto the place and fort: both which we carried, or possessed ourselves of, with no great difficulty and an inconsiderable loss on our side, consisting only of three men, though several others were wounded. Of the Spaniards we killed and wounded above 100. The fort was encompassed with palisades, called also by the Spaniards *estacadas* or huge strong and thick pales of wood. Having taken the fort and town, and examined our prisoners very severely concerning the treasure we there expected to find, all that we got out of them was very inconsiderable, in view of the huge expectations we had conceived in our minds. For the Spaniards, having timely notice of our march, had conveyed away unto remoter places, towards Panama, some few days before, all that was valuable upon the place; so that our disappointment here in this particular was very great, and all that ever we could rob and pillage, either in the town or fort, scarce amounted unto twenty pound weight of gold and some small quantity of silver.

Our stay here at Santa Maria was but short, not above the space of two days, our resolutions being to seek revenge for the huge loss, or rather disappointment, we had sustained of our vast expectations. We had here intelligence given us of some mine or mines of gold that were somewhere to be found farther on about this place, called St Maries River, but whether it might prove to be worth our time and labour to go seek them (especially considering we knew how not to come at the gold when we should find them out, and that the Spaniards and miners, or slaves, would be all fled, transporting with them what was already digged out) we could not easily determine. Hereupon we all unanimously agreed to visit the South Sea, unto which we were already very near, in those canoes we had brought with us, which were sufficient for our number, concluding either to attack Panama and ransack it anew, as Sir Henry Morgan had done before us, or at least that we should meet with some considerable prize in that Sea where ships do navigate so quietly and but few pirates were ever seen.

Thus, having taken in what provisions we thought necessary, we fell down the river in our canoes, taking the opportunity of the tide, and arrived the next day at the mouth of the river in sight of the South Sea. Here we were all in danger of being lost with our canoes, the wind blowing extremely hard and causing a violent storm, which overwhelmed one of our canoes with seven or eight men, who had all inevitably perished had they not been taken up with the utmost extremity of danger of others who ventured their lives to save them. This river we went down into the South Sea I think was called Darien, though I cannot be very positive herein. Being now come into the Pacific, or South Sea, we sailed, or rowed, along the shore towards Panama, which is not far distant from the mouth of the river, where we disembogued[1], touching at several places or little islands in our way to take in water or search for provisions for our fleet of canoes. All this while we had in our company the Emperor and his son Golden-Cap, together with the Indians they brought into the field, so that we were a pretty considerable fleet of fisher-boats or canoes: each canoe had six, eight, or ten men on board, yea some had fourteen and more. At Plantin Isle, which isle lies between the mouth of the river we came out at and Panama, we seized a Spanish bark, which had a considerable number of men on board her, I believe above 100, but nothing else that was worth our acceptance. This vessel we took in hopes of a good prize, and withal to mend ourselves in shipping, for this was now the biggest bottom we had.

By this time those of Panama had received advice of our adventures at Santa Maria, as also of our coming into the South Sea either in quest of that city or of some other hazardous attempt. They were, therefore, infinitely alarmed at these news, and in great haste had thrust out to sea three or four small vessels or barks, though withal pretty well manned, which they called *La Armadilla*, or The Little Fleet, out of design to guard their coasts and oppose our attempts. Thus the very next day we came into the South Sea one of these barks belonging to the Armadilla came up with us,

[1] See note 2 on p. 309.

and very briskly fired at our fleet, as if they would fight us all; but soon tacked about and bid us adieu, having killed [of] us one man and wounded six or seven more. Two days after we met with three more of these barks belonging to the Armadilla of Panama, whereof the one had on board, as well as I can remember, 90 men; another had fourscore; and the third threescore and five. These small men-of-war met with us at a great disadvantage, for that morning we had sent away the Spanish bark which we had taken at Plantin Isle, to seek for fresh water at some places, we having been disappointed of it where we had sought for it before; and, to the intent she might go the safer and peradventure bring us some good purchase by the way, we had put on board her above 100 of our best men: so that what bottoms we had left were only canoes, and in them not above 200 good fighting-men, for of the Indians we made no great account, as wanting both our arms and experience to manage them. The Armadilla came up with full sail unto us, and engaged us very stoutly, thinking to take or destroy every canoe in our fleet; but we, knowing scarce any quarter could be expected at their hands especially in those seas, were resolved never to surrender, and do the utmost of our endeavour to destroy them or make them fly. Thus, after the first volleys of shot, we presently encompassed one of these little men-of-war with our canoes, and as desperately ran him aboard with sword and pistol in hand, causing him suddenly to surrender. Being in possession of him, we took another of their small number, and forced the third to fly away towards the town of Panama with all the sail he could make: this rencounter, or engagement, though but short, yet was very bloody—especially on the Spaniards' side—and sharp; for in it we had a dozen of our men killed outright, and almost forty who were desperately wounded. How many the Spaniards lost or had wounded among them we could not learn—especially in the third vessel, which fought us all along very briskly and stood close to it for a good while even after the other two were taken; so that we could not do otherwise than commend the courage of those Spaniards.

The Armadilla being destroyed, we proceeded to the road of Panama, which we instantly blocked up with our canoes and other vessels, which now were three or four. Here in the harbour, and at the mouth thereof, we took five or six vessels more, or rather ships, between great and small—but no great booty in them: amongst these only was one, called *La Trinidad*, or *The Blessed Trinity*, which was a ship of four-hundred tons and in which we found about threescore-thousand pieces-of-eight, that were sent to pay the garrison of the town or for some other effect. In this ship, being a good, strong and tight vessel, we came afterwards for England. The dividend of this prize amounted unto above 240 pieces-of-eight to each man; yet had we good fortune in not being disappointed of this purchase, as we had been oftentimes before in other adventures; for though we had blocked up the mouth of the road, and lay, as I have said, before Panama, yet this ship gave us the slip, and got into the harbour in the dark of the night both unseen and unknown to us. However, we having intelligence thereof, entered the harbour when they thought themselves in safety, and had the good luck to seize and make a prize of her, though not without some small loss of men. Both in this and other skirmishes we lost in all before Panama 40 men, and had about 50 more wounded; so that now our small number was almost, if not quite, reduced unto two-third parts thereof. The wounded we all put into one vessel, which we appointed to be the hospital of our fleet, and the other vessels we manned as well as our number would afford to do it. After having stayed some days before Panama and blocked up the road, we weighed anchor, and went unto a little island named Tobago, there to provide ourselves with several necessaries, which were at that instant something scarce with us. As for the town of Panama itself, we dared not to attempt it with so small a number of men, they being well provided to give us a hot reception: only once we landed 150 men, which were as many as we could well spare from manning and defending our fleet of canoes and ships; but found we could do no good against the town, being repulsed with some damage, which notwithstanding we made a good retreat unto our fleet.

Being almost ready to raise the blockade of Panama, Captain John Coxon (or Croxen) began to vary in his resolutions, and at last openly to mutiny against the rest of the Company: the effect hereof was that he departed from us and returned back with the Emperor and his son King Golden-

Cap and all the Indians and canoes they had brought with them, carrying also with him 50 of our English company and the best surgeon of the fleet, who belonged unto him and who would not go without his instruments to work withal, that is to say the medicaments, which we very much wanted for our wounded men. What medicines he left behind were not considerable in comparison of what he carried away; but this point we knew not till afterwards, or we should have torn in pieces the said surgeon and his master rather than have parted with those things of which we had so much necessity. This piece of dishonesty of Captain Coxon weakened much our forces and diminished in great measure our number; for, had he taken care of or carried away our wounded men, we should not much have resented his departure, the Indians being of no considerable help unto us. But here, that he may be known, I will not omit to tell you that the chief occasion of his grudge against us was because we reproached him for his ill-behaviour in the engagement we had with the Armadilla of Panama; for in that dangerous action, to speak it all in a word, he shewed himself more like a coward than one of our profession, that is to say a true Buccaneer. What adventures he and his company met withal after they separated from us I cannot give any just account thereof; only that as we learned afterwards he went back unto the mouth of the river, and over land much by the same way he had come before, till he came to the North Sea (where doubtless he found the ships we had left behind us), being civilly entertained all along by those Indians and the good Emperor Andræas and his son, though he had done them no great service—which sheweth the civility of those Indians, and what inclinations they had for us English rather than the Spaniards, their ancient masters. Thus we disengaged from the pretended service we had proffered unto that Emperor—I call it pretended, forasmuch as any one would easily guess that the real intent thereof was only to serve ourselves with gold and silver, and learn intelligence from those Indians where it was to be had, or, what is more obvious, to be led by them unto it—especially considering that, had we gone any other way about this matter, it might have cost us every one of our lives; for these Indians of Darien are very fierce withal, and are the same people that killed and tore in pieces that famous Buccaneer L'Ollonais (of whom you may read many notable exploits in the History of the Buccaneers) and many other of his companions, for landing upon and offering violence to their country and habitations.

But our constant resolutions were, not to go back nor return homewards until such time as we had made a diligent search into those Southern Seas, and freighted, if possible, our vessels with gold, or at least as much silver as they could carry : such vast expectations had we framed now unto ourselves, in the vain ideas of our minds. Captain Coxon, who commanded in chief, being separated or departed from us, we chose in his place Captain Sawkins and Captain Sharp to lead us, and were now reduced unto 200 men, whereof many, as was said before, lay dangerously wounded in the hospital-vessel.

Having, therefore, refitted ourselves at the island of Tobago, which is situated over-against the road of Panama, we sailed thence about the middle of May, 1680, in quest of some other purchase or design, coasting the shore towards the Northern parts of America commonly called California. We persisted in our course the space of eight or ten days, in all which time nothing remarkable happened unto us ; till at the end thereof we arrived at the isles of Quiblo, where there is a town called by the Spaniards Puebla Nueva.

Here we landed to seek provisions, and by the by to plunder what we could get ; but, the country being alarmed since our blocking up the road of Panama, they had put themselves into an indifferent good posture of defence, and hereupon watched for our coming, and were resolved to entertain us as warmly as they could. Captain Sawkins therefore, landing before the rest, as being a man of undaunted courage, and running up with a small party to some breast-works they had made before the town, was here unfortunately killed, more through his own temerity and the rashness of his conduct than any other cause. Those who followed could not possibly rescue him, as being not yet quite landed : besides him, two or three more were killed and five or six wounded, which caused the residue of those he had led up to retreat unto the waterside as fast as they could. Thus we were beaten off from the place, and got nothing but blows for our pains.

But this disaster occasioned a second mutiny amongst our men : our Commanders were not thought to be leaders fit enough for such great and hard enterprizes. Now Captain Sharp was left in chief, and he was censured by many. The contest grew so hot and came to that degree that we divided again into parties, and about threescore-and-ten more of our men fell off from us, separated, and returned back overland, as Coxon and the others had done before. Others who commanded vessels threw up their commissions (I can only name unto you Captain Cook for one), in whose room others were placed to command their ships. Thus all things were in great distraction, and our company decreased daily; yet others held constant to their resolutions, and were still determined to be buried in those seas rather than to return home without the gold they had fought for so long and through so many dangers. At the mouth of the river belonging to this place we surprised a bark, or great boat, which was laden with maize, or Indian wheat, which stood us in very good stead at that present; for provisions now again began to grow somewhat scarce with us. Our Commander now was Captain Sharp, and our number was only of 130, or not quite 140.

We sailed from Puebla Nueva, and steered our course for the islands called De los Galapagos, or in English Tortoise Islands, from the huge number of tortoises which there are to be found. These islands, which are seven or eight, all comprehended under the same name, lie very close unto, if not under, the equinoctial line: there we intended to careen our vessels and seek more provisions; but, the winds proving contrary for a long while, we could not reach them, and were constrained to take up for the same purpose with another little island called Gorgona, where indifferent good accommodation was found for refitting our ships. Here we careened and got in provisions, staying here for these two intents above a month, so that it was towards the latter end of July before we departed thence. Three or four days after we set out from Gorgona we lost Captain Sharp in the dark of the night, and with him the best vessel we had, which was the *Trinity*, the same ship which we had taken out of the harbour of Panama. This loss occasioned sundry distractions in our minds, not knowing what would become of us after so many misfortunes: he was gone from us a whole fortnight or thereabouts; neither had we any hopes of finding him any more, till at last, we happening to put in at Drake's Isle to seek for provisions, he happily arrived there three days after, which caused in us infinite joy, he having the best vessel and stoutest men on board: yes, we had missed of him this time likewise, and perhaps for ever, had we not, by a misfortune of sinking our canoe, which was sent ashore, tarried there one day longer than we determined.

Having sailed from Drake's Isle, we arrived in seven or eight days after over against Guayaquil. Hereabouts, by night, we took a little Spanish man-of-war, like unto the vessel of the Armadilla of Panama; who was come out from Guayaquil, and in a true blue Spanish bravado had undertaken to take or destroy us with that little tool and only 30 or 40 men. The Captain's name was Don Thomas de Argandona, of which name and family, as I am credibly informed, there have been several sea-commanders in this age who were both skilful and courageous men. The vessel we thought fit to sink, as being of no use unto us and wanting men to man her. In the fight we lost none of our men, and only three were wounded; what the Spaniards lost I do not remember. The prisoners told us that some of our men who had deserted us at Puebla Nueva had landed in a bark not far from Guayaquil, and that all of them were killed by the inhabitants of an island where they landed, excepting one: what became of the rest, I have not yet learned. This was the occasion of fitting out this bark against us, little thinking perhaps that we had a ship of four-hundred ton under us, and only being persuaded they should meet with some such little bark or canoe as that was, whose men their neighbours had destroyed a little before.

About a week or ten days after, we took another prize more valuable than the former: this was a ship of three-hundred ton called *St Peter*, and was loaden with coco-nuts, broad-cloth, timber, and other goods, and was bound for Lima, which is the capital city of Peru. We took out of her what we most wanted, or thought fit for our designs, and, having cut down the main mast, let her go with all the prisoners we had, and most of the provisions that was on board her. This was about the beginning of September, 1680, as my notes tell me.

Towards the latter end of October we descried the land of Arica, having sustained beforehand for many days infinite hunger and thirst. For provisions at length grew so scarce with us that we were allowed only five ounces of meal, and one pint of water to each man, the Captain himself having no more allowance than the rest : yea, at last, some were found among us who gave 30 pieces-of-eight for a pint of water, and very glad they were to get it, so near starving we were when we came to Arica. Here we could land no men, the sea was so big, which made us go to a port close by called He lo he.

At this port we landed, and found some provisions, especially at a sugar-works not far distant thence. Here we refreshed, and feasted ourselves pretty well for three or four days. The Spaniards came unto us with a flag of truce, and promised to bring us in good store of beeves and hogs, as many as we demanded, provided we would spare their *ingenio de azucar*, or sugar-works, and not pull it down ; which we promised to do. But, two days after, these treacherous Spaniards sent 300 horsemen against us, instead of bringing the cattle, with full intent to destroy us if possibly they could. We drew out our men into a plain, and at the first volley killed several of them, which made them wheel about and instantly retire, though at first they came very fiercely against us. With this we retired to our vessels, knowing no more good was to be done there at that time, nor at Arica ; for by this body of horse we perceived all the country was alarmed against us.

From He lo he that day month we arrived at Coquimbo, upon which place we resolved to revenge our former affronts at Arica. Here we met with a body of 150 horse just at our landing, which always watch the bay ; who instantly set upon us with great fury, and made a circle about the first party of our men that were landed, thinking to make sure of our destruction and cut us all in pieces. But we stood to our arms very courageously, killed and wounded several of them, and routed them soon, having only one man wounded on our side. We followed them close at their heels into the town, which we instantly took with no loss at all. This action was performed with only four-score men, a few more or less, and the first party that fought the horse were under 40. When we came into the town, we found it was of a considerable bigness, and had no less than eight or nine churches, which made us fear there were more inhabitants than we could master, as being so few in number that it were impossible to fight our way through them, should they come to a head and make any resistance. As therefore we met the inhabitants, we told them they must repair to the church or churches, or else expect no quarter from them that were following us who were many hundreds in number; for we were only the forerunners of a greater body of Pirates that were at our heels. Having so done, and got several churches full of the inhabitants, we placed at each door a barrel of gunpowder with a train to it and a man standing with a lighted match, who told them that, if they offered to stir out, he would presently give fire; but none offered to attempt it. So that by this means, while the inhabitants remained in that confinement, we plundered the town at our leisure. Here we found great store of provisions of all sorts; for the town is very pleasant and finely adorned with orchards of fruit, vineyards, and gardens. At Coquimbo is also gold-dust to be found in a river that runneth close by the place. Here another piece of treachery was put upon us by the Governor of the town. After a flag of truce and some complements sent to and fro between us, he came to an amicable parley with our Captain and only two more, one on each side, where they drank very friendly together upon a hill close by the town, he keeping the fields with his horsemen and all those that were fled out of the town. There he promised to ransom the town from fire, for 95,000 pieces-of-eight, which should be sent us in within a day or two. But that night or the next they contrived to fire our ship, an Indian swimming aboard under the stern with a ball of combustible matter, which he fixed there unseen to our men; so that, had it not been discovered by the stink before it burst out into a flame, we had all, both on shore and land, inevitably perished. The next day they half-drowned the town by letting in many sluices of water upon us; by which acts of hostility and treachery we perceived no faith nor money more than what we had already got was to be expected from them. Thus we set fire to the town, staying as long as we could till it was all in a flame, locked up the doors of the churches, and marched out, fighting our way down to our boats, which we easily did, for they made no great opposition after the first volleys of our shot, which killed some few of them. Here we set Captain Argandona on shore, Captain Peralta, who was taken in the ship that was bound for Lima, and other prisoners which we had still remaining on board our vessel, and whom we all along entertained very well. We were in possession of the town of Coquimbo only four or five days, and for our booty we brought away five-hundred pound weight of plate, besides jewels, goods, and other things.

From Coquimbo we sailed to the isles of Juan Fernandez, where we kept our Christmas that year 1680, finding there good plenty of provisions, and as much dissention among our men—who would not return home that year, as our Captain would have them to do, but make a farther search for gold, or golden prizes, into those seas. But the true occasion of their grudge was that Captain Sharp had got by these adventures, as it was said, almost a-thousand pound, whereas many of our men were scarce worth a groat: and good reason there was for their poverty, for at the Isle of Plata, called by us Drake's Isle, and other places, they had lost all their money to their fellow Buccaneers at dice—so that some had a great deal, and others just nothing. Those who were thrifty men sided with Captain Sharp, and were for returning home; but the others chose another Commander, by name John Watling, and turned Sharp out of his commission, pretending they could do it as being a free election. And so they might do, for they were the greatest number by far; and power may pretend to any thing. This contest had like to have come to blows among us; but some prudent men moderated the matter, and persuaded Captain Sharp's party to have patience for a while—at least seeing they were the fewest, and had moneys to lose, which the other party had not.

By order of our new Commander Watling we set sail presently after the beginning of the New Year 1681 from the isles of Juan Fernandez, and were resolved to go and plunder Arica, both to find employment for our discontented party, as being a vastly rich place, and to remember them for the shams put upon us at He lo he or Ylo. Just as we were ready to sail, three men-of-war came upon us, one of eight, another of twelve, and the third of sixteen guns. We had not so much as one gun, for all our vessel was of four-hundred ton or more. Neither had we now more than one ship, we having sunk the *Mayflower*, wherein Captain Cox sailed, upon the coast of Guayaquil, by reason we had broken her bowsprit with the stern of the *Trinity*, which had her in a tow, and could not fit her with another. These ships now being three against one, and we not able to divide them, as we endeavoured to do, by running on board their Admiral before the rest could come up, we thought fit to run for it. So we did, bidding them adieu in the night, and steering directly, as I have mentioned, for Arica.

We landed at Arica, and fought the town with 93 men, which number was all we could conveniently spare. We got into the town and took several of their breast-works, yet were repulsed from the castle, and afterwards beaten out of the town by the country-people, who poured in upon us in huge numbers ; so that we were forced to retreat unto our boats, fighting our way through above 1000 men who were gathered against us : this was the hardest shock we had in all the South Sea. Captain Watling, our Commander-in-chief, was here killed ; through whose ill-conduct, as it was thought, this misfortune happened unto us. For, had he assaulted the fort in time, before the people and soldiers that ran out of the town were got into it, we had undoubtedly carried all before us. But he trifled away his time in giving quarter and taking prisoners upon the breastworks, till at last we had more prisoners than we could command. We placed some of these prisoners before the front of our men, when we assaulted the castle, just as Sir Henry Morgan did the nuns and friars at Porto Bello ; but the Spaniards fired as well at them as at us. In a word, we lost here 40 men, nine of which were taken prisoners, being our surgeons and others, while they were dressing the wounded at the hospital ; which loss of our surgeons increased our damage very much, and only 42 or 43 were left serviceable to fight our way through so many hundred of foot and horse unto our boats, we not losing one man by the way, though several were wounded : so much did we awe them with our fuzees, and so afraid were they to break in upon us, though we were almost three miles from our boats. This repulse we resented more than any other we ever sustained before, since here was more plate and gold than we could well carry away, by reason it is the *embarcadero*, or place where all the vast riches that are brought from the mountains of Potosy are shipped off for Panama, whence it goes into Spain. Now Captain Sharp was chosen again, his conduct being thought safer than any other man's, and they having had trial of another leader. Our surgeons we left behind had quarter from the enemy, they being able to do good service in that country ; but our wounded men were all knocked on the head, as we understood afterwards. This misfortune fell to us on the 30th of January, being King Charles' day, as I can remember by some tokens.

Having set sail from Arica, we cruized to and fro for the space of six weeks, but could meet with nothing that was to our purpose. By this time provisions grew scarce again, and our men began to mutiny anew; some being for going home, and others for staying longer till they had got more moneys. To find them employment we put in at a place called Guasco. Here we landed some of our men, took some prisoners, and got in provisions, but did nothing else considerable. We landed again afterwards within two leagues of Ylo, or He lo he, where we took many prisoners, and thanked them for their former kindness unto us, which we had not yet forgotten, as they found by experience this time.

After this, about the middle of April, 1681, our dissentions grew so high among us that above 40 more of our men deserted us, and in boats and canoes rowed away from us, to go home overland through the province of Darien, as their companions had done before. They steered their course in quest of St Maries River, belonging to that country, as was mentioned before: their chief grudge was against Captain Sharp, whom they envied and would not obey; neither would we be brought to choose another Commander, knowing that neither by that means we should ever be able to keep them quiet. Thus we parted with them, allowing them what was necessary for their voyage, or they rather taking it away with them; but we would not quarrel about it. Now our company and forces were extremely weakened, but our hearts as yet were good; and, though we had met with many disappointments in several places, yet we hoped that at last, by some means or other, we should attain the ends of our desires, which was to enrich ourselves.

Finding it very cold and bad weather in the latitude where we were, we sailed Northward, and about the beginning of May we came to the Gulf of Nicoya, where we anchored at an island called Chero. Here we took down our upper-deck, and sank our quarter-deck, and fitted ourselves very well to sea again. This was all performed by help of a Spanish carpenter and six or seven of his men, who were building some vessels in a river close by. We rewarded them for their pains with one of our barks, which we gave them, and for their sakes turned loose all our prisoners, excepting some negroes, which we detailed to do our drudgery. One man was lost here, who was drowned, our drunken men overturning the boat as they came from shore.

From Chero we went to the island of El Cavallo, where we lost our interpreter, who had done us good service all along, and at this place ran away from us, as we judged, unto the Spaniards, leaving behind him all that he had purchased in the voyage, which was worth nigh 500 pound in money and goods. What should be his intent in this action we could not know, except to betray us unto that nation.

He was a Dutchman by birth, and his name James Marquis, and was very intelligent in the Spanish *lingua*, and besides that in several others. After his departure we had no great use for an interpreter, neither now did we much want one; yet, in what occasions we had, we made use of one Mr. Ringrose, who was with us in all this voyage, and being a good scholar and full of ingeniosity had also good skill in languages. This gentleman kept an exact and very curious *Journal* of all our voyage from our first setting out to the very last day; took also all the observations we made, and likewise an accurate description of all the ports, towns, and lands we came to. His papers, or rather his diary, with all his drafts, are now in the hands of a person of my acquaintance at Wapping in London, and, as he telleth me, are very nigh being printed, which, if it be so, as I hope he will not fail to do it, I shall refer you for the truth of what I have here said, unto those papers; for I desire to be corrected by them, if in any thing here delivered my memory has failed me, for I am certain he kept all along the best and truest account of all things that happened, beyond any man about us, and observed more particularities than any one else. Yet I am sure I have not much deviated from the truth in what is here set down; only that, perhaps, I have omitted many things which I have forgotten, my notes being very short concerning all the voyage.

In June, 1681, we cleaned our vessel in the gulf called Dulce, which we had not done so long before, and you may easily believe was by this time very foul. Having sailed thence, towards El Cabo de San Francisco, or Cape St Francis, somewhere about that Cape in July we took a ship that was bound for Panama and was laden with cacao-nuts, and had besides some small quantity of plate on board her. We took out of her the plate and goods, and what else we pleased, cut down the main-mast, and so let her go before the wind towards the port she was bound unto. About a fortnight after, at Cabo del Paffao, we took another small prize which was bound for Paita or Lima, that being the harbour, or landing-place, of all that goes up to that great city, the head of Peru. This was only a kind of packet-boat that was going from Panama to Paita: she ran in under the shore when we gave her chase, and most of the passengers and other people got to land; but we took the greatest part of them, and dismissed them the next day, not knowing what to do with them, so they were forced to foot it overland back again to Panama. The vessel likewise we turned loose before the wind, the next day after we had rummaged her pretty well, as having no farther service for her. The next after, we came up with another sail at Cape Paffao (where we took the packet-boat), which proved to be one of the greatest adventures of this whole voyage, if not the greatest of all, had we but known our own happy fortune, and how to make good use of it. This was a ship called *El Santo Rosario*, or *The Holy Rosary*, of an indifferent big burthen and loaded with brandy and oil, wine and fruit, besides good store of other provisions. They fired at us first, but we came up-board to board with them, and gave them such volleys of small shot that they were soon forced to surrender, having several of their men wounded, their Captain killed, and one only man more. In this ship, besides the lading above-mentioned, we found also almost 700 pigs of plate, but we took them to be some other metal, especially tin: and under this mistake they were slighted by us all, especially the Captain and seamen, who by no persuasions used by some few, who were for having them rummaged, could not be induced to take them into our ship, as we did most of the other things. Thus we left them on board the *Rosario*, and, not knowing what to do with the bottom in that scarcity of men we were under, we turned her away loose unto the sea, being very glad we had got such good belly-timber out of her and thinking little what quantity of rich metal we left behind. It should seem this plate was not yet thoroughly refined and fitted for to coin; and this was the occasion that deceived us all. One only pig of plate, out of the whole number of almost 700, we took into our ship, thinking to make bullets of it ; and to this effect, or what else our seamen pleased, the greatest part of it was melted or squandered away. Afterwards, when we arrived at Antigua, we gave the remaining part of it, which was yet about one-third thereof, unto a Bristol man, who knew presently what it was (though he dissembled with us), brought it to England, and sold it there for seventy-five-pound sterling, as he confessed himself afterwards to some of our men. Thus we parted with the richest booty we had gotten in the whole voyage, through our own ignorance and laziness.

In this ship, the *Rosario*, we took also a great book full of sea-charts and maps, containing a very accurate and exact description of all the ports, sounding, creeks, rivers, capes, and coasts belonging to the South Sea, and all the navigations usually performed by the Spaniards in that ocean. This book, it seemeth, serveth them for an entire and complete *Wagender*[1], in those parts, and for its novelty and curiosity was presented unto His Majesty after our return into England. It has been since translated into English, as I hear, by His Majesty's order, and the copy of the translation, made by a Jew, I have seen at Wapping ; but withal the printing thereof is severely prohibited, lest other nations should get into those seas and make use thereof, which is wished may be reserved only for England against its due time. The seaman who at first laid hold on it, on board the *Rosario*, told us the Spaniards were going to cast this book overboard, but that he prevented them, which notwithstanding we scarce did give entire credit unto, as knowing in what confusion they all were. Had the Captain himself been alive at that time, his story would have deserved more belief ; yet, howsoever, if the Spaniards did not attempt to throw this book into the sea, at least they ought to have done it for the reasons that are obvious to every man's understanding and are hinted at before. We parted with the *Rosario* and her plate the last day of July, 1681.

Here it was, at Cape Paffao, immediately after our turning away to sea the *Rosario*, and on the first or second day of August, 1681, that we set up our resolutions to seek no farther into those seas, but to come away for England round about the Strait of Magellan or by Strait Le Maire. This voyage

[1] Lucas Wagenaer, *Den Nieuwen Spieghel der Zeevaert . . . in diversche Zeecaerten begrepen ;* folio, Amsterdam 1596.

we thought less dangerous by far, seeing others had performed it before us, than to go overland, as our companions went, through such great and imminent dangers both of Indians and Spaniards; through which nations, peradventure, we should be forced to fight our way almost every step we made: after which, when we came to the North Sea, we knew not how to get any shipping to convey us unto Jamaica; for we could not question but our own ships were either departed long before that time or at least taken up and carried away by our companions and deserters; besides that we had too much goods and luggage to carry overland, taken out of our several prizes, which we were unwilling to lose. Our chief motives for this sudden departure for England were the huge scarcity of men we had at that present; for now our whole number was reduced unto 64 men, whereof many were not fit to bear arms, as being negroes and others, that had only courage or skill to do our drudgery: this number, we feared, by any farther encounters might be so far lessened as scarce to be able to man our ship, at least to convey us home in safety; whereby, should we weaken it more, we might come to lose all we had got. And now we had purchased in the *Rosario* good store of provisions, especially of wine and brandy, sufficient to last, as we hoped, for such a voyage; which, should we diminish upon farther adventures, we knew not when we should be so well provided again. The last motive was that most of our men had gotten pretty well by this voyage, and were afraid to lose by farther adventures what they had already purchased; for, though some of our men had made away or lost all their money at play, yet others were so much the richer by their losses. For these reasons we set sail from Cape Paffao on the third day of August, to seek for the Strait of Magellan, or that of Le Maire, thereby to return into England, or at least unto the Leeward Islands.

This voyage round about the Strait of Magellan, or rather beyond it, as also beyond the Strait of Le Maire, we performed in just six months, a day or two more or less, till we arrived at Antego at the end of January, 1681, having set forth from Cape Paffao, in the South Sea, at the beginning of August, 1681, as was said before. In all this long and tedious voyage very little happened unto us that was remarkable, neither had we any encounter with enemies either by sea or land that is worth rehearsing—only two or three things I shall hint unto you by the by.

At Paita, which is the landing-place, or harbour, belonging to the court of Lima, situated some few miles distant from the sea, we endeavoured to land some of our men upon the side of the bay. Having manned already our canoes for this intent with 30 or 40 men, which was now the greatest number we could spare, we descried many hundred men, both horse and foot, drawn up into battle-array, who waited for our landing. By this sight we perceived that we were discovered, and that the whole country was alarmed against us, whereby we judged it would be the greatest piece of rashness in the world to go ashore and throw ourselves, being so few, into the mouths of so many enemies. Hereupon we gave over the design we had against that rich place, went back into our ship, and sailed away for the Strait of Fernando de Magellan.

In October we had very hard weather, that we had much ado to keep the seas. This was, if I well remember, about 50 degrees and a half of Southern latitude. Here, in this stress of weather, we spied a high land, unto which we made, and came to an anchor in a good harbour, where we moved our ship to the land. Here we stayed all the remaining part of that month, which was about three weeks, fishing and fowling for our maintenance, as much as the weather would permit us—thereby to save our other provisions. We took one Indian prisoner, but could not learn of him what country that was, as not understanding his language: we sought for others, but they were fled. These Indians are very wild, and do eat raw flesh. Unto this place we gave the name of the Duke of York's Island, more by guess than anything else; for whether it were an island or continent we could not tell—only we conceived it to be so, and that other islands there might be adjoining unto it. One of our company, whose name was Shergall, was drowned as we went into the harbour, falling overboard from the sprit-sail-top.

About the beginning of November, we set forth again hence, seeking for the Straits either of Magellan or Le Maire, but could find neither of them. The hardness of the weather was such that we missed both of them, and were driven many degrees beyond them: neither could we make any land, but came round about such a way as peradventure never any mortals came before us. Yet nothing remarkable did we see or meet withal, except hard weather, and here and there some floats of ice of two or three leagues long. We were very nigh 60 degrees of Southern latitude: this is all I can remember, not having any Journal nor the particular observations by me that were taken when the weather permitted.

Thus we arrived, by God's infinite mercy, in safety at the island of Barbados, just at the latter end of January, 1681. Here a boat came off to us that belonged to the *Richmond* frigate: we were afraid of the said frigate, lest she should seize us for pirateering, and strip us of all we had got in the whole voyage. Hereupon we stood away for the isle of Antigua, but could not get leave to come into the harbour, though to obtain it we sent a present of jewels unto the Governor's lady; but he would not grant it, and our jewels were returned us very civilly. Hence we resolved every one to shift for ourselves: the ship in which we came home, which was the *Trinity*, as I have said before, taken by us at Panama, we gave away to seven or eight of our men who had payed away all their money. Thus we dispersed, some of our company coming to England, others going to Jamaica, Barbados, New England, Virginia, and other places. The island of Barbados was the very first land we descried in the whole voyage of three-months' time, that is ever since we set out from the Duke of York's Island, as we named the place at the beginning of November. This navigation, performed by us, proves that several degrees more to the South of the Strait of Magellan, or that of Le Maire—especially about 58, 59, or 60 degrees of Southern latitude—there is a much easier passage from the North unto the South Sea than through either of these two Straits. Also that there is no such continent as *Terra Australis incognita*, as is named and described in all the ancient maps: so that it is but steering many degrees higher to the South and one may go as easily into the South Sea, or come thence into the North Sea, as we can go from England to Jamaica, only that the voyage, peradventure, will be something longer than by the Strait of Magellan, which makes not much to the purpose, but is rather much better seeing it is performed through an open sea and with less danger by far than through either of those Straits. All these things I hope will very distinctly be made out in the papers, maps, and drafts of that ingenious man Mr Ringrose above-mentioned, unto which I must of necessity refer you, against the time of their coming forth in print.

Captain Sharp our Commander, myself, and several others came for England, soon after the performance of this voyage. Here several of us were put into prison and tried for our lives, at the suit of Don Pedro de Ronquillo, the Spanish Ambassador, for committing piracy and robberies in the South Sea; but we were acquitted by a jury after a fair trial, they wanting witnesses to prove what they intended: neither had they had any at all against us, were it not for two or three villains of our own company, among which were two negroes who turned cat in the pan[1], and had a spleen against Captain Sharp and others that had profited more by the voyage than they had done. One chief article against us was the taking of the *Rosario* and killing the Captain thereof and another man; but it was proved the Spaniards fired at us first, as I have hinted at above, and thus it was judged we ought to defend ourselves. During the space of our imprisonment and trial several others of our company were forced to abscond and keep themselves concealed very close, for fear of being taken and brought under the same indictment. Also at Jamaica three of our company who arrived there were taken and cast into prison, and one of them was hanged who was wheedled into an open confession of his crime: the other two stood it out, and escaped, as I suppose, for want of witnesses to prove the fact against them. Our trial was at the Marshalsea in Southwark, by a Court of Admiralty.

Thus far I have given you an account of our adventures in the South Sea. But here you inquire of me what is become of Captain Sharp since the time of his trial? I must tell you I could wish I had a better account to give of him than what I have at present: he wasted all his money here in good fellowship in a short while after that he was set at liberty; much he spent also while he was under confinement, so that he was soon reduced low, as most of the Buccaneers use to be after their voyages, according to what is truly enough related of them in that History. Having spent all his money, he resolved to go seek for more, and that by the same means he

[1] An old proverbial saying (occurring in Heywood's *Proverbes*, 1546): to prove perfidious, to change sides—probably a culinary metaphor, from *cate* (cake).

had used formerly; yet an order there was, either from the Privy Council or the Court of Admiralty, that no Commander should carry him into those parts of the West Indies again, fearing lest he should do more mischief unto the Spaniards, contrary to the articles, beyond the line, for they had notice given them he intended to return thither to make new discoveries upon those coasts, and unto this effect had already taken up his passage in one of His Majesty's frigates—but this order prevented him. As for merchant-ships, they refused to carry him, fearing he would tempt the men to revolt against the masters, and by this means run away with the ship to privateering, as he had done before.

Not finding, therefore, any means to get out of England, he got together a little money, and with this he bought an old boat, which, as I am told, used to lie above London Bridge, for the sum of £20 sterling. Into this boat he put a small quantity of butter and cheese, and a dozen or two pieces of beef: these were his provisions: his crew were only 16 men. With this equipage he sailed down the river, and came unto the Downs: hereabouts, as 'tis said, he met with a French vessel, which he clapt aboard, seized, and made himself master thereof. Presently after he sank his own boat, which he intended to carry no farther than until he could provide himself with a better bottom. Upon Romney Marsh he espied some cattle, and thereupon sent some men ashore to provide what they thought fit for the present victualling of their vessel. Thus he is gone out of England, but whither, upon what design, or what adventures he has met withal since, I cannot tell you.

THE

BUCCANEERS OF AMERICA

THE SECOND VOLUME

CONTAINING THE DANGEROUS VOYAGE AND BOLD ATTEMPTS

OF

CAPTAIN BARTHOLOMEW SHARP

AND OTHERS

PERFORMED UPON THE COASTS OF THE

SOUTH SEA FOR THE SPACE OF TWO YEARS

From the Original Journal of the said Voyage

written by

MR BASIL RINGROSE, GENT.

Who was all along present at those Transactions

A DESCRIPTION of The South Sea & Coasts of AMERICA Containing y whole Navigation and all those places at which Capt. SHARP and his Companions were in the years 1680 & 1681
The Tropick of Cancer
Tropick of Capricorn
SINUS MEXICANUS
Bahama Islands
Hispaniola
Jamaica
Barbados
MARE BRAZILIÆ
BRAZIL
AMERICA Meridio: PERU
CHI: CAS :nalis CHILE
MAR DEL ZUR
MARE MAGALLANICUM
Sharpe's Passage
Sharpe's Redditus

PART IV

CONTAINING THE DANGEROUS VOYAGE AND BOLD ASSAULTS OF CAPTAIN BARTHOLOMEW SHARP AND OTHERS, PERFORMED IN THE SOUTH SEA, FOR THE SPACE OF TWO YEARS, ETC.

THE PREFACE TO THE READER

THE general applause wherewith the *History of the Buccaneers* has been received could have no other effect than easily to persuade the Publisher of that piece to undertake the Second Volume thereof, especially considering that the same points which deserved the credit and commendation of the first did seem to subsist for the like esteem and reception of the second. These were the fidelity of the relations both here and there published, the authors having been not only eye-witnesses but also actors in the transactions they report; the candour and sincerity of the style; the variety and pleasantness of these voyages; the greatness of the attempts here related; the unparalleled courage of the Buccaneers; the strangeness of their performances; the novelty of their exploits; and, withal, the glory and grandeur of valour which here is seen to be inherent to our English nation, and as pregnant of great actions in the present as in the former ages. Unto which points may be added in this Second Volume for its recommendation the grand discovery of a new passage into the South Sea, beyond the Straits of Magellan and Le Maire through an open and in no wise dangerous ocean without those formidable perils from rocks, currents, and shoals which hitherto have rendered the two passages aforementioned altogether inaccessible to trading: a navigation performed by Captain Sharp and his companions, many degrees beyond what Sir Francis Drake, Jacob Le Maire, Noord, or Magellan himself, who first circumnavigated the world, ever reached unto in their sailings. This discovery alone, as hugely beneficial to mankind, so may it seem sufficient of itself to recommend the present piece unto the public, even as extremely necessary to all such as navigate the ocean, and no less delightful unto those persons whose studies are directed to the search of nature, to the arts of mathematics or navigation. Besides which point, both of art, curiosity, and usefulness, we have given unto us here by Mr Ringrose an exact account of many places in the South Sea; the very draughts and maps of many ports, islands, bays, gulfs, points, and coasts, hitherto unknown to the greatest part of Europe—their appearance at sea, their surroundings, landings, and bearings; together with what variety of winds and weather, of currents and calms, and other observations the Buccaneers experimented in those parts. All which things, as they manifest unto us the inquisitiveness of the author, so ought we highly to applaud his curiosity and genius, who all along the course of this voyage not only fought with his sword in the most desperate engagements and battles of the Buccaneers against the Spaniards, but with his pen gave us a true account of those transactions, and with his pencil has delineated unto us the very scenes of those tragedies. Thus we find him totally employed towards our information and instruction at home while he endured the greatest fatigues and hardship abroad: at the same time making quadrants at sea that others sat idle and murmuring upon the decks; at the same time shipwrecked and almost naked and starving upon a desert island, and yet describing, even more exactly than the Spaniards themselves, the Gulf of Ballona (otherwise called of San Miguel), where he was cast away. These things, I say, as they are not undeserving of the highest praise and commendation in this ingenious gentleman, Mr Ringrose their author, so shall the curios of nature and posterity itself be his eternal debtors for their acquaintance with these writings.

Some imperfect account of these transactions, both short and in many things defective, I gave last year unto the public, at the end of the second impression of the *History of the*

Buccaneers. But, such as that relation was, I had no better then to give; neither had I then seen the present Journal of Mr Ringrose, and that same account being received from the hands of some of the Buccaneers themselves at Wapping, it was esteemed fit, both by me and others, to be published at that time. But as the author of those papers, mistrusting both his own memory and sufficiency, remits himself in that narrative unto the Journal of Mr Ringrose, and desires by this alone to be corrected or supplied either in what he was mistaken or deficient—so now, this Diary being published, I hope I have vindicated myself from any fault in history, having brought these papers to light by which those others were beforehand both acknowledged and desired to be amended.

As to my other Journal of this voyage, I shall not concern myself in the least with their veracity, nor meddle with their relations—knowing that, if any other person did take it, that no person in the voyage was so able as Mr Ringrose. Yet I know that divers narratives, in many points differing from one another, have at several times been made public of one and the same battle, one and the same siege, voyage, journey, or other transaction. And indeed all human affairs, wheresoever reported by various persons, though all were present at the times and places of their circumvolution, are necessarily subject to some diversity in the rehearsal—one person observing, omitting, contracting, dilating, understanding, or mistaking one particular point or part of any transaction more than another.

Having premised this much, I shall here only declare that what is here asserted shall be supported by Mr Ringrose himself whenever he returns into England—yea, and owned for truth by Captain Bartholomew Sharp, as the chiefest actor in these affairs, as soon as he comes home again; and, if any other person can show unto the world any Journal of the same voyage more complete, more exact, more elaborate, more curious and informing than Mr Ringrose has done, he shall deserve the laurel for me.

The case being thus stated concerning the present narrative or Journal, I hope no person for the future will asperse or misconstrue the sincerity of my intentions in relation to the public. This I speak under that due resentment I ought to have for being traduced the last year by some persons who, being transported with too much passion and partiality, would have nobody else to be an admirer of the person and valorous actions of Sir Henry Morgan or the rest of the Buccaneers but themselves. As if to publish a translation of the unparalleled exploits of that Jamaican hero—to give him this commendable title; to say that both he and his companions had acted beyond mortal men in America; to compare them to Alexander, Julius Cæsar, and the Nine Worthies of Fame; to propose them unto our English nation as the truest patterns of undaunted and exemplary courage that it ever produced, were to disparage the conduct of Sir Henry Morgan and his companions—as if all this were intended only to diminish the glory of his actions and eclipse the splendour of his and their valorous triumphs. Methinks, if envy reach thus far, with the same reason or unjust measure those persons may say that to publish this present Journal is to divulge nothing else than a satire against Captain Sharp; and that Mr Ringrose, who everywhere admires his conduct and extols his actions to the skies—yea, and was present himself and concerned in the same affairs—did mean nothing else than to traduce his own and Captain Sharp's name as infamous unto posterity. For my part, I judge myself so far distant from blemishing[1] in the least or disparaging Sir Henry Morgan or his heroic actions, that I believe I have showed myself to be the greatest admirer of his personal valour and conduct—yea, I think I have done more towards the advantage both of the honour and credit of that great commander, by soliciting and publishing that translation, than all the authors of our English nation besides. And I could unfeignedly wish that these persons who pretend to be so passionate for Sir Henry Morgan and his huge deserts as to misinterpret the sincere respects and service I have endeavoured to perform unto his merits would outdo that I have already done in this particular, and give us either a more full, exact, and true account of his exploits, or the best panegyric of his prowess that ever was written; and then experiment whether I did not readily embrace the printing such a thing at my own cost and charge, or rather render them ten thousand thanks for his commendations than carp at their actions for perusing and printing the same.

[1] Aspersing: cf. Mrs. Hutchinson, *Memoirs of Col. Hutchinson*, ed. 1846, p. 51: "Blemish not a man that is innocent."

For what if the French or Dutch author of the *History of the Buccaneers* did mistake himself in two or three points relating to Sir Henry Morgan? Must therefore the Publisher be blamed for faithfully printing what was most faithfully translated? Must the saddle be set upon the wrong horse, and the faults of the author be imputed unto the printer? Thus, if Mr Ringrose should happen to commit any mistake in these present papers, that blame should be presently mine; and happy should be all authors if so readily their errors could be discharged upon the Publishers. Besides, what authors can there be found so accurate in all things as not to be subject now and then to some little lapses of their pen? Were it so in John Esquemeling; as he ought to be pardoned for any small *peccadillo* shot wittingly nor willingly committed, concerning what he relates of Sir Henry Morgan, so am I hitherto persuaded that he never designed to offend that great person, or falsely traduce his memory in the least. My argument is: Because he himself had the hand of a private Buccaneer in those affairs, he himself was a sharer in those booties, an actor in those enterprizes, and could no more blame Sir Henry Morgan for leading unto those attempts than blemish himself for following unto them. Another reason, even more prevalent, is that he all along speaks more honourably of Sir Henry Morgan than of any other Commander of the Buccaneers though they were his own countrymen, either Francis L'Ollonais or Roche Brasiliano, whereof the one was a Dutchman and the other was born in France. So that to say that he represents the English Buccaneers as the worst of men is plainly to forget that he relates ten times greater villainies of his own nation and countrypeople; and that the partiality they accuse him of, if any such can be found in that author, is rather bent against the French and other nations than the English. Does he in any place of his *History* lay all the faults and cruelties of the English Buccaneers upon Sir Henry Morgan? Or do we believe that, if committed without order, as in most armies many things are so done, the General or Commander-in-Chief ought to be accountable for them? Or, if those things were performed by order, that the Spaniards had not deserved them at the hands of the Buccaneers?

Aye, but he mistakes the pedigree of Sir Henry Morgan. Truly a great fault, and unpardonable in John Esquemeling, a foreigner to our nation and an illiterate Buccaneer, that he should not be better read in our English history! So did he also mistake his very name, calling him Captain John Morgan (for Henry); but that fault was rectified in the translation. As if every private soldier ought to be thoroughly acquainted with the Christian name of his General, and know whether he was baptized John or Thomas, Richard or William! Now what dishonour can it be refuted unto the merits of Sir Henry Morgan to be misrepresented by John Esquemeling, for the son of a rich yeoman in Wales, whereas at the same time he says that he was of good quality in that country even as most who bear that name in Wales are known to be? Does not all our English nation know the family of the Morgans to be one of the ancientest and best qualified in all Wales or England, and that to be descended of a rich yeoman of the same family is as great an honour and as honourable a pedigree as any private gentleman needs to pretend to?

But then Sir Henry Morgan did not burn Panama. And what disgrace was it to that worthy person if he had set fire unto it, for those reasons he knew best himself? Certainly no greater dishonour than to take and plunder the said city. Thus are all these persons so far transported with passion towards Sir Henry Morgan as to bereave him of the glory of his greatest actions, whether true or false. For, whether he fired the town or not (for that question I shall not make mine), this I am sure, that it was constantly so reported and believed here in England, viz. that *the English had set fire unto it,* that unto this day the Buccaneers do believe it to be so; and consequent unto this belief Mr Ringrose in these papers says plainly in some place or other that Panama was once burnt by Sir Henry Morgan; that the Spaniards themselves never believed or reported this fact otherwise, neither will they easily be persuaded to the contrary unto this very day, as I am credibly informed by those persons who lived in Spain at the same time that the news of the taking of Panama was brought into Spain, and who have been resident there many years since. For what concerns what now is published that the Governor of Panama fired the town himself is rather believed by the Spaniards to be a sham of the Governor's making—thereby to save his own bacon—against whom they rail as the greatest coward that ever was, for deserting the town and flying to the mountains at the approach of the English. How then, say they, could he fire it himself, or give orders to have it fired, when we know he was upon the spur 30 or 40 miles distant from there ? Had he done it, he would have set fire unto every house before he had left the town and not so many hours after the English were in possession of the place and be at such a distance from it. Thus, both the English nation and the Spanish having agreed to give the honour of this action, either truly or falsely, to Sir Henry Morgan, I cannot but admire that those who pretend to be the greatest admirers of his merits should endeavour to divest him of it.

What concerns two or three points more relating to Sir Henry Morgan in the *History of the Buccaneers :* I shall not undertake to apologize for John Esquemeling, in case he has misrepresented them. All I shall say is this : that that worthy person is not the first General or Chief Commander whose actions have been misconstrued or misunderstood by the common soldiers, and consequently ill represented by them at home. Neither is anything in this world more subject to glosses and false representations than the heroic actions of great men by their servants or inferiors. If this be the case of John Esquemeling, and that he was mal-contented with his fortune at Panama, what is that to me ? What fault was that of mine ? Meanwhile, why have not these persons so zealous of the honour of Sir Henry Morgan given us the true Journal of his huge exploits, but rather suffer his famous actions to lie dormant for so many years in England at the same time that other nations have published them abroad ? And then why must I be blamed by these persons, his admirers, for doing for the renown of Sir Henry Morgan what I could, if I could not do so much as I would willingly have done ?

[THE PUBLISHER].

PART IV

CHAPTER I

Captain Coxon, Sawkins, Sharp, and others set forth in a fleet towards the province of Darien, upon the continent of America. Their designs to pillage and plunder in those parts. Number of their ships, and strength of their forces by sea and land

At a place called Boca del Toro was the general rendezvous of the fleet, which lately had taken and sacked Porto Bello the second time—that rich place having been taken once before, under the conduct of Sir Henry Morgan, as is related in the *History of the Buccaneers*. At this place also were two other vessels, the one belonging to Captain Peter Harris, and the other to Captain Richard Sawkins ; both Englishmen and privateers. Here, therefore, a report was made to the fleet of a peace concluded between the Spaniards and the Indians of the land of Darien, who for the most part wage incessant wars against one another. Also, that since the conclusion of the said peace they had been already tried and found very faithful unto Captain Bournano, a French commander, in an attempt on a certain place called Chepo, near the South Sea. Further, that the Indians had promised to conduct him to a great and very rich place named Tocamora ; upon which he had likewise promised them to return in three months time with more ships and men. Hereupon we all agreed to go and visit the said place, and thus dispersed ourselves into several coves (by the Spaniards called *cuèvas*, or hollow creeks under the coasts), there to careen and fit our vessels for that purpose. In this place, Boca del Toro, we found plenty of fat tortoises, the pleasantest meat in the world. When we had refitted our vessels, we met at an island called by us the Water-key; and this was then our strength, as follows:—

	Tons	Guns	Men
Captain Coxon, in a ship of	80	8	97
Captain Harris	150	25	107
Captain Bournano	90	6	86
Captain Sawkins	16	1	35
Captain Sharp	25	2	40
Captain Cook	35	0	43
Captain Alleston	18	0	24
Captain Row	20	0	25
Captain Mackett	14	0	20

We sailed thence March 23rd, 1679, and in our way touched at the islands called Samballas. These are certain islands, reaching eight leagues in extent and lying fourteen leagues Westward of the river of Darien. Being here at anchor, many of the Indians, both men and women, came to see us. Some brought plantains, others other fruits and venison, to exchange with us for beads, needles, knives, or any trifling bauble whereof they stand in need. But what they most chiefly covet are axes and hatchets to fell timber withal. The men here go almost naked, as having only a sharp and hollow tip, made either of gold, silver, or bark, into which they thrust their privy members, which tip they fasten with a string about their middle. They wear as an ornament in their noses a golden or silver plate, in shape like a half-moon, which, when they drink, they hold up with one hand while they lift the cup with the other. They paint themselves sometimes with streaks of black; as the women do in like manner with red. These have in their noses a pretty thick ring of gold or silver; and for clothing they cover themselves with a blanket. They are generally well-featured women: among them I saw several fairer than the fairest of Europe, with hair like the finest flax. Of these it is reported they can see far better in the dark than in the light.

These Indians misliked our design for Tocamora, and dissuaded us from it, asserting it would prove too tedious a march, and the way so mountainous and uninhabited that it would be extremely difficult to get provisions for our men. Withal they proffered to guide us, undescried, within a few leagues of the city of Panama, in case we were pleased to go thither, where we could not choose but ourselves know we should not fail of making a good voyage. Upon these and other reasons which they gave us, we concluded to desist from the journey of Tocamora and to proceed to Panama. Having taken these resolutions, Captain Bournano's and Captain Row's vessels separated from us, as being all French and not willing to go to Panama, they declaring themselves generally against a long march by land. Thus we left them at the Samballas. Thence an Indian Captain, or Chief Commander, named Andræas, conducted us to another island called by the English The Golden Island, situated somewhat to the Westward of the mouth of the great river of Darien. At this island we met, being in all seven sail, on April 3rd, 1680.

Here at The Golden Island the Indians gave us notice of a town called Santa Maria, situated on a great river which bears the same name and which runs into the South Sea by the Gulf of San Miguel. In the town was kept a garrison of 400 soldiers; and from this place much gold was carried to Panama which was gathered from the mountains thereabouts. In case we should not find sufficient purchase there, we might thence proceed by sea to Panama, where we could not easily fail of our designs. This motion of the Indians we liked so well that we landed 331 men, on April 5th, 1680, leaving Captains Alleston and Mackett with a party of seamen to guard our ships in our absence with which we intended to return home.

The men that were landed had each of them three or four cakes of bread (called by the English doughboys[1]) for their provision of victuals; and for drink the rivers afforded enough. At the time of our landing Captain Sharp was very faint and weak, having had a great fit of sickness lately, from which he had scarcely recovered. Our several companies that marched were distinguished as follows. First,

[1] A nautical term for hard dumplings boiled in sea-water: cf. Dampier, *Voyages* (1697), ed. 1729, i, 5, 110: "This we served instead of butter, to eat with the Dough-boys or dumplins." Still in use in the navy: cf. *Pall Mall Budget*, 22 Aug., 1887, p. 13, col. 2: "Each man had also a dough-boy made with ¼ lb. of flour and boiled in the soup." The modern use of the word to designate an American private soldier refers to the shape of the buttons on his tunic.

Captain Bartholomew Sharp with his company had a red flag, with a bunch of white and green ribbons. The second division, led by Captain Richard Sawkins with his men, had a red flag striped with yellow. The third and fourth, led by Captain Peter Harris, had two green flags, his company being divided into two several divisions. The fifth and sixth, led by Captain John Coxon, who had some of Alleston's and Mackett's men joined to his, made two divisions or companies, and had each of them a red flag. The seventh was led by Captain Edmund Cook, with red colours striped with yellow, with a hand and sword for his device. All or most of them were armed with fuzee, pistol, and hanger.

CHAPTER II

They march towards the town of Santa Maria with design to take it. The Indian King of Darien meets them by the way. Difficulties of this march, with other occurrences till they arrive at the place

BEING landed on the coast of Darien, and divided into companies as was mentioned in the preceding chapter, we began our march towards Santa Maria, the Indians serving us for guides in that unknown country. Thus we marched at first through a small skirt of a wood, and then over a bay almost a league in length. After that, we went two leagues directly up a woody valley, where we saw here and there an old plantation, and had a very good path to march in. There we came to the side of a river, which in most places was dry, and built us houses, or rather huts, to lodge in.

Unto this place came to us another Indian, who was a chief commander and a man of great parts, named Captain Antonio. This Indian officer encouraged us very much to undertake the journey to Santa Maria, and promised to be our leader, saying he would go along with us now but that his child lay very sick. However, he was assured it would die by the next day, and then he would most certainly follow and overtake us. Withal he desired we would not lie in the grass for fear of monstrous adders, which are very frequent in those places. Breaking some of the stones that lay in the river, we found them shine with sparks of gold. These stones are driven down from the neighbouring mountains in time of floods. This day four of our men tired, and returned to the ships. So we remained in all 327 men, with 6 Indians to conduct us. That night some showers of rain fell.

The next day of our march we mounted a very steep hill, and on the other side at the foot thereof we rested on the bank of a river, which Captain Andræas told us ran into the South Sea, being the same river on which the town of Santa Maria was situated. Hence we continued our march until noon, and then ascended another mountain very much higher than the former. Here we ran much danger oftentimes and in many places, the mountain being so perpendicular and the path so narrow that but one man at a time could pass. We arrived by the dark of the evening to the other side of the mountain, and lodged again by the side of the same river, having marched that day, according to our reckoning, about 18 miles. This night likewise some rain fell.

The next morning being April 7th, we marched all along the river aforementioned, crossing it often, almost at every half-mile, sometimes up to the knees and at other times up to the middle in a very swift current. About noon we came to a place where we found some Indian houses. These were very large and neat : the sides were built with cabbage-trees, and the roofs of wild canes thatched with palmetto royal, but far neater than ours at Jamaica. They had many divisions into rooms, though no ascent by stairs into chambers. At this place were four of these houses together, that is, within a stone's throw one of another, each of them having a large plantain-walk before it. At the distance of half-a-mile from this place lived the King or chief Captain of these Indians of Darien, who came to visit us in royal robes with his queen and family. His crown was made of small white reeds, which were curiously woven, having no other top than its lining, which was of red silk. Round about the middle of it was a thin plate of gold, more than two-inches broad, laced behind—whence did stick two or three ostrich-feathers. About this plate went also a row of golden beads, which were bigger than ordinary peas ; underneath which the red lining of the crown was seen. In his nose he wore a large plate of gold in the form of a half-moon, and in each ear a great golden ring, nearly four-inches in diameter, with a round thin plate of gold of the same breadth, having a small hole in the centre by which it hung to the ring. He was covered with a thin, white, cotton robe, reaching to the small of his legs, and round its bottom a fringe of the same, three-inches deep. So that by the length of this robe our sight was impeded, that we could see no higher than his naked ankles. In his hand he had a long bright lance, as sharp as any knife. With him he had three sons, each of them having a white robe, and their lances in their hands, but standing bareheaded before him; as also were eight or nine persons more of his retinue, or guard. His queen wore a red blanket, which was closely girt about her waist, and another that came loosely over her head and shoulders, like our old-fashioned striped hangings. She had a young child in her arms, and two daughters walked by her, both marriageable, with their faces almost covered with stripes or streaks of red, and almost laden about their neck and arms with small beads of several colours. These Indian women of the province of Darien are generally very free, airy, and brisk, yet withal very modest, and cautious in their husbands' presence, of whose jealousy they stand in fear. With these Indians we made an exchange, or had a truck as it is called, for knives, pins, needles, or any other such like trifles; but in our dealing with them we found them to be very cunning. Here we rested ourselves for the space of one day, and withal chose Captain Sawkins to lead the *Forlorn*, to whom, for that purpose, we gave the choice of four-score men. The King ordered us each man to have three plantains, with sugar-canes to suck, by way of a present. But, when these were consumed, if we could not truck we must have starved, for the king himself did not refuse to deal for his plantains. This sort of fruit is first reduced to mash, then laid between leaves of the same tree, and so used with water; after which preparation they call it *miscelaw*.

On April 9th we continued our march along the banks of the river above-mentioned, finding on our way here and there a house. The owners of the said houses would most commonly stand at the door, and give, as we passed by, to every one of us either a ripe plantain or some sweet cassava-root. Some of them would count us by dropping a grain of corn for each man that passed before them, for they know no greater number, nor can count no farther, than twenty. That night we arrived at three great Indian houses, where we took up our lodgings, the weather being clear and serene all night.

The next day Captain Sharp, Captain Coxon, and Captain Cook, with about threescore-and-ten of our men, embarked themselves in fourteen canoes upon the river, to glide down the stream. Among this number I also embarked, and we had in our company our Indian Captain Andræas, of whom mention was made above, and two Indians more in each canoe, to pilot or guide us down the river. But, if we had been tired whilst travelling by land before, certainly we were in a worse condition now in our canoes. For at the distance of almost every stone's cast we were constrained to quit and get out of our boats, and haul them over either sands or rocks, and at other times over trees that lay across and filled up the river so that they hindered our navigation; yea, several times over the very points of land itself. That very night we built ourselves huts for shelter upon the riverside, and rested our wearied limbs until next morning.

This being come, we prosecuted our journey all day long with the same fatigue and toil as we had done the day before. At night came a tiger and looked on us for some while, but we did not dare to fire at the animal, fearing we should be descried by the sound of our fuzees—the Spaniards, as we were told, not being at any great distance from that place.

But the next day, which was April 12th, our pain and labour was rather doubled than diminished—not only for the difficulties of the way, which were intolerable, but chiefly for the absence of our main body of men, from whom we had parted the day before. For now, hearing no news of them, we grew extremely jealous of the Indians and their councils, suspecting a design of those people thus to divide our forces and then, by cutting us off, to betray us to the Spaniards, our implacable enemies. That night we rested ourselves by building huts, as we had done and as has been mentioned before.

On Tuesday morning, the next ensuing day, we continued our navigation down the river, and arrived at a beachy point of land, at which place another arm joins the same river. Here, as we understood, the Indians of Darien did usually rendezvous whensoever they drew up in a body with intention to fight their ancient enemies, the Spaniards. Here also we made a halt, or waited for the rest of our forces and company, the Indians having now sent to seek them, as being themselves not a little concerned at our dissatisfaction and jealousies. In the afternoon our companions came up with us, and were hugely glad to see us, they having been in no less fear for us than we had been at the same time for them. We remained and rested there that night also, with design to fit our arms for action, which now, as we were told, was near at hand.

We departed thence early the next morning, which was the last day of our march, having in all now the number of threescore-and-eight canoes, wherein were embarked 327 of us Englishmen, and 50 Indians, who served us for guides. To the point above-mentioned the Indians had hitherto guided our canoes with long poles or sticks; but now we made ourselves oars and paddles to row with, thus to make what speed we could. Thus we rowed with all haste imaginable, and upon the river we happened to meet two or three Indian canoes that were laden with plantains. About midnight we arrived and landed at the distance of half-a-mile more or less from the town of Santa Maria, whither our march was all along intended. The place where we landed was deeply muddy, insomuch that we were constrained to lay our paddles on the mud to wade upon, and withal lift ourselves up by the boughs of the trees to support our bodies from sinking. Afterwards we were forced to cut our way through the woods for some space, where we took up our lodgings for that night, for fear of being discovered by the enemy, to whom we were so near.

CHAPTER III

They take the town of Santa Maria with no loss of men, and but small booty of what they fought for. Description of the place, country, and river adjacent. They resolve to go and plunder for the second time the city of Panama

THE next morning, which was Thursday, April 15th, about break of day, we heard from the town a small arm discharged, and after that a drum beating *à travailler*. With this we were roused from our sleep, and, taking up our arms, we put ourselves in order and marched towards the town. As soon as we came out of the woods into the open ground, we were descried by the Spaniards, who had received intelligence beforehand of our coming, and were prepared to receive us, having already conveyed away all their treasure of gold and sent it to Panama. They ran immediately into a large palisaded fort, having each pale or post twelve-foot high, and began to fire very briskly at us as we came. But our vanguard ran up to the place, and, pulling down two or three of their palisades, entered the fort incontinently, and made themselves masters thereof. In this action not fifty of our men had come up before the fort was taken, and on our side only two were wounded, and not one killed. Notwithstanding, within the place were found two hundred and three-score men, besides which number two-hundred others were said to be absent, having gone up into the country to the mines to fetch down gold, or rather to convey away what was already in the town. This golden treasure comes down another branch of this river to Santa Maria from the neighbouring mountains, where are thought to be the richest mines of the Indies, or at least of all these parts of the Western world. Of the Spaniards we killed in the assault 26, and wounded to the number of 16 more. But their governor, their priest, and all or most of their chief men made their escape by flight.

Having taken the fort, we expected to find here a considerable town belonging to it. But it proved to be only some wild houses made of cane, the place being chiefly a garrison designed to keep in subjection the Indians, who bear a mortal hatred towards, and are often apt to rebel against, the Spaniards. But, bad as the place was, our fortune was much worse. For we came only three days too late to meet with three-hundred-weight of gold, which was carried thence to Panama in a bark that is sent thence twice or thrice every year to fetch the gold brought to Santa Maria from the mountains. This river, called by the name of the town, is hereabouts twice as broad as the river Thames at London, and flows above three-score miles upwards, rising to the height of two-fathom-and-a-half at the town itself. As soon as we had taken the place, the Indians who belonged to our company and had served us for guides came up to the town. For whilst they heard the noise of the guns they were in great consternation and dared not approach the palisades, but hid themselves closely in a small hollow, so that the bullets, while we were fighting, flew over their heads.

Here we found and redeemed the eldest daughter of the King of Darien, of whom we made mention above. She had, as it should seem, been forced away from her father's house by one of the garrison (which rape had hugely incensed him against the Spaniards), and was with child by him. After the fight the Indians destroyed as many of the Spaniards as we had done in the assault, by taking them into the adjoining woods and there stabbing them to death with their lances. But, so soon as we learnt of this barbarous cruelty, we hindered them from taking any more out of the fort, where we confined them every one prisoners. Captain Sawkins, with a small party of ten more, put himself into a canoe and went down the river, to pursue and stop, if it were possible, those that had escaped, for they were the chief people of the town and garrison. But now, our great expectations of taking a huge booty of gold at this place being totally vanished, we were unwilling to have come so far for nothing, or to go back empty-handed, especially considering what vast riches were to be had at no great distance. Hereupon we resolved to go to Panama, [in] which place, if we could take [it], we were assured we should get treasure enough to satisfy our hungry appetite for gold and riches, that city being the receptacle of all the plate, jewels, and gold that is dug out of the mines of all Potosi and Peru. Unto this effect, therefore, and to please the humours of some of our company, we made choice of Captain Coxon as our General or Commander-in-chief. Before our departure we sent back what small booty we had taken here by some prisoners under the charge of twelve of our men, to convey it to the ships.

Thus we prepared to go forward on that dangerous enterprise of Panama. But the Indians who had conducted us having got from us what knives, scissors, axes, needles, and beads they could, would not stay any longer, but all, or the greater part of them, returned to their home. Which notwithstanding, the king himself, Captain Andræas, Captain Antonio, the king's son, called by the Spaniards Bonéte de Oro, or King Golden-Cap, as also his kinsman, would not be persuaded by their falling off to leave us, but resolved to go to Panama, out of the desire they had to see that place taken and sacked. Yea, the king promised, if there should be occasion, to join 50,000 men to our forces. Besides which promises, we had also another very considerable encouragement to undertake this journey. For the Spaniard who had forced away the king's daughter, as was mentioned above, fearing lest we should leave him to the mercy of the Indians, who would have but little mercy on him, having shown themselves so cruel to the rest of his companions, for the safety of his life had promised to lead us not only into the town but even to the very bedchamber door of the governor of Panama, and that we should take him by the hand and seize both him and the whole city before we should be discovered by the Spaniards, either before or after our arrival.

CHAPTER IV

The Buccaneers leave the town of Santa Maria, and proceed by sea to take Panama. Extreme difficulties, with sundry accidents and dangers of that voyage

HAVING been in possession of the town of Santa Maria only the space of two days, we departed thence on Saturday, April 17th, 1680. We all embarked in 35 canoes and a *periagua*[1], which we had taken here lying at anchor before the town. Thus we sailed, or rather rowed, down the river in quest of the South Sea, upon which Panama is seated, towards the Gulf of Ballona, whereat we were to disembogue[2] into that ocean. Our prisoners, the Spaniards, begged very earnestly that they might be permitted to go with us and not be left to the mercy of the Indians, who would show them no favour and whose cruelty they so much feared. But we had much ado to find a sufficient number of boats for ourselves, the Indians that left us having taken with them, either by consent or stealth, so many canoes. Yet, notwithstanding this, they found soon after either bark logs, or old canoes, and by that means shifted so well for their lives as to come along with us. Before our departure we burnt both the fort, the church, and the town, which was done at the request of the King, he being extremely incensed against it.

Among these canoes it was my misfortune to have one that was very heavy, and consequently sluggish. By this means we were left behind the rest a little way, there being only four

[1] A corruption of Span. *piragua*, a West-Indian canoe, a pirogue: cf. ". . . six peryagoes, which are huge great trees formed as your canowes, yut so laid out on the sides with boords, they will seeme like a little gally." Capt. John Smith, *Works* [1629] (edn. 1884, p. 901).

[2] Discharge from the mouth—from Span. *desembocar*. Cf. Beaumont and Fletcher, *Knight of Malta* [c. 1626], i, 3: "My ships ride in the bay ready to disembogue."

men besides myself that were embarked therein. As the tide fell, it left several shoals of sand naked, and hence, we not knowing of the true channel amongst such a variety of streams, happened to steer within a shoal for above two miles before we perceived our error. Hereupon we were forced to lay by until high water came, for to row in such heavy boats against the tide is totally impossible. As soon as the tide began to turn, we rowed away in prosecution of our voyage, and withal made what haste we could; but all our endeavours were in vain, for we could neither find nor overtake our companions. Thus at about ten o'clock at night, the tide being low, we stuck up an oar in the river, and slept by turns in our canoe, several showers of rain falling all the night long which pierced us to the skin.

But, the next morning, no sooner had day come than we rowed away down the river as before, in pursuit of our people. Having gone about the space of two leagues, we were so fortunate as to overtake them. For they had lain that night at an Indian hut, or *embarcadero*, that is to say landing place, and had been taking in water till then. Being arrived at the place, they told us that we must not omit to fill our jars there with water, otherwise we should meet with none in the space of six days' time. Hereupon we went every one of us the distance of a quarter-of-a-mile from the *embarcadero* to a little pond to fill our water in calabashes, making what haste we could back to our canoe. But, when we returned, we found not one of our men, they all being departed and already got out of sight. Such is the procedure of these wild men that they care not in the least whom they lose of their company or leave behind. We were now more troubled in our minds than before, fearing lest we should fall into the same misfortune we had so lately overcome.

Hereupon we rowed after them as fast as we possibly could, but all in vain. For here are found such huge numbers of islands, greater and lesser, as also quays about the mouth of the river, that it was not difficult for us, who were unacquainted with the river, to lose ourselves a second time amongst them. Yet notwithstanding, though with much trouble and toil, we found at last that mouth of the river that is called by the Spaniards Boca Chica, or The Little Mouth. But, as it happened, it was now young flood, and the stream ran very violently against us; so that, though we were not above a stone's cast from the said mouth, and this was within a league broad, yet we could not by any means come near it. Hence we were forced to put ashore, which we did accordingly, until high-water. We hauled our canoe close by the bushes, and, when we got out, we fastened our rope to a tree, which the tide had almost covered, for it flows here nearly four-fathom deep.

As soon as the tide began to turn, we rowed away from there to an island, distant about a league and a half from the mouth of the river, in the Gulf of San Miguel. Here in the gulf it went very hard with us whensoever any wave dashed against the sides of our canoe, for it was nearly twenty-feet in length and yet not quite one-foot-and-a-half in breadth where it was at the broadest, so that we had only just room enough to sit down in her, and a little water would easily have both filled and overwhelmed us. At the island aforesaid we took up our resting-place for that night, though it was, from the loss of our company and the great dangers we were in, the sorrowfullest night that until then I had ever experienced in my whole life. For it rained impetuously all night long, insomuch that we were wet from head to foot and had not one dry thread about us; neither, through the violence of the rain, were we able to keep any fire burning wherewith to warm or dry ourselves. The tide ebbs here a good half-mile from the mark of high-water, and leaves bare wonderfully high and sharp-pointed rocks. We passed this heavy and tedious night without one minute of sleep, being all very sorrowful to see ourselves so far and remote from the rest of our companions, as also totally destitute of all human comfort; for a vast sea surrounded us on one side and the mighty power of our enemies, the Spaniards, on the other. Neither could we descry at any hand the least thing to relieve us, all that we could see being the wide sea, high mountains, and rocks; while we ourselves were confined to an egg-shell, instead of a boat, without so much as a few clothes to defend us from the injuries of the weather. For at that time none of us had a shoe to our feet. We searched the whole quay to see if we could find any water, but found none.

CHAPTER V

Shipwreck of Mr Ringrose, the author of this narrative. He is taken by the Spaniards, and miraculously by them preserved. Several other accidents and disasters which befell him after the loss of his companions till he found them again. Description of the Gulf of Vallona

ON Monday, April 19th, at break of day, we hauled our canoe into the water again, and departed from the island aforementioned: wet and cold as we were, we rowed away towards the Punta de San Lorenzo, or Point St Lawrence. In our way we met with several islands which lie straggling thereabouts. But now we were again so hard put to it by the smallness of our vessel and being in an open sea, that it had become the work of one man, yea sometimes of two, to cast out the water, which came in on all sides of our canoe. After struggling for some time with these difficulties, as we came near one of those islands a heavy sea overturned our boat, by which means we were all forced to swim for our lives. But we soon got to the shore, and to the same place our canoe came tumbling after us. Our arms were very fast lashed to the inside of the boat, and our locks were as well cased and waxed down as was possible; so were also our cartouche-boxes and powder-horns. But all our bread and fresh water was utterly spoilt and lost.

Our canoe being tumbled on shore by the force of the waves, our first business was to take out and clear our arms. This we had scarcely done when we saw another canoe fall into the same misfortune at a little distance to leeward of us, amongst a great number of rocks that bounded the island. The persons that were cast away proved to be six Spaniards of the garrison of Santa Maria, who had found an old canoe and had followed us to escape the cruelty of the Indians.

They presently came to us, and made us a fire; which being done, we got our meat and broiled it on the coals, and all of us ate amicably together. But we stood in great need of water, or other drink to our victuals, not knowing in the least where to get any. Our canoe was thrown up by the waves to the edge of the water, and there was no great fear of its splitting, being full six inches in thickness, on the sides thereof. But that in which the Spaniards came split itself against the rocks, being old and slender, into an hundred pieces. Though we were thus shipwrecked and driven ashore, as I have related, yet otherwise and at other times is this Gulf of San Miguel a mere mill-pond for smoothness of water.

My company was now altogether for returning and proceeding no farther, but rather for living amongst the Indians, in case we could not reach the ships we had left behind us in the Northern Sea. But with much ado I prevailed with them to go forward at least one day longer, and, in case we found not our people the next day, that then I would be willing to do anything which they should think fit. Thus we spent two or three hours of the day in consulting about our affairs, and withal keeping a man to watch and look out on all sides for fear of any surprisal by the Indians or other enemies. About the time that we were come to a conclusion in our debates, our watchman by chance spied an Indian, who, as soon as he saw us, ran into the woods. I sent immediately two of my company after him, who overtook him, and found that he was one of our friendly Indians. Thus he led them to a place not far distant where seven more of his company were with a great canoe which they had brought with them. They came to the place where I was with the rest of my company, and seemed to be glad to meet us on that island. I asked them by signs for the main body of our company, and they gave me to understand that if we would go with them in their canoe, which was much bigger than ours, we should be up with the party by the next morning. This news, as may easily be supposed, not a little rejoiced our hearts.

Presently, after this friendly invitation, they asked who the other six men were whom they saw in our company, for they easily perceived us not to be all of one and the same coat and *lingua*. We told them they were 'Wankers', which is the name they commonly give to the Spaniards in their own language. Their next question was, if they should kill those Spaniards ; but I answered them : *No, by no means ; I would not consent to have it done.* With which answer they seemed to be satisfied for the present. But, a little while after, my back being turned, my company thinking that they should thereby oblige the Indians, beckoned to them to kill the Spaniards. With this the poor creatures, perceiving the danger that threatened them, made a sad shriek and outcry, and I came in time to save all their lives. But withal I was forced to give way and consent that they should have one of them for to make their slave. Hereupon I gave the canoe that I came in to the five Spaniards remaining, and bid them get away and shift for their lives, lest those cruel Indians should not keep their word, and they should run the same danger again they had so lately escaped. Having sent them away whilst I rested myself here, I took a survey of this gulf and the mouth of the river, which I finished the same day, and do here present to the view of the reader.

But now, thanks be to God, joining company with those Indians, we got into a very large canoe, which for its bigness was better able to carry twenty men than our own that we had brought to carry five. The Indians had also fitted a very good sail to the said canoe, so that, having now a fresh and strong gale of wind, we set sail thence, and made therewith brave way, to the infinite joy and comfort of our hearts, seeing ourselves so well accommodated and so happily rid of the miseries we but lately had endured. We had now a smooth and easy passage after such tedious and laboursome pains as we had sustained in coming so far since we left Santa Maria. Under the point of St Lawrence, mentioned above, is a very great rippling of the sea, occasioned by a strong current which runs hereabouts, and which often almost filled our boat with its dashes as we sailed. This evening, after our departure from the island where we were cast away, it rained vehemently for several hours, and the night proved to be very dark. About nine o'clock that night we descried two fires on the shore of the continent over against us. These fires were no sooner perceived by the Indians of our canoe than they began to shout for joy and cry out, *Captain Antonio, Captain Andræas*, the names of their Indian Captains and leaders ; and to affirm they were assured those fires were made by their companions. Hence they made for the shore towards those fires as fast as they could drive. But, so soon as our canoe came among the breakers nigh the shore, out came from the woods about three-score Spaniards with clubs and other arms, and, laying hold of our canoe on both sides thereof, hauled it out of the water quite dry; so that by this means we were all suddenly taken and made their prisoners. I laid hold of my gun, thinking to make some defence for myself; but all was in vain, for they suddenly seized me between

four or five of them and hindered me from action. Meanwhile our Indians leaped overboard, and got away very nimbly into the woods, my companions standing amazed at what had happened and the manner of our surprisal. I asked them presently if any of them could speak either French or English; but they answered: *No.* Hereupon, as well as I could I discoursed to some of them, who were more intelligent than the rest, in Latin, and by degrees came to understand their condition. These were Spaniards who had been turned ashore here by our English party, who left them upon this coast lest by carrying them nearer to Panama any of them should make their escape and discover our march towards that city. They had me, presently after I was taken, into a small hut which they had built, covered with boughs, and made there great shouts for joy, because they had taken us, designing in their minds to use us very severely for coming into those parts, and especially for taking and plundering their town of Santa Maria. But, while the captain of those Spaniards was examining me, in came the poor Spaniard that was come along with us, and reported how kind I had been to him and the rest of his companions, by saving their lives from the cruelty of the Indians.

The captain, having heard him, arose from his seat immediately and embraced me, saying that we Englishmen were very friendly enemies and good people, but that the Indians were very rogues and a treacherous nation. Withal he desired me to sit down by him, and to eat part of such victuals as our companions had left them when they were turned ashore. Then he told me that for the kindness I had showed to his countrymen he gave us all our lives and liberties, which otherwise he would certainly have taken from us. And, though he could scarcely be persuaded in his mind to spare the Indians' lives, yet for my sake he pardoned them all, and I should have them with me in case I could find them. Thus he bid me likewise take my canoe, and go in God's name, saying withal he wished us as fortunate as we were generous. Hereupon I took my leave of him, after some little stay, though he invited me to tarry all night with him. I searched out, and at last found, my Indians, who for fear had hid themselves in the bushes adjoining to the neighbouring woods where they lay concealed. Having found them, the Captain led me very civilly down to the canoe, bidding my companions and the Indians get in after me: as they at first hauled us ashore, so now again they pushed us off to sea, by a sudden and strange vicissitude of fortune. All that night it rained very hard, as was mentioned above; neither durst we put ashore any more at any place, it being all along such as by mariners is commonly called an "iron coast".

The next morning being come, we sailed, and paddled, or rowed, till about ten o'clock. At which time we espied a canoe making towards us with all speed imaginable. Being come up with us, and in view, it proved to be of our own English Company, who, mistaking our canoe for a Spanish *periagua*, was coming in all haste to attack us. We were infinitely glad to meet them, and they presently conducted us to the rest of our company, who were at that instant coming from a deep bay which lay behind a high point of rocks, where they had lain at anchor all that night and morning. We were all mutually rejoiced to see one another again, they having given both me and my companions up for lost.

CHAPTER VI

The Buccaneers prosecute their voyage, till they come within sight of Panama. They take several barks and prisoners by the way. Are descried by the Spaniards before their arrival. They order the Indians to kill the prisoners

FROM the place where we rejoined our English forces we all made our way towards a high hummock of land, as it appeared at a distance, but was nothing else than an island seven leagues distant from the bay aforementioned. On the highest part of this island the Spaniards keep a watch or 'look-out' (for so it is termed by the seamen) for fear of pirates or other enemies. That evening we arrived at the island, and, being landed, went up a very steep place till we came to a little hut where the watchman lodged. We took by surprizal the old man who watched in the place but happened not to see us till we were got into his plantain walk before the lodge. He told us in his examination that we were not as yet descried by the Spaniards of Panama or any others that he knew, which relation of the old fellow much encouraged us to go forwards with our design of surprising that rich city. This place, if I took its name rightly, is called Farol de Plantanos, or, in English, Plantain-Watch.

Here, not long before it was dark that evening, a certain bark came to an anchor at the outward side of the island which instantly was descried by us. Hereupon we speedily manned out two canoes, who went under the shore and surprised the said boat. Having examined the persons that were on board, we found she had been absent the space of eight days from Panama, and had landed soldiers at a point of land not far distant from this island, with intention to fight and curb certain Indians and negroes who had done much hurt in the country thereabouts. The bark being taken, most of our men endeavoured to get into her, but more especially those who had the lesser canoes. Thus there embarked thereon to the number of 137 of our company, together with that sea-artist and valiant commander, Captain Bartholomew Sharp. With him went also on board Captain Cook, whom we mentioned at the beginning of this history. The remaining part of that night we lay at the quay of the said island, expecting to prosecute our voyage the next day.

Morning being come, I changed my canoe and embarked myself on another, which, though it was something lesser than the former, yet was furnished with better company. Departing from the island, we rowed all day long over shoal-water, at the distance of about a league from land, having sometimes not above four-foot water and white ground. In the afternoon we descried a bark at sea, and instantly gave her chase. But the canoe wherein was Captain Harris happened to come up the first with her, who, after a sharp dispute, took her. Being taken, we put on board the said bark 30 men. But the wind would not suffer the other bark, in chasing, to come up with us. This pursuit of the vessel did so far hinder us in our voyage, and divide us asunder, that, night soon coming on, we lost one another and could no longer keep in a body together. Hereupon we laid our canoe ashore, to take up our rest for that night at the distance of two miles, more or less, from high-water mark, and about four leagues to leeward of the island of Chepillo, to which place our course was then directed.

The next morning, as soon as the water began to float us, we rowed away for the forementioned island Chepillo, where by assignation our general rendezvous was to be. On our way as we went, we spied another bark under sail, as we had done the day before. Captain Coxon's canoe was now the first that came up with this vessel. But, a young breeze freshening at that instant, she got away from him after the first onset, killing in the said canoe one Mr Bull and wounding two others. We presently conjectured that this bark would get before us to Panama, and give intelligence of our coming to those of the town ; all which happened as we had foreseen. It was two o'clock in the afternoon before all our canoes could come together and join one another, as it was assigned at Chepillo. We took at that island fourteen prisoners, between negroes and mulattos; also great store of plantains and good water, together with two fat hogs. But now, believing that ere this we had been already descried at Panama by the bark aforementioned, we resolved among ourselves to waste no time, but to hasten away from the said island, to the intent we might at least be able to surprise and take their shipping, and by that means make ourselves masters of those seas, in case we could not get the town which now we judged almost impossible to be done. At Chepillo we took also a *periagua* which we found at anchor before the island, and presently we put some men on board her. Our stay here was only of few hours, so that about four o'clock in the evening, which now was coming on, we rowed away, designing to reach Panama before the next morning, to which place we had now only seven leagues to go, it being no farther distant from Chepillo. But, before we departed from the said island, it was judged convenient by our Commanders, for certain reasons which I could not dive into, to rid their hands of the prisoners which we had taken. And hereupon orders were given unto our Indians, who they knew would perform them very willingly, to fight, or rather to murder and slay, the said prisoners upon the shore, and that in view of the whole fleet. This they instantly went about to do, being glad of this opportunity to revenge their hatred against their enemies, though in cold blood. But the prisoners, although they had no arms wherewith to defend themselves, forced their way through those barbarous Indians, in spite of their lances, bows, and arrows, and got into the woods of the island, only one man of them being killed. We rowed all night long, though many showers of rain ceased not to fall.

CHAPTER VII

They arrive within sight of Panama. Are encountered by three small men-of-war. They fight them with only 68 men, and utterly defeat them, taking two of the said vessels. Description of that bloody fight. They take several ships at the isle of Perico before Panama

THE next morning, which was on April 23rd, 1680, that day being dedicated to St George, our Patron of England, we came before sunrise within view of the city of Panama, which makes a pleasant show to the vessels that are at sea from off the shore. Soon after we saw also the ships belonging to the said city which lay at anchor at an island called Perico, distant only two leagues from Panama. On the aforesaid island are to be seen several storehouses which are built there, to receive the goods delivered out of the ships. At that present there rode at anchor at Perico five great ships and three pretty big barks, called Barcos de la Armadilla, or little men-of-war; the word *Armadilla* signifying a *Little Fleet*. These had been suddenly manned with design to fight us, and prevent any further attempts we should make upon the city or coasts of those seas. As soon as they spied us, they instantly weighed anchor and got under sail, coming directly to meet us whom they expected very shortly, according to the intelligence they had received of our coming. Our two *periaguas* being heavy could not row so fast as we that were in the canoes, and hence we were got pretty far before them. In our five canoes (for so many we were now in company) we had only 36 men, in a very unfit condition to fight, being tired with so much rowing, and so few in number in comparison with the enemy that came against us. They sailed towards us directly before the wind, insomuch that we feared lest they should run us down before it. Hereupon we rowed up into the wind's eye, as the seamen term it, and got close to windward of them. While we were doing this, our lesser *periaguas*, in which were 32 or more of our company, came up with us. So that we were in all 68 men that were engaged in the fight of that day, the King himself, who was in the *periagua* aforementioned, being one of our number. In the vessel that was admiral of these three small men-of-war were fourscore and six Biscayners, who have the repute of being the best mariners and also the best soldiers amongst the Spaniards. These were all volunteers, who came designedly to show their valour, under the command of Don Jacinto de Barahona, who was High Admiral of those seas. In the second were 77 negroes, who were commanded by an old and stout Spaniard, a native of Andalusia in Spain, named Don Francisco de Peralta. In the third and last were 65 *mestizos* or mulattos or tawnymores, commanded by Don Diego de Carabaxal. So that in all they made the number of 228 men. The Commanders had strict orders given them, and their resolution was to give quarter to none of the Pirates or Buccaneers. But such bloody commands as these seldom or never do happen to prosper.

The canoe of Captain Sawkins, and also that wherein I was, were much to leeward of the rest; so that the ship of Don Diego de Carabaxal came between us two, and fired presently on me to windward, and on him to leeward, wounding with these broadsides four men in his canoe and one in that I was in; but he paid so dear for his passage between us that he was not very quick in coming about again and making the same way. For we killed with our first volley of shot several of his men upon the decks. Thus we also got to windward, as the rest were before. At this time the Admiral of the *Armadilla*, or *Little Fleet*, came up with us suddenly, scarce giving us time to charge, and thinking to pass by us all with as little or less damage as the first of his ships had done. But, as it happened, it fell out much worse with him, for we were so fortunate as to kill the man at the helm, so that his ship ran into the wind, and her sails lay a-back, as is usually said in marinery. By this means we had time to come all up under his stern, and, firing continually into his vessel, we killed as many as came to the helm, besides which slaughter we cut asunder his main sheet and brace with our shot. At this time the third vessel, in which Captain Peralta was, was coming up to the aid of their general. Hereupon Captain Sawkins, who had changed his canoe and was gone into the *periagua*, left the Admiral to us four canoes (for his own was quite disabled) and met the said Peralta. Between him and Captain Sawkins the dispute, or fight, was very hot, lying board on board together, and both giving and receiving death unto each other as fast as they could charge. While we were thus engaged, the first ship tacked about, and came up to relieve the Admiral. But we, perceiving that and foreseeing how hard it would go with us if we should be beaten from the Admiral's stern, determined to prevent his design. Hereupon two of our canoes, to wit Captain Springer's and my own, stood off to meet him. He made up directly towards the Admiral, who stood upon the quarter-deck waving to him with a handkerchief so to do. But we engaged him so closely in the middle of his way, that had he not given us the helm and made away from us, we had certainly been on board him. We killed so many of them that the vessel had scarce men enough left alive or unwounded to carry her off. Yet, the wind now blowing fresh, they made shift to get away from us, and hereby saved their lives.

The vessel which was to relieve the Admiral being thus put to flight, we came about again upon the Admiral, and all together gave a loud halloo, which was answered by our men in the *periagua*, though at a distance from us. At that time we came so close under the stern of the Admiral that we wedged up the rudder; and withal killed both the Admiral himself and the chief pilot of his ship, so that now they were almost quite disabled and disheartened likewise, seeing what a bloody massacre we had made among them with our shot. Hereupon, two-thirds of their men being killed and many others wounded, they cried for quarter, which had several times been offered unto them and as stoutly denied until then. Captain Coxon entered on board the Admiral, and took with him Captain Harris, who had been shot through both his legs, as he boldly adventured up along the side of the ship. This vessel being thus taken, we put on board her also all the rest of our wounded men, and instantly manned two of our canoes to go and aid Captain Sawkins, who now had been three times beaten from on board by Peralta, such valiant defence had he made. And indeed, to give our enemies their due, no men in the world did ever act more bravely than these Spaniards.

Thus coming up close under Peralta's side, we gave him a full volley of shot, and expected to have the like return from him again, but on a sudden we saw his men blown up that were abaft the mast—some of them falling on the deck, and others into the sea. This disaster was no sooner perceived by their valiant Captain Peralta than he leaped overboard, and, in spite of all our shot, got several of them into the ship again, though he was much burnt in both his hands himself. But, as one misfortune seldom comes alone, whilst he was recovering these men to reinforce his ship withal and renew the fight, another jar of powder took fire forward, and blew up several others upon the forecastle. Among this smoke, and under cover thereof, Captain Sawkins laid them on board and took the ship. Soon after they were taken, I went on board Captain Peralta, to see what condition they were in, and indeed such a miserable sight I never saw in my life, for not one man there was found but was either killed, desperately wounded, or horribly burnt with powder, insomuch that their black skins were turned white in several places, the powder having torn it from their flesh and bones. Having compassionated their misery, I went afterwards on board the Admiral, to observe likewise the condition of his ship and men. Here I saw what did much astonish me, and will scarcely be believed by others than ourselves who saw it. There were found on board this ship but 25 men alive, whose number before the fight had been four-score-and-six, as was said above. So that three-score-and-one, out of so small a number, were destroyed in the battle. But, what is more, of these 25 men only eight were able to bear arms, all the rest being desperately wounded, and by their wounds totally disabled to make any resistance or defend themselves. Their blood ran down the decks in whole streams, and scarce one place in the ship was found that was free from blood.

Having possessed ourselves of these two *Armadilla* vessels, or *little men-of-war*, Captain Sawkins asked the prisoners how many men there might be on board the greatest ship that we could see, lying in the harbour of the island of Perico above-mentioned, as also in the others that were something smaller. Captain Peralta, hearing these questions, dissuaded him as much as he could from attempting them, saying that in the biggest alone there were 350 men, and that he would find the rest too well provided for defence against his small number. But one of his men, who lay a-dying upon the deck, contradicted him as he was speaking, and told Captain Sawkins there was not one man on board any of those ships that were in view; for they had all been taken out of them to fight us in these three vessels called the *Armadilla*, or *Little Fleet*. Unto this relation we gave credit, as proceeding from a dying man; and, steering our course to the island, we went on board them, and found, as he had said, not one person there. The biggest ship of these, which was called *La Santissima Trinidad*, or *The Blessed Trinity*, they had set on fire, made a hole in her, and loosened her foresail; but we quenched the fire with all speed, and stopped the leak. This being done, we put our wounded men on board her, and thus constituted her for the time being our hospital.

Having surveyed our own loss and damages, we found that 18 of our men had been killed in the fight, and 22 were wounded. These three Captains against whom we fought were esteemed by the Spaniards to be the valiantest in all the South Seas. Neither was this reputation undeservedly conferred upon them, as may easily be inferred from the relation we have given of this bloody engagement. As the third ship was running away from the fight, she met with two more that were coming out to their assistance, but gave them so little encouragement that they returned back and dared not engage us. We began the fight about half-an-hour after sunrise, and by noon had finished the battle and quite overcome them. Captain Peralta, while he was our prisoner, would often break out in admiration of our valour, and say: *Surely we Englishmen were the valiantest men in the whole world, who designed always to fight open, whilst all other nations invented all the ways imaginable to barricade themselves, and fight as close as they could.* And yet, notwithstanding, we killed more of our enemies than they of us.

Two days after our engagement, we buried Captain Peter Harris, a brave and stout soldier and a valiant Englishman, born in the county of Kent; whose death we very much lamented. He died of the wounds he received in the battle, and besides him only one man more: all the rest of our wounded men recovered. Being now come before Panama, I here inquired of Don Francisco de Peralta, our prisoner, many things concerning the state and condition of this city and the neighbouring country, and he satisfied me in manner following.

CHAPTER VIII

Description of the state and condition of Panama, and the parts adjacent. What vessels they took while they blocked up the said Port. Captain Coxon with 70 more return home. Sawkins is chosen in chief

THE famous city of Panama is situated in the latitude of 9 degrees North. It stands in a deep bay, belonging to the South Sea. It is in form round, excepting only that part where it runs along the sea-side. Formerly it stood four miles more to the East, when it was taken by Sir Henry Morgan, as is related in the *History of the Buccaneers*. But then, being burnt, and three times more since that time by casualty, they removed it to the place where it now stands. Yet, notwithstanding, there are some poor people still inhabiting the old town, and the cathedral church is still kept there, the beautiful building whereof makes a fair show at a distance, like that of St Paul's in London. This new city of which I now speak is much bigger than the old one, and is built for the most part of brick, the rest being of stone, and tiled. As for the churches belonging thereto, they are not as yet finished. These are eight in number, whereof the chief is called Santa Maria. The extent of the city comprehends better than a mile-and-a-half in length, and above a mile in breadth. The houses for the most part are three stories in height. It is well walled round about, with two gates belonging thereto, excepting only where a creek comes into the city, the which at high-water lets in barks, to furnish the inhabitants with all sorts of provisions and other necessaries. Here are always 300 of the King's soldiers to garrison the city; besides which number, their militia, of all colours, are 1100. But, at the time that we arrived there, most of their soldiers were out of town, insomuch that our coming put the rest into great consternation, they having had but one night's notice of our being in those seas. Hence we were induced to believe that, had we gone ashore instead of fighting their ships, we had certainly rendered ourselves masters of the place; especially considering that all their chief men were on board the Admiral—I mean such as were undoubtedly the best soldiers. Round about the city, for the space of seven leagues, more or less, all the adjacent country is Savanna, as they call it in the Spanish language, that is to say, plain and level ground, as smooth as a sheet, for this is the signification of the word Savanna. Only here and there is to be seen a small spot of woody land, and everywhere this level ground is full of *vacadas* or *beef stantions*[1], where whole droves of cows and oxen are kept, which serve as well as so many look-outs, or watch-towers, to descry if an enemy is approaching by land. The ground whereon the city stands is very damp and moist, which renders the place of bad repute for the concern of health. The water is also very full of worms, and these are much prejudicial to shipping; which is the cause that the King's ships lie always at Lima, the capital city of Peru, unless when they come down to Panama to bring the King's plate, which is only at such times as the fleet of *galleons* comes from Old Spain to fetch and convey it thither. Here, in one night after our arrival, we found worms of three-quarters of an inch in length, both in our bedclothes and other apparel.

At the island of Perico above-mentioned we seized in all five ships; of these, the first and biggest was named, as was said before, the *Trinidad*, and was a great ship, of the burden of 400 tons. Her lading consisted of wine, sugar, sweetmeats (whereof the Spaniards in those hot countries make infinite use), skins, and soap. The second ship was of about 300 tons burden, and not above half laden with bars of iron, which is one of the richest commodities that are brought into the South Sea. This vessel we burnt with the lading in her, because the Spaniards pretended not to want that commodity, and therefore would not redeem it. The third was laden with sugar, being of the burden of one-hundred and four-score tons, more or less. This vessel was given to be under the command of Captain Cook. The fourth was an

[1] Spanish *estancia*, a dwelling, 'station' for cattle.

old ship of sixty tons burden, which was laden with flour of meal. This ship we likewise burnt with her lading, esteeming both bottom and cargo at that time to be useless to us. The fifth was a ship of 50 tons, which, with a *periagua*, Captain Coxon took along with him when he left us.

Within two or three days after our arrival at Panama, Captain Coxon being much dissatisfied with some reflections which had been made upon him by our company, determined to leave us and return back to our ships in the Northern Seas by the same way he came thither. Unto this effect he persuaded several of our company, who sided most with him and had had the chief hand in his election, to fall off from us, and bear him company in his journey or march overland. The main cause of those reflections was his backwardness in the last engagement with the *Armadilla*, concerning which point some sticked not to defame, or brand, him with the note of cowardice. He drew off with him threescore-and-ten of our men, who all returned back with him in the ship and *periagua* above-mentioned towards the mouth of the river of Santa Maria. In his company also went back the Indian King, Captain Antonio, and Don Andræas, who, being old, desired to be excused from staying any longer with us. However, the King desired we would not be less vigorous in annoying their enemy and ours, the Spaniards, than if he were personally present with us. And, to the intent we might see how faithfully he intended to deal with us, he at the same time recommended both his son and nephew to the care of Captain Sawkins, who was now our newly-chosen General or Commander-in-Chief in the absence of Captain Sharp. The two *Armadilla* ships which we took in the engagement we burnt also, saving no other thing of them both but their rigging and sails. With them also we burnt a small bark which came into the port laden with fowls and poultry.

On Sunday, which was April 25th, Captain Sharp with his bark and company came in and joined us again. His absence was occasioned by want of water, which forced him to bear up to the King's Islands. Being there, he found a new bark, which he at once took, and burnt his old one. This vessel did sail excellently well. Within a day or two after the arrival of Captain Sharp came in likewise the people of Captain Harris who were still absent. These had also taken another bark, and cut down the masts of their old one by the board, and thus without masts or sails turned away the prisoners they had taken in her. The next day we took in like manner another bark which arrived from Nata, being laden with fowls, as before. In this bark we turned away all the meanest of the prisoners we had on board us.

Having continued before Panama for the space of ten days, being employed in the affairs aforementioned, on May 2nd we weighed from the island of Perico, and stood off to another island, distant two leagues farther from thence, called Tavoga. On this island stands a town which bears the same name, and consists of a hundred houses, more or less. The people of the town had all fled on seeing our vessels arrive. While we were here, some of our men being drunk on shore happened to set fire to one of the houses; which consumed twelve houses more before any could get ashore to quench it. To this island came several Spanish merchants from Panama, and sold us what commodities we needed, buying also of us much of the goods we had taken in their own vessels. They gave us likewise 200 pieces-of-eight for each negro we could spare them of such as were our prisoners. From this island we could easily see all the vessels that went out or came into the Port of Panama; and here we took likewise several barks that were laden with fowls.

Eight days after our arrival at Tavoga we took a ship that was coming from Truxillo and bound for Panama. In this vessel we found 2000 jars of wine, 50 jars of gunpowder, and 51,000 pieces-of-eight. This money had been sent from that city to pay the soldiers belonging to the garrison of Panama. From the said prize we had information given us that there was another ship coming from Lima with 100,000 pieces-of-eight more; which ship was to sail ten or twelve days after them, and which they said could not be long before she arrived at Panama. Within two days after this intelligence we took also another ship laden with flour from Truxillo, belonging to certain Indians, inhabitants of the same place or thereabouts. This prize confirmed what the first had told us of that rich ship, and said, as the others had done before, that she would be there in the space of eight or ten days.

Whilst we lay at Tavoga, the President, that is to say the

Governor, of Panama, sent a message by some merchants to us to know what we came for into those parts. To this message Captain Sawkins made answer: *That we came to assist the King of Darien, who was the true Lord of Panama and all the country thereabouts. And that since we were come so far, there was no reason but that we should have some satisfaction. So that if he pleased to send us 500 pieces-of-eight for each man, and 1000 for each Commander, and not any farther to annoy the Indians but suffer them to use their own power and liberty as became the true and natural lords of the country, that then we would desist from all further hostilities and go away peaceably; otherwise, that we should stay there, and get what we could, causing to them what damage was possible.* By the merchants also that went and came to Panama we understood there lived then as Bishop of Panama one who had been formerly Bishop of Santa Martha, and who was prisoner to Captain Sawkins when he took the said place about four or five years past. The Captain having received this intelligence, sent two loaves of sugar to the Bishop as a present. On the next day the merchant who carried them, returning to Tavoga, brought to the Captain a gold ring for a retaliation of said present. And withal he brought a message to Captain Sawkins from the President above-mentioned, to know farther of him, since we were Englishmen, *from whom we had our commission, and to whom he ought to complain for the damages we had already done them.* To this message Captain Sawkins sent back for answer: *That as yet all his company were not come together; but that when they were come up we would come and visit him at Panama, and bring our commissions on the muzzles of our guns, at which time he should read them as plain as the flame of gunpowder could make them.*

At this island of Tavoga Captain Sawkins would fain have stayed longer, to wait for the rich ship above-mentioned that was coming from Peru; but our men were so importunate for fresh victuals that no reason could rule them, nor their own interest persuade them to anything that might conduce to this purpose. Hereupon, on May 15th, we weighed anchor, and sailed thence to the island of Otoque. Being arrived there, we lay by it while our boat went ashore and fetched off fowls and hogs and other things necessary for sustenance. Here at Otoque I finished a draft from point Garachine to the bay of Panama, etc. Of this I may dare to affirm that it is in general more correct and true than any the Spaniards have themselves, for which cause I have here inserted it, for the satisfaction of those that are curious in such things.

From Otoque we sailed to the island of Cayboa, which is a place very famous for the pearl-fishery thereabouts, and is at the distance of eight leagues from another place called Puebla Nueva, on the mainland. In our way to this island we lost two of our barks, the one whereof had fifteen men in her, and the other seven. Being arrived, we cast anchor at the said island.

CHAPTER IX

Captain Sawkins, Chief Commander of the Buccaneers, is killed before Puebla Nueva. They are repulsed from the said place. Captain Sharp chosen to be their leader. Many more of their company leave them and return home overland

WHILE we lay at anchor before Cayboa our two Chief Commanders, Captain Sawkins and Captain Sharp, taking with them threescore men, more or less, went in the ship of Captain Cook to the mouth of the river where Puebla Nueva is situated. The day of this action, as I find it quoted in my Journal, was May 22nd, 1679. When they came to the river's mouth, they put themselves into canoes, and were piloted up the river towards the town by a negro who was one of our prisoners. I was chosen to be concerned in this action, but happened not to land, being commanded to remain in Captain Cook's ship while they went up to assault the town. But here at Puebla Nueva the inhabitants were too well prepared for the reception of our party. For a distance of a mile below the town they had cut down great trees and laid them across the river, with design to hinder the ascent of any boats. In like manner on shore before the town itself they had raised three strong breastworks, and made other things for their defence. Here, therefore, Captain Sawkins, running up to the breastworks at the head of a few men, was killed: a man who was as valiant and courageous as any could be, and likewise, next to Captain Sharp, the best beloved of all our company or the most part thereof. Neither was this love undeserved by him, for we ought justly to attribute to him the greatest honour we gained in our engagement before Panama with the Spanish *Armadilla*, or *Little Fleet*, especially, considering that, as has been said above, Captain

Sharp was by accident absent at the time of that great and bloody fight.

We that remained behind on board the ship of Captain Cook carried her within the mouth of the river of Puebla Nueva, and entered close by the East shore, which here is crowned with a round hill. Here within two stone's cast of shore we had four fathom water. Within the point opens a very large and fine river, which falls from a sandy bay at a small distance thence. But, as we were getting in, being strangers to the place we unwittingly ran our ship aground, nigh to a rock which lies on the Westward shore: for the true channel of the said river is nearer to the East than the West shore. With Captain Sawkins, in the unfortunate assault of this place, there died two men more, and three were wounded in the retreat, which they performed to the canoes in pretty good order. On their way down the river Captain Sharp took a ship, whose lading consisted of indigo, otto, manteca, or butter, and pitch, and likewise burnt two vessels more, as being of no value. With this he returned on board our ships, much troubled in his mind, and grieved for the loss of so bold and brave a partner in his adventures as Sawkins had constantly shown himself to be. His death was much lamented, and occasioned another party of our men to mutiny and leave us, returning overland as Captain Coxon and his company had done before.

Three days after the death of Captain Sawkins, Captain Sharp, who was now Commander-in-Chief, gave the ship which he had taken in the river of Puebla Nueva, which was of the burden of one hundred tons, more or less, to Captain Cook, to command and sail in—ordering withal that the old vessel which he had should go with those men that designed to leave us, their mutiny and our distraction being now grown very high. Hereupon Captain Sharp coming on board *La Trinidad*, the greatest of our ships, asked our men in full council who of them were willing to go or stay, and prosecute the design Captain Sawkins had undertaken, which was to remain in the South Sea and there to make a complete voyage; after which, he intended to go home round about America, through the Strait of Magellan. He added withal that he did not as yet fear, or doubt in the least, but to make each man who should stay with him worth one thousand pounds by the fruits he hoped to reap of that voyage. All those who had remained after the departure of Captain Coxon, for love of Captain Sawkins and only to be in his company and under his conduct, thinking thereby to make their fortunes, would stay no longer, but pressed to depart. Among this number I acknowledge myself to have been one, being totally desirous in my mind to quit those hazardous adventures, and return homewards with those who were now going to leave us. Yet, being much afraid and averse to trust myself among wild Indians any farther, I chose rather to stay, though unwilling, and venture on that long and dangerous voyage. Besides which danger of the Indians, I considered that the rains were now already up, and it would be hard passing so many gullies, which of necessity would then be full of water and consequently create more than one single peril to the undertakers of that journey. Yet, notwithstanding, 63 men of our company were resolved to encounter all these hardships, and to depart from us. Hereunto they took their leave of us, and returned homewards, taking with them the Indian King's son and the rest of the Indians for their guides overland. They had, as was said above, the ship wherein Captain Cook sailed to carry them, and out of our provisions as much as would serve for treble their number.

Thus on the last day of May they departed, leaving us employed about taking in water and cutting down wood at the island of Cayboa aforementioned, where this mutiny happened. Here we caught very good tortoises and red-deer. We killed also alligators of a very large size, some of them being above twenty-feet in length. But we could not find but that they were very fearful of a man, and would fly from us very hastily when we hunted them. This island lies S.S.E. from the mouth of the river above-mentioned. On the South-east side of the island is a shoal, or spit, of sand, which stretches itself the space of a quarter-of-a-league into the sea. Here, therefore, just within this shoal, we anchored in fourteen fathom water. The island on this side thereof makes two great bays, in the first of which we watered at a certain pond not distant above the cast of a stone from the bay. In this pond, as I was washing myself and standing under a mançanilla tree, a small shower of rain happened to fall on the tree, and thence dropped on my skin. These drops caused me to break out all over my body into red spots, of which I was not well for the space of a week after. Here I ate very large oysters, the biggest that ever I ate in my life, insomuch that I was forced to cut them into four pieces, each quarter of them being a good mouthful[1].

Three days after the departure of the mutineers Captain Sharp ordered us to burn the ship that they hitherto had sailed in, only out of design to make use of the ironwork belonging to the said vessel. Withal, we put all the flour that was her lading into the last prize, taken in the river of Puebla Nueva, and Captain Cook, as was said before, was ordered to command her. But the men belonging to his company would not sail any longer under his command. Hereupon he quitted his vessel and came on board our Admiral, the great ship above-mentioned, called *La Trinidad*, determining to rule over such unruly company no longer. In his place was put one whose name was John Cox, an inhabitant of New England, who forced kindred, as was thought, upon Captain Sharp, out of old acquaintance, in this conjuncture of time, only to advance himself. Thus he was made, as it were, Vice-Admiral to Captain Sharp. The next day three of our prisoners, viz. an Indian, who was Captain of a ship, and two mulattos ran away from us, and made their escape.

After this it was thought convenient to send Captain Peralta prisoner in the Admiral, on board the ship of Mr Cox. This was done to the intent he might not hinder the endeavours of Captain Juan, who was Commander of the money-ship we took, as was mentioned, at the island of Tavoga. For this man had now promised to do great things for us, by piloting and conducting us to several places of great riches, but more especially to Guayaquil, where he said we might lay down our silver and lade our vessels with gold. This design was undertaken by Captain Sawkins, and had not the head-strongness of his men brought him to the island of Cayboa, where he lost his life, he had certainly effected it before now. That night we had such thunder and lightning as I never had heard before in all my life. Our prisoners

[1] It does not seem to occur to the writer that his 'red spots' were more probably due to the oysters than to the rain!

told us that in these parts it very often causes great damages both by sea and land. And my opinion led me to believe that our mainmast received some damage on this occasion. The rainy season being now entered, the wind for the most part was at N.W., though not without some calms.

CHAPTER X

They depart from the island of Cayboa to the isle of Gorgona, where they careen their vessels. Description of this isle. They resolve to go and plunder Arica, leaving their design of Guayaquil

HAVING got in all things necessary for navigation, we were now in readiness to depart on Sunday, June 6th, 1680. That day some rain fell, which now was very frequent in all places. About five o'clock in the evening we set sail from the island of Cayboa, with a small breeze, the wind being at S.S.W. Our course was E.S. by E. and S.E. having all night a very small, or little, wind. The same calmness of weather continued all the next day, insomuch, that we lay and drove only as the current horsed us to N.W.

Little better than a calm we had also the third day of our navigation. Meanwhile a current drove us to the Westward. About sunrising we descried Quicara, which at that time bore N.W. by W. from us at the distance of five leagues, more or less. With the rising of the sun an easy gale of wind sprang up, so that at noon we had altered our bearing, which was then N. by E. being six leagues distant, and appearing thus, as is underneath demonstrated.

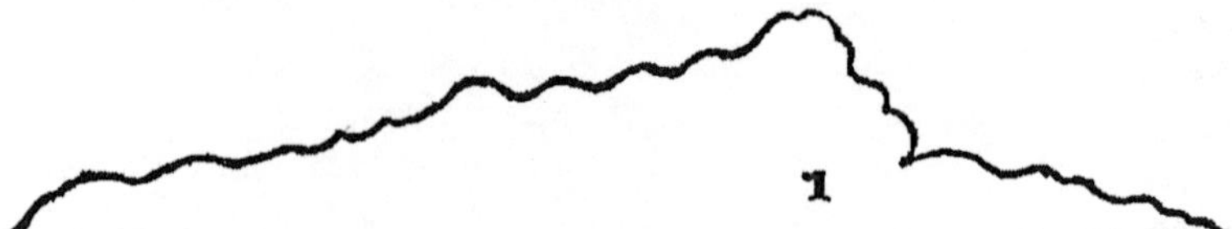

QUICARA LAT. 7 DEG. 4°. N.

These are two several islands, whereof the least is to the Southward of the other. The land is a low table-land, these islands being more than three leagues in length. About six o'clock that evening we were nigh ten leagues distant W.S.W. from them. Much like the former weather we had the fourth day of our sailing, with little wind in the forenoon and rather less than more in the afternoon. I judged, about the middle of the day, we were at the distance of twenty leagues S.S.W. from the said islands.

Thursday, June 10th, we had very small and variable winds. This day I reckoned that we had made hitherto a S. by E. way, and a S. by W. from our departure, being driven by a current, according to the observation I made, into lat. 6° 30'.

This day we saw many tortoises floating upon the sea. Hereupon we hoisted out our boat, and came to one of them, who offered not to stir until she was struck, and even then not to sink to the bottom but rather to swim away. The sea hereabouts is very full of several sorts of fish, as dolphins, bonitos, albicores[1], mullets, and old wives[2], etc., which came swimming about our ship in whole shoals. The next day, which was Friday, we had likewise very little wind, which was no more than we had all Thursday night, with some showers of rain. That day we had an observation which was lat. 6° N. In the evening a fresh wind came up at S.W., our course being S.S.E. On Saturday we had in like manner, about seven in the morning, a fresh breeze at S. So we stood W.S.W. with cloudy weather, and several showers of rain. This day our Spanish prisoners informed us we must not expect any settled wind until we came within the latitude of three degrees, for all along the Western shore of these seas there is little wind, which is the cause that those ships that go from Acapulco to the islands called De las Philipinas, do coast along the shore of California, until they get into the height of 45 degrees, yea, sometimes of 50 degrees latitude. As the wind varied, so we tacked several times, thereby to make the best of our way that was possible to the Southward.

As our prisoners had informed us, so we found it by experience. For on the next day, which was Sunday, June 13th, we had very little wind, and most commonly none, for the space of twenty-four hours. That day we tried the current

[1] Span. *albacore*, a large species of tunny found in West Indian seas: cf. Hakluyt, *Voyages* [1579], vol. II, ii, 100: ". . . the fish which is called *albocore*, as big as a salmon."

[2] The wrasse, or sea-cream. Monfet, *Health's Improv.* [1655]: "Of fresh-water fish. . . . Old wives (because of their mumping and soure countenance." P. Browne, *Jamaica* [1756]: "A saying That an Old Wife is the best of fish, and worst of flesh."

of the sea, and found it very strong to the eastward. The same day we had much rain, and in the afternoon a small breeze at W., and W.S.W., but mostly at W. Yet, notwithstanding all this calmness of weather, the next day in the morning very early, by a sudden gale of wind which arose we made shift to split our main top-sail. We had all the night before and that day continued and incessant showers of rain, and made a S.W. and by S. way; seeing all along as we went a multitude of dolphins, bonitos, and several other sorts of fish floating upon the seas, whereof in the afternoon we caught many, the weather being now changed from stormy to calm again—insomuch that we could fish as we sailed along, or rather as we lay tumbling in the calm.

Tuesday, June 15th, the morning continued calm as the day before; and this day also we saw multitudes of fish of several sorts, whereof we caught some for our table, as we were wont to do. By an observation which was made this day, we found ourselves to be now in lat. 4° 21′. At this time the course of our navigation and our whole design was to go and careen our vessels at the islands commonly called by the Spaniards De los Galapagos, that is to say 'of the Tortoises', being so denominated from the infinite number of those animals swarming and breeding thereabouts. These islands are situated under the equinoctial line at the distance of 100 leagues, more or less, from the main continent of America, in the South Sea. In the afternoon of this day we had a small breeze to push us forwards.

June 16th, being Wednesday, we made our way this day, and for the four-and-twenty hours last past, E.S.E., with much rain, which ceased not to fall, as in all this voyage, since our departure from Cayboa. This day likewise we caught several dolphins and other sorts of fish, but in the evening we had again a fresh breeze at S. by W., our course being, as was just now said, E.S.E.

The next day, which was June 17th, about five in the morning we descried land, which appeared all along to be very low, and likewise full of creeks and bays. We instantly asked our pilot what land that was before us; but he replied he knew it not. Hereupon, being doubtful of our condition, we called Mr Cox on board us, who brought Captain Peralta with him. This gentleman, being asked, presently told us the land we saw was the land of Barbacoa, being almost a wild country all over. Withal he informed us that to leeward of us, at the distance of ten leagues or thereabouts, did lie an island called by the name of Gorgona, which island, he said, the Spaniards did shun, and very seldom come nigh to, by reason of the incessant and continual rains there falling, scarce one day in the year being dry at that place. Captain Sharp, having heard this information of Captain Peralta, judged the said island might be the fittest place for our company to careen at, considering that, if the Spaniards did not frequent it, we might in all probability lie there undescried, and our enemies the Spaniards in the meantime might think that we were gone out of those seas. At this time it was that I seriously repented my staying in the South Seas and that I did not return homewards in company of them that went before us. For I knew, and could easily perceive, that by these delays the Spaniards would gain time and be able to send advice of our coming to every port all along the coast, so that we should be prevented in all or most of our attempts and designs wheresoever we came. But those of our company who had got money by the former prizes of this voyage over-swayed the others who had lost all their booty at gambling. Thus we bore away for the island aforesaid of Gorgona, and at the distance of six leagues and a half, at S.W.I. observed it to make the appearance following.

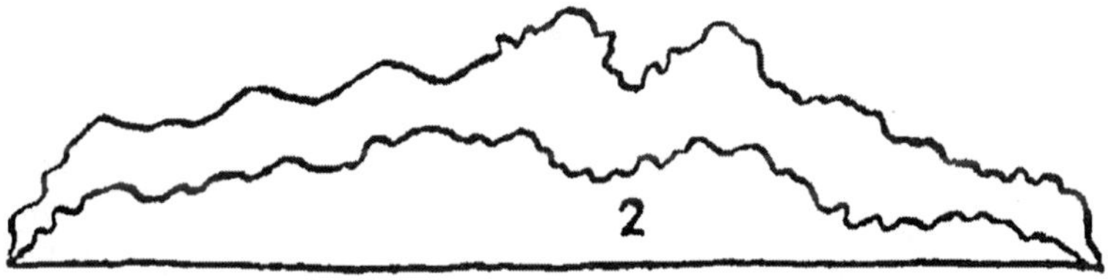

GORGONA *LAT. 1. 0°. N.*

On the mainland over against this island of Gorgona we were told by our prisoners that up a great laguna, or lake, is seated an Indian town, where they have great quantity of sand-grains of gold. Moreover, that, five days' journey up a river belonging to the said laguna, do dwell four Spanish superintendents, who have each of them the charge of overseeing 50 or 60 Indians who are employed in gathering that gold which slips from the chief collectors, or finders, thereof. These are at least threescore and ten or fourscore Spaniards, with a great number of slaves belonging to them, who dwell higher up than these four superintendents, at a distance of twenty-five or thirty days' journey on the said river. That once every year, at a certain season, there comes a vessel from Lima, the capital city of Peru, to fetch the gold that here is gathered, and to bring to these people such necessaries as they want. By land it is nothing less than six-weeks' travel from thence to Lima.

The mainland to windward of this island is very low and full of rivers. All along the coast it rains most desperately. The island is only 4 leagues distant from the continent. While we lay at it, I took the whole circumference thereof, which is according to what is here underneath described.

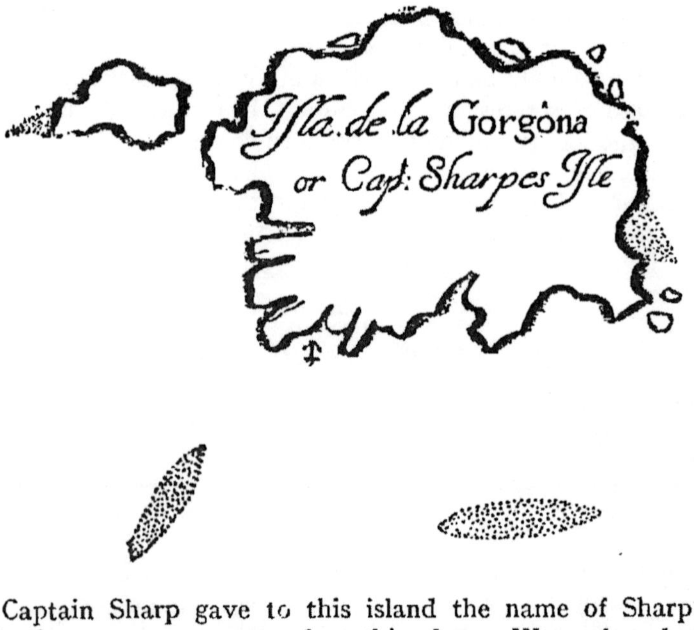

Captain Sharp gave to this island the name of Sharp's Isle, by reason we careened at this place. We anchored on the South side of the island, at the mouth of a very fine river, which there disgorges itself into the sea. There belong to this island about thirty rivers and rivulets, which all fall from the rocks on the several sides of the island. The whole circumference thereof is about three-leagues-and-a-half, being all high and mountainous land, excepting only on that side where we cast anchor. Here therefore we moored our ship in the depth of eighteen or twenty fathom water, and began to unrig the vessel. But we were four or five days' space before we could get our sails dry so as to be able to take them from the yards, there falling a shower of rain almost every hour of the day and night. The mainland to the East of the island, and so stretching northward, is extremely high and towering, and perpetually clouded, excepting only at the rising of the sun, at which time the tops of those hills are clear. From the South side of this island where we anchored, as was said above, we could see the lowland of the main, at least a point thereof which lies nearest to the island. The appearance it makes is as it were of trees growing out of the water.

Friday, July 2nd, as we were heaving down our ship, our mainmast happened to crack. Hereupon our carpenters were constrained to cut out large fishes, and fish it, as the usual terms of that art do name the thing.

On the next day after the mischance of our mainmast, we killed a snake which had fourteen inches in circumference and eleven feet in length. About the distance of a league from this island runs a ledge of rocks, over which the water continually breaks—the ledge being about two miles, more or less, in length. Had we anchored but half-a-mile more northerly, we had ridden in much smoother water; for here where we were the wind came in upon us in violent gusts. While we were there, from June 30th to July 3rd, we had dry weather, which was esteemed as a rarity by the Spaniards, our prisoners. And every day we saw whales and grampuses, who would often come and dive under our ship. We fired at them several times, but our bullets rebounded from their bodies. Our choice and best provisions here were Indian conies, monkeys, snakes, oysters, conchs, periwinkles, and a few small turtle, with some other sorts of good fish. Here in like manner we caught a sloth, a beast well deserving that name, given it by the Spaniards, by whom it is called *pereza*, from the Latin word *pigritia*.

At this island died Josephe Gabriel, a Spaniard, born in Chile, who was to have been our pilot to Panama. He was the same man who had stolen and married the Indian King's daughter, as was mentioned above. He had all along been very true and faithful to us in discovering several plots and conspiracies among our prisoners, either to get away or destroy us. His death was occasioned by a calenture, or malignant fever, which killed him after three days' sickness, having lain two days senseless. During the time of our stay at this island we lengthened our topsails, and got up topgallant masts; we made two staysails, and refitted our ship very well. But we wanted provisions extremely, as having nothing considerable of any sort but flour and water. Being almost ready to depart, Captain Sharp, our Commander, gave us to understand he had changed his resolution concerning the design of going to Guayaquil, for he thought it would be in vain to go thither considering that in all this time we must of necessity have been descried before now. Yet notwithstanding he himself before had persuaded us to stay. Being very doubtful among ourselves what course we should take, a certain old man who had long time sailed among the Spaniards told us he could carry us to a place called Arica, to which town, he said, all the plate was brought down from Potosi, Chiquisaca, and several other places within the land, where it was dug out of the mountains and mines, and that he doubted not but that we might get there of purchase at least 2000 pounds every man. For all the plate of the South Sea lay there, as it were, in store, being deposited at the said place until such time as the ships did fetch it away. Being moved with these reasons, and having deliberated thereupon, we resolved in the end to go to the said place. At this island of Gorgona afore-mentioned we likewise took down our round-house coach, and all the high carved work belonging to the stern of the ship, for, when we took her from the Spaniards before Panama, she was high as any third-rate ship in England.

CHAPTER XI

The Buccaneers depart from the isle of Gorgona, with design to plunder Arica. They lose one another by the way. They touch at the Isle of Plate, or Drake's Isle, where they meet again. Description of this isle. Some memoirs of Sir Francis Drake. An account of this voyage and the coasts all along. They sail as far in a fortnight as the Spaniards usually do in three months

ON Sunday, July 25th, in the afternoon, all things being now in readiness for our departure, we set sail, and stood away from the island of Gorgona, or Sharp's Isle, with a small breeze which served us at N.W. But as the sun went down that day, so our breeze died away by degrees. Yet already we could begin to experiment that our ship sailed much better since the taking down of her round house and the other alterations which we made in her.

The next day about two o'clock in the morning we had a land-breeze to help us, which lasted for the space of six hours, more or less. So that at noon we found ourselves to be five-leagues-and-a-half distant to the South-West from Gorgona. This day the Spaniards, our prisoners, told us, in common discourse, that in most part of this lowland coast they find three-score fathom water. In the afternoon we had a very strong land-breeze: meanwhile we continued making short trips off and in. That night we had much rain for the greatest part of the night, which occasioned the next morning, being the third day of our navigation, to be very cloudy until ten o'clock. About that hour it cleared up, and then we saw the island of Gorgona at E.N.E., being distant about 12 leagues more or less from us. We had the wind all this day at S.W., where it continued, seldom varying above two points of the compass to the westwards. Night being come, about two o'clock Captain Sharp ordered me to speak to Captain Cox and bid him go about and stand off from the shore, for he feared less Cox should come too nigh unto it. But he replied he knew well that he might stand in until two o'clock. The next day very early in the morning we saw him not, the morning being cloudy and stark calm. Yet notwithstanding at eight o'clock it cleared up, and neither then could we see him. Hence we concluded, and so it proved, that we had lost him in the obscurity of the night, through his obstinacy in standing in too long and not coming about when we spoke to him. Thus our Admiral's ship was left alone, and we had not the company of Captain Cox any longer in this voyage, till we arrived at the Isle of Plate, where we had the good fortune to find him again, as shall be mentioned hereafter. The weather being clear this morning, we could see Gorgona, at a distance of at least 15 or 16 leagues to the E.N.E. All this day it continued calm till about four in the afternoon, at which time we had a W.S.W. wind, which continued to blow all that night.

Thursday, July 29th, 1679. This day the wind continued pretty fresh all day long. About four in the afternoon we came within sight of the island Del Gallo, which I guessed to be nigh 28 leagues distant from that of Gorgona, the place of our departure S.W. It is about nine leagues distant E. from the main; so that the island with the mainland S.W. from it appears thus :—

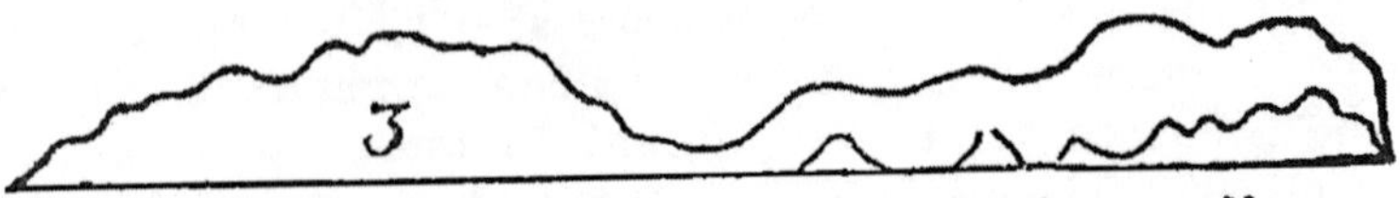

GALLO *LAT. 2. 12. N.*

All this day the weather continued clear, and the wind W.S.W.

The next day, July 30th, the wind blew very fresh and brisk, insomuch that we were in some fear for the heads of our low masts, being very sensible that they were but weak. About three or four in the afternoon we saw another island, 6 or 7 leagues distant from Gallo, called Gorgonilla. At E. by S. from us it made the appearance which I have here adjoined. All the mainland hereabouts lies very low and flat, and is in very many places overflowed and drowned every high-water.

GORGONILLA

On Saturday, July 31st, in the morning the island Del Gallo, at E.N.E. being distant about 8 leagues, gave us this appearance :—

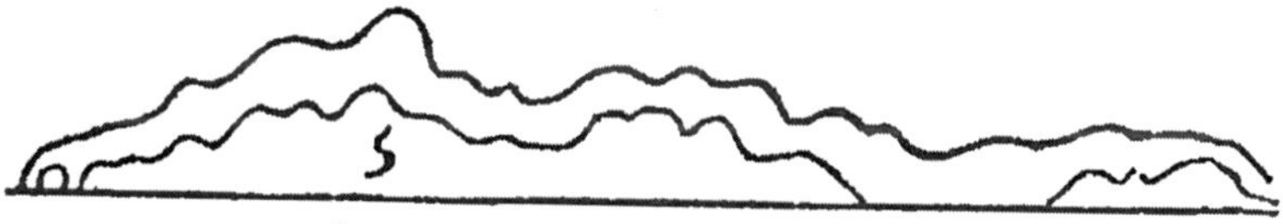

GALLO. Another Prospect thereof

The point of Mangroves is a low and level point, running out S.S.W. This day, and the night before it, we lost by our computation 3 leagues of our way, which I believe happened because we stood out too far from the land, having stood off all night long.

August 1st, which was Sunday, we had a very fresh wind at W.S.W. This was joined also with several small showers of rain which fell that day. In the meanwhile we got pretty well to windward with it, by making small trips to and fro, which we performed most commonly, by standing in three glasses and as many out.

The next day, August 2nd, in the morning, we came up into the highland of Santiago, where begins the highland of this coast. We kept at the distance of ten leagues from it, making continual short trips, as was mentioned before. The next day likewise we continued to do the same. But the weather was cloudy and for the most part full of rain.

Wednesday, August 4th, we continued still turning in the wind's eye, as we had done for two days before. This day, in the afternoon, we discovered three hills at E.N.E. of our ship. These hills make the land of San Matteo, which gives this following appearance :—

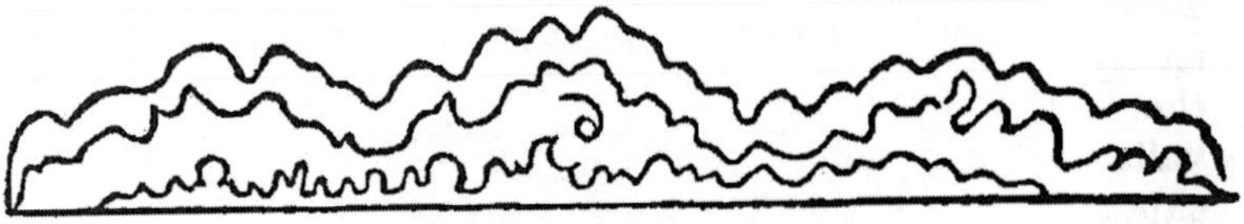

San Matteo

All the coast along hereabouts is highland. That evening also we saw the cape of San Francisco. At first this cape appeared like two several islands. But two hours after, at the distance of 12 leagues, at S. by W. it looked thus :—

Cape of San Francisco

Thursday, August 5th, we being then about the cape, it looked very like unto Beachy Head in England. It is full of white cliffs on all sides. The land turns off here to E. of S., and makes a large and deep bay, the circumference whereof is full of pleasant hills. In the bight of the bay are two high and rocky islands, which represent exactly two ships with their sails full. We were now come out of the rainy countries into a pleasant and fair region, where we had for the most part a clear sky and dry weather. Only now and then we could here find a small mist, which soon would vanish away. In the meanwhile every night a great dew used to fall, which supplied the defect of rain.

The two next days following we continued plying to windward with fair weather, nothing else remarkable happening in them which might deserve any notice to be taken thereof.

On Sunday, August 8th, we came close under a wild and mountainous country. This day likewise we saw Cape Passao at the distance of 10 leagues, more or less, to windward of us. Ever since we came on this side Mangrove point we had observed a windward current did run all along as we sailed. Under shore the land is full of white cliffs and groves, lower towards the pitch of the cape.

The next day we had both a fair day and a fresh wind to help us on our voyage. We observed that Cape Passao makes three points, between which are two bays. The leeward-most of the two is of the length of 3 leagues, and the other of 4. Adjoining unto the bays is seen a pleasant valley. Our prisoners informed us that northward of these capes live certain Indians, who sell maize and other provisions to any ships that happen to come in there. The Cape itself is a continuous cliff, covered with several sorts of shrubs and low bushes. Under these cliffs lies a sandy bay of the depth of 40 feet. The Spaniards say that the wind is always here between the S.S.W. and W.S.W. The cape represents with much likeliness the brow of an alligator or cayman. At S. Cape Passao appears thus :—

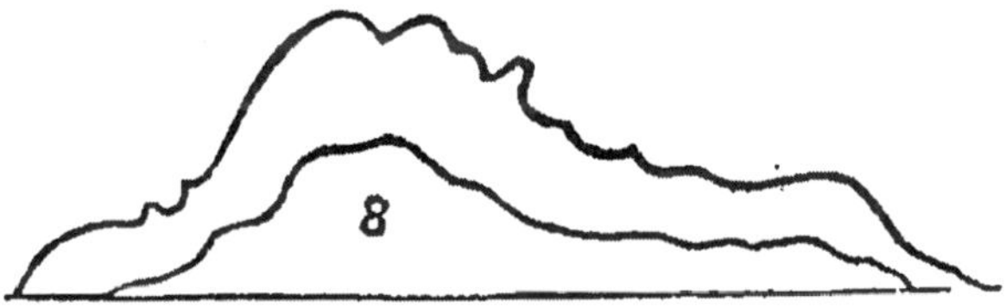

CAPE PASSAO *LAT. 1. 30. S.*

Tuesday, August 10th. This morning the sky was so thick and hazy that we could not see the highland, though it were just before us, and not altogether two leagues distant from us. But, as soon as it cleared up, we stood in towards the land until we came within a mile of the shore. Here, having sounded, we found seven-fathom-and-a-half of water, under which was a light and clayey ground. The coast all along is very mountainous and likewise full of high and towering cliffs. When we sounded, the tide was almost at low-water. Here it ebbs and flows nearly four fathom perpendicular. From this cape the land runs along S.E. for the space of three or four leagues, with huge highland cliffs, like those of Calais over against England. Being past this cape, the highland S. from us is Cape St Lawrence.

August 11th we found ourselves N.N.W. from Monte de Christo, a very high and round hill. Thence to windward is seen a very pleasant country, with spots here and there of woody land, which cause the country all over to look like so many enclosures of ripe cornfields. To leeward of the said hill the land is all high and hilly, with white cliffs at the seaside. The coast runs S.W. till it reaches to a point of land within which is the port of Manta, as it is called. This port of Manta is nothing else than a settlement of Spaniards and Indians together where ships that want provisions call in and are furnished with several necessaries. About 6 or 7 leagues to windward of this port is Cape St Lawrence, butting out into the sea, being in form like the top of a church. Monte de Christo gives this appearance at sea :—

MONTE DE CHRISTO LAT. 50. S.

The cape rises higher and higher from the port of Manta. As we sailed along we saw multitudes of grampuses every day ; also water-snakes of divers colours. Both the Spaniards and Indians are very fearful of these snakes, believing there is no cure for their bitings. At the distance of eight leagues, or thereabouts, to leeward of Cape St Lawrence it appears thus :—

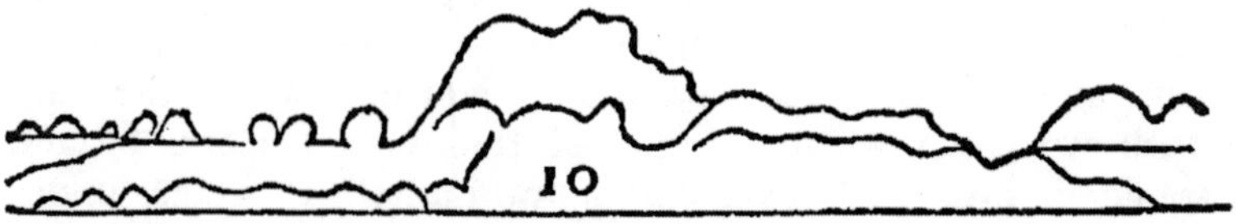

CAPE ST. LAWRENCE LAT. 55. S.

This day before night we came within sight of Manta. Here we saw the houses of the town belonging to the port, which were not above twenty or thirty Indian houses, lying under the windward and the mount. We were not willing to be descried by the inhabitants of the said place, and stood off to sea again.

On Thursday, August 12th, in the morning, we saw the Island of Plate at S.W. at the distance of five-leagues, more or less. It appeared to us to be an even land. Having made this island, we resolved to go thither and refit our rigging, and get some goats which there run wild up and down the country. For, as was said before, at this time we had no other provision than flour and water. The island itself is indifferent highland and off at sea looks thus, as is here described :—

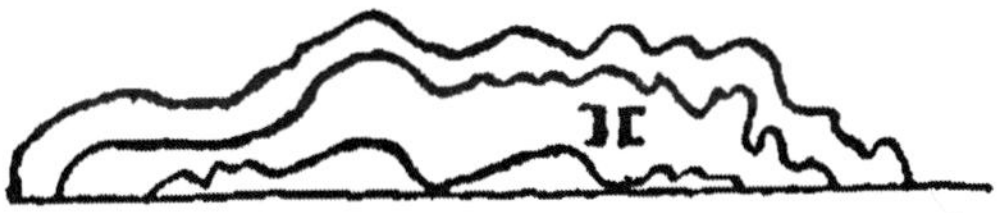

ISLE OF PLATE LAT. 2. 42. S.

But the highland of Cape Passao, of which we have spoken before, at the distance of 15 leagues to N., gives in several hummocks this appearance :—

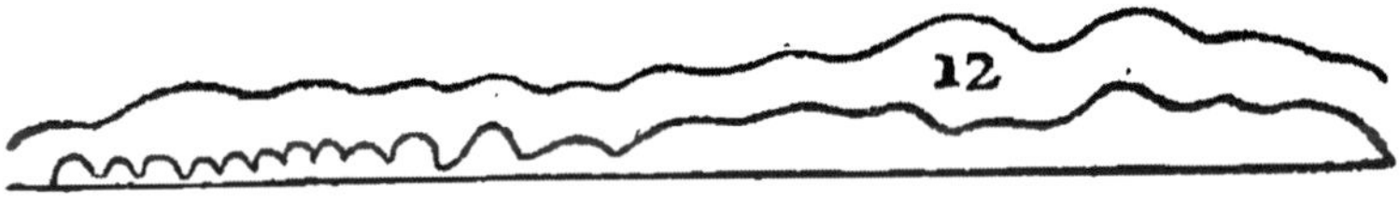

HIGHLAND OF CAPE PASSAO

The land of Cape St Lawrence is all white cliffs, the head of the cape running N. and S. This day several great whales came up to us, and dived under our ship. One of these whales followed our ship from two in the afternoon till dark night.

The next morning very early, at about six o'clock, we came under the aforesaid Isle of Plate, and here unexpectedly, to our great joy, we found at anchor the ship of Captain Cox with his whole company, whom we had lost at sea for the space of a whole fortnight before. We found they had reached this island, and had been there at anchor four days before us, being now just ready to depart thence. At about seven we came to anchor, and then the other vessel sent us a live tortoise and a goat to feast upon that day, telling us withal of great store of tortoises to be found ashore upon the bays and of much fish to be caught hereabouts. The island is very steep on all sides, insomuch that there is landing only on the N.E. side thereof, where is a gully, nigh unto which we anchored in 12 fathom water. Here at the distance of a furlong, or little more, from the shore as you go to land, you will see on the left hill a cross still standing there erected in former times. No trees are to be found on the whole island, but only low shrubs, on which the goats feed, which cattle is here very numerous. The shore is bold and hard, neither is there any water to be found upon it, excepting only on the S.W. side of the island, where it cannot be come at, lying so much enclosed by the rocks and too great a sea hindering the approach to it in boats.

This island received its name from Sir Francis Drake and his famous actions, for here it is reported by tradition that he made the dividend, or sharing, of that quantity of plate which he took in the *Armada* of this sea, distributing it to each man of his company by whole bowls full. The Spaniards affirm to this day that he took at that time twelve-score tons of plate and 16 bowls of coined money a man, his number then being 45 men in all—insomuch that they were forced to heave much of it overboard, because his ship could not carry it all. Hence was this island called by the Spaniards themselves the Isle of Plate, from this great dividend; and by us Drake's Isle.

All along as we sailed we found the Spanish pilots to be very ignorant of the coasts. But they plead thus much for their ignorance, that the merchants, their employers, either of Mexico, Lima, Panama, or other parts, will not entrust one pennyworth of goods on that man's vessel that corks her, for fear she should miscarry. Here our prisoners told us likewise that in the time of Oliver Cromwell, or the Commonwealth of England, a certain ship was fitted out of Lima with 70 brass guns, having on board her no less than thirty millions of dollars, or pieces-of-eight, all which vast sum of money was given by the merchants of Lima, and sent as a present to our gracious King (or rather his father) who now reigneth, to supply him in his exile and distress; but that this great and rich ship was lost by keeping along the shore in the Bay of Manta above-mentioned, or thereabouts. What truth there may be in this history I cannot easily tell: at least it seems to me as scarce deserving any credit.

At this island we took out of Mr Cox's ship the old Moor (for of that nation he was) who pretended he would be our pilot to Arica. This was done lest we should have the misfortune of losing the company of Cox's vessel, as we had done before, our ship being the biggest in burden and having the greatest number of men. Captain Peralta admired oftentimes that we were got so far to windward in so little space of time; whereas they had been, he said, many times three or four months in reaching to this distance from our departure. Their long and tedious voyages, he added, were occasioned by their keeping at too great a distance from the shore. Moreover, he told us, that had we gone to the islands of Galapagos, as we were once determined to do, we had met in that voyage with many calms and such currents that many ships have by them been lost and never heard of to this day. This Island of Plate is about two-leagues in length, and very full of both deep and dangerous bays, as also such as we call gullies in these parts. The circumference and description of the said island is exactly thus :—

We caught at this island and salted good number of goats and tortoises. One man standing here on a little bay in one day turned 17 tortoises, besides which number our mosquito-strikers brought us in several more. Captain Sharp, our Commander, showed himself very ingenious in striking them, he performing it as well as the tortoise-strikers themselves. For these creatures here are so little fearful that they offer not to sink from the fishermen, but lie still until such time as they are struck. But we found that the tortoises on this side were not so large, nor so sweet to the taste, as those on the North side of the island. Of goats we have taken, killed, and salted, above 100 in a day, and that without any labour. While we stayed here we made a square maintopsail yard. We cut also six feet off our bowsprit, and three feet more off our head. Most of the time that we remained here we had hazy weather. Only now and then the sun would happen to break out, and then to shine so hot that it burnt the skin off the necks of several of our men. As for me, my lips were burnt in such a manner that they were not well in a whole week afterwards.

CHAPTER XII

Captain Sharp and his company depart from the Isle of Plate in prosecution of their voyage towards Arica. They take two Spanish vessels by the way, and learn intelligence from the enemy. Eight of their company destroyed at the Isle of Gallo. Tediousness of this voyage, and great hardships they endured. Description of the coast all along, and their sailings

HAVING taken in at the isle of Plate what provisions and other necessaries we could get, we set sail thence on Tuesday, August 17th, 1679, in prosecution of our voyage and designs above-mentioned, to take and plunder the vastly rich town of Arica. This day we sailed so well, and the same we did for several others afterwards, that we were forced to lie by several times, besides reefing our topsails, to keep our other ship company, lest we should lose her again.

The next morning, about break of day, we found ourselves to be at the distance of 7 or 8 leagues to the Westward of the island whence we had departed, standing W. by S. with a S. by W. wind. About noon that day we had laid the land. After dinner the wind came S.S.W. at which time we were forced to stay more than once for the other vessel belonging to our company.

On the following day we continued in like manner a West course all the day long. Sometimes this day the wind would change, but then in a quarter-of-an-hour it would return to S.S.W. again. Hereabouts where we now were we observed great ripplings of the sea.

August 20th, yesterday in the afternoon about six o'clock, we stood in S.E., but all night and all this day, we had very small winds. We found still that we gained very much on the small ship, which did not a little both perplex and hinder us in our course.

The next day likewise we stood in S.E. by S., though with very little wind, which sometimes varied, as was mentioned above. That day I finished two quadrants, each of which were two-feet-and-a-half radius. Here we had in like manner, as has been mentioned on other days of our sailings, very many dolphins, and other sorts of fish swimming about our ship.

On the morning following we saw again the island of Plate at N.E. of our ship, giving us this appearance at that distance of prospect :—

ISLE OF PLATE

The same day at the distance of six-leagues, more or less, from the said island, we saw another island, called Solango. This isle lies close in by the mainland. In the evening we observed it to bear E.N.E. from us. Our course was S.E. by S. and the wind at S.W. by S. This day likewise we found that our lesser ship was still a great hindrance to our sailing, being forced to lie by, and stay for her two or three hours every day. We found likewise that, the farther from shore we were, the less wind we had all along, and that under the shore we were always sure of a fresh gale, though not so favourable to us as we could wish it to be. Hitherto we had used to stand off 40 leagues, and yet notwithstanding, in the space of six days, we had not got above ten leagues on our voyage, from the place of our departure.

August 23rd: this day the wind was S.W. by S. and S.S.W. In the morning we stood off. The island of Solango, at N.E. by N. appears thus :—

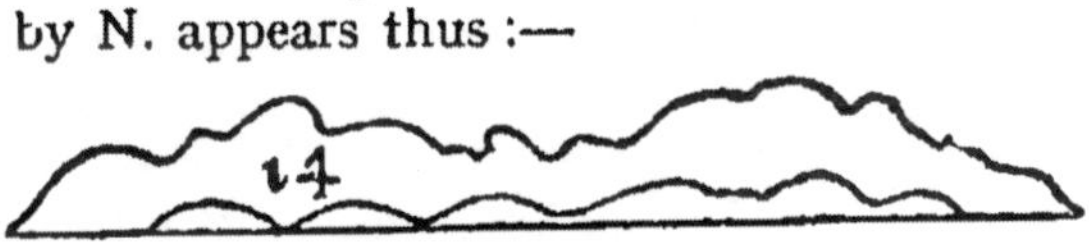

ISLE OF SOLANGO

As S. by W., and about six leagues distance from us, we descried a long and even hill. I took it to be an island, and conjectured it might be at least eight leagues distant from the continent. But afterwards we found it was a point of land joining to the main, and is called Point St Helena, being continued by a piece of land which lies low, and in several places is almost drowned from sight, so that it cannot be seen at two leagues distance. In this lowland the Spaniards have conveniences for making pitch, tar, salt, and some other things, for which purpose they have several houses here, and a friar who serves them as their chaplain. From the island of Solango to this place are reckoned eleven leagues, more or less. The land is hereabouts indifferent high, and is likewise full of bays. We had this day very little wind to help us in our voyage, excepting what blasts came now and then in snatches. These sometimes would prove pretty fair to us, and allow us for some little while a South course. But our chief course was S.E. by S. The point of St Helena at S. half E. and at about 6 leagues distance gives exactly this appearance as follows :—

PUNTA DE SANTA HELENA

Here we found no great current of the sea to move anyway. At the isle of Plata, afore-described, the sea ebbs and flows nearly 13 feet perpendicular. About four leagues to leeward of this point is a deep bay, having a quay at the mouth of it which takes up the better part of its width. In the deepest part of the bay on shore we saw a great smoke, which was at a village belonging to the bay, to which place the people were removed from the point above-mentioned. This afternoon we had a small Westerly wind, our course being S.S.W. Hereabouts it is all along a very bold shore. At three o'clock in the afternoon we tacked about to clear the point. Being now a little way without the point, we spied a sail, which we conceived to be a bark. Hereupon we hoisted out our canoe, and sent in pursuit of her, which made directly for the shore. But the sail proved to be nothing else than a pair of bark-logs [1], which, arriving on shore, the men spread their sail on

[1] The modern *balsa, balza*: cf. Hakluyt, *Voyages* [1600], vol. iii, p. 416: " . . . it was so well peopled with Indians, which had so many canoas of wood, as we might discerne, and not raftes or balsas, for so they call those floats which are made all flat with canes."

the sand of the bay to dry. At the same time there came down on the shore an Indian on horseback, who hallooed to our canoe, which had followed the logs. But our men, fearing to discover who we were, in case they went too near the shore, left the design and returned back to us. In these parts the Indians have no canoes, nor any wood indeed that may be thought fit to make them of. Had we been descried by these poor people, they would in all probability have been very fearful of us. But they offered not to stir, which gave us to understand they knew us not. We could perceive from the ship a great path leading to the hills, so that we believed this place to be a look-out, or watch-place, for the security of Guayaquil. Between four and five we doubled the point, and then we descried the Point Chandy, at the distance of six leagues S.S.E. from this point. At first sight it seemed like to a long island, but withal, lower than that of St Helena.

Tuesday, August 24th, at noon, we took the other ship, wherein Captain Cox sailed in tow, she being every day a greater hindrance than before to our voyage. Thus, about three in the afternoon we lost sight of land, in standing over for Cape Blanco. Here we found a strong current to move to the S.W. The wind was at S.W. by S., our course being S. by E. At the upper end of this gulf, which is framed by the two capes aforementioned, stands the city of Guayaquil, being a very rich place, and the *embarcadero*, or sea-port, to the great city of Quito. To this place likewise many of the merchants of Lima do usually send the money they design for Old Spain in barks, and by that means save the custom that otherwise they would pay to the King by carrying it on board the fleet. Hither comes much gold from Quito, and very good and strong broadcloth, together with images for the use of the churches, and several other things of considerable value. But more especially coco-nut, whereof chocolate is made, which is supposed here to be the best in the whole universe. The town of Guayaquil consists of about 150 great houses, and twice as many little ones. This was the town to which Captain Sawkins intended to make his voyage, as was mentioned above. When ships of greater burden come into this gulf, they anchor outside Lapina, and then put their lading into lesser vessels to carry it to the town. Towards the evening of this day a small breeze sprang up, varying from point to point, after which, about nine o'clock at night, we tacked about, and stood off to sea, W. by N.

As soon as we had tacked, we happened to spy a sail N.N.E. from us. Hereupon we instantly cast off our other vessel which we had in tow, and stood round about after them. We came very near to the vessel before the people saw us, by reason of the darkness of the night. As soon as they spied us, they immediately clapped on a wind, and sailed very well before us, insomuch that it was a pretty while before we could come up with them and within call. We hailed them in Spanish, by means of an Indian prisoner, and commanded them to lower their top-sails. They answered they would soon make us to lower our own. Hereupon we fired several guns at them, and they as thick at us again with their harquebuses[1]. Thus they fought us for the space of half-an-hour or more, and would have done it longer, had we not killed the man at the helm, after which none of the rest dared to be so hardy as to take his place. With another of our shot we cut in pieces and disabled their main-top halliards. Hereupon they cried out for quarter, which we gave them, and entered their ship. Being possessed of the vessel, we found in her five-and-thirty men, of which number 24 were natives of Old Spain. They had one-and-thirty firearms on board the ship for their defence. They had only fought us, as they declared afterwards, out of bravado, having promised on shore so to do, in case they met us at sea. The Captain of this vessel was a person of quality, and his brother, since the death of Don Jacinto de Barabona, killed by us in the engagement before Panama, was now made Admiral of the sea-armada. With him we took also in this bark five or six other persons of quality. They did us in this fight, though short, very great damage in our rigging, by cutting it in pieces, besides which they wounded two of our men, and a third man was wounded by the negligence of one of our own men, occasioned by a pistol which went off unadvisedly. About eleven o'clock this night we stood off to the west.

[1] An early kind of hand-gun. Other early spellings are: arkbusshe, ha(c)quebute, hargubush, harquebuz(e), herquebuze, hagabus, etc!

The next morning, about break of day, we hoisted out our canoe, and went aboard the bark which we had taken the night before. We transported on board our own ship more of the prisoners taken in the said vessel, and began to examine them, to learn what intelligence we could from them. The Captain of the vessel, who was a very civil and meek gentleman, satisfied our desires in this point very exactly, saying to us :

Gentlemen, I am now your prisoner-at-war by the over-ruling providence of fortune, and, moreover, am very well satisfied that no money whatsoever can procure my ransom, at least for the present at your hands. Hence I am persuaded it is not my interest to tell you a lie, which if I do I desire you to punish me as severely as you shall think fit. We heard of your taking and destroying our Armadilla and other ships at Panama, about six weeks after that engagement, by two several barks which arrived here thence. But they could not inform us whether you designed to come any farther to the southward, but, rather, desired we would send them speedily all the help by sea that we could. Hereupon we sent the noise and rumour of your being in these seas by land to Lima, desiring they would expedite what succours they could send to join with ours. We had at that time in our harbour two or three great ships, but all of them very unfit to sail. For this reason at Lima the Viceroy of Peru pressed three great merchant ships, into the biggest of which he put 14 *brass guns, into the second* 10, *and in the other* 6. *To these he added two barks, and put* 750 *soldiers on board them all. Of this number of men they landed eight-score at Point St Helena, all the rest being carried down to Panama, with design to fight you there. Besides these forces, two other men-of-war, bigger than the aforementioned, are still lying at Lima, and fitting out there in all speed to follow and pursue you. One of these men-of-war is equipped with* 36 *brass guns, and the other with* 30. *These ships, besides their complement of seamen, have* 400 *soldiers added to them by the Viceroy. Another man-of-war belonging to this number, and lesser than the aforementioned, is called the* Patache. *This ship consists of* 24 *guns, and was sent to Arica to fetch the King's plate thence. But the Viceroy, having received intelligence of your exploits at Panama, sent for this ship back from there with such haste that they came away and left the money behind them. Hence the* Patache *now lies at the port of Callao, ready to sail on the first occasion or news of your arrival thereabouts, they having for this purpose sent to all parts very strict orders to keep a good look-out on all sides, and all places along the coasts. Since this, from Manta they sent us word that they had seen two ships at sea pass by that place. And from the Goat Key also we heard that the Indians had seen you, and that they were assured one of your vessels was the ship called* La Trinidad, *which you had taken before Panama, as being a ship very well known in these seas. Hence we concluded that your design was to ply, and make your voyage thereabouts. Now this bark wherein you took us prisoners, being bound for Panama, the Governor of Guayaquil sent us out before her departure, if possible to discover you, which, if we did, we were to run the bark on shore and get away, or else to fight you with these soldiers and firearms that you see. As soon as we heard of your being in these seas, we built two forts, the one of six guns, and the other of four, for the defence of the town. At the last muster taken in the town of Guayaquil we had there* 850 *men of all colours, but when we came out, we left only* 200 *men that were actually under arms.*

Thus ended the relation of that worthy gentleman. About noon that day we unrigged the bark which we had taken, and after so doing sunk her. Then we stood S.S.E., and afterwards S. by W. and S.S.W. That evening we saw point St Helena at N. half E., at the distance of nine leagues, more or less.

The next day, being August 26th, in the morning we stood S. That day we cried out all our pillage, and found that it amounted to 3,276 pieces-of-eight, which was accordingly divided by shares amongst us. We also punished a friar, who was chaplain to the bark aforementioned, and shot him upon the deck, casting him overboard before he was dead. Such cruelties, though I abhorred very much in my heart, yet here was I forced to hold my tongue and contradict them not, as having not authority to oversway them. At ten o'clock this morning we saw land again, and the pilot said we were sixteen leagues to leeward of Cabo Blanco. Hereupon we stood off and on, close under the shore, which all appeared to be barren land.

The morning following we had very little wind, so that we advanced but slowly all that day. To windward of us we could perceive the continent to be all high land, being whitish clay, full of white cliffs. This morning, in common discourse, our prisoners confessed to us and acknowledged the destruction of one of our little barks, which we lost on our way to the island of Cayboa. They stood away, as it appeared by their information, for the Goat Key, thinking to find us there, as having heard Captain Sawkins say that he would go thither. On their way they happened to fall in with the island of Gallo, and understanding its weakness by their Indian pilot, they ventured on shore and took the place, carrying away three white women in their company. But, after a small time of cruising, they returned again to the aforesaid island, where they stayed two or three days, after which they went out to sea again. Within three or four days they came to a little quay four leagues distant from this isle. But, whilst they had been out and in thus several times, one of their prisoners made his escape to the mainland, and brought off thence 50 men with firearms. These, placing themselves in ambush, at the first volley killed six of the seven men that belonged to the bark. The other man that was left took quarter of the enemy, and he it was that discovered to them our design upon the town of Guayaquil. By an observation which we made this day we found ourselves to be in lat. 3° 50″. At this time, our prisoners told us there was an embargo laid on all the Spanish ships, commanding them not to stir out of the ports, for fear of their falling into our hands at sea.

Saturday, August 28th. This morning we took out all the water, and most part of the flour that was in Captain Cox's vessel. The people in like manner came on board our ship. Having done this, we made a hole in the vessel and left her to sink, with a small old canoe at her stern. To leeward of Manta, a league from shore, in 18 fathom water, there runs a great current outwards. About eleven in the forenoon we weighed anchor, with a wind at W.N.W. turning it out. Our number now in all being reckoned, we found ourselves to be 140 men, two boys, and 55 prisoners, being all now in one and the same bottom. This day we got six or seven leagues in the wind's eye.

All the day following we had a very strong S.S.W. wind, insomuch that we were forced to sail with two reefs in our main-top sail and one also in our fore-top sail. Here Captain Peralta told us that the first place which the Spaniards settled in these parts, after Panama, was Tumbes, a place that now was to leeward of us, in this gulf where we now were. That there a priest went ashore with a cross in his hand, while

10,000 Indians stood gazing at him. Being landed on the strand, there came out of the woods two lions; and he laid the cross gently on their backs, and they instantly fell down and worshipped it: and moreover, that two tigers, following them, did the same—whereby these animals gave to the Indians to understand the excellency of the Christian religion, which they soon after embraced. About four in the evening we came abreast the cape, which is the highest part of all. The land hereabouts appeared to be barren and rocky. At 3 leagues distance east from us the cape showed thus:—

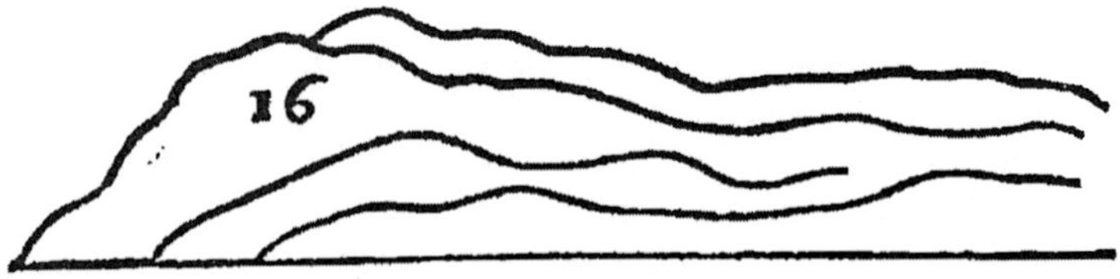

CAPE BLANCO

Were it not for a windward current which runs under the shore hereabouts, it were totally impossible for any ships to get about this cape, there being such a great current to leeward in the offing. In the last bark which we took, of which we spoke in this chapter, we made prisoner one Nicolas Moreno, a Spaniard by nation, who was esteemed to be a very good pilot of the South Sea. This man did not cease continually to praise our ship for her sailing, and especially for the alterations we had made in her. As we went along, we observed many bays to lie between this cape and Point Parina, of which we shall soon make mention hereafter.

In the night the wind came about to S.S.E. and we had a very stiff gale of it; so that by break of day the next morning we found ourselves to be about 5 leagues distant to windward of the cape aforementioned. The land hereabouts makes three or four several bays, and grows lower and lower the nearer we came to Punta Parina. This point looks at first sight like two islands. Between four and five of the clock that evening we were W. from the said point.

The next day likewise, being the last day of August, the wind still continued S.S.E. as it had done the whole day before. This day we thought it convenient to stand farther out to sea, for fear of being descried at Paita, which now was not very far distant from us. The morning proved to be hazy—but about eleven we spied a sail, which stood then just as we did E. by S. Coming nearer to it, by degrees we found her to be nothing else than a pair of bark-logs under a sail, which were going that way. Our pilot advised us not to meddle with those logs, nor mind them in the least, for it was very doubtful whether we should be able to come up with them or not, and then by giving chase to them we should easily be descried and known to be the English pirates, as they called us. These bark-logs sail excellently well for the most part, and some of them are of such a size that they will carry 250 packs of meal from the valleys to Panama without wetting any of it. This day, by an observation made, we found ourselves to be in lat. 4° 55′ S. Point Parina at N.E. by E., and at the distance of 6 leagues, more or less, gives this following appearance :—

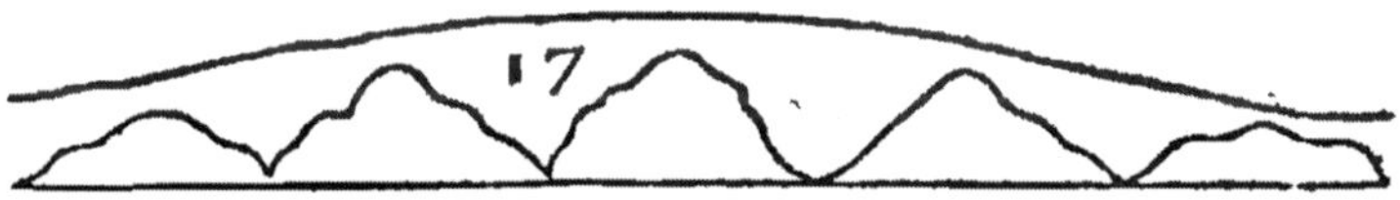

Punta Parina

At the same time La Silla de Paita bore from us S.E. by E., being distant only 7 or 8 leagues. It had the form of a high mountain, and appeared thus to us :—

La Silla de Paita

The town of Paita itself is situated in a deep bay, about 2 leagues to leeward of this hill. It serves for an *embarcadero*, or port-town, to another great place which is distant thence about 13 leagues higher in the country and is called Piura, seated in a very barren country.

On Wednesday, September 1st, our course was S. by W. The midnight before this day we had a land-wind that sprang up. In the afternoon La Silla de Paita, at the distance of 7 leagues, at E. by N. appeared thus :—

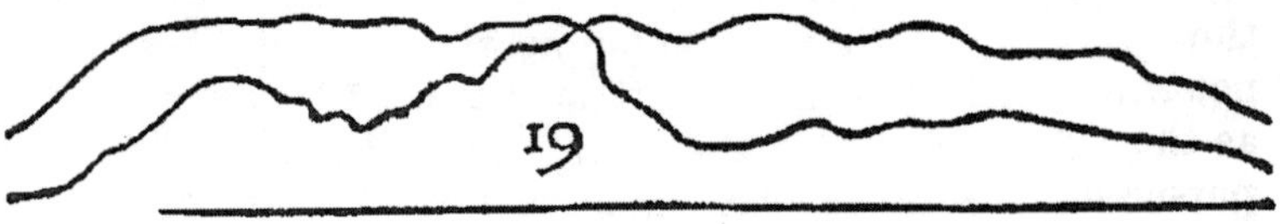

LA SILLA DE PAITA

All along hereabouts is nothing but barren land, as was said before: likewise, for three or four days last past, we observed along the coasts many seals.

That night as we sailed we saw something that appeared to us to be as it were a light. And the next morning we spied a sail, whence we judged the light had come. The vessel was at the distance of six leagues from us, in the wind's eye, and thereupon we gave her chase. She stood to windward as we did. This day we had an observation, which gave us lat. 5° 30′ S. At night we were about 4 leagues to leeward of her, but so great a mist fell that we suddenly lost sight of her. At this time the weather was as cold with us as in England in November. Every time we went about with our ship the other did the like. Our pilot told us that this ship set forth from Guayaquil eleven days before they were taken, and that she was laden with rigging, woollen and common cloth, and other manufactures made at Quito. Moreover, that he had heard that they had spent a mast, and had put into Paita to refit it.

The night following they showed us several lights through their negligence, which they ought not to have done, for by that means we steered directly after them. The next morning she was more than 3 leagues in the wind's eye distant from us. Had they suspected us, it could not be doubted but they would have made away towards the land, but they seemed not to fly nor stir for our chase. The land here all along is level, and not very high. The weather was hazy, so that at about eleven o'clock that morning we lost sight of her. At this time we had been for the space of a whole week, at an allowance of only two draughts of water each day, so scarce were provisions with us. That afternoon we saw the vessel again, and at night we were not full two leagues distant from her, and not more than half-a-league to leeward. We made short trips all the night long.

On Saturday, September 4th, about break of day, we saw the ship again at the distance of a league, more or less, and not above a mile to windward of us. They stood out as soon as they espied us, and we stood directly after them. Having pursued them for several hours, about four o'clock in the afternoon, we came up within the distance of half our small-arms shot, to windward of them. Hereupon they, perceiving who we were, presently lowered all their sails at once, and we cast dice among ourselves for the first entrance. The lot fell to larboard, so that 20 men belonging to that watch entered her. In the vessel were found 50 packs of coco-nut, such as chocolate is made of, many packs of raw silk, Indian cloth, and thread stockings : these things being the principal part of her cargo. We stood out S.W. by S. all the night following.

The next day being come, we transported on board our ship the chief part of her lading. In her hold we found some rigging, as had been told us by Nicholas Moreno, our pilot, taken in the former vessel off Guayaquil ; but the greatest part of the hold was full of timber. We took out of her also some osnaburgs[1], of which we made top-gallant sails, as shall be said hereafter. It was now nineteen days, as they told us, since they had set sail from Guayaquil, and then they had only heard there of our exploits before Panama, but did not so much as think of our coming so far to the southward, which did not give them the least suspicion of us, though they had seen us for the space of two or three days before at sea and always steering after them—otherwise they had made for the land, and endeavoured to escape our hands.

The next morning, likewise, we continued to take in the remaining part of what goods we desired out of our prize. When we had done, we sent most of our prisoners on board the said vessel, and left only their foremast standing, all the rest being cut down by the board. We gave them a foresail to sail withal, all their own water, and some of our flour to serve them for provisions, and thus we turned them away, not caring to be troubled or encumbered with too many of their company. Notwithstanding, we detained still several

[1] Coarse linens, originally exported from Osnaburg, in Germany.

of the chief of our prisoners. Such were Don Thomas de Argandona, who was Commander of the vessel taken before Guayaquil, Don Christoval, and Don Baltazar, both gentlemen of quality taken with him, Captain Peralta, Captain Juan Moreno, the pilot, and twelve slaves, of whom we intended to make good use, to do the drudgery of our ship. At this time I reckoned that we were about the distance of 35 leagues, little more or less, from land ; moreover, by an observation made this day, we found lat. 7° 1′ S. Our plunder being over and our prize turned away, we sold both chests, boxes, and several other things at the mast, by the voice of a crier.

On the following day we stood S.S.W. and S.W. by S. all day long. That day one of our company died, named Robert Montgomery, the same man who was shot by the negligence of one of our own men with a pistol through the leg at the taking of the vessel before Guayaquil, as was mentioned above. We had an observation also this day, by which we now found lat. 7° 26′ S. On the same day likewise we made a dividend, and shared all the booty taken in the last prize. This being done, we hoisted into our ship the launch which we had taken in her, as being useful to us. All these days last past it was observed that we had every morning a dark cloud in the sky, which in the North Sea would certainly foretell a storm—but here it always blew over.

Wednesday, September 8th, in the morning, we threw our dead man above-mentioned into the sea, and gave him three French volleys for his funeral ceremony. In the night before this day we saw a light belonging to some vessel at sea, but we stood away from it, as not desiring to see any more sails to hinder us in our voyage towards Arica, whither now we were designed. This light was undoubtedly from some ship to leeward of us, but on the next morning we could descry no sail. Here I judged we had made a S.W. by S. way from Paita, and by an observation found 8° 00′ S.

CHAPTER XIII

A continuation of their long and tedious voyage to Arica, with a description of the coasts and sailings thereunto. Great hardship they endured for want of water and other provisions. They are descried at Arica, and dare not land there—the country being all in arms before them. They retire thence, and go to Puerto de Hilo, close by Arica. Here they land, take the town with little or no loss on their side, refresh themselves with provisions, but in the end are cheated by the Spaniards, and forced shamefully to retreat thence

On September 9th we continued still to make a S.W. by S. way, as we had done the day before. By a clear and exact observation, taken the same day, we found now lat. 8° 12′ S. All the twenty-four hours last past afforded us but little wind, so that we advanced but little on our voyage, and were forced to tack about every four or five hours.

The next day, by another observation taken, we found then lat. 9° 00′ S. Now the weather was much warmer than before, and with this warmth we had small and misty rains that frequently fell. That evening a strong breeze came up at S.E. by E.

The night following, likewise, we had a very great dew that fell, and a fresh wind continued to blow. At this time we were all hard at work to make small sails of the osnaburgs we had taken in the last prize, as being much more convenient for their lightness. The next morning being Saturday, September 11th, we lay by to mend our rigging. These last twenty-four hours we had made a S. by W. way. And now we had an observation that gave us lat. 10° 9′ S. I supposed this day that we were west from Cosmey, about the distance of eighty-nine leagues and a half.

September 12th. This day we reckoned a S.S.W. way,

and that we had made 34 leagues and three-quarters, or thereabouts. Also that all our westing from Paita was eighty-four leagues. We supposed ourselves now to be in lat. 11° 40′ S. But, the weather being hazy, no observation could be made.

September 13th. Yesterday in the afternoon we had a great eclipse of the sun, which lasted from one o'clock till three after dinner. From this eclipse I then took the true judgment of our longitude from the Canary Islands, and found myself to be 285° 35′, in lat. 11° 45′ S. The wind was now so fresh that we took in our top-sails, making a great way under our courses and sprit-sail.

September 14th we had a cloudy morning, which continued so all the first part thereof. About eight it cleared up, and then we set our fore-topsail and, about noon, our main-topsail likewise. This was observable, that all this great wind precedent did not make anything of a great sea. We reckoned this day that we had run by a S.W. by W. way, 26 leagues and two-thirds.

The next day, in like manner, we had close weather, such as the former morning. Our reckoning was twenty-four leagues and two-thirds, by a S.W. by W. way. But, by observation made, I found myself to be 23° S. of my reckoning, as being in the lat. of 15° 17′ S.

On the 16th we had but small and variable winds. For the twenty-four hours last past we reckoned 24 leagues and two-thirds, by a S.W. by S. way. By observation we had lat. 16° 41′. That evening we had a gale at E.S.E. which forced us to hand our top-sails.

The 17th, likewise, we had many gusts of wind at several times, forcing us to hand our top-sails often. But in the forenoon we set them with a fresh gale at E.S.E. My reckoning this day was 31 leagues, by a S.S.W. way. All day long we stood by our top-sails.

On the 18th we made a S. by W. way. We reckoned ourselves to be in lat. 19° 33′ S. The weather was hazy, and the wind began to die this day by degrees.

The next day, being the 19th, we had very small wind. I reckoned 13 leagues and a-half, by a S.W. by S. way, and our whole westing from Paita to be 164 leagues in lat. 20° 06′ S. All the afternoon we had a calm, with drizzling rain.

Monday, September 20th. Last night we saw the clouds, which are so famous among the Magellan mariners of these Southern seas. The least of these clouds was about the bigness of a man's hat. After this sight the morning was very clear. We had run at noon at E.S.E. 13 leagues and a-half, and, by an observation then made, we found lat. 20° 15′ S. This day the wind began to freshen at W. by S. Yet, notwithstanding, we had a very smooth sea.

But on the next morning the wind came about to S.W., and yet slackened by degrees. At four this morning it came to S. by E., and at ten the same day to S.E. by S. We had had this day a clear observation, and by it lat. 20° 25′ S. We stood now E. by N., with the wind at S.E.

September 22nd. This morning the wind was at E.S.E. By a clear observation we found lat. 19° 30′ S. Likewise on a N.E. by E. way.

September 23rd. We had a fresh wind and a high sea. This morning early the wind was at E. and about ten at E.N.E. From a clear observation we found our latitude to be 20° 35′ S. The way we made was S. by W. That morning we happened to split our sprit-sail.

Next morning the wind was variable and inconstant, and the weather but hazy. We reckoned a S. by E. way: this day we bent a new main-topsail, the old one serving for a fore-topsail. In the afternoon we had but little wind, whereupon we lowered our top-sails, having in like manner a very smooth sea.

The following day, likewise, brought us calm and warm weather, which occasioned us to set up our shrouds both fore and aft. An observation taken this day afforded us lat. 21° 57′. That evening we bent a sprit-sail.

On September 26th an observation gave us lat. 22° 05′ S. At noon we had a breeze at N.N.E., our course being E.S.E. In the afternoon we set up a larboard top-sail studding-sail. In the evening the wind came about at N. pretty fresh.

The next day we had a smooth sea, and took in four studding-sails. For yesterday in the afternoon we had put out, besides that above-mentioned, another studding-sail and two main studding-sails more. This day we had by observation 22° 45′ S., having made by an E.S.E. way thirty-five leagues and a-half—our whole meridian difference 68 leagues and a-half.

September 28th. All the forenoon we had very little wind, and yet withal a great southern sea. By observation we had lat. 22° 40′ S.

September 29th. All the night past we had much wind, with three or four fierce showers of rain. This was the first that we could call rain, ever since we left Cape Francisco above-mentioned. This day our allowance was shortened, and reduced to three-pints-and-a-half of water, and one cake of boiled bread to each man for a day. An observation this day gave us lat. 21° 59′ S. by a N.E. by E. way.

On September 30th we had a cloudy day, and the wind very variable, the morning being fresh. Our way was N.E. half N., wherein we made 18 leagues.

October 1st. All the night past and this day we had a cloudy sky and not much wind. We made a N.E. by E. way, and by it 17 leagues and two miles. This day we began at two-pints-and-a-half of water for a day.

The 2nd, we made a E.N.E. way, and by it 26 leagues, more or less. Our observation this day gave us lat. 20° 29′ S. I reckoned now that we were 10 leagues and a-half to E. of our meridian, the port of Paita, so that henceforward our departure was eastward. The wind was this day at S.E. by S.

On the 3rd we had both a cloudy morning, a high sea, and drizzling weather. An observation which we had this day gave us lat. 19° 45′ S. In the afternoon the wind blew so fresh that we were forced to hand our top-sails and sprit-sail.

The 4th, likewise, we had a high sea and a cold wind. At break of day we set our top-sails. An observation made afforded us lat. 19° 8′ S. Here we supposed ourselves fifty-nine leagues D.M.

The 5th, we had still a great sea, and sharp and cold winds, forcing us to our low sails. By a N.E. by E. way we reckoned this day 26 leagues and a-half.

But on the 6th we had great gusts of wind. Insomuch that this morning our ring-bolts gave way which held our main-stay, and had like to have brought our main-mast by the board. Hereupon we ran three or four glasses west before the wind. By an observation we found lat. 19° 4′ S.

On October 7th the wind had somewhat fallen. We had both a cloudy day and variable winds.

The 8th of the said month we had again a smooth sea and small whiffling winds. This morning we saw a huge shoal of fish, two or three water-snakes, and several seals.

On the next day we had in like manner a very smooth sea, and withal a cloudy day. Our course was E.

October 10th. We had likewise a cloudy day, with small and variable winds, and, what is consequent to these, a smooth sea. Our way was S. by E. This day we spied floating upon the sea several tufts of sea-grass, which gave us good hopes that we were not far from shore. In the afternoon we had a N.E. by E. wind that sprang up: the night was very cold and cloudy.

On the 11th we had a fresh wind at S.E. and E.S.E. together with a cloudy day, such as we had experienced for several days before. We reckoned this day 32 leagues by a N.E. by E. way. Here our pilot told us that the sky is always hazy near the shore upon these coasts where we now were.

On October 12th we had a clear day, and N.E. way.

The 13th we had but little wind. This day we saw a whale, which we took for an infallible token that we were not far distant from land, which now we hoped to see in a few days. We made an E.S.E. way, and by it we reckoned nineteen leagues. All the evening was very calm.

Thursday, October 14th, we had both a calm and close day until the afternoon. Then the weather became very hot and clear. This day we saw several land-fowls, being but small birds, concerning which our pilot said that they use to appear about one or two days' sail from the land. Our reckoning was 11 leagues by an E.S.E. way. In the evening of this day we thought that we had seen land, but it proved to be nothing else than a fog-bank.

October 15th. Both the night past and this day was very clear. We made an observation this day, which gave us lat. 18° 00′ S.

The 16th. Last night and this day were contrary to the former, both cloudy. Our way was N.E. by E. whereof we reckoned 13 leagues.

Sunday, October 17th, the wind blew very fresh, our course being E.N.E. About five that morning we saw land, but the weather was so hazy that at first we could scarce perceive whether it was land or not. It was distant from us about eight leagues, and appeared as a high and round hill, being in form like a sugar-loaf. We saw land afterwards all along to the S.E. by E. from it. In the evening, we being then within 5 leagues of the shore, the land appeared very high and steep.

October 18th. All the night last past we stood off to sea with a fresh wind. This morning we could just see land at N.N.E. We reckoned a S.E. by E. way, and by observation we found lat. 17° 17′ S.

Tuesday, October 19th. We had very cloudy weather, finding what our pilot had told us to be very true concerning the haziness of this shore. We saw all along as we went very high land, covered with clouds, insomuch that we could not see its top.

On Wednesday, the next day, we had likewise cloudy weather, and for the most part calm. The same weather being very cloudy, as before, continued in like manner on Thursday.

Friday, October 22nd. This morning we saw the land plain before us. Our pilot, being asked what land that was, answered it was the Point of Hilo. At N.N.E. and about 6 or 7 leagues distance it appeared thus to us:—

PUNTA DE HILO LAT. 18° 4′ S.

There is every morning and evening a brightness over the point which lasted for two or three hours, being caused by the reflection of the sun on the barren land, as it is supposed. This day we had but little wind, and the huge want of water we were now under occasioned much disturbance among our men. As for my part, I must acknowledge I could not sleep all night long through the greatness of my drought. We could willingly have landed here to seek for water, but the fear of being discovered and making ourselves known hindered us from so doing. Thus we unanimously resolved to endure our thirst for a little longer. Hereabouts is a small current that runs under the shore. This morning we had but little wind at S., our course being E.S.E. The point at the distance of 5 leagues N.E. looks on the following side thus:—

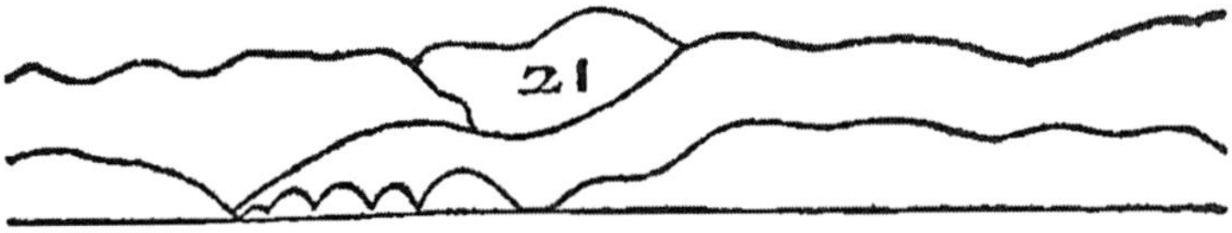

PUNTA DE HILO

Our wind continued to blow not about six hours each day. We reckoned the difference of our meridian to be this day 180 leagues. Very great was our affliction now for want of water, we having but half-a-pint a day to our allowance.

October 23rd. This day we were forced to spare one measure of water, thereby to make it hold out the longer, so scarce it became with us. At three this afternoon the point looked thus:—

PUNTA DE HILO MORA DE SAMA

Here the point looks like an island, and Mora de Sama to the southward thereof, gives this appearance:—

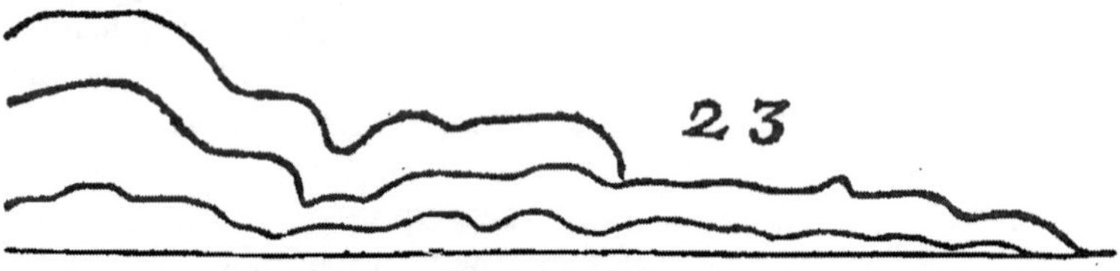

MORA DE SAMA

At about nine o'clock at night we had a land wind, and with it we stood S.E. by S., but all the night after we had but little wind.

October 24th. All the night past we had very cloudy and dark weather, with mizzling rain. The morning being come it cleared up, but all the land appeared covered with clouds. Yet, notwithstanding, in the afternoon it gave us again this appearance :—

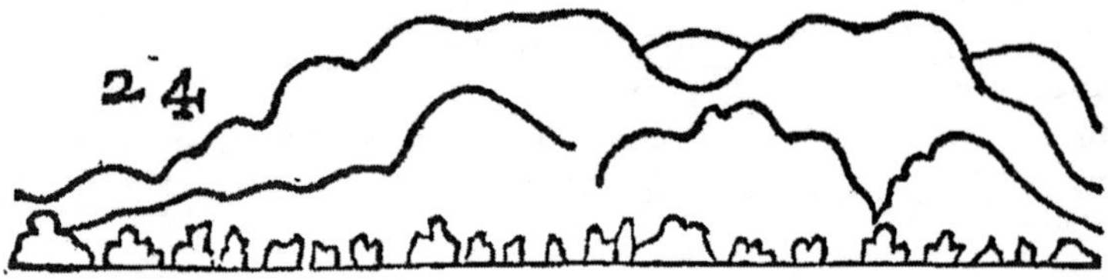

MORA DE SAMA *LAT.* 18° 29′ S.

Under the hill of Mora de Sama are eighteen or nineteen white cliffs, which appear in the form thus described. This day we resolved that 112 men should go ashore, and at about eight this evening we sent our launch and four canoes, with four-score men, to take three or four fishermen at a certain river, close by Mora de Sama, called El Rio de Juan Diaz, with intent to gain what intelligence we could as to how affairs stood at present on the coast and country thereabouts.

Monday, October 25th. Last night being about the distance of one-league-and-a-half from shore, we sounded, and found forty-five fathom water, with a hard ground at the bottom. This morning our people and canoes that were sent to take the fishermen returned, not being able to find either their houses or the river. They reported withal they had had a very fresh wind all the night long under shore, whereas we had not one breath of wind all night on board.

Tuesday, October 26th. Last night, being the night before this day, about six o'clock we departed from the ship to go to take Arica, resolving to land about the distance of a league to windward of the town. We were about 6 leagues distant from the town when we left our ship, whereby we were forced to row all night, that we might reach the place of our landing before day. Towards morning the canoes left the launch, which they had had all night in tow and wherein I was, and made all the speed they possibly could for the shore, with design to land before the launch could arrive. But, being come nigh the place where we designed to land, they found to our great sorrow and vexation that we were descried, and that all along the shore and through the country they had certain news of our arrival. Yet, notwithstanding our discovery, we would have landed if we could by any means have found a place to do it in. But the sea ran so high, and with such a force against the rocks, that our boats must have each been staved into one thousand pieces, and we in great danger of wetting our arms, if we should adventure to go on shore. The bay all round, and likewise the tops of the hills, was possessed by several parties of horse which seemed to be gathered there by a general alarm through the whole country, and they waited only for our landing, with design to make a strong opposition against us. They fired a gun at us, but we made them no answer, but rather returned to our ship, giving over this enterprise until a fairer opportunity. The hill of Arica is very white, being occasioned by the dung of multitudes of fowls that nest themselves in the hollow thereof. To leeward of the said hill lies a small island at the distance of a mile, more or less, from the shore. About half-a-league from that island we could perceive six ships to ride at anchor, four of which had their yards taken down from their masts, but the other two seemed to be ready to sail. We asked our pilot concerning these ships, and he told us that one of them was mounted with six guns, and the other with only four. Being disappointed of our expectations at Arica, we now resolved to bear away thence to the village of Hilo, there to take in water and other provisions, as also to learn what intelligence we could obtain. All that night we lay under a calm.

On October 27th, in the morning, we found ourselves to be about a league to windward of Mora de Sama. Yet, notwithstanding, the weather was quite calm, and we only drove with the current to leeward. The land between Hilo and Mora de Sama forms two several bays, and the coast runs along N.W. and S.E., as may appear by the following demonstration. Over the land we could see from our ship, as we drifted, the coming or rising of a very high land, at a great distance far up in the country.

October 28th. The night before this day we sent away our four canoes with 50 men in them, to seize and plunder the town of Hilo. All that day was very calm, as the day before.

The next morning, about break of day, a fair breeze sprang up, with which we lay right in with the port. About one in the afternoon we anchored, and the port lies thus, as is here described :—

PORT OF HILO

We cast anchor at the distance of two miles from the village, and then we perceived two flags, which our men had put out, having taken the town and set up our English colours. The Spaniards were retreated to the hills, and there had done the same. Being come to an anchor, our Commander, Captain Sharp, sent a canoe on board of us, and ordered that all the men our ship could spare should come ashore. Withal they told us that those of our party that landed the morning before were met by some horsemen on the shore, who only exchanged some few volleys of shot with our men, but were soon put to flight. That hereupon our forces had marched directly to the town, where the Spaniards, expecting we should have landed at first, had made a breastwork, thirty paces long, of clay and banks of sand. Here, in a small skirmish, we happened to kill an Indian, who told us before he died that they had received news of our coming nine days ago, from Lima, and but one day before from Arica. Having taken the town, we found therein great quantity of pitch, tar, oil, wine, and flour, with several other sorts of provisions. We endeavoured to keep as good a watch as the Spaniards did on the hills, fearing lest they should suddenly make an attempt to destroy us.

On the next day, October 30th, we chose out three-score men of them who were the fittest to march, from among the rest, and ordered them to go up and search the valley adjoining and belonging to the town. We found the said valley to be very pleasant, being all over set with fig, olive, orange, lemon, and lime-trees, with many other fruits agreeable to the palate. About four miles up, within the valley, we came to a great sugar-works, or *ingenio d'azucar*, as it is called by the Spaniards, where we found great store of sugar, oil, and molasses, but most of the sugar the owners had hidden from us in the cane itself. As we marched up the valley the Spaniards marched along the hills, and observed our motion. From the tops of the hills they often tumbled down great stones upon us, but with great care we endeavoured to escape those dangers, and the report of our gun would suddenly cause them all to hide their heads. From this house, I mean the sugar-works above-mentioned, Mr Cox, myself, and one Cannis, a Dutchman (who was then our interpreter), went to the Spaniards with a flag of truce. They met us very civilly, and promised to give us four-score beeves as ransom of the sugar-work upon condition that it should not be spoilt nor demolished. We agreed with them that they should be delivered to us at the port next day at noon. Hereupon Captain Sharp, in the evening, sent down to the port 20 men, with strict orders that our forces there should offer no violence to those that brought down the beeves.

Sunday, October 31st. This day being employed in casting up some accounts belonging to our navigation, I reckoned that Hilo was to the eastward of Paita one hundred and eighty-seven leagues. This morning the Captain of the Spaniards came to our Commander, Captain Sharp, with a flag of truce, and told him that sixteen beeves were already sent down to the port and that the rest should certainly be there the next morning. Hereupon we were ordered to prepare ourselves to retreat, and march back to the port, and there embark ourselves on board our ship. My advice was to the contrary, that we should rather leave 20 men behind to keep the house of the sugar-works, and that others should possess themselves of the hills, thereby to clear them of the Spaniards and their look-out. But, my counsel not being regarded, each man took away what burden of sugar he pleased, and thus we returned to our vessel. Being come there, we found no beeves had been brought down at all, which occasioned us much to suspect some double-dealing would in the latter end be found in this case.

The next morning, November 1st, our Captain went to the top of the hills aforementioned, and spoke with the Spaniards themselves concerning the performance of their agreement. The Spaniards made answer that the cattle would certainly come down this night, but, in case they did not, that the master or owner of the sugar-works had now returned from Potosi, and we might go up and treat with him, and make, if we pleased, a new bargain for the preservation of his house and goods, it being his interest more than theirs to save it from being demolished. With this answer our men returned to us, and we decided to wait until the next day for the delivery of the beeves.

On the following day, about eight in the morning, there came in to us a flag of truce from the enemy, telling us that the winds were so high that they could not drive the cattle, otherwise they had been delivered before now. But withal that by noon we should in no manner fail to have them brought to us. Noon being come and no cattle appearing, we, now having filled our water and finished other concerns, resolved to be revenged on the enemy, and do them what mischief we could, at least by setting fire to the sugar-works. Hereupon three-score men of us marched up the valley, and burnt both the house, the canes, and the mill belonging to the *ingenio*. We broke likewise the coppers, coggs, and multitudes of great jars of oil that we found in the house. This being done, we brought away more sugar, and returned to the port over the hills or mountains, which we found to be very pleasant, smooth, and level after once we had ascended them. It fell out very fortunately to us that we returned back this way, for otherwise our men at the seaside had inevitably been cut off and torn in pieces by the enemy, they being at that time dispersed and straggling up and down in parties of two and three. For from the hills we spied coming from the northward of the bay above 300 horsemen, all riding at full speed towards our men, who had not as yet descried them and little thought of any such danger from the enemy so nigh at hand. Being alarmed with this sight, we threw down what sugar we had and ran incontinently to meet them, thereby to give our other men time to rally and put themselves into a posture of defence. We being in good rank and order, fairly proffered them battle upon the bay; but, as we advanced to meet them, they retired and rode towards the mountains to surround us and take the rocks from us, if they possibly could. Hereupon, perceiving their intentions, we returned back and possessed ourselves of the said rocks, and also of the lower town, as the Spaniards themselves did of the upper town (at the distance of half-a-mile from the lower), the hills and the woods adjoining thereunto. The horsemen, being now in possession of these quarters, we could perceive as far as we could see more and more men resort to them, so that their forces increased hourly to considerable numbers. We fired one at another as long as we could reach and the day would permit. But in the meanwhile we observed that several of them rode to the watch-hill, and looked out often to the sea-board. This gave us occasion to fear that they had more strength and forces coming that way which they expected every minute. Hereupon, lest we should speed worse than we had done before, we resolved to embark silently in the dark of the night, and go off from the coast where we had been so early descried and the enemy was so much prepared against us. We carried off a great chest of sugar, whereof we shared seven-pound-weight-and-a-half each man, thirty jars of oil, and great plenty of all sorts of garden herbs, roots, and most excellent fruit.

CHAPTER XIV

The Buccaneers depart from the Port of Hilo, and sail to that of Coquimbo. They are descried before their arrival. Notwithstanding they land; are encountered by the Spaniards; and put them to flight. They take, plunder, and fire the City of La Serena. A description thereof. A stratagem of the Spaniards, in endeavouring to fire their ship, discovered and prevented. They are deceived again by the Spaniards, and forced to retire from Coquimbo without any ransom for the City or considerable pillage. They release several of their chief prisoners

THE next morning, being Wednesday, November 3rd, 1679, about seven o'clock, we set sail from Hilo, standing directly off to sea, with a small land-wind. Upon the shore we could not discover this morning above 50 men of our enemies' forces, which caused us to suspect the rest were run away from their colours and had deserted in the dark of the night. If this were so, we were equally afraid of each other, and, as we quitted the land being jealous of their multitudes, so they abandoned their stations for fear of our encounters. All the while we lay in the Port of Hilo, we had a fresh wind, but now, being come out thence, we found it was almost stark calm. Hereabouts runs a great sea all along this coast, as we experimented at Arica, insomuch that there is no landing except under the favour of some rock or other.

November 4th, in the morning, we saw the Port of Hilo at E.N.E., at the distance of 9 leagues, more or less, from the land. The white sand gives a bright reflection over the land, which we could see after we had lost sight of the land itself.

The next day to this we had an indifferent fresh wind at S.S.E. We reckoned a S.W. half W. way, and, by it, that we had made 20 leagues. The day was very fair and sunshiny and the sea very smooth.

November 6th. We had a clear night the last past, and the day proved very fair and clear, like the former. We reckoned by a S.W. by W. way about 21 leagues. In the afternoon it was almost stark calm.

On the following day we had in like manner very little wind, no more than the last twenty-four hours. We were now about this time many of us very much troubled and diseased with the scurvy. It proceeded, as we judged, from the great hardship and want of provisions which we had endured for several months past, as having had only bread and water, as was mentioned above. Only at Hilo we killed a mule, which gave to those who would eat of the flesh a very good meal, as we esteemed it, the Spaniards having swept away with them all other provisions of flesh. But there we had plundered some small quantity of good chocolate, whereof the Spaniards make infinite use. So that now we had each morning a dish of that pleasant liquor, containing almost a pint.

Next day likewise we had very little wind, as before. We made an observation this day, and found lat. 20° 05′ S.

November 9th we had still very little wind, and that variable. We took almost every hour an observation, and found ourselves to be in lat. 20° 18′ S.

The 10th we had in like manner but little wind, as for so many days before. We observed an E.S.E. current, or nearest to it, to run hereabouts. This day we saw the homing of a very high land, which we much admired, for at this time I conceived we could not be less than 35 or 40 leagues distant from land. We supposed it to be Mora Tarapaca. That day we set up our shrouds.

Upon the 11th an indifferent gale of wind sprang up at S.W. by S., by which we made twenty-five leagues and one-third. We had now a great S.S.W. sea. In the night the wind we found came one or two points from the land. This morning we saw the like homing of land, whereby we were made sensible that it was no land which we had seen the day before.

On the 12th we had several mists of rain, with windy weather. We made by a S.S.W. half S. way, 25 leagues and one-third. We had likewise a great and rolling S.S.W. sea, as the day before.

The 13th of the said month we had both cloudy and misty weather. We made a S.S.W. and one-quarter S. way, by which we ran 50 leagues.

But the next day fair and clear weather came about again. We had likewise an easy gale of wind, by which we made a S.W. way and advanced 22 leagues and-a-half.

On November 15th, we had also clear weather and an indifferent gale of wind. Our way was S.W. by W., by which we reckoned 18 leagues. Likewise that our westing from Hilo, whence we had set forth, was 114 leagues and one-third. By observation we found lat. 23° 25′. I took now the declination-table used and made by the cosmographer of Lima.

Tuesday, November 16th. Last night we had a shower or two of rain. By observation we found lat. 23° 35′ S.

The 17th we made a S.W. by W. half S. way. By observation we found lat. 23° 46′ S. with very little wind.

The 18th upon a S.W. by W. way we made 21 leagues. By observation we found lat. 24° 20′ S.

Friday, November 19th, 1680. This morning about an hour before day we observed a comet to appear a degree N. from the bright in Libra. The body thereof seemed dull, and its tail extended itself 18 or 20 degrees in length, being of a pale colour and pointing directly N.N.W. Our prisoners hereupon reported to us that the Spaniards had seen very strange sights, both at Lima, the capital city of Peru, Guayaquil, and other places, much about the time of our coming into the South Seas. I reckoned this day we had run 20 leagues by a S.W. way.

The day following the appearance of the comet we had many storms of wind at S.S.E. and E.S.E. Our reckoning by a S.W. by W. way was 22 leagues.

Sunday, November 21st, we had likewise many gusts of wind, such as the day before, with frequent showers of rain. The wind varied to and fro, according as the clouds drew it here and there. We reckoned a S.S.W. way, and, by it, 21 leagues and a-half. In all, W. from Hilo, we judged ourselves to be 178 leagues and two-thirds. We had this day a great

S.W. Sea, and cloudy weather. I supposed our latitude to be 26° 53′ S.

November 22nd we had in like manner cloudy weather, and now but little wind. We reckoned a S. way, and 51 leagues.

The 23rd we had very little wind, all the storm after the appearance of the comet being now quite allayed. We reckoned we had made a S.E. by E. way. By observation found lat. 27° 46′ S.

Wednesday, November 24th. All the last twenty-four hours we had a N.W. wind. Our way was S.E. half S., by which we reckoned 31 leagues and one-third.

The 25th. Last night the wind blew at W.S.W., but this morning it came about again at N.W. as the day before. Our reckoning this day was a S.E. and one-quarter E. way, 29 leagues and one-third. Lat., by observation 39° 57′ S. Our difference of meridian 135⅓.

November 26th. In the night the wind started to S.S.W., but this day at noon we had little better than a calm. I reckoned an E.S.E. half E. way, and, by it, 23 leagues.

Saturday, 27th. Yesterday in the evening the wind came to S. I reckoned an E. and something S. way, and, by that, 23 leagues, as the day before this.

November 28th. All the last twenty-four hours we enjoyed a fresh wind at S.S.E., having a high S.W. sea. Our reckoning was an E. by N. and half N. way, and withal 24 leagues. By observation lat. 30° 16′ S. and meridian distance 88 leagues. At noon the wind came at S. half E.

On the 29th we had a very great S.W. sea, and withal cloudy weather. My reckoning was by an E. one-third S. way, 20 leagues and one-third. This day we happened to see two or three great fowls flying in the air, concerning which our pilot told us that they used to appear 70 or 80 leagues off from the island called Juan Fernandez. The day before this Captain Peralta, our prisoner, was taken very frantic, his distemper being occasioned, as we thought, through too much hardship and melancholy. Notwithstanding, this present day he became indifferent[1] well again.

The following day we had likewise cloudy weather. We made, according to our account, an E. half N. way, and by

[1] See note on p. 87.

it 16 leagues and two-thirds. Our meridian difference 52 leagues.

December 1st. We had hazy weather, and withal an indifferent good wind at S., yea, sometimes S. by W. Our way was E. by S., by which we reckoned 22 leagues. The night before this day we sailed over white water like banks, of a mile in length or more. But these banks, upon examination, we found to be only great shoals of anchovies.

On December 2nd, very early in the morning, we espied land, which appeared to be very high. About noon this day we were 6 leagues distance from it. All the preceding night we had so much wind that we were forced to make use only of a pair of courses. By an observation made this day, we found lat. 30° 35′ S. We went away largely, driving better than nine leagues every watch. With this wind we made all the sail we possibly could, designing by this means to get into Coquimbo, upon which coast we now were, before night. But the wind was so high that sometimes we were forced to lower all our sail, it blowing now a mere fret of wind. Towards the evening it abated by degrees, insomuch that at midnight it was stark calm again. At that time we hoisted out our launch and canoes, and, putting into them 100 men, we rowed away from the ship with design to take by surprisal a considerable city, situated nigh unto the coast, called by the Spaniards La Ciudad de la Serena.

Friday, December 3rd, 1679. When we departed from the ship, we had above 2 leagues, more or less, to row to the shore. But, as it happened, the launch (wherein I was) rowed so heavily in comparison to the canoes that we could not keep pace with the said boats. For this reason and no other, it was broad day before we got to a certain storehouse situated upon the shore, which we found our men had passed by in the dark of the night, without perceiving it. They, being landed, immediately marched away from their canoes towards the city aforementioned of La Serena, but they had not proceeded far on their march when they found, to the great sorrow and chagrin of us all, that we were discovered here also, as we had been at the other two places before, to wit Arica and Hilo. For, as they marched in a body together being but thirty-five men in all, who were all those that were landed out of the canoes, they were suddenly encountered and engaged by a whole troop of an hundred Spanish horse. We that were behind, hearing the noise of the dispute, followed them at their heels, and made all the haste we possibly could to come up to their relief. But, before we could reach the place of battle, they had already routed the Spaniards and forced them to fly away towards the town.

Notwithstanding this rout given to the horse, they rallied again at a distance of about a mile from that place, and seemed as if they did wait for us and would engage us anew. But, as soon as all our forces were come together, whereof we could make but fourscore-and-eight men in all, the rest being left behind to guard the boats, we marched towards them and offered them battle. As we came nigh unto them, we clearly found they designed no such thing, for they instantly retired and rode away before us, keeping out of the reach of our guns. We followed them as they rode, being led by them designedly clear out of the road that went to the town, that we might not reach nor find it so soon. In this engagement with the horse our company had killed three of their chief men and wounded four more, killing also four of their horses. When we found that we had been led by this stratagem of the enemy out of the way of the town, we left the bay and crossed over the green fields to find it, wading oftentimes over several branches of water, which there serve to enclose each plot of ground. Upon this march we came to several houses, but found them all empty and swept clean both of inhabitants and provisions. We saw likewise several horses and other heads of cattle in the fields, as we went along towards the City. This place of La Serena our pilot had reported to us to be but a small town, but, being arrived there, we found in it no fewer than seven great churches and one chapel belonging thereto. Four of these churches were monasteries or convents, and each church had its organ for the performance of divine service. Several of the houses had their orchards of fruit and gardens belonging to them, both houses and gardens being as well and as neatly furnished as those in England. In these gardens we found strawberries as big as walnuts and very delicious to the taste. In a word, everything in this city of La Serena was most excellent and delicate, and far beyond what we could expect in so remote a place. The town was inhabited by all sorts of tradesmen, and besides them had its merchants, some of which were accounted to be very rich.

The inhabitants of La Serena, upon our approach and discovery, were all fled, carrying with them whatever was most precious of their goods and jewels, or less cumbersome to them. Much of their valuable things they had likewise concealed or buried, having had time since we were first discovered so to do. Besides, they had had warning enough to beware of us, sent them over land from Arica and several other places where we had landed or been descried at sea. Notwithstanding, we took in the town one friar and two

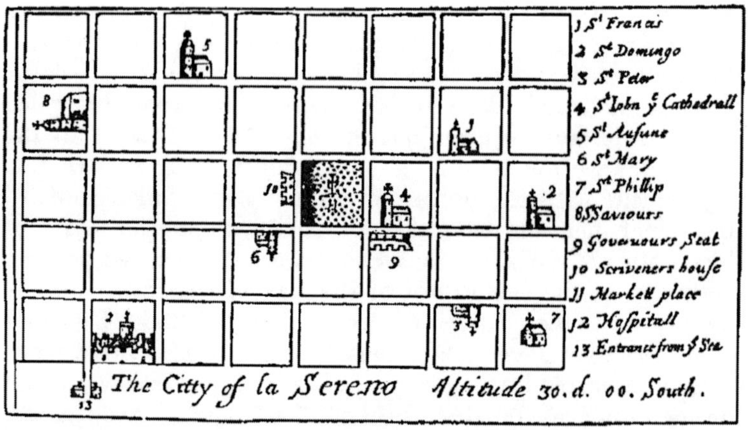

Chilenos, or Spaniards, natives of the Kingdom of Chile, which adjoins that of Peru, towards the Strait of Magellan. These prisoners related to us that the Spaniards, when they heard of our coming, had killed most of the Chilian slaves, fearing lest they should run or revolt from them to us. Moreover, that we had been descried from their coasts four days before our arrival or descent upon land—all which time they had employed in carrying away their plate and goods. To this information they added that for their defence they had received a supply of 60 men from Arica. Having taken possession of the town, that evening there came a negro to us, running away from the Spaniards. He likewise informed us that, when we were before Panama, we had taken a negro who was esteemed to be the best pilot in all the South Sea, but more especially for this place and all the coasts of Coquimbo. Moreover, that if the Spaniards had not sent all the negroes belonging to this city farther up into the country out of our reach and communication, they would all undoubtedly have revolted to us.

That night about midnight our boatswain, accompanied by 40 men and having a Chilian for their guide, went out of the town some miles within the country, with design to find out the places where the Spaniards lay concealed, and had hid their goods and plate. But, before they came, the Spaniards had received intelligence thereof from some secret spies they had in the town, and both the men and their women were all fled to places that were more occult and remote. So that by this search they only found an old Indian woman and three children, but no gold nor plate, nor yet any other prisoners. This morning our ship came to an anchor, by the storehouse above-mentioned, named Tortuga, at the distance of a furlong from shore, in seven fathom water. While we were quartered in the town, I took this following ground-plate thereof.

The next morning, being Saturday, December 4th, there came into the town a flag of truce from the enemy. Their message was to proffer a ransom for the town to preserve it from burning, for now they began to fear we would set fire to it, as having found no considerable booty or pillage therein. The Captains, or chief Commanders, of both sides met about this point, and agreed betwixt them for the sum of 95,000 pieces-of-eight to be the price of the whole ransom. In the afternoon of this day I was sent down to the bay of Coquimbo, with a party of 20 men, to carry thither both goods taken in the town and provisions for the ship. It is two-leagues-and-a-half from the town to the port—one league on the bay, the rest being a very great road, which leads from the bay to the city. The Spaniards promised that the ransom should be collected and paid in by the next day. This day also there died one of our negro slaves on board the ship.

The following day in the morning I returned back to the town with the men I had brought down the day before. Only six of them I left behind, to look after our canoes at the end of the bay. When I came up into the city, I found that the Spaniards had broken their promise, and had not brought in the ransom they had agreed for; but had begged more time until to-morrow at eight in the forenoon. This evening another party of our men went down to the ship, to carry goods, such as we had pillaged in the town. Moreover, that night about nine o'clock happened an earthquake, which we were very sensible of, as we were all together in the church of San Juan, where our chief rendezvous and *corps du garde* was kept. In the night the Spaniards opened a sluice, and let the water run in streams about the town, with intent either to overflow it and thereby force us out of the place, or at least that they might the easier quench the flame, in case we should fire the town.

On the next morning we set fire to the town, perceiving it to be overflowed and that the Spaniards had not performed, or rather that they never designed to perform their promise. We fired, as nigh as we could, every house in the whole town, to the intent it might be totally reduced to ashes. Thus we departed from La Serena, carrying with us what plunder we could find, having sent two parties before, loaded with goods to the ship, as was mentioned above. As we marched down to the bay, we beat up an ambuscade of 250 horse, which lay by the way in private, with an intent to fall on our men, in case we had sent down any other party again with goods to the ship. When we came to the sea-side, being half-way to our ship, we received advice that the Spaniards had endeavoured, by an unusual stratagem, to burn our ship and by these means destroy us all. They acted thus: They blew up a horse's hide like a bladder, and upon this float a man ventured to swim from shore and come under the stern of our ship. Being arrived there, he crammed oakum and brimstone, and other combustible matter, between the rudder and the stern-post. Having done this, he fired it with a match, so that in a small time our rudder was on fire and all the ship in a smoke. Our men both alarmed and amazed with this smoke, ran up and down the ship, suspecting the prisoners to have fired the vessel, thereby to get their liberty and seek our destruction. At last they found out where the fire was, and had the good fortune to quench it before its going too far. As soon as they had put it out, they sent the boat ashore, and found both the hide aforementioned and the match burning at both ends, whereby they became acquainted with the whole matter. When we came to the storehouse on the shore-side, we set at liberty the friar, our prisoner, and another gentleman who was become our hostage for the performance of the ransom. Moreover, when we came aboard, we sent away and set at liberty Captain Peralta, Don Thomas de Argandona, Don Baltazar, Don Christoval, Captain Juan, the Pilot's Mate, the old Moor, and several others of our chief prisoners. To this release of our prisoners we were moved partly because we knew not well what to do with them, and partly because we feared lest by the example of this stratagem they should plot our destruction in earnest, and by the help of so many men, especially persons of quality, be able to go through with it.

CHAPTER XV

The Buccaneers depart from Coquimbo for the isle of Juan Fernandez. An exact account of this voyage. Misery they endure, and great dangers they escape very narrowly there. They mutiny among themselves, and choose Watling to be their chief commander. Description of the island. Three Spanish men-of-war meet with the Buccaneers at the said island, but these outbrave them on the one side and give them the slip on the other

BEING all embarked again, as was mentioned in the preceding chapter, the next morning, which was Tuesday, December 7th, twenty of us were sent ashore to observe the motion of the enemy. We went to the look-out, or watch-hill, but could learn nothing thence. Hereupon about noon we returned on board the ship, and at two in the afternoon we weighed anchor and set sail, directing our course for the isle of Juan Fernandez, not far distant from the coast of Coquimbo. At night we were five leagues distant thence at N.W. by N.

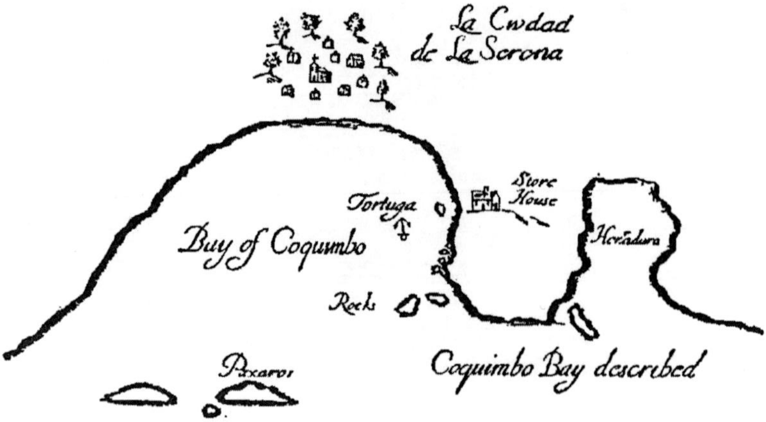

The southermost island of those, which are called De los Paxaros, or the Islands of Birds, was then N.N.W. from us. Before our departure I took this draft of the bay of Coquimbo and city of La Serena.

December 8th we had but very little wind and a lee-ward current here, which we perceived did heave us to the Northward. The aforementioned island, De los Paxaros, at three in the afternoon bore N.E. of us. At the distance of 3 leagues, more or less, it appeared thus :—

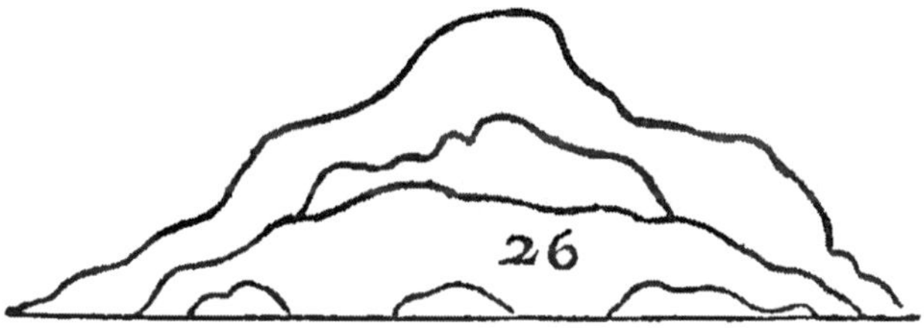

ISLE DE LOS PAXAROS

It is distant from the main continent four leagues, and from the next island of the same name about two. The mainland is extremely high and mountainous hereabouts. At evening we were west from the said island five leagues. About 8 or 9 leagues to windward of Coquimbo are certain white cliffs which appear from the shore to those that are off at sea.

On December 9th we had likewise but little wind, as the day before. I supposed myself this day to be about thirteen leagues W. from the island above-mentioned. The weather was cloudy, with mizzling rain, so that no observation could be taken. However, this day it was thought convenient to put us to an allowance of water, for we had taken in little or none at Coquimbo. The same weather, or very like it, we had the next day, being the 10th—that is to say, stark calm and cloudy.

On December 11th we had some small rain in the forepart of the day. But in the afternoon it cleared up, so that the weather was very hot. We had still but little wind.

The next day, December 12th, we had very fair weather, and by a clear observation made this day we found lat. 30° 06′ S.

December 13th. By a W.S.W. way we made forty-two leagues. By observation we found lat. 30° 45′ S. D.M. 4 leagues and two-thirds.

On the 14th, in the morning, we had a handsome shower of rain, which continued for some while. Then, about eight o'clock, there sprang up a S.S.W. breeze. My reckoning was by an E.S.E. way 14 leagues. And by observation we found this day 30° 30′ S. In the afternoon of this day died one of our men whose name was William Cammock. His disease was occasioned by a surfeit, gained by too much drinking on shore at La Serena, which produced in him a *calenture*, or malignant fever, and a hiccough. Thus in the evening we buried him in the sea, according to the usual custom of mariners, giving him three French volleys for his funeral.

The following day we had an indifferent fresh wind on both tacks. Our way was W.S.W., and by it we reckoned 34 leagues. So likewise by an observation we had lat. 30° 42′ S. All the afternoon blew a S. by W. wind very fresh, with a short topping S.W. sea.

But on the next ensuing day we had no small breeze, but rather hard gusts of wind. These grew so high that they forced us to take in our top-sails. We made a S.W. half S. way, and 45 leagues.

On the 17th we had likewise high winds, and withal a S.W. sea. Our way W. by S. By observation this day lat. 30° 51′ S. In the afternoon we had a S.S.E. wind, our course being S.W.

December 18th. This day we had the same high winds as before, at S.S.E. We reckoned by a W.S.W. way forty-five leagues. At noon the wind was somewhat fallen, and then we had some rain.

The 19th we had both cloudy and windy weather. My reckoning was a S.W. by S. way, and hereupon fifty-eight miles. Yesterday we were assured by our pilot that we were now in the meridian of the island of Juan Fernandez, whither our course was directed for the present. What occasioned him to be so positive in his assertion was the seeing of those great birds of which we made mention in the foregoing chapter.

On the 20th we had cloudy weather in the morning on both tacks. We made a S.W. and half S. way, and by it 52 leagues. By observation this day lat. 32° 20′ S. D.M. 123 leagues.

The next day likewise we had cloudy weather, yet by observation we found a W. way. On the 22nd by observation we found an E. way proved.

Thursday, December 23rd. All the night past we had a fresh wind. But, in the morning from top-mast head we descried a hummock of land. In the evening we saw it again. We found afterwards that what we had seen was the Westernmost island of Juan Fernandez—which is nothing but a mere rock, there being no riding, nor scarce landing, near to it.

Friday, December 24th. This morning we could descry the island of Juan Fernandez itself S. by E., it being at sixteen leagues distance when we saw it yesterday. At seven this morning the island stood E., the wind being N.W. or by N. At eight the same morning the island at the distance of five leagues, little more or less, appeared thus :—

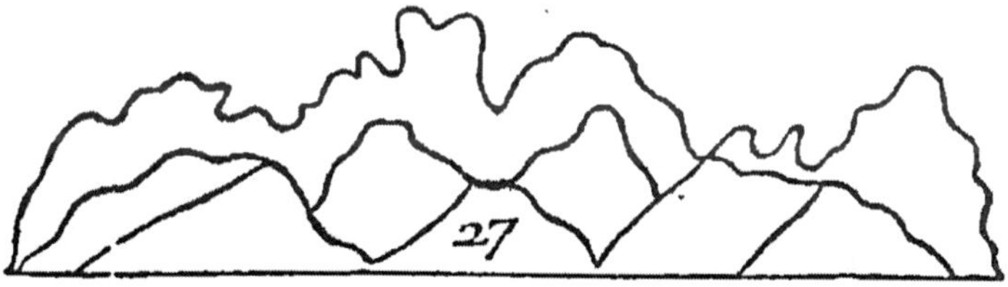

ISLE DE JUAN FERNANDEZ

Here my observation was that I could see neither fowl nor fish near this island ; both which things are usually to be seen about other islands. Having told my observation to our pilot, he gave me for answer that he had made many voyages by this island and yet never saw either fowl or fish any more than I. Our reckoning this day was an E.S.E. way, and hereby 36 leagues. By observation lat. 33° 30′ S.

Saturday, December 25th. Yesterday, in the afternoon at three o'clock, we saw the other island making two or three hummocks of land. This morning we were about eight leagues distant from it, the island bearing E.S.E. from us. At eight the same morning we were right abreast with it. Here, therefore, are two islands together, the biggest whereof is 3 leagues and a-half in length nearest N.W. and S.E., the other (and lesser) is almost one league and no more in circumference. At ten o'clock we sent off from the ship one of our canoes to seek for the best landing and anchoring for our vessel. As we approached, both islands seemed to us nothing but one entire heap of rocks. That which lies more to the N. is the highest, though we could not now see the tops thereof for the clouds which covered it. In most places it is so steep that it becomes almost perpendicular.

This day being Christmas-day, we gave in the morning early three volleys of shot for solemnization of that great festival. I reckoned an E. by S. way. By a clear observation from the middle of the island lat. 33° 45′ S., and M.D. 99 leagues. In the evening of this day we came to an anchor at the South end of the island in a stately bay that we found there, but which lies open from the S. to the S.E. winds. We anchored in eleven fathom water, and at the distance of only one furlong from the shore. Here we saw multitudes of seals covering the bay everywhere, insomuch that we were forced to kill them to set our feet on shore.

Sunday, December 26th. This day we sent a canoe to see if we could find any riding secure from the southerly winds, these being the most constant winds that blow on these coasts. The canoe being gone, our Commander sent likewise what men we could spare on shore, to drive goats, whereof there is great plenty in this island. They caught and killed that day to the number of three-score or thereabouts. The canoe, returning to the ship, made report that there was good riding in another bay, situate on the North side of the island, in fourteen fathom water and not above one-quarter-of-a-mile from the shore. Moreover, that there was much wood to be had, whereas in the place where we had first anchored not one stick of wood nor tuft of grass was to be found.

The next day, being the 27th, between two and four o'clock in the morning we had a tempest of violent winds and fierce showers of rain. The same day we got in two-hundred jars of water, bringing them the full distance of a league from the place of our riding. In the meanwhile others were employed to catch goats, as they had done the day before.

On the 28th of the said month, in the morning, I went with ten more of our company and two canoes, to fetch water from the land. Being come thither and having filled our jars, we could not get back to the ship by reason of a Southerly wind that blew from off the ocean and hindered our return. Thus we were forced to lie still in a water-hole, and wait till the winds were over for a safer opportunity. Meanwhile, the violence of the wind increasing, our ship was forced to get under sail and make away, not without danger of being forced ashore. Hereupon she sailed out of the harbour, to seek another place of anchoring. At noon I ventured out, to try if I could follow the ship, but was forced in again by the wind and a raging sea. Thus we lay still for some while longer till the evening came on. This being come, we ventured out again both canoes together, but the winds were then so high that we were forced to throw all our jars of water overboard to lighten our boats—otherwise we had inevitably perished. I ought to bless and praise God Almighty for this deliverance, for, in all human reason, the least wave of that tempest must have sunk us. Notwithstanding, we came that night to our place, or harbour, where we expected to have found our ship (called *False Wild Harbour*)—but found her not. Hereupon, not knowing what to do, we went ashore, and hauled up our canoes dry. Having done this, we ascended higher within the island, along a gulley, for the space of half-a-mile, there to clear ourselves of the noise and company of the seals, which were very troublesome on the shore. Here we kindled a fire, dried our clothes, and rested ourselves all night, though with extremely hungry bellies, having eaten very little or nothing all the day before. In the sides of the hill under which we lay we observed many holes like coney-holes. These holes are the nests and roosting-places of multitudes of birds that breed in this island—called by the Spaniards *pardelas*. One of these birds, as we lay drying and warming ourselves, fell down into our fire.

The next morning being come, very early before sunrise we went farther to the northward, to seek for our ship, which we feared we had lost. But we were not gone far when we soon spied her at sea. Hereupon we passed a point of land and entered a certain bay, which was about a mile deep and not above half-a-league over. Into this bay we put, and instantly made a fire, thereby to show the ship whereabouts we were. Here we found good watering and wooding close to the shore. In this bay also we saw another sort of amphibious animal, which I imagined to be the same that by some authors is called a 'Sea-Lion'[1]. These animals are six times bigger than seals. Their heads are like that of a lion, and they have four fins not unlike a tortoise. The hinder parts of these creatures are much like fins, but are drawn after them, being useless upon the shore. They roared as if they had been lions, and were full of a certain short and thick hair, which was of a mouse colour, but that of the young ones was somewhat lighter. The old ones of these sea-lions are between 12 and 14 feet long and about 11 or 12 feet in circumference. A seal is very easily killed, as we often experimented, but two of our men with great stones could not kill one of these animals.

That day in the afternoon there came a canoe from on board the ship with provisions for us, they fearing lest we should be starved. In like manner the launch came with men to cut wood. They told us that the ship came to an anchor in the other bay, but that within half an hour the cable broke, and they were forced to leave their anchor behind them and get out to sea again. Night being come, we made our beds of fern, whereof there is huge plenty upon this island, together with great multitudes of trees like our English box, which bear a sort of green berries, smelling like pimento, or pepper. All this day the ship was forced to ply off at sea, not being able to get in.

December 30th. The morning of this day we employed in filling water and cutting down wood. But in the afternoon eight of us eleven went aboard the ship all in one and the same canoe, sending her ashore again with provisions for the men that were there. This day in like manner we could not get into the harbour, for no sooner the ship came within the parts of land but the wind coming out of the bay blew us clear out again. Thus we were forced to ply out all that night and great part of the following day.

On the next day, having overcome all difficulties and many dangers, we came to an anchor in the afternoon in fifteen fathom water, at the distance of a cable's length from shore. Here it was observable that we were forced to keep

[1] Probably the seal, *Otaria jubata*, of the Pacific Ocean, which has a large crest or mane, on its neck. Cf. Dampier, *Voyages* (1697), ed. 1729, i, 90: "The Sea Lion is a large creature about 12 or 14 foot long." It must not be confused with the walrus, as is frequently done.

men ashore on purpose to beat off the seals, while our men filled water at the sea-side, at high-water mark, for the seals covet hugely to lie in fresh water. About this island fish is so plentiful that in less than one hour's time two men caught enough for our whole company.

Saturday, January 1st, 1681. This day we put up a new main-top, larger than the old one, and we caught cray-fish that were bigger than our English lobsters.

The next day, being January 2nd, died a chief man of our company, whose name was John Hilliard. This man, until our weighing anchor from the port of Coquimbo, had been our Master all the space of this voyage. But from that time we chose John Cox for the starboard, and John Fall for the larboard, watch. The disease whereof he died was the dropsy. That evening we buried our dead companion, and gave him a volley for his funeral, according to the usual custom.

On January 3rd we had terrible gusts of wind from the shore every hour. This day our pilot told us that many years ago a certain ship was cast away upon this island, and only one man saved, who lived alone upon the island five years before any ship came this way to carry him off. The island has excellent land in many valleys belonging thereunto. This day, likewise, we fetched our anchor which we left in the other bay when the ship broke her cable.

Tuesday, January 4th, 1681. This day we had such terrible flaws of wind that the cable of our ship broke, and we had undoubtedly been on shore had not the other held us fast. At last it came home, and we drove outward. By the way it caught hold of a rock, and held some time, but at last we hauled it up, and the wind came with so much violence that the waves flew as high as our main-top and made all the water of a foam.

January 5th the same huge gusts of wind continued all the night last past, notwithstanding which this day at noon it was brave and calm. But in the morning the anchor of our ship gave way again, and we drove to the Eastward more than half-a-mile, till at last we happened to fasten again in 60 fathom water. Here in this bay where we rode at anchor did run a violent current, sometimes into and at other times out of the bay, so that all was uncertain with us. But our greatest discomfort was that our men were all in a mutiny against each other, and much divided among themselves, some of them being for going home towards England or our foreign plantations, and that round about America through the Strait of Magellan, as Captain Sawkins had designed to do; others of them being for staying longer and searching farther into those seas till such time as they had got more money. This day at noon our anchor drove again, whereupon, to secure ourselves from that dangerous place, we sailed thence into the West bay, anchored there in twenty-five fathom water, and moored our ship one-quarter-of-a-mile from shore.

On Thursday, January 6th, our differences being now grown to a great height, the mutineers made a new election of another person to be our chief Captain and Commander, by virtue whereof they deposed Captain Sharp, whom they protested they would obey no longer. They chose therefore one of our company whose name was John Watling, to command in chief, he having been an old privateer and gained the esteem of being a stout seaman. The election being made, all the rest were forced to give their assent to it, and Captain Sharp gave over his command, whereupon they immediately made articles with Watling, and signed them.

The following day, being the 7th, we burnt and tallowed the starboard side of our ship. In this bay where we now anchored we found a cross cut in the bark of a tree and several letters besides. Hereupon, in another tree up the gulley, I engraved the two first letters of my name, with a cross over them. This day, likewise, William Cook, servant to Captain Edmund Cook, being searched, we found a paper with all our names written in it, which it was suspected he designed to have given to the Spanish prisoners. For these reasons this evening our Captain thought it convenient to put him in irons, which was accordingly done. The next day we finished the other side of our ship.

Sunday, January 9th. This day was the first Sunday that ever we kept by command and common consent since the loss and death of our valiant commander, Captain Sawkins. This generous-spirited man threw the dice overboard, finding them in use on the said day.

January 10th. This day the weather was very clear and settled again. We caught every day in the bay where we now were great plenty of fish, and I saw the same day a shoal of fish a mile and more long.

On the next day, being the 11th, we filled our water and carried our wood on board the ship. Moreover, our two canoes went to the other side of the island to catch goats, for on the barren side thereof are found and caught the best, and by land it is impossible to go from one side of the island to the other.

Wednesday, January 12th. This morning our canoes returned from catching goats, firing guns as they came towards us to give us warning. Being come on board, they told us they had espied three sail of ships, which they conceived to be men-of-war, coming about the island. Within half-an-hour after this notice given by our boats, the ships came in sight to leeward of the island. Hereupon we immediately slipped our cables and put to sea, taking all our men on board that were ashore at that time. Only one, William, a Mosquito Indian, was then left behind on the island, because he could not be found at this our sudden departure. Upon the Island of Juan Fernandez grow certain trees that are called by the name of bilby-trees. The tops of these trees are excellent cabbage, and of them is made the same use that we do of cabbage in England. Here fish abound in such quantity that on the surface of the water I have taken fish with a bare and naked hook, that is to say unbaited. Much fish is taken here of the weight of twenty pounds, the smallest that is taken in the bay being almost two pound weight. Very good timber for building of houses and other uses is likewise found upon the island. It is distant from the main continent ninety-five leagues or thereabouts, being situate in 33° 40′ S. The plats of the island lie N.W. and S.E.

Being got out of the bay, we stood off to sea, and kept to windward as close as we could. The biggest of these Spanish men-of-war, for such they proved to be, was of the burden of 800 tons, and was called *El Santo Christo*, being mounted with twelve guns. The second, named *San Francisco*, was of the port of 600 tons, and had ten guns. The third was of the carriage of 350 tons, whose name I have forgotten. As soon as they saw us, they instantly put out their bloody flags, and we, to show them that we were not as yet daunted, did the same with ours. We kept close under the wind, and were, to confess the truth, very unwilling to fight them, by reason they kept all in a knot together and we could not single out any one of them or separate him from the rest—especially considering that our present Commander, Watling, had showed himself at their appearance to be faint-hearted. As for the Spaniards themselves, they might have easily come to us, since we lay by several times, but undoubtedly they were cowardly given, and peradventure as unwilling to engage us as we were to engage them.

The following day, being January 13th, in the morning we could descry one of the forementioned men-of-war under the leeward side of the island, and we believed that the rest were at anchor thereabouts. At W. by S. and at the distance of seven leagues the island appeared thus :—

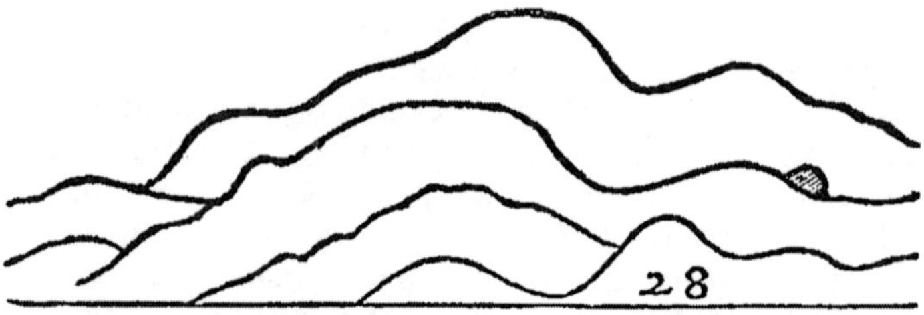

Isle of Juan Fernandez *LAT.* 33° 40′ *S.*

At noon that day we stood towards the island, making as if that we intended to be in with them. But in the afternoon our Commander propounded the question to us whether we were willing now that the fleet was to windward, to bear away from them. To this we all agreed with one consent. And hereupon, night being come, with a fresh wind at S.S.E. we stood away N.E. by N., and thus gave them handsomely the slip, after having outbraved them that day and the day before.

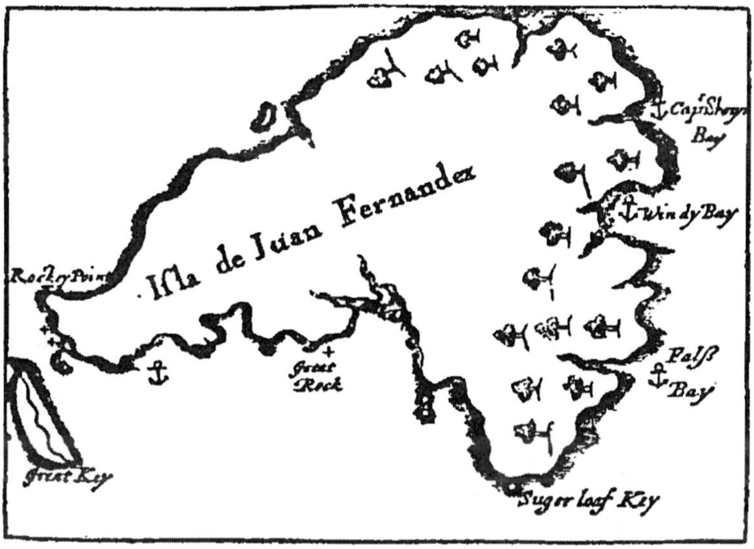

CHAPTER XVI

The Buccaneers depart from the isle of Juan Fernandez to that of Iquique. Here they take several prisoners, and learn intelligence of the posture of affairs at Arica. Cruelty committed upon one of the said prisoners who had rightly informed them. They attempt Arica the second time, and take the town, but are beaten out of it again before they could plunder—with great loss of men, many of them being killed, wounded, and made prisoners. Captain Watling, their chief Commander, is killed in this attack, and Captain Sharp presently chosen again, who leads them off, and through mountains of difficulties makes a bold retreat to the ship

HAVING bid our enemies adieu, after the manner as was said in the preceding chapter, the next morning, being January 14th, we bore N.E. We reckoned this day a N.N.E. one quarter S. way, and by it 30 leagues. We were four leagues E. from the island of Juan Fernandez, when I took our departure.

Saturday, January 15th, we had hazy weather. This day we made by a N.E. by N. way 11 leagues. The same hazy weather continued in like manner the 16th. But about ten that morning the wind died away. Our reckoning was a N.E. by N. way, and 36 leagues.

On the 17th we had a soft gale, and a clear observation. We found by it lat. 28° 47′ S. easting 70 leagues. The next day we had likewise a clear day, and we reckoned by a N.E. by N. way 31 leagues. By observation lat. 27° 29′ S.

Wednesday, January 19th, we had a clear day, as before, and reckoned a N.E. by N. way, and 35 leagues and two-thirds. By observation we took lat. 25° 00′ S. This day we put up our top-gallant masts and sails, which we had taken down at the island of Juan Fernandez, when we thought to have gone directly thence for the Strait of Magellan. But now our resolutions were changed, and our course was bent for Arica, that rich place, the second time, to try what good we could do upon it by another attempt, in order to make all our fortunes there. In the evening of this day we saw land at a great distance.

January 20th, about midnight, we had a small land-wind that sprang up and reached us. At break of day we could descry land again, at the distance of 9 or 10 leagues, more or less. This day was very hot and calm, easting 92 leagues.

On the 21st we had very little wind, and all along as we went we could descry high land, and that barren. We sailed N. by E., and N.N.E. along the coast of the continent.

The next day being Saturday, January 22nd, we had very hot weather. This day we sailed N. and N. by E., and looked out continually for the island of Iquique, which our pilot told us was hereabouts. We kept at a just distance from land for fear of being descried by the enemy.

On the following day, Sunday, 23rd, we sailed in like manner N.N.E. along the coast, which seems to be very full of bays hereabouts. By observation this day we took lat. 21° 49′ S.

Monday, January 24th. This day we had an indifferent gale of wind, and we stood N. and by E., the wind being S.S.E. By observation lat. 21° 02′ S. Our whole easting I reckoned to be 92 leagues and a-half. In the afternoon of this day Captain Watling, our Commander, and 25 men more departed from the ship in two canoes, with design to seek for and take the island of Iquique, and there to gain intelligence of the posture of affairs at Arica. We were at the distance of twelve leagues from shore when they went away from the ship.

The next day by a clear observation lat. 20° 40′ S. At four in the afternoon this day one of our canoes returned, bringing word that they could not find the island, though they had searched for it very diligently. At night came the other, being brought back by a wrong sign given us by the first canoe. This second canoe had landed upon the continent, and there found a track, which they followed for some little space. Here they met a dead whale, with whose bones the Spaniards had built a hut, and set up a cross. There lay also many pieces of broken jars. They observed likewise that hereabouts upon the coast were many bays, good landings, and anchoring for ships. That evening, about seven o'clock, a fresh gang departed from the ship to seek for the same island, while we lay becalmed all night, driving about a league to leeward.

Wednesday, January 26th, we had extremely hot weather. This day the Spanish pilot told us that on the continent over against us, and at the distance of a very little way within the land, are many rich mines of silver, but that the Spaniards dared not open them for fear of an invasion from some foreign enemy or other. We sailed N., at the distance of about 2 leagues from shore. At noon by observation found lat. 20° 21′ S. At four o'clock we saw a smoke made by our men, close by a white cliff, which proved to be the island. Hereupon we immediately sent away another canoe with more men, to supply them in their attempts. But in the meanwhile the first canoe, which had departed the evening before this day, came aboard, bringing with them four prisoners, two old white men and two Indians.

The other canoe, which set out last, brought back molasses, fish, and two jars of wine. To windward of the said island is a small village of eighteen or twenty houses, having a small chapel near it built of stone, and for adornment thereof it is stuck full of hides or the skins of seals. They found about 50 people in this hamlet, but the greatest part of them made their escape at the arrival of the canoe. To this island frequently come barks from Arica, which city is not far distant, to fetch clay, and they have already transported away a considerable part thereof. The poor Indians, inhabitants or natives of this island, are forced to bring all the fresh water they use the full distance of eleven leagues, that is to say from a river named Camarones, which lies to leeward of the island. The barque wherein they used to bring it was gone for water when our men landed upon the place. The island all over is white, but the bowels thereof are of a reddish sort of earth. From the shore is seen here a great path which leads over the mountains into the country. The Indians of this island eat much and often a sort of leaves that are of a taste much like our bay-leaves in England, insomuch that their teeth are dyed a green colour by the continual use of it. The inhabitants go stark naked, and are very robust and strong people, yet notwithstanding they live more like beasts than men.

Thursday, January 27th. This morning on board the ship we examined one of the old men who were taken prisoners upon the island the day before. But, finding him in many lies, as we thought, concerning Arica, our Commander ordered him to be shot to death, which was accordingly done. Our old Commander, Captain Sharp, was much troubled in his mind and dissatisfied at this cruel and rash proceeding, whereupon he opposed it as much as he could. But, seeing he could not prevail, he took water and washed his hands, saying: *Gentlemen, I am clear of the blood of this old man; and I will warrant you a hot day for this piece of cruelty, whenever we come to fight at Arica.* These words were found at the latter end of this expedition of Arica to contain a true and certain prophecy, as shall be related hereafter.

The other old man, being under examination, informed us that the island of Iquique aforementioned belonged to the Governor of Arica, who was proprietor thereof; and that he allowed these men a little wine and other necessaries, to live upon for their sustenance. That he himself had the superintendence of forty or fifty of the governor's slaves, who caught fish and dried it for the profit of the said governor, and he sold it afterwards to the inland towns, and reaped a considerable benefit thereby. That by a letter received from Arica eight days ago they understood there was then in the harbour of Arica three ships from Chile, and one bark. That they had raised there a fortification mounted with 12 copper guns. But that when we were there before, they had conveyed out of the town to the neighbouring stations all their plate, gold, and jewels, burying it there in the ground and concealing it after several manners and ways, which, whether it were now returned or not, he could not easily tell. That there were two great places, the one at ten, the other at twenty-five, leagues distance from Arica, at which towns lay all their strength and treasure. That the day before had passed a post to declare our having been at Coquimbo. That the embargo laid on all vessels going northward was now taken off, so that a free passage was allowed them. That by land it was impossible to go hence to Arica in less than four or five days, forasmuch as they must carry water for themselves and horses for the whole journey. And, lastly, that those arms that were brought from Lima to Arica, as was mentioned above, were now carried away to Buenos Ayres. All these things pleased us mighty well to hear. But, however, Captain Sharp was still much dissatisfied because we had shot the old man. For he had given us information to the full, and, with all manner of truth, how that Arica was greatly fortified, and much more than before; but our misfortune was that we took his information to be all contrary to the truth.

The leaves of which we made mention above are brought down to this island in whole bales, and then distributed to the Indians by a short allowance given to each man. This day we had very hot weather, and a S.W. sea. By observation we found lat. 20° 13′ S. Besides the things abovementioned, our prisoners informed us that at Arica the Spaniards had built a breastwork round about the town, and one also in every street, that, in case one end of the town were taken, they might be able to defend the other. We stood off and on for the greatest part of this day. In the afternoon we were 8 leagues and a-half distant from shore, with a fresh wind. That morning, moreover, we took the bark that was at the river of Camarones, to fill water for the island.

Friday, January 28th. Last night about midnight we left the ship, and embarked ourselves in the bark aforementioned, the launch, and four canoes, with design to take Arica by surprise. We rowed and sailed all night, making in for the shore.

Saturday, January 29th. About break of day we got under shore, and there hid ourselves among the rocks for all the day long, fearing lest we should be descried by the enemy before we came to Arica. At this time we were about 5 leagues to southward of Arica, near Quebrada de San Vitor, a place so-called upon that coast. Night being come, we rowed away from there.

Sunday, January 30th, 1680. This day (being the day that is consecrated in our English Calendar to the Martyrdom of our glorious King Charles the First) in the morning about sunrise, we landed amongst some rocks at some distance of 4 miles, more or less, to the southward from Arica. We put on shore 92 men in all, the rest remaining in the boats to keep and defend them from being surprised by the enemy, with the intent we might leave behind us a safe retreat in case of necessity. To these men we left strict orders that, if we made one smoke from the town or adjoining fields, they should come after us towards the harbour of Arica with one canoe; but, in case we made two, that they should bring all away, leaving only 15 men in the boats. As we marched from our landing-place towards the town, we mounted a very steep hill, and saw thence no men nor forces of the enemy; which caused us to hope we were not as yet descried, and that we should utterly surprise them. But, when we were come about half of the way to the town, we spied three horsemen, who mounted the look-out hill; and, seeing us upon our march, they rode down full-speed towards the city, to give notice of our approach. Our Commander, Watling, chose out 40 of our number to attack the fort, and sent us away first thitherwards, the rest being designed for the town. We that were appointed for the fort had ten hand grenades among us when we gave the assault, and with them, as well as with our other arms, we attacked the castle, and exchanged several shot with our enemies. But at last, seeing our main body in danger of being overborne with the number of our enemies, we gave over that attempt on the fort, and ran down in all haste to the valley, to help and assist them in the fight. Here the battle was very desperate, and they killed three and wounded two more of our men from their out-works, before we could gain upon them. But, our rage increasing with our wounds, we still advanced, and at last beat the enemy out of all, and filled every street in the city with dead bodies. The enemy made several retreats to several places, from one breastwork to another; and we had not a sufficient number of men wherewith to man all places taken. Insomuch that we had no sooner beat them out of one place than they came another way, and manned it again with new forces and fresh men.

We took in every place where we vanquished the enemy great number of prisoners, more indeed than peradventure we ought to have done or knew well what to do with; they being too many for such a small body as ours was to manage. These prisoners informed us that we had been descried no less than three days before from the island of Iquique, whereby they were in expectation of our arrival every hour, knowing we still had a design to make a second attempt upon that place. That into the city were come 400 soldiers from Lima, who, besides their own, had brought 700 arms for the use of the country-people; and that in the town they had 600 armed men, and in the fort 300.

Being now in possession of the city, or the greatest part thereof, we sent to the fort, commanding them to surrender; but they would not vouchsafe to send us any answer. Hereupon we advanced towards it, and gave it a second attack, wherein we persisted very vigorously for a long time. Not being able to carry it, we got upon the top of a house that stood near it, and from there fired down into the fort, killing many of their men and wounding them at our ease and pleasure. But, while we were busied in this attack, the rest of the enemy's forces had taken again several posts of the town, and began to surround us in great numbers, with design to cut us off. Hereupon we were constrained to desist the second time as before from assaulting the fort, and make head against them. This we no sooner had done than, their numbers and vigour increasing every moment, we found ourselves to be overpowered, and consequently we thought it convenient to retreat to the place where our wounded men were, under the hands of our surgeons, that is to say our Hospital. At this time our new Commander, Captain Watling, both our quartermasters, and a great many others of our men were killed, besides those that were wounded and disabled. So that now, the enemy rallying against us and beating us from place to place, we were in a very distracted condition, and in more likelihood to perish every man than escape the bloodiness of that day. Now we found the words of Captain Sharp to bear a true prophecy, being all very sensible that we had had a day too hot for us, after that cruel heat in killing and murdering in cold blood the old Mestizo Indian whom we had taken prisoner at Iquique, as before was mentioned.

Being surrounded with difficulties on all sides and in great disorder, having no head or leader to give orders for what was to be done, we were glad to turn our eyes to our good and old Commander, Captain Bartholomew Sharp, and beg of him very earnestly to commiserate our condition and carry us off. It was a great while that we were reiterating our supplications to him before he would take any notice of our request in this point, so much was he displeased with the former mutiny of our people against him, all which had been occasioned by the instigation of Mr Cook. But Sharp is a man of an undaunted courage and of an excellent conduct, not fearing in the least to look an insulting enemy in the face, and a person that knows both the theory and practical parts of navigation as well as most do. Hereupon, at our request and earnest petition, he took upon him the Command-in-chief again, and began to distribute his orders for our safety. He would have brought off our surgeons, but that they had been drinking while we assaulted the fort, and thus would not come with us when they were called. They killed and took of our number 28 men—18 more that we brought off were desperately wounded. At this time we were extremely faint for want of water and victuals, whereof we had had none all that day. Moreover, we were almost choked with the dust of the town, this being so much raised by the work that their great guns had made that we could scarcely see each other. They beat us out of the town, and then followed us into the Savannas, or open fields, still charging us as fast as they could. But when they saw that we rallied again, resolving to die one by another, they then ran from us into the town, and sheltered themselves under their breastworks. Thus we retreated in as good order as we could possibly observe in that confusion. But their horsemen followed us as we retired, and fired at us all the way, though they would not come within reach of our guns, for their own reached farther than ours, and outshot us more than one-third. We took the sea-side for our greater security; which, when the enemy saw, they betook themselves to the hills, rolling down great stones and whole rocks to destroy us. In the meanwhile those of the town examined our surgeons and other men whom they had made prisoners. These gave them our signs that we had left to our boats that were behind us, so that they immediately blew up two smokes, which were perceived by the canoes. This was the greatest of our dangers. For, had we not come at the instant that we did to the sea-side, our boats had been gone, they being already under sail, and we had inevitably perished every man. Thus we put off from the shore, and got on board about ten o'clock at night, having been involved in a continual and bloody fight with the enemy all that day long.

CHAPTER XVII

A description of the Bay of Arica. They sail hence to the Port of Guasco, where they get provisions. A draft of the said port. They land again at Hilo to revenge the former affronts, and take what they could find

HAVING ended our attempt at Arica, the next day, being January the last, we plied to and fro in sight of the port, to see if they would send out the three ships we had seen in the harbour to fight us. For upon them we hoped to revenge the defeat and disappointment we had received at the town the day before. But our expectations in this point also were frustrated, for not one of those vessels offered to stir.

The houses of this town of Arica are not above eleven-feet high, being built of earth and not of brick or timber. The town itself is four-square in figure, and at one corner stands the castle, which may easily be commanded even with small arms from the hill which lies close to it. This place is the *embarcadero*, or port-town, of all the mineral towns that lie hereabouts, and hence is fetched all the plate that is carried to Lima, the head city of Peru. I took the bay of Arica as it appeared to me.

On Tuesday, February 1st, we had a clear observation, and by it we found lat. 19° 06′ S. This day we shared the old remains of our plate, taken in some of our former booties. Our shares amounted only to 37 pieces-of-eight to each man.

N.B.—*Here I would have my reader take notice that from this day forward I kept no constant Diary or Journal as I had done before, at least for some considerable space of time, as you see hereafter—my disease and sickness at sea being the occasion of intermitting what I had never failed to do in all the course of this voyage till now. Only some few memorandums as my weakness gave leave I now and then committed to paper, which I shall give you as I find them, towards a continuance of this history. Thus :—*

Monday, February 14th. This night between eleven and twelve o'clock died on board our ship William Cook, who was the servant aforementioned to Captain Edmund Cook, of whom likewise mention has been often made in this Journal.

February 16th, 1680. This day we found ourselves to be in lat. 27° 30′ S. We had a constant breeze at S.E. and S.S.E. till we got about 200 leagues from land. Then, at the eclipse of the moon, we had a calm for two or three days ; and then a breeze at N. for the space of two days ; after which we had a calm again for two or three days more.

March 1st. By observation, lat. 34° 01′ S. At this time begins the dirty weather in these seas. We lay under a pair of courses, the wind being at S.E. and E.S.E., with a very great sea at S.S.E.

March 3rd. All hands were called up, and a council held ; wherein, considering it was now dirty weather and late in the year, we bore up the helm and resolved to go to the main for water, and thence to leeward, and so march overland towards home or at least to the North Sea. But God directed us from following this resolution, as you shall hear hereafter. We being thus determined that day, we stood N.E. with a strong wind at S.E. and E.S.E.

On March 5th died our Coquimbo Indian. The seventh we had a West-wind, our course being E. by N. The eighth of the said month we were put to an allowance, having only one cake of bread a day. March 10th, we had a strong South-wind.

On March 12th we fell in with the mainland, somewhat to leeward of Coquimbo. Within the island of Paxaros are double lands, in whose valleys are fires for the melting of copper, with which metal these hills abound. Off to seaboard it is a rocky land, and within it is sandy. About the distance of eight leagues to leeward is a rocky point with several quays or rocks about it. About one half-mile to leeward of this point turns in the port of Guasco. Right against the anchoring are three rocks, close under the shore.

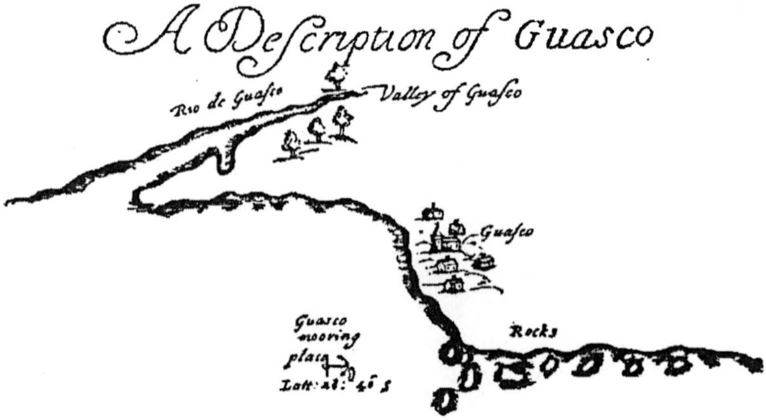

Being arrived here, we landed on shore three-score men of our company, with design to get provisions and anything else that we could purchase. The people of the country all ran away as soon as they saw us. There was building on shore in this port a fire-bark of 16 or 18 tons burden, with a cock-boat belonging to it. We took one Indian prisoner, and with him went up the space of six or seven miles into the country to an Indian town of three-score or four-score houses. Thence we came back to the church, which is distant four miles from the sea-side; and lodged there all night. Here are multitudes of good sheep and goats in the country adjoining this port, and it is watered with an excellent fresh-water river; but the getting of the water is very difficult, the banks being very high or otherwise inaccessible. However, we made a shift to get in 500 jars of water. Furthermore, we brought away 120 sheep and four-score goats, with which stock we victualled our vessel for a while. As for oxen, they had driven them away farther up into the country. The jurisdiction of Guasco itself is governed by a Tenente, or Deputy-Governor, and a Friar, and is in subjection to the city of La Serena above-mentioned, being a dependence upon it. Here grows corn, peas, beans, and several other sorts of grain; and for fruits this place is not inferior to Coquimbo. Here we found likewise a mill to grind corn, and about 200 bushels thereof ready ground, which we conveyed on board our ship. Every house of any account has branches of water running through its yards or courts. The inhabitants had hidden their wine and other best things, as plate and jewels, having descried us at sea before our landing—so that our booty here, besides provisions, was inconsiderable. However, we caught some few fowls, and eat five or six sheep, and likewise a great hog, which tasted very like our English pork. The hills are all barren, so that the country which bears fruit is only an excellent valley, being four times as broad as that of Hilo above-mentioned. These people of Guasco serve the town of Coquimbo with many sorts of provisions. We gave the Indian whom we had taken his liberty, and I took the port of Guasco.

Tuesday, March 15th, 1680. This morning we departed from the port of Guasco aforementioned, with very little wind, having done nothing considerable there, excepting only the taking in the few provisions above-related. We were bent therefore to seek greater matters, having experienced but ill success in most of our attempts hitherto. On March 20th, Moro de Horse, being high doubled land, and at E. by N. appeared thus to us, in lat. 24° S. :—

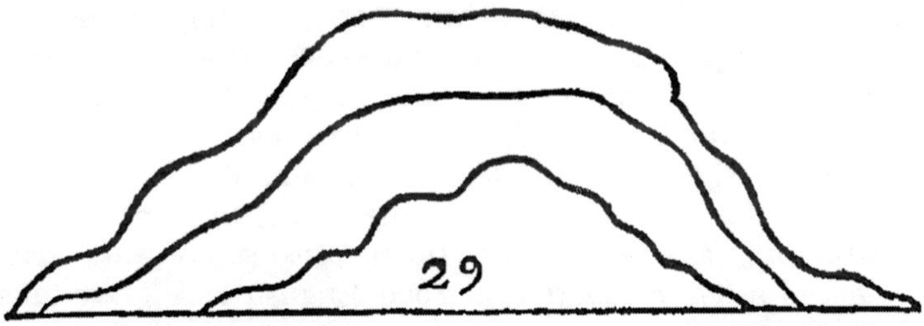

MORO DE HORSE LAT. 24° S.

At N., and at the distance of ten leagues, more or less, we saw the great and high hill of Moro Moreno, being so called from its colour. It is a dark hill, but much higher and bigger than the other aforementioned, and appears like an island, thus :—

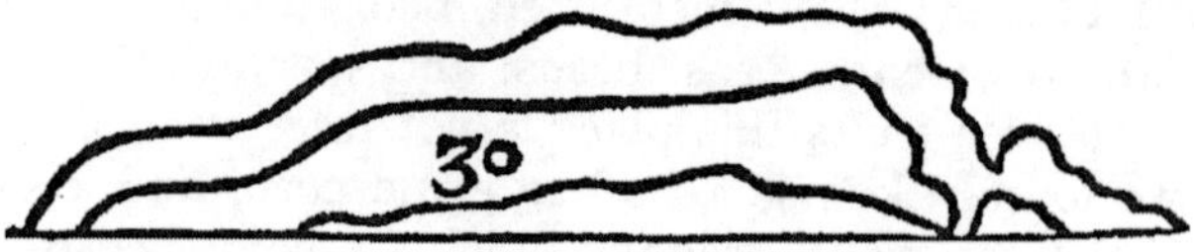

MORO MORENO *LAT.* 23° 30′ *S.*

We had now very dark weather all along the coast. On March 21st we were W. from the bay of Mexillones. The point of this bay one league upwards represents exactly a sugar-loaf.

March 22nd. This day our boat and canoes went from the ship, well manned, to find the river Loa. They went also about two leagues to leeward of it, to a fishing village, but could find no place fit for landing ; whereupon they returned without doing anything. The next day another canoe of our company went out upon the same exploit, but found the same success. Yet, notwithstanding, here Sir Francis Drake watered, and built a church, as we were told by our pilot. This church is now standing on the sea-side by the river, whose mouth is now dry. There are several huts to windward of it ; and from the said church or chapel a great path goes up the hills ; which leads to Pica.

On Thursday, March 24th, by observation lat. 20° 10′ S. This day also we saw land at 18 leagues distance, more or less.

Sunday, March 27th, we saw Mora de Sama and Lacumba at some distance. The same day we had an observation, and found by it lat. 18° 17′ S. That evening we departed from the ship with our boats and canoes towards the coast of Hilo, upon which we now were. We landed and took the village of Hilo undescried, they scarce suspecting we could have any design upon that place the second time. We caught the friar who was chaplain to the town, and most of the inhabitants, asleep, making them prisoners-of-war. Here we heard a flying report that 5000 English had lately taken Panama the second time, and kept it. But this rumour, as it should seem, proved to be a falsity. At this time the river came out, and was overflowed, it being near the time of the freshes. Here the prisoners told us that in Arica ten of our men were still alive, whereof three were surgeons, all the rest being dead of their wounds. The Spaniards sent word to Hilo that we had killed 70 men and wounded three times as many of their forces. Here the inhabitants said that of 45 men sent to the relief of Arica from hence there came home but only two alive. We filled what water we pleased here, but a small boat that we brought from Guasco broke loose from us and was staved to pieces on the rocks. Here we took 18 jars of wine, and good store of new figs. On Tuesday following we went up to the sugar-works mentioned in our former expedition against Hilo, and found all fruits just ripe and fit for eating. There we laded seven mules downwards with molasses and sugar. The inhabitants told us, moreover, that those who came to fight us when we were here the first time were most of them boys, and had only 50 firearms amongst them, they being commanded by an English gentleman who is married at Arequipa. Likewise, that the owner of the sugar-works aforementioned was now engaged in a suit-at-law against the town of Hilo, pretending it was not the English who robbed him and spoilt his *ingenio*, when we were there before, but the townsmen themselves. This day in the evening we sailed from Hilo with dark weather and little wind, which continued for several days afterwards.

CHAPTER XVIII

They depart from the Port of Hilo to the Gulf of Nicoya, where they take down their decks and mend the sailing of their ship. Forty-seven of their companions leave them, and go home overland. A description of the Gulf of Nicoya. They take two barks and some prisoners there. Several other remarks belonging to this voyage

FROM the time that we set sail from the port of Hilo until Sunday, April 10th, 1681, nothing happened to us that might be accounted remarkable; neither did I take any notes all this while, by reason of my indisposition aforementioned. This day we could hear distinctly the breaking of the seas on the shore, but could see no land, the weather being extremely dark and hazy. Notwithstanding, about noon it cleared up, and we found ourselves to be in the bay called De Malabrigo. The land in this bay runs due E. and W. By an observation made, we found this day 6° 35′ S. We saw from here the leeward island of Lobos, or Seals, being nothing but a rocky and scraggy place. On the S.W. side thereof is a red hill, which is a place about the said island which the Indian fishermen much frequent. It is situated in lat. 6° 15′ S. This day likewise in the evening we saw the point called Aguja.

On Saturday, April 16th, we came within a league distance of the West-end of the island of Plate, above described. The next day to this, being Sunday, April 17th, 1681, our mutineers broke out again into an open dissension, they having been much dissatisfied all along the course of this voyage, but more especially since our unfortunate fight at Arica, and never entirely reconciled to us since they chose Captain Watling and deposed Sharp at the isle of Juan Fernandez, as was related above. Nothing now could appease them nor serve their turn but a separation from the rest of the company and a departure from us. Hereupon this day they departed from the ship, to the number of 47 men, all in company together, with design to go overland by the same way they came into those seas. The rest who remained behind did fully resolve and faithfully promise to each other they would stick close together. They took five slaves in their company, to guide and do them other service in that journey. This day we had lat. 1° 30′ S. We sailed N.N.W. before the wind.

The next day after their departure, being April 18th, we began to go to work about taking down one of our upper decks, thereby to cause our ship still to mend her sailing. We now made a N.W. by N. way, by observation lat. 25° N., the wind being at S.W.

On April 19th we made a N.W. by N. way. By observation lat. 2° 45′ N. In the afternoon we had cloudy weather. The following day likewise we made the same way, and by it 70 miles, according to my reckoning.

On the 21st in the morning we had some small showers of rain, and but little wind. We saw some turtle upon the surface of the water, and great quantity of fish. We caught twenty-six small dolphins. By a N.W. by N. way, we reckoned this day forty miles.

April 22nd. This day we caught seven large dolphins and one bonito. We saw likewise whole multitudes of turtle swimming upon the water, and took five of them. By observation lat. 5° 28′ N. Hereabouts runs a great and strong current. This day we lowered the quarter-deck of our ship, and made it even to the upper deck.

The following day we had but small wind, and yet great showers of rain. Hereupon every man saved water for himself, and a great quantity was saved for the whole company. In the morning of this day we caught eight bonitos, and in the evening ten more.

On April 24th we had both cloudy and rainy weather. By observation lat. 7° 37′ N.; M.D. 92 leagues. This morning we caught forty bonitos, and in the evening thirty more. In the afternoon we stood N., the wind being at S.W. by S.

Monday, April 25th. All the night before this day we had huge gusts of wind and rain. At break of day we were close in with land, which upon examination proved to be the island of Cano. To westward thereof is very high land. About noon this day it cleared up, and we had lat. 8° 34′ N. In the evening we sent a canoe to search the island. In it they found good water, and even ground, but withal an open road. At night we stood off the first watch, and the last we had a land wind.

The next day following at daylight we stood in, and about noon we came to an anchor at the East side of the island aforementioned, which is not in breadth above one league. In the afternoon we removed from our former anchoring place, and anchored again within shot of the N.E. point of the island. In this place grows great number of coco trees all over the greatest part of the isle. On the North side thereof are many rivulets of good water to be found in sandy bays. We saw moreover some good hogs on shore, whereof we killed one, and two pigs. Here are great numbers of turtle-doves, and huge store of fish, but withal, very shy to be caught. To Northward of the island it looks thus :—

ISLA DEL CANO *LAT.* 8° 45′ *N.*

April 27th we had some rain and wind the forepart of the day, but the afternoon was fair. The next day in like manner we had great quantity of rain. On Saturday, the 30th, about seven o'clock in the morning we weighed anchor from the aforesaid island with little wind, and stood N.W. That day fell much rain, with great thunder and lightning.

Monday, May 2nd. This day we observed and found lat. 9° N. The coast all along appeared to us very high and mountainous, and scarce six hours did pass but we had thunder, lightning, and rain ; the like continued for the two days following, wherein we had nothing but almost continual thunder and rain.

On May 5th we had an indifferent fair day, and that evening we were right off of the Gulf of Nicoya.

Friday, May 6th. This morning we saw the cape very

plain before us. N. by E. from it, are certain quays at eight leagues distance close under the main. We steered N.N.W. towards the biggest of them, at whose E.S.E. side are two or three small rocks. The main eastward is fine savanna, or plain and even land, through which goes a very great road, which is to be seen from the sea. At noon the port of Caldero, commonly called Puerto Caldero, bore N. from us. At which time the ebb forced us to sound in the middle of the gulf, where we found fourteen fathom water. After this we anchored nearer to the eastern quays, in 19 fathom, where we had oozy ground.

Saturday, May 7th. The night before this day was very fair all night long. In the morning we went in a canoe, being several in company, to seek for a place to lay our ship in. Amongst the islands along the shore we found many brave holes, but little or no water in them, which caused us to dislike what we had found. On one of the said islands we happened to find a hat, and many empty jars of water, which showed us that some people had been lately there. About eight in the evening our ship weighed anchor at young flood, and about three in the afternoon we anchored again in six-fathom water.

Sunday, May 8th, 1681. The night before this day, we had much rain, with thunder and lightning. The morning being come, our Commander, Captain Sharp, departed from the ship in two canoes, with 22 men in his company, out of design to surprise any vessels or people they could meet hereabouts. In the meanwhile, in the evening, we drove up with the tide (there being no wind) in the ship, for the space of two or three leagues higher, till we found but three fathom at high water. Here we backed astern. At this time we saw one of our canoes coming off from the island that was ahead of us (which was named Chira), calling for more men and arms, and saying there were two ships to be seen higher up the gulf. Hereupon eight of us went away with them ashore, whereof two joined the party aforementioned, and the six remaining were appointed to guard the prisoners they had taken. To these we showed ourselves very kind, as finding that they were very sensible of the cruelties of the Spaniards towards them and their whole nation. Here we found eight or nine houses and a small chapel standing. These people have been in former times a considerable and great nation, but are now almost destroyed and extinguished by the Spaniards. We ascended a creek of the sea for a league, or thereabouts, and took two barks by surprisal, which were the two sail they had told us of before. One of these barks was the same we had taken before at Panama, of which I made mention at the beginning of this history.

On Monday following this day we weighed anchor with our barks, and drove down the creek, with the tide at ebb, towards our ship. The prisoners that we had taken here informed us that, when we were to westward in these seas before, there lay 100 men at the port of Santa Maria. That our men who left us at the island of Cayboa, as was mentioned above, met the other bark that we lost at sea, as we were sailing thither, and thus all went overland together. That in the North Seas, near Porto Bello, they had taken a good ship, and that for this cause, ever since, the Spaniards had kept at the mouth of the river of Santa Maria three *Armadilla* barks, to stop and hinder others from going that way. On Monday night our Captain, with 24 men, went from the ship into another creek, and there took several prisoners, among whom was a shipwright and his men, who were judged able to do us good service in the altering of our ship: these carpenters being there actually building two great ships for the Spaniards. Having taken these men, they made a float of timber to bring down the tools and instruments they were working withal. Here it happened that they put several tools and some quantity of iron-work into a dory, to be conveyed down the river with the float. But this dory sank by the way, being overladen with iron, and one of our company, by name John Alexander, a Scotchman, was unfortunately drowned by this means.

On Thursday following, May 12th, we sent a canoe from the ship, and found the dory that had been sunk. That evening likewise drove down the body of our drowned man aforementioned. Hereupon we took him up, and on Friday morning following threw him overboard, giving him three French volleys for his customary ceremony. Both this day and the day before we fetched water from a point near the houses on the island of Chira aforementioned. From the ship also we sent away a Spanish merchant whom we had taken among the prisoners, to fetch a certain number of beeves that might serve for a ransom of the new bark taken here. This day the weather was fair, but on Sunday following it rained from morning until night.

On Monday, May 16th, we began to work all hands together on our ship. On Tuesday an Indian boy named Peter ran away from us. He belonged to Captain Sawkins, and waited on him as his servant. On Wednesday died an Indian slave, whose name was Salvador. On Thursday we heard thirty or forty guns fired on the main, which caused us to think that these would also turn to Hilo beeves. On Friday we caught cockles, which were as large as both our fists. At night there fell such dreadful rain, with thunder, lightning, and wind, that for the space of two hours the air was as light as day; the thunder not ceasing all the while. On Sunday we continued to work; the night before which day we had more thunder, lightning, and rain.

Wednesday, May 25th. This day we finished our great piece of work, viz. the taking down the deck of our ship. Besides which, the length of every mast was shortened; and all was now served and rigged, insomuch that it would seem incredible to strangers, could they but see how much work we performed in the space of a fortnight or less. The same day likewise we set at liberty our Spanish carpenters, who had been very serviceable to us all this while, the old pilot, the old Spaniard taken at the isle of Iquique, and several others of our Spanish prisoners and slaves. To these people, but chiefly to the Spanish carpenters as a reward for their good service, we gave the new bark which we had taken at this place. But the old bark we thought fit to keep, and sail in our company, as we did, putting into her for this purpose six of our own men and two slaves. The next day we fell down as low as Vanero, a place so called hereabouts, and would have sailed away again that very evening but that our tackle gave way in hoisting our anchor, whereby we lay still. In the Gulf of Nicoya we experienced most commonly a fresh breeze, and at night a land wind.

Friday, May 27th. This day likewise we drove down with the tide as low as Cavallo, another place so named in the gulf. Here we stayed and watered that day; and here one Cannis Marcy, our interpreter, ran away from us.

On May 28th in the morning we sailed thence, and came within 29 leagues of that rich and rocky shore. Yet, notwithstanding, we had but seven fathom water. Here I saw this day a white porpoise. Behind this island is a town called New Cape Blanco. At Puerto Caldero, above-mentioned, is but one storehouse to be seen. We came to an anchor in the depth of seven-fathom water, at the distance of a league from shore, and caught five turtle.

May 29th. This day we saw Cape Blanco. Both this day and the day following we continued tacking out of the gulf against a South wind. Here I took the ensuing demonstration of the Gulf of Nicoya, which, for the use of the reader, I have hereunto annexed.

CHAPTER XIX

They depart from the Gulf of Nicoya to Golfo Dulce, where they careen their vessel. An account of their sailings along the coast; also a description of Golfo Dulce. The Spaniards force the Indians of Darien to a peace by a stratagem contrived in the name of the English

Wednesday, June 1st, 1681. This day we had very fair weather, and yet but little wind. Hereupon the tide, or current, drove us to the Westward of Cape Blanco. Off this Cape, and at the distance of two miles within the sea, is situate a naked and nothing but barren quay. At E. by N., and at 4 leagues distance, Cape Blanco gave us this appearance :—

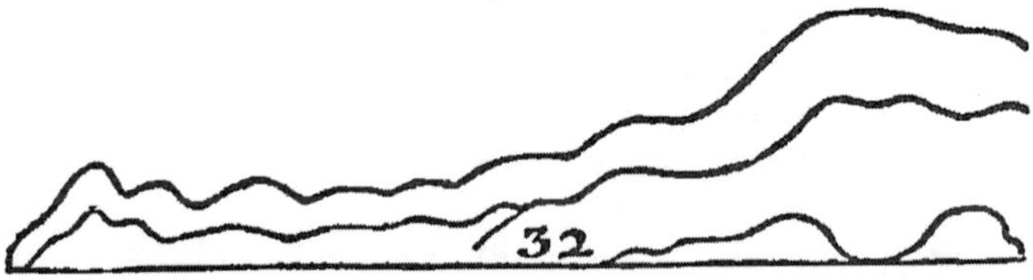

CABO BLANCO *LAT. 9° 30′ N.*

The coast here along runs N.W. half W., and grows lower and lower towards Cape Guyones. This cape at 7 leagues distance, and at N.W. by N., appeared thus to us :—

CABO DE GUYONES *LAT. 10° 00′ N.*

At first sight the cape appeared very like two islands. The latter part of this day was cloudy, which hindered much our prospect.

June 2nd. This morning we saw land, which appeared like several quays to us at N.W. by N., and at 7 leagues distance. It was the land of Puerto de Velas, and appeared thus:—

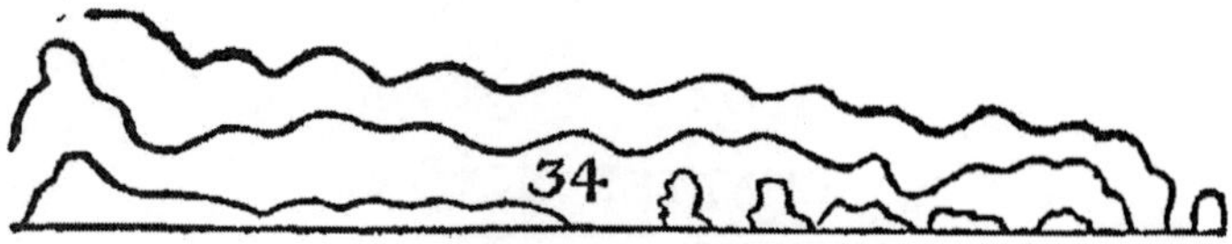

Puerto de Velas

This evening our Captain called us together and asked our opinions concerning the course we ought to steer. Having discussed the points by him proposed amongst us, we all resolved to bear up for Golfo Dulce, and there careen our vessels. This being done, we concluded to go thence to the cape, and cruise thereabouts under the equinoctial. We observed this day that our bark taken at the gulf of Nicoya sailed much better than our ship.

Friday, June 3rd. The night before this day was very fair, and we had a fresh wind, our course being S.E. This morning we saw no land. In the evening the wind came about at S.S.W. and S.W. by S.

June 4th. This day we stood E. and E. by N., the wind being W. and W. by N. In the evening we stood N.E., and descried land at the distance of 24 leagues, more or less, from Cape Blanco.

Sunday, June 5th. Last night we lay by for all, or the greater part thereof. This morning we saw the island of Cano above described, which bore E.S.E. from us. We saw likewise multitudes of fish, but they would not bite. Also water-snakes of divers colours.

June 6th. All last night we had rain, and with it but little wind—yea, scarce enough to carry us clear off from the island aforementioned. Towards morning we had a fresh wind at N.N.W. So then we stood out S. until morning, and, this being come, we stood N.E. by E. The land runs from Punta Mala to Golfo Dulce and Punta Borrica, E.S.E. half S. At 9 leagues distance we laid the island of Cano. Punta Borrica at the same distance, or thereabouts, looks thus:—

PUNTA BORRICA *LAT. 8° 00′ N.*

The West end of Golfo Dulce is very high land, and a high rock lies close off it. Besides which, two other rocks lie farther out ; the outermost of which is a mile distant from the shore. The East side is also high, but breaks into small points and bays, growing lower and lower to Punta Borrica. We came about a mile within the mouth of the gulf ; then anchored in eight-fathom-and-a-half water. The mouth of the gulf is almost 3 leagues over.

The next day, being June 7th, we weighed anchor again at young flood, and got about 2 leagues higher. At evening we came again to anchor in seven-fathom-and-a-half water. It rained this day until eight o'clock, more like the pouring down of water from the clouds than the usual falling of drops.

Wednesday, June 8th, at daybreak we weighed anchor again, with a fresh sea-breeze. The higher up we went, the deeper we found the gulf, and at last no ground even with thirty-fathom of line. This day we sent our canoe away to seek water and a good place to lay our ship in. Having landed, they found one Indian and two boys, which they made prisoners and brought aboard ; we used them very kindly, giving them victuals and clothes, for they had no other than the bark of a tree to cover their nakedness withal. Being examined, they informed us that a Spanish priest had been amongst them, and had made peace with their nation, ordering them strictly not to come near any ship nor vessel that had red colours, forasmuch as that they were Englishmen, and would certainly kill them. Being asked where now the priest was, they answered that he was gone to a great Spanish town, which was distant thence four sleeps up in the country. After this the Indian left the two boys, his children, with us, and went to fetch more Indians to us, from a plantain-walk, or grove, situated by a river a league off, or thereabouts. We came to an anchor in a bay close by one of the Indian quays, where two fresh rivers were within a stone's-throw of each other, in twenty-seven-fathom-and-a-half water, and at a cable's length from the mark of low water. The Indians whom our prisoner went to seek came to us several times, selling to us honey, plantains, and other necessaries that we usually bought of them or trucked for with other things. We also made use of their bark-logs in tallowing our ship, in which concern they did us good service. Their darts are headed with iron as sharp as any razor.

Here one of the prisoners which we took at the Gulf of Nicoya informed us by what means, or rather stratagem of war, the Spaniards had forced a peace upon the Indians of the province of Darien since our departure thence. The manner was as follows: A certain Frenchman who ran from us at the island of Tavoga to the Spaniards was sent by them in a ship to the river's mouth, which disembogues from that province into the South Sea. Being arrived there, he went ashore by himself in a canoe, and told the Indians that the English who had passed that way were come back from their adventures in the South Sea. Withal he asked them if they would not be so kind and friendly to the Englishmen as to come aboard and conduct them on shore. The poor deceived Indians were very joyful to understand this good news, and thus 40 of the chief men among them went on board the Spanish vessel, and were immediately carried prisoners-of-war to Panama. Here they were forced to conclude a peace, though upon terms very disadvantageous to them, before they could obtain their liberty.

These poor and miserable Indians of Golfo Dulce would come every day into our company, and eat and drink very familiarly with us all the time we were there. We laid our ship on ground, but the water did not ebb low enough to see her keel. Whilst we were careening our vessel, we built a house upon the shore, both to lodge and eat in, and every day we caught plenty of good fish. On Sunday, June 12th, the work of careening our ship going on in due order, we came to cleanse our hold, and here on a sudden both myself and several others were struck totally blind with the filth and nastiness of the said place. Yet soon after we recovered our sight again without any other help than the benefit of the fresh and open air, which dissipated those malignant vapours that had oppressed our eyes. On June 14th we had a great and fierce tornado, with which our cable broke, and, had it not then happened to be high water at that instant, we had been lost inevitably. However, we had the good fortune to shore her up again, and by that means secure ourselves from farther danger. On June 21st we weighed anchor again, and went a league higher than the former place. Here we watered, and in the meanwhile left men below to cut wood.

Thursday, June 23rd. This day ran away from us two negroes. The name of one of them was Hernando, who was taken with Don Thomas de Argandona on the coast of Guayaquil, as was mentioned above. The other was named Silvestre, having been taken at the town of Hilo. Following the example of these aforementioned, on Monday, June 27th, that is, four days after, two more of our prisoners endeavoured to make their escape, both of them slaves. One of these was named Francisco, who was a negro, and had been taken in the coco-ship mentioned before. The name of the other was also Francisco, and he was an Indian born, who was taken before Panama. Their attempts to escape succeeded not, for we caught them both again before they got on shore. On Tuesday following I went to sail up and down the gulf in the little bark belonging to our ship; and, having viewed all places, took this description of Golfo Dulce here inserted. Our captain gave this gulf the name of King Charles, his Harbour.

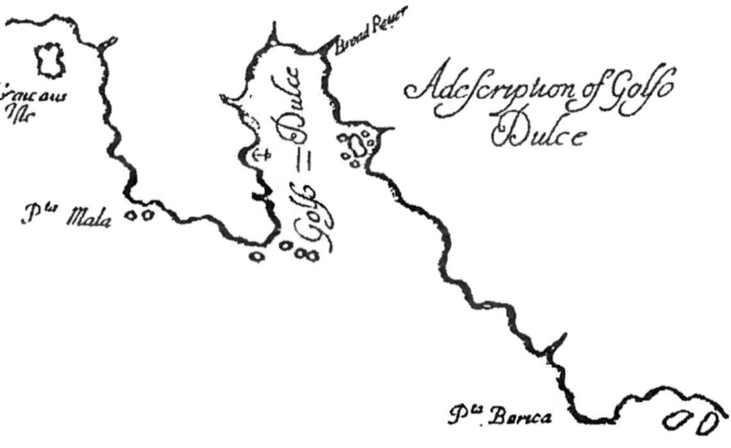

CHAPTER XX

They depart from Golfo Dulce, to go and cruize under the equinoctial. Here they take a rich Spanish vessel with 37,000 pieces-of-eight, besides plate and other goods. They take also a packet-boat bound from Panama to Lima. An account of their sailings and the coast along

OUR vessel being now careened and all things in a readiness for our departure, on Tuesday, June 28th, in the afternoon, we weighed anchor to go to sea again, turning out towards the mouth of Golfo Dulce. Our design was to cruize under the equinoctial, as had been concluded upon before, thereby to get what purchase we could by sea, seeing the greatest part of our attempts on land had proved hitherto very unsuccessful to us.

Wednesday, June 29th. Both the night last past and this day we had rainy weather. About three in the afternoon a fresh gale sprang up at S.W. and S.S.W., our course being S.E. and S.E. by S. At five this evening the gulf bore N.W. by W., 7 leagues distant, and Punta Borrica 3 leagues and a-half distant.

Thursday, June 30th. All night past we enjoyed a fresh gale at S.S.W. We sailed in the bark (where I was) better than the man-of-war, for so we called the Trinity vessel, notwithstanding that she was newly cleansed and tallowed. This day we had hazy weather, and I reckoned myself from Punta Borrica S.S.E. 18 leagues and a-half.

July 1st, 1681. Last night we had two or three tornados. I reckoned this day a S.S.E. way, and by a clear observation found lat. 6° 10′ N. We saw great quantities of fish as we sailed this day.

July 2nd. We made a S.E. way, and our reckoning was 64 by it. By observation I found lat. 5° 20′ N. At noon the same day we had a fresh gale at S.W., with some rain.

July 3rd. We had hazy weather. We made a S.E. by S. way, and 37.

Monday, July 4th. The night just past was windy, with rain, which forced us to hand our top-sails. Our reckoning this day was a S.E. way, and 100 miles.

July 5th. We had a clear night, and withal a fresh gale. By this we made a S.E. way. Our latitude this day gave us 2° 20′ N. This morning we saw land Southward of us, lying in low hummocks. It was the point, so called, of Manglares.

Wednesday, July 6th. We turned up along shore, and by observation took this day lat. 2° 02′ N. Hereabouts with every new moon is experienced a windward current. In the evening of this day we were close in with low land. We had windy weather and a great sea.

Thursday, July 7th. This day by observation we found lat. 01° 48′ N. In the evening of the said day we lost sight of the said ship.

The next day, being July 8th, we saw the ship again, whose loss began to create some concern in our minds. This day we made very high land all along as we went. And the port, or rather bay, of San Matteo, or St Matthew, appeared to us like several islands.

Saturday, July 9th. This morning we stood fair in with the port of Tucames. Off the highest part of the land there seems to lie a quay. At the North-east point of the port it appears exactly thus :—

PUERTO DE TUCAMES

This day at noon we had a clear observation, which gave us lat. 01° 22′ N.

Sunday, July 10th. Last night we stood off to sea, thereby to keep clear of the shore. This day observation showed us lat. 01° 31′ N. About noon the same day we happened to spy a sail, to which immediately we gave chase. We bore up one point of the compass, thereby to hinder her lasking away ;

but notwithstanding in the evening lost sight of her again. However, our great ship got up with her, and at about eight o'clock at night made her a prize. She proved to be the same ship, named *San Pedro*, which we had taken the last year, being then bound from Truxillo to Panama, and laden with wine, gunpowder, and pieces-of-eight, whereof mention was made in its due place. Thus this same bottom became doubly fortunate to us, being twice taken by us in the space of fourteen months. For she had on board her now 21,000 pieces of eight, in eight chests, and in bags 16,000 more, besides plate.

Monday and Tuesday, the 11th and 12th of the said month, we made in for the shore. Our prize was so deeply laden that she seemed to be buried in the water. She had 40 men on board her, besides some merchants and friars. On Tuesday an observation gave us lat. 1° 20′ N.

Wednesday, July 13th. This day we dared not adventure into the bay of San Matteo, because we saw some Indians, who had made a great fire on shore, which, as we judged, was designedly done to give intelligence of our arrival. Hereupon we bore away for the river of Santiago, six leagues distant, more or less, from the bay aforementioned, to the North-east. Thursday, Friday, and Saturday of the said week we spent in taking out what parcels of coco-nut we thought fit from on board the prize, which was chiefly laden with the said commodity. This being done, we cut down the main-mast by the board, and gave them only their main-sail, and thus turning the ship loose sent away in her all our old slaves, for the good service they had done us, taking new ones from the prize in their room. One only we still detained, who was Francisco, the negro that attempted to run away by swimming ashore, as was mentioned above.

Sunday, July 17th. This day we went from the ship, and found the river of Santiago above-mentioned. At the mouth of this river we stayed Monday and Tuesday following to take in water, which we now much wanted. On the sides of the river we found good store of plantains. Our fresh water we fetched the distance of four miles up the river. We saw several Indians, but could not speak with them they were so shy of us, being forewarned by the Spaniards not to come near us.

On Wednesday, July 20th, we shared our plunder among

ourselves, or rather this day made part of the dividend of what we had taken, the rest being reserved to another day. Our prisoners being examined, informed us that the Spaniards had taken up our anchors and cables which we left behind us at the isle of Juan Fernandez. Also that they had surprised the Mosquito Indian that we left behind us there on shore, by the light of a fire which he made in the night upon the isle.

Tuesday, July 21st. All the last four-and-twenty hours we stood off and on. The next day we shared the rest of our things taken in the prize, as also the money that was in the bags; the rest we laid up to divide upon another occasion, especially after such time as we were got through the Strait of Magellan. Our dividend amounted to the sum of 234 pieces-of-eight to each man. Our prisoners informed us this day that a new Viceroy of Peru was arrived at Panama, and that he dared not adventure up to Lima in a ship of 25 guns that was at Panama for fear of meeting with us at sea, but had chosen rather to wait until the Armada came down from Lima to safeguard and conduct him thither.

July 23rd we had a fresh breeze at S.W., and the next day a clear observation, which gave us only latitude 14′ N. This day Cape San Francisco at N.E. appeared thus to us:—

CABO DE SAN FRANCISCO

Monday, July 25th. This day we observed latitude 01° 20′ S., and we had a south-west wind.

July 26th. This morning we had a very great dew fallen in the night last past. The weather in like manner was very close.

On Wednesday, July 27th, Cape Passao, at S.S.W. and at 6 leagues distance appeared thus:—

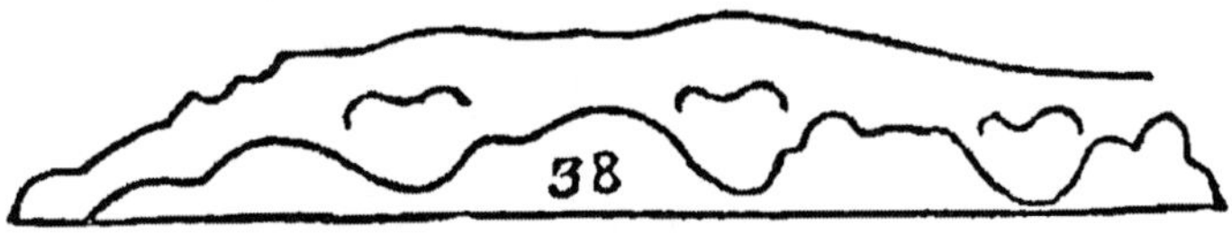

CABO PASSAO

The same morning about seven o'clock we spied a sail E.S.E. from us, under the shore. We presently gave her close chase, as eagerly as we could, and about noon came up with her. But several of the people belonging to her were already got on shore, whereby they made their escape from being taken our prisoners. These were chiefly a friar, who was either a passenger or chaplain to the vessel, and five negroes. She proved to be a *barco d'adviso,* or packet-boat, that was going with letters from Panama to Lima. In this bark we took among other prisoners two white women who were passengers to the same place. Both these and the rest of the prisoners told us they had heard at Panama that we were all gone out of these seas homewards overland, and that made them adventure now up towards Lima—otherwise they had not come. This day and the Thursday following we spent in taking out of the packet-boat what we could find in her, which all were things of no considerable value, they having scarce brought any thing with them but the packet. They told us, moreover, that the new Viceroy of Peru, of whom we made mention above, was setting forth from Panama under the conduct of three sail of ships, the one of 16, the other of 8, and the third of 6 guns. That a general peace was all over Europe, excepting only that the English had wars with the Algerines by sea and the Spaniards by land. Having got what we could out of the prisoners and the vessel, we gave them their liberty, and sent them away in the same bark, being desirous not to encumber ourselves with more than we could well manage. That night we stood out to sea all night long, most of our men being fuddled.

CHAPTER XXI

They take another Spanish ship richly laden under the equinoctial. They make several dividends of their booty among themselves. They arrive at the isle of Plate, where they are in danger of being all massacred by their slaves and prisoners. Their departure thence for the port and bay of Paita, with design to plunder the said place

THE next morning after we had turned away the packet-boat aforementioned, the weather being very close, we spied another sail creeping close under our lee. This vessel looked mighty big, so that we thought she had been one of their chief men-of-war who was sent to surprise or destroy us. Notwithstanding, our brave Commander, Captain Sharp, resolved to fight her, and either to take the said vessel, though never so big, or that she should take us. To this effect, coming nearer to her, we easily perceived she was a merchant-ship of great bulk, as most of your Spanish vessels are, and very deeply laden. Being up with them, those within her fired three or four guns at us first, thinking to make their party good against us. But we answered them briskly with a continual volley of small arms, so that they soon ran down into the hold, and surrendered, crying aloud for quarter. As it should seem, we had killed in that volley their Captain and one seaman, and also wounded their boatswain : which loss of their commander daunted them so suddenly, he being a man of good repute in those seas. Captain Sharp, with twelve more of our company, entered her the first. In this vessel I saw the most beautiful woman that I ever saw in all the South Sea. The name of the captain of this vessel was Don Diego Lopez, and the ship was called *El Santo Rosario*, or *The Holy Rosary*. The men we found on board her were about the number of 40, more or less.

Having examined our prisoners, they informed us that the day before they set sail from El Callao, from which port they were going towards Panama, our men whom they had taken prisoners at Arica were brought into that place and very civilly entertained there by all sorts of people, but more especially by the women. That one of our surgeons, whom we suspected to be Mr Bullock, was left behind, and remained still at Arica.

We lay at anchor from Friday, July 29th, which was the day we took this prize, until Wednesday following, at the same place under Cape Passao as we anchored before. Here we sank the bark that we had taken at the Gulf of Nicoya, being willing to make use of what rigging she had, and also to contract our number of men. In the meanwhile we took out of the prize much plate and some money ready coined, besides 620 jars of wine and brandy, and other things. Thus, leaving only the fore-mast standing in the said vessel, we turned her away, as we had done the others before, together with all the prisoners in her, giving them their liberty not to be encumbered with them, being desirous to spare our provisions as much as we could. We detained only one man, named Francisco, who was a Biscayner, because he reported himself to be the best pilot of those seas. This being done, we shared all the plate and linen taken in our prize, and weighed thence, standing S.S.E. with a fresh wind that sprang up.

Friday, August 4th. This day we shared the ready money taken in *The Rosario*, our last prize. Our dividend came to 94 pieces-of-eight each man. Cape Passao, under which all these prizes were taken, at N.E. appears thus :—

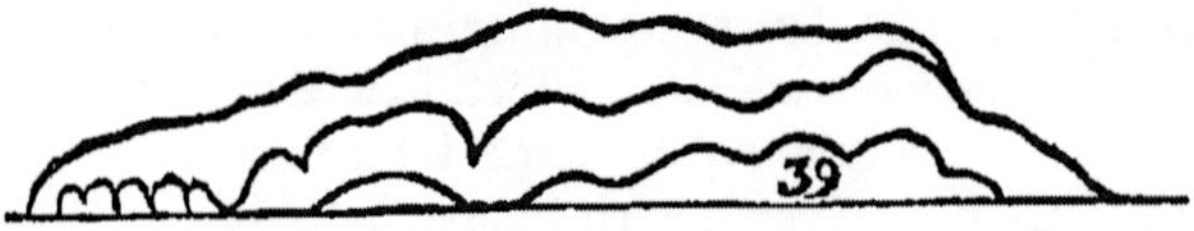

CABO PASSAO

The land runs S.E., and is for 5 leagues together to windward of this cape, all mountainous and high land.

The next day, being August 5th, we completed our dividends, sharing this day all our odd money, ready-coined, and plate, with some other things.

Saturday, August 6th. This day perusing some letters taken in the last prize, I understood by them that the Spaniards had taken prisoner one of the last party of our men that left us. Also that they were forced to fight all their way overland as they went, both against the Spaniards and the Indians, these having made peace with the Spaniards since our departure, as was mentioned above. That our Englishmen had killed, amongst other Spaniards, the brother of Captain Assientos and Captain Alonso, an officer so named. Moreover, that ten sail of privateers were coming out of the North Sea, with intent to march over-land into the South Sea, as we had done before, but that they were prevented, being forced back by the great rains that fell near the islands called Samballas.

On August 7th we had very fair weather, notwithstanding some strong winds from shore, and also a strong current to leeward. This ran so fierce against us the next day, August 8th, that in the space of the last four-and-twenty hours we lost three leagues.

Tuesday, August 9th, we saw the port and town of Manta, this being nothing but sixteen or seventeen straggling houses, with a large and high brick church belonging to it. What we got in the day by the help of the wind we lost in the night by the current. The same fortune we had the next day, for we still gained no way all this while.

Thursday, August 11th. All last night we had but little wind; this day we had a violent current to windward, as before, with some gusts of wind. However, by the help of these we made shift to get to windward of the isle of Plate.

August 12th, in the morning, we came to an anchor at the aforesaid isle. We sent our boat ashore with men, as we had done formerly, to kill goats, but we found them to be extremely shy and fugitive compared with what they were the last year. Here it was that our quartermaster, James Chappel, and myself fought a duel together on shore. In the evening of this day our slaves agreed among themselves and plotted to cut us all in pieces, not giving quarter to any, when we should be buried in sleep. They conceived this night afforded them the fittest opportunity by reason that we were all in drink. But they were discovered to our Commander by one of their own companions, and one of them named Santiago, whom we brought from Iquique, leapt overboard;

who, notwithstanding, was shot in the water by our Captain, and thus punished for his treason. The rest laid the fault on that slave, and so it passed, we being not willing to inquire any farther into the matter, having terrified them with the death of their companion. We lay at this isle until Tuesday following, and in the meanwhile gave our vessel a pair of boots and tops[1], being very merry all the while with the wine and brandy we had taken in the prize.

On Tuesday, August 16th, in the afternoon, we weighed thence with a S.W. wind. The island at N.W. from us gave us this following appearance :—

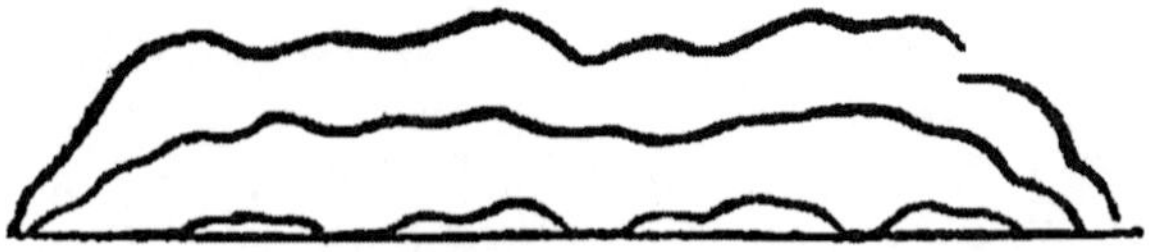

Isle de la Plata

Wednesday, August 17th, the island at E., this morning and at 2 leagues and a-half distance appeared thus :—

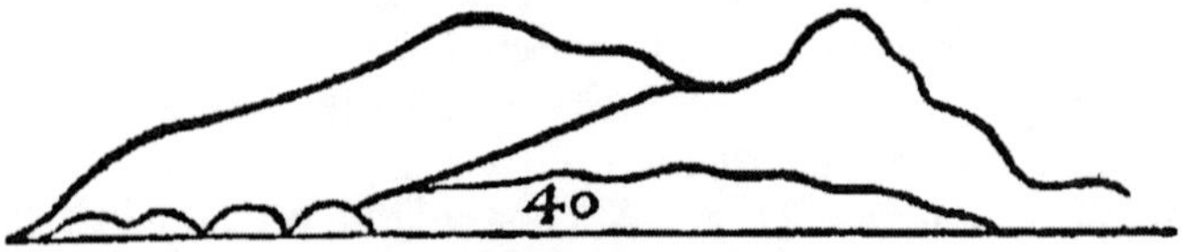

Island of Plate

All the day long until the evening we had a leeward current, but then I could not perceive any.

Thursday, August 18th. This morning we were to windward of the island of Solango. In the night before we had continual misty rain. At noon the aforesaid island bore N. by E. of us, and at 3 leagues distance appeared thus :—

Isle de Solango

[1] Perhaps a play upon the phrase 'topsy-boosy' = drunk. A person very drunk is said to be 'in his boots', which Bishop Kennet (*Glossary*—

About 3 leagues from Solango are two rocks, called Los Ahorcados. They appear both high and black to the view. Besides this N.N.E. from Point St Helena is a high rock, which to windward thereof runs shoaling for the space of half-a-mile under water. It is distant about eight leagues, more or less, from the said point, and is called Chanduy. At this place, and upon this rock, was lost the ship aforementioned that was ordered from these seas to the aid of our most gracious Sovereign, King Charles the First, late King of England. Said ship had on board, as the Spaniards relate, to the sum of many millions of pieces-of-eight; all which quantity of plate was sent as a present to our King, being then in his troubles, by the worthy merchants of Lima. The rock aforementioned lies about two leagues distant from the mainland.

August 19th. This day our pilot told us that, since we were to windward, a certain ship that was coming from Lima bound for Guayaquil ran ashore on Santa Clara, losing there in money to the value of 100,000 pieces-of-eight; which otherwise, peradventure, we might very fortunately have met with. Moreover, that the Viceroy of Peru had beheaded their great Admiral Ponce, for not coming to fight and destroy us while we were at Gorgona. This evening we saw point St Helena at the distance of ten leagues to S.S.E. from us.

August 20th. This day we had both misty and cold weather. In the afternoon we saw Point St Helena, at N.E. by N. and at 7 leagues distance, more or less.

On Sunday, August 21st, we had a fair and clear day. I reckoned myself this day to be about 25 leagues to the Southward of St Helena.

August 22nd. This morning about two o'clock we came close in with the shore. We found ourselves to leeward of a certain point called Punta de Mero, which is nothing else than a barren and rocky point. Here runs an eddy current under the shore.

Tuesday, August 23rd. This day in the morning we had but little wind. At noon it blew fresh again. We made all day but short trips, and reefed topsails.

in his *Parochial Antiquities*, 1695) calls "a country proverb". Cf. 'to go to bed in one's boots', i.e. very drunk.

Wednesday, August 24th. This morning a great dew fell. At noon we were W. from Cape Blanco. We found by observation lat. 4° 13′ S. We resolved now to bear up for Paita, and take it by surprise if possible, thereby to provide ourselves with many necessaries that we wanted.

CHAPTER XXII

They arrive at Paita, where they are disappointed of their expectations, as not daring to land, seeing all the country alarmed before them. They bear away for the Strait of Magellan. Description of the bay and port of Paita, and Colan. An account of their sailings towards the Strait aforementioned

Thursday, August 25th. The night before this day we stood off to sea for fear of the shore and lest we should be descried from the coast of Paita, to which we were now pretty nigh. About noon this day we began to stand in again, and saw the homing of the land, though with hazy weather. The next day, being August 26th, we had cold winds, great dews, and dry weather.

Saturday, August 27th. All this day, but more especially in the morning, we had many fogs. In the afternoon we saw la Silla de Paita at W.S.W., being about five leagues distant from it.

Sunday, August 28th. Last night about ten o'clock we were close into land, at the distance of half-a-league, more or less, to leeward of the island of Lobos. We continued our course all that night, and about break of day found ourselves close under Pena Horadada, a high and steep rock so called. Hence we sailed with a land-wind, and sent away from the ship two canoes well manned and armed, with good hopes to have taken the town of Paita undescried. But, as it should seem, they had already received news of our coming or being upon that coast, and also had received supplies of forces that were sent them from the city of Piura, distant thence 12 leagues up-country. These supplies consisted chiefly of three companies of horse and foot, all of them being armed with firearms. Besides this, they had made a breastwork along the sea-side for the defence of the town and the great church, which lies at the outermost part of the town. From these places, as also from a hill that covers the town, they fired at our men, who were innocently rowing towards shore with their canoes. This preposterous firing was the preservation of our people, for, had the Spaniards permitted our men to come ashore, they had assuredly destroyed them every man. But fear always hinders that nation of victory, at least in most of our attempts.

Our men, perceiving themselves to be discovered and the enemy prepared for their reception, hereupon retreated, and came on board the ship again without attempting to land or do anything else in relation to the taking of the place. We judged there could not be less than 150 fire-arms, and four times as many lances upon the shore, all in readiness to hinder our people from landing. Within the town our pilot told us there might be 150 families.

Being disappointed of our expectations at Paita, we stood down the bay towards Colan. This is another town so called, and which exceeds Paita three times. It is chiefly inhabited by fishermen, and thence they send fish to most inland towns of Peru, and also serve Paita with water from the river Colan, not far distant from the town. It is two leagues, more or less, from the town of Paita aforementioned to Colan, and thence to the river one league, although the houses of Colan do reach almost to the river. The town of Colan itself is inhabited only by Indians, and these are all rich because they will be paid in ready money for everything they do for the Spaniards. But the town of Paita is chiefly inhabited by Spaniards, though there be also some Indians; but the Spaniards do not suffer the Indians to be any great gainers or grow rich under them.

About ten o'clock a young breeze sprang up, and with that we stood away W., and W. by S. Within a little while it blew so fresh that we were forced to reef our topsails, the weather being very dark and hazy. I took the port of Paita and bay of Colan, as they lay exactly situated (see map).

Monday, August 29th. All our hopes of doing any further good upon the coasts of the South Sea being now frustrated, seeing we were descried before our arrival wherever we came, we resolved unanimously to quit all other attempts and bear away for the Strait of Magellan, in order to return homewards either for England or some of our plantations in the West Indies. This day we had a great dew, and I reckoned myself W.S.W. from Paita 13 leagues and a-half, with very little wind. So we stood E.

The next day, August 30th, we had misty weather. We made a W.S.W. way, and by it 5 leagues and one-third. In the afternoon of this day the wind freshened again, having been but little before, and we stood E.S.E.

The last day of August we had very fair weather. I believed now that the wind was settled at S.E. and S.S.E. We made a S.S.W. way, and 21 leagues and two-thirds.

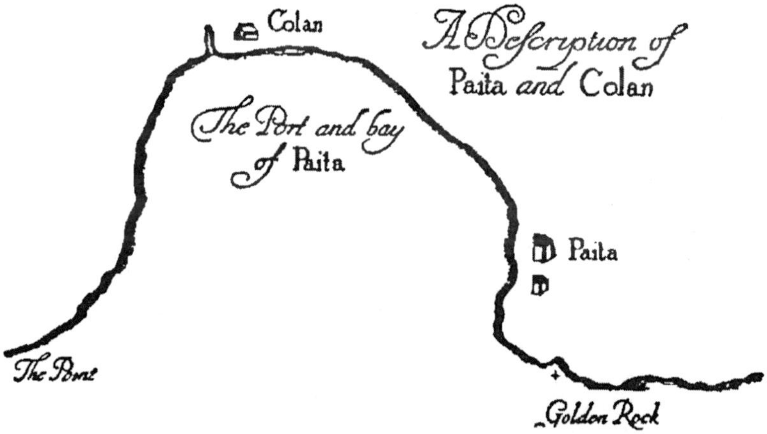

September 1st. Last night was very cloudy, but withal we had a fresh gale. Our reckoning was a S.W. by S. way, and that we had made 16 leagues and two-thirds.

September 2nd. We reckoned a S.W. way, and by it 26 leagues and two-thirds. This day we had an observation and found lat. 7° 40′ S.

September 3rd brought us both cloudy and misty weather. We made a W.S.W. way, and 14 leagues.

September 4th. This day the wind was at E.S.E. and sometimes E., coming in many flaws. We had a S.W. by S. way, and reckoned 23 leagues and two-thirds. We had a great sea from S.

Monday, September 5th, we had great winds, and a high and short sea. Our way was S.S.W. and half-W. by which we reckoned 28 leagues and two-thirds of a league.

September 6th we had a very fresh wind at S.E. by E. with an indifferent smooth sea. By observation we found this day latitude 12° 00′ S. We made a S.W. by S. way, and 28 leagues and one-third.

Wednesday, September 7th, we had a very fresh wind. We reckoned a S.W. by S. way, and 36 leagues. We observed latitude 13° 24′ S. We make now for each mess a plum-pudding of salt water and wine lees.

On the 8th we enjoyed a fresh gale of wind, though with hazy weather. Our reckoning was a S.W. by S. way, and hereby 25 leagues and one-third of a league.

September 9th we made a S.W. by S. way, and 21 leagues and a-third. In the afternoon the wind came about something more S., allowing us a S.W. course.

Saturday, September 10th. All last night past and this morning the wind was very fresh at E. Our way was S.S.W. and by our reckoning 35 leagues and one-third. The weather now was warm. An observation this day gave us latitude 16° 40′ S.

September 11th we had whiffling winds. A S.W. half S. way, and thereby 12 leagues and two-thirds. By an observation we found 17° 10′ S. Now we had a very great sea, so that we took in our sprit-sail.

September 12th. All the night before this day we were under a pair of courses; yet this morning we heaved out main-topsail. We made a W.S.W. way, and 17 leagues and one-third. By observation we found lat. 17° 30′ S.

The 13th. During last night we had huge and great storms of wind. In the morning our goose-head gave way, so that at about noon we were forced to lie by till four in the afternoon to mend it. Our course was S.W. half W. and our reckoning 29 leagues and two-thirds of a league. Lat. by observation 18° 12′ S.

Wednesday, September 14th. This day we had very hazy weather. We made a S.S.W. way, and 20 leagues.

September 15th. This day likewise we had a S.S.W. way, and reckoned 23 leagues and one-half. Our observation taken this day gave us 20° 09′ S.

On September 16th we had a clear day, a S.W. half S. way, and made 16 leagues and two-thirds. We found by observation lat. 20° 48′ S.

The 17th. Last night was very calm. Also this day, it being a full moon. We reckoned a S.W. way, and only by reason of the calmness of the weather 9 leagues and one-third of a league. We had an observation which afforded us 21° 08′ S. lat.

Sunday, September 18th. Last night a wind sprang up at S.S.E. which the morning of this day freshened at S.E. We made a W.S.W. way, and by it 18 leagues. Moreover, this day we had a clear observation that showed us lat. 21° 30′ S.

September 19th. All last night we had a very fresh wind, but this morning it came about to E. by S. and E.S.E. with hazy weather. I reckoned a S.W. by S. way, and 22 leagues.

September 20th. This day gave us a fresh wind, hazy weather, a S. by W. way, and hereupon 23 leagues and one-third.

September 21st. This day also the fresh gale continued, with cloudy, and sometimes misty, weather. Our reckoning showed us a S. by W. way as the day before, and by it 28 leagues and one-third. By an observation made we found lat. 25° 15′ S.

Thursday, September 22nd. This day we had a very fresh wind. We reckoned a S. half W. way, and by that 29 leagues and two-thirds. An observation taken gave us lat. 26° 42′ S. We observed this day a N.E. sea, which seemed very strange to us.

The next day we had several showers of small rain. My reckoning was a S. by W. way, and thereupon 26 leagues. We found by observation lat. 27° 57′ S.

September 24th. We had hazy weather, and the wind not so fresh at E.S.E., with a smooth sea. We made a S.S.W. way half-westerly, and 23 leagues and two-thirds. This day also an observation gave us lat. 28° 57′ S. I reckoned now that we were distant from Paita 302 leagues and two-thirds.

Sunday, September 25th. This day we had not much wind, and hazy weather. At noon the wind came E., then E.N.E., and then again N.E. by E. We reckoned a S. by E. way, half-E. and 55.

Monday 26th. We had hazy weather and a fresh wind at N.E. We reckoned a S.E. half S. way, and 24 leagues. In the afternoon we experienced a N.N.E. sea, and then soon after a N.N.E. wind. After this a N. wind, and that but very little.

September 27th. All the night before this day we had a fresh wind at N.N.E. About eight this morning it came about again to N.N.W. We made a S.E. by S. way, and 38 leagues. By observation I found lat. 32° 30′ S. Now we enjoyed a very smooth sea and fair weather.

Wednesday, September 28th. In the night past a very fresh wind at N.N.W. and N.W. At break of day we had a wind heaving us a-back at once. At noon again the wind was at S.W., our course being S.E. This morning we took down our top-gallant masts. We made a S.E. by E. way, and on this road 27 leagues and two-thirds. By observation lat. 33° 16′ S., a S.W. sea.

On the 29th we had very windy and hazy weather, with some rain now and then. All last night we handed our main-top-sail. We made a S.E. by E. way, and 32 leagues and two-thirds. We had a S.W. sea and wind.

Friday, September 30th. This day we had fresh winds between S.W. and W. We reckoned a S.E. half-S. way, and thereupon 44 leagues. By observation we found lat. 35° 54′ S.

October 1st. The wind this day was not very fresh, but varying. My reckoning was a S.E. half-S. way, and twenty-four leagues. An observation gave us 36° 50′ S. This day I finished another quadrant, being the third I finished in this voyage. We had a S.W. sea, with showers of rain and gusts of wind.

Sunday, October 2nd. The wind this day was hanging between W.N.W. and N.W. by N. We made a S.E. by S. way, and 33 leagues and two-thirds. By observation we found 38° 14′ S. About noon we had a fresh wind at N.W. and S.W.

October 3rd. Last night in the fore-part thereof was clear, but the latter was rainy. The wind very fresh at N.W. by N., but this day we had little wind, and cloudy weather, a S.W. by W. wind, and a S.E. by S. way, by which we reckoned 33 leagues and one-third.

October 4th. We had a clear night and very fresh wind. We reckoned a S.E. by S. way, and thereby 43 leagues. By observation, lat. 41° 34′ S. This day also fell several showers of rain.

October 5th. We had a windy night, and a clear day. We reckoned a S.S.E. half E. way, and 44 leagues and two-thirds. By observation lat. 43° 26′ S. The weather now was very windy, causing a huge tempestuous sea. The wind at N.W. and N.W. by N. blowing very high.

October 6th. This day the wind was still at N.W., and yet not so fresh as it was yesterday; the weather very foggy and misty. As for the wind, it came in gusts, so that we were forced to hand our top-sails, and sprit-sail. We reckoned a S.E. half S. way, and thereby 43 leagues and one-third. The seas now were not so high as for some days past. In the evening we scudded away under our fore-course.

Friday, October 7th. Last night was very cloudy, and this day both dark and foggy weather with small rain. We made a S.E. way, and 30 leagues and two-thirds. A fresh wind at N.N.W. and N.W. We keep still under a fore-course, not so much for the freshness of the wind as the closeness of the weather.

October 8th. We had a clear night the night before this day, and a strong gale, insomuch that this day we were forced to take in our fore-sail, and loosen our mizzen, which was soon blown to pieces. Our eldest seamen said that they were never in the like storm of wind before—the sea was all in a foam. In the evening it dulled a little. We made a S.E. half E. way, and 18 leagues, with very dark weather.

Sunday, October 9th. All the past night we had a furious W.N.W. wind. We set our sail a-drough[1], and so drove to the southward very much, and almost incredibly if an observation had not happened, which gave us lat. 48° 15′ S. We had a very stiff gale at W.N.W. with a great sea from W., which met with a S.S.W. sea as great as it. Now the weather was very cold, and we had one or two frosty mornings. Yesterday in the afternoon we had a very great storm of hail. At noon we bent another mizzen.

Monday, October 10th. This day brought us a fresh wind at N.W. and N.N.W. We made a S.E. half-E. way, and by it 44 leagues. By observation we found lat. 49° 41′ S. I reckoned myself now to be east from Paita 69 leagues and a-half.

[1] Southwards. This is the only example of the use of this adverb given in *N.E.D.*

Tuesday, Oct. 11th. Last night we had a small time calm. This day was both cloudy and rainy weather. The wind at S.W. and S.S.W. so furious that at ten o'clock this morning we scudded under a main-sail. At noon we lowered our fore-yard while we sailed. We made a S.E. by E. way, and 30 leagues.

CHAPTER XXIII

The Buccaneers arrive at a place incognito, to which they give the name of the Duke of York's Islands. A description of the said islands and of the gulf, or lagoon, wherein they lie, so far as it was searched. They remain there many days by stress of weather, not without great danger of being lost. An account of some other remarkable things that happened there

Wednesday, October 12th. All the night before this day we had many high winds. I reckoned an E.S.E. way, and twenty leagues, for our vessel drove at a great rate. Moreover, we were in lat. 50° 50′ S., so that our easting from Paita by my account ought to be 101 leagues, or thereabouts.

This morning, about two hours before day, we happened by great accident to spy land. It was the great mercy of God, which had always attended us in this voyage, that saved us from perishing at this time, for we were close ashore before we saw it; and our foreyard, which we most needed on this occasion, was taken down. The land we had seen was very high and towering; and here appeared to be many islands scattered up and down. We steered in with what caution we could, between them and the main, and at last, God be praised, arrived at a place, or rather bay, where we perceived ourselves to be land-locked, and, as we thought, pretty safe from the danger of those tempestuous seas. From here we sent away our canoe to sound and search the fittest place for anchoring. At this time one of our men, named Henry Shergall, as he was going into our sprit-sail-top, happened to fall into the water, and was drowned before any help could be had, though we endeavoured it as much as we possibly could. This incident several of our company interpreted as a bad omen of the place, which proved not so, through the providence of the Almighty, though many dangers were not wanting here to us, as I shall relate.

We came to an anchor in the depth of 40 fathom, more or less, and yet at no greater distance than a stone's-cast from shore. The water where we anchored was very smooth, and the high lands round about all covered with snow. Having considered the time of the year and all other circumstances, we resolved that, in case we could find a sufficient stock of provisions here, we would stay longer, that is until summer came or something more, before we prosecuted our intended voyage homewards through the Strait of Magellan; which now we began to be careful how to find. That day of our anchoring in this bay we shot six or eight brave geese and some smaller fowl besides. Here we found also many hundreds of mussel-banks, all which were very plentifully stocked with that kind of fish. We buried our dead man on the shore, giving him several volleys for his funeral rites, according to the custom. In the night of this day our anchor came home, so that we were forced to let go a-grappling to secure ourselves. But still every flaw of wind drove us. Hereupon we set our sprit-sail, and ran about a mile into another bay, where we let go another anchor, and thus anchored again. The first anchor, which was also the biggest in our ship, we lost by this accident, the cable being cut by the rocks. To these islands aforementioned our captain gave the name of His Royal Highness the Duke of York's Islands.

Thursday, October 13th. This day we began to moor our ship, she driving as we easily could perceive with every flaw of wind that blew. The tide flows here full seven-feet up and down. We moored our vessel into a rocky point, being a quay, whereof there are many in the circumference of this bay. The ground of the bottom of the said bay we found was hard and sandy, being here and there rocky. This evening we brought on board great store of limpets, of which we made a kettle of broth, that contained more than all our company could eat.

On Friday, October 14th we killed several geese, as also many of another sort of fowl like an eagle but having a bigger beak, with their nostrils rising from the top of the middle of their beak by a hand-trunk. This fowl lives on fish; but we saw none. Yesterday in the evening there fell a great sleet of snow on the hills round about the bay, but none where we were at anchor. Moreover, this day in the evening we caught limpets in great quantity, being three times as many as we could eat. Our men, in ranging the quays for game, found grass plaited above a fathom long, and a knot tied at the end thereof. In like manner on other quays they found mussels and limpet-shells. From these things we presently concluded that these countries were inhabited, and that some Indians or others were to be found hereabouts.

Saturday, October 15th. Last night we had much rain, with large hailstones. About midnight the wind came to north with such great fury that the tree to which our cable was fastened on shore gave way and came up by the roots. All those gusts of wind were mixed with violent storms of rain and hail. Thus we fastened again to other trees. But here it happened that, our ship coming up to the shore, our rudder touched, and thereupon broke our goose-neck. Great was now our extremity, and greater it will be, if God send not better weather. Scarce a minute now passed without flaws of wind and rain.

Sunday, October 16th. Last night was rainy, as before. About nine o'clock our biggest hawser gave way and broke. All this day likewise we had rain, with several showers of hail, and but little wind to W. of N.

Monday, October 17th. All last night, until five this morning, it ceased not to rain. Then until ten it snowed. On the hills it snowed all the night long. This day we hunted on the shore many tracks of people hereabouts, but could find none hitherto, they having fled and concealed themselves for fear of us, as we supposed.

October 18th. In the past night we had much rain and hail. But the day was very clear. Hereupon we made an observation, which gave us lat. 50° 40′ S. Moreover, this day we had pretty warm weather.

October 19th. Both clear and frosty last night. This day was hazy, and somewhat windy from the north quarter. Every day we had plenty of limpets and mussels of a very large size.

October 20th. Last night was rainy, and this day windy, with very great gusts of wind at N.N.W. until the afternoon. Then we had wind at N.W., being very fresh and in gusts.

October 21st. All the past night was tempestuous, with huge gusts of wind and showers of hail. Yesterday in the evening we carried a cable ashore, and fastened it to a tree. This being done, at midnight our biggest cable broke in the middle. Towards morning we had much snow. In the day, great gusts of wind with large hailstones; and also great plenty of limpets.

October 22nd. Last night we had strange gusts of wind from N.W., together with much hail and rain. This day we killed a penguin; and also began to carry water on board.

October 23rd. All the last twenty-four hours we had much rain. The wind was but little at W. and W.S.W.

October 24th. All this time until noon nothing but rain. At that time it held up fair for the space of half-an-hour, or thereabouts, and then it rained again all the rest of the day.

October 25th. All this while we had not one minute fair. Towards evening it held up from raining, but the weather was cloudy, and withal much warmer than when we came hither at first.

Wednesday, October 26th. All the past night and this forenoon we had fair weather. But afternoon it rained again. We found cockles like those we have in England.

Thursday, October 27th. Last night we had much rain, with very great gusts of wind, lasting for the whole space thereof. Yet, notwithstanding, this day proved to be the fairest that we ever had since we came into this place. In the evening of this day our canoe, which was gone to search the adjacent places for Indians or what else they could find, returned to the ship with a dory at her stern. They had gone, as it should seem, beyond the old bay where we first anchored, and thereabouts happened to meet with this dory. In it were three Indians, who, perceiving themselves near being taken, leaped overboard to make their escape. Our men in pursuing them unadvisedly shot one of them dead. A second, being a woman, escaped their hands. But the third, who was a lusty boy about eighteen years of age, was taken, and him they brought on board the ship. He was covered only with a seal's skin, having no other clothing about him. His eyes squinted, and his hair was cut pretty short. In the middle of the dory they had a fire burning, either for dressing victuals or some other use. The dory itself was built sharp at both ends, and flat-bottomed. They had a net to catch penguins, and a club like our bandies, called by them a tomahawk. His language we could not understand, but he pointed up the lagoon, giving us to understand that there were more people thereabouts. This was confirmed by our men, who also said they had seen more. They had darts to throw against an enemy, pointed with wood.

On the next day, being October 28th, in the evening our canoe went from the ship again to seek for more Indians. They went into several lagoons, and searched them narrowly. But they could find nothing but two or three huts, all the natives being fled before our arrival. In the evening they returned to the ship, bringing with them very large limpets, and also mussels which were six-inches-and-a-half long. Our Indian prisoner could open these mussels with his fingers, which our men could not so readily do with their knives. Both the night past and this day we had very fair weather.

On the 29th we had in like manner a very fair day, and also a smooth wind at S.S.E. Our Indian this day pointed to us that there were men in this country, or not far off from here, with great beards. He appeared to us by his actions to be very innocent and foolish. But by his carriage I was also persuaded that he was a man-eater. This day likewise we caught limpets enough to suffice us for the morrow.

Sunday, October 30th. This day was fair, and there blew a small S.S.E. wind. In the morning we sent a canoe over to the eastward shore, to seek either for provisions or Indians. I myself could not go as I desired, being, with two or three more, at that time very much tormented with the gripes. I am persuaded that this place where we now were is not so great an island as some hydrographers lay it down, but rather an archipelago of smaller islands. We saw this day many penguins, but they were so shy that we could not come near them. They paddle on the water with their wings very fast, but their bodies are too heavy to be carried by the said wings. The sun now made the weather very warm, insomuch that the snow melted apace.

October 31st. Both last night and this day were very fair. At noon our canoe returned from the Eastern shore, bringing word that they had found several good bays and harbours, that were deep even close to the shore, only that there lay in them several sunken rocks, which we had also where we were. But these rocks are not dangerous to shipping, by reason that they have weeds which lie two fathoms in circumference about them. This morning blew a small wind at N.N.E.

November 1st. This day was also fair, and we had a small wind as before, at N.N.E.

November 2nd. Last night I took the polar distance of the South star of the cock's foot, and found it to be 28° 25′. I observed also the two Magellan clouds, of which I made mention in this Journal before, and found them to be as follows, viz. the lesser 14° 05′, and the greater 14° 25′. The morning of this day we hoisted on end our top-masts, and also brought too a main-top-sail and fore-sail, and finished our filling all the water we needed. At the same time the wind hung easterly: and I was still much tormented with the gripes as before.

November 3rd. This morning we hung our rudder, the greatest piece of work we had to do, after those violent storms above-mentioned. In the afternoon we hauled in our two biggest hawsers, and also our biggest cable from the shore. For the last three days we had a very great and dark fog between us and the Eastward shore. We had now very little wind in the cove where we were, but abroad at sea there blew at the same time a stiff gale at S.S.E. Moreover, we could perceive now, the stormy weather being blown over, much small fry of fish about the ship, whereof we could see none, as was mentioned before. This day we had a very clear and calm evening.

November 4th. Both all last night and this day we had very calm weather. And this morning a small breeze sprang up at N. and N.N.E., which afterwards wheeled about to S. and S.S.E. This morning we hoisted our main and fore-yards, and likewise fetched off from the shore our other hawser and cable, into eleven-fathom water. Our resolutions were now changed for a departure, in order to seek the mouth of the Strait of Magellan, seeing that we could not winter here for want of provisions, which we could not find either on the continent or about these islands aforementioned.

The weather now was very warm, or rather hot, and the birds sung as sweetly as those in England. We saw here both thrushes and blackbirds, and many other sorts of those that are usually seen in our own country.

Saturday, November 5th. This morning brought us a wind at N.N.E. hereupon: we warped to a rocky point, thereby to get out of the cove where we lay. For our anchor came home to us as we were carrying our warp out. At this time a second breeze came up very fresh in our stern, so that we took the opportunity thereof, and went away before it. By noon this day we hoisted in our canoes, and also turned away loose to the sea our Indian dory. As for the Indian

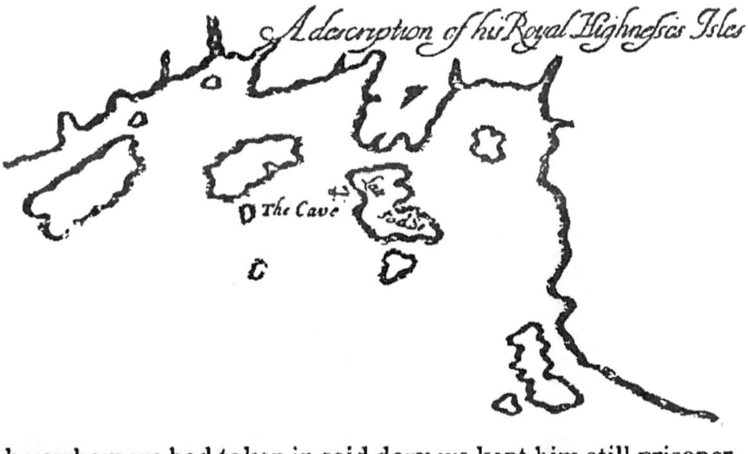

boy whom we had taken in said dory we kept him still prisoner, and called him Orson. Our cove at our departure from this place looked thus, as I took then the description thereof. When we were come out into the channel, the weather grew dead calm—only now and then we had a small breeze, sometimes from one quarter and then from another. By this slackness of wind we observed that the current hoisted us to the Southward. On the East side of this lagoon we perceived the Indians make a great smoke at our departure.

We had a very fair day till six in the evening: when we got without the mouth of the gulf, it blew so hard that in an hour it forced us to hand our top-sails. Having now a fit gale at N.W. and N.N.W., we stood S.W. by W. to clear ourselves of some breaks which lie four leagues from the gulf's mouth at S. and S.S.E. Hereabouts we saw many reefs and rocks, which occasioned us to stand close-hauled. I have drawn here and given to my reader so much as I have seen of the gulf itself; the rest must be completed in due time by them that have greater opportunities of making a farther search into it than I had at the time of our stay here under such tempestuous weather as I have described, and the distemper which hung upon me at the same time.

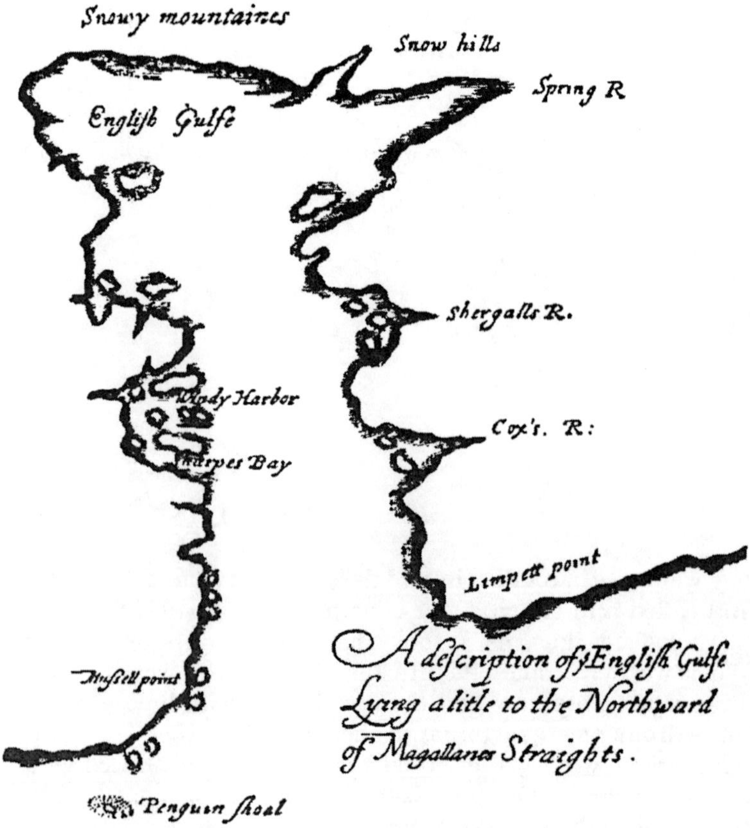

CHAPTER XXIV

They depart from the English Gulf in quest of the Strait of Magellan, which they cannot find. They return home by an unknown way, never navigated before

Sunday, November 6th. This morning we had lost the sight of land, so that we could see it no more. All the last night, and this day, we were under our two courses and sprit-sail. The weather this day was hazy. My reckoning was a S.W. half S. way, and by it 21 leagues. We had now an indifferently high sea, and a fresh wind at N.N.W.

November 7th. Last night was both rainy and foggy; but in the morning it cleared up. The wind for the most part was at W. and W.N.W. But at noon it came about at W.S.W. Our reckoning was a S.W. by S. way, and by it 20 leagues. We found by observation lat. 52° 03′. We now steered away S.S.E., the wind being at that time at W.S.W. In the evening of this day I found a variation of the needle to N.E. to the number of 15° or better. I was still troubled with the gripes as I had been before.

November 8th. Last night was fair. About midnight the wind came to N.N.W. At the break of day we all were persuaded that we had seen land, but at noon we saw that it was none, but only a cloud. The wind was now at N. My reckoning was a S.E. half-E. way, and 32 leagues and one-third. We had an observation that gave us 53° 27′ S. The whole day was very fine and warm, and we saw great numbers of fowls and seals.

November 9th. Yesterday in the evening the weather was cloudy. Hereupon we lay by under a main course. After midnight we sailed East, and E. by N., with a fresh wind at W.N.W. and not any great sea. The day itself was cloudy, and toward noon we had some rain. So at two in the afternoon we lay by under a main course, the wind being fresh at N.W. I reckoned an E.N.E. way, and thereby 28 leagues.

Thursday, November 10th. All last night we lay under a main course, with a mere fret of wind at N.W. and N.N.W. Day being come, the wind rather increased, insomuch that about noon our sail blew to pieces. Hereupon we were forced to lower the yard and unbend the sail, lying for a little while under a mizzen. But that also soon gave way; so that all the rest of this day we lay a hull in very dark weather, foggy and windy, with a huge sea, which oftentimes rolled over us. In the afternoon it seemed to abate for some space of time; but soon after it blew worse than before, which compelled us to lower our fore-yard.

November 10th. All last night we had furious windy and tempestuous weather, from the points of N.W. and N.N.W., together with seas higher and higher. In the evening we set our mizzen: at which time the sun appeared very watery; but the wind now abated by degrees, and the seas also.

November 12th. This morning little wind was stirring, but only some rain fell. About ten it cleared up, by observation lat. 55° 25′. The sea was now much fallen, and a fresh wind sprang up at W. and W.S.W. We experienced also a very great current to the S.W. In the afternoon of this day we set our sails again, resolving now unanimously to make for the Straits of St Vincent, otherwise called the Strait of Fernando de Magellan. We had a fresh wind at W.N.W., our course being S.S.E., under our sprit-sail, fore-sail, and fore-top-sail. This day we saw many fishes, or rather fowls, who had heads like Muscovy ducks, as also two feet like them. They had two fins like the forefins of turtles; white breasts and bellies; their beak and eyes being red. They are full of feathers on their bodies, and their hinder parts are like those of a seal; wherewith they cut the water. The Spaniard calls these fowls *paxaros ninos*. They weigh most commonly about six or seven pounds, being about one-foot, a little more or less, in length. Our Commander, Captain Sharp, had so much dexterity as to strike two of them. In the evening we set also our mainsail, the wind now coming to S. of W.

Sunday, November 13th. All last night we had a fresh wind between S.W. and W.N.W., with sometimes mists of small rain. In the evening we enjoyed a fine leading gale at

W.N.W. together with both clear and wholesome weather. We made a S.E. way, and by it 42 leagues and two-thirds. This day an observation gave us lat. 56° 55′ S. We still experienced a great S.W. current. In the afternoon of this day we steered E.S.E., and in the evening had whiffling-winds.

November 14th. Both last night and this morning we had cloudy weather. About eight it cleared up. My reckoning was a S.E. by E. way, and by it 32 leagues. Our observation gave us lat. 57° 50′ S. This day we could perceive land, and at noon were due W. from it. In the evening we stood E. by S.

November 15th. All the past night was very cloudy. We judged now that we should be close in with the land we had seen the day before, but the morning being come we could see none. In the night much snow fell, and in the day we had great sleets thereof, the weather being very cold and cloudy. I reckoned an E.S.E. way, and hereby 29 leagues and two-thirds; moreover, that our lat. was 58° 25′ S. The wind was now so fresh at N. that we were forced to lie under our two courses and sprit-sail.

November 16th. Most of this time we had still rain and snow, but now no night at all, though the weather was dark. The wind was various, but from midnight before this day the wind was at S.E. and S.S.E. We now lay E.N.E. I reckoned a N.E. by E. way, and 23 leagues. About four in the afternoon two of our fore-shrouds' bolts broke, but were presently mended. This afternoon also we saw a very large whale. In the evening we handed in our fore-top-sail, and lay under our pair of courses and sprit-sail, the evening being very clear.

November 17th. In the past night there was a very hard frost. At four this morning we saw two or three islands of ice at the distance of two or three leagues to the S. of us. Soon after this we saw several others, the biggest of them being at least 2 leagues round. By observation lat. 58° 23′ S. We had now a vehement current to the S. At noon I saw many others of these islands of ice aforementioned, of which some were so long that we could scarce see the end of them, and extended about 10 or 12 fathom above-water. The weather in the meanwhile was very clear, and the wind cold. I found variation of the needle 18 degrees to the N.E.

November 18th. All last night was very fair. I must call it night, for otherwise it was not dark at all. The sea was very smooth, and the wind at N. and N.N.W. I reckoned a N.E. by N. way, and by the same 22 leagues. At ten it grew dead calm, which held all the afternoon of this day. But at night we had a wind again at N. and N. by E.

November 19th. This day was cloudy with snow, and a frosty night preceding it. The wind now was so fresh at N. that we were forced to take in our topsails, and lie all day under our courses and sprit-sail. We made by an E.S.E. way 18 leagues and two-thirds.

November 20th. We had a cloudy night, together with mizzling rain and snow. This morning fell so great a fog that we could not see from stem to stern of our ship. From ten o'clock last night we had also calm and very cold weather. But, what was worse than all this, we were now kept to a very short allowance of our sorry victuals, our provisions growing very scanty with us. About ten this morning we had a very small breeze at N. Several of our men were not able to endure the cold, so fierce it was; whereby they were forced to lie and keep themselves as close as they could. We made an E. way, and by the same 16 leagues. This day at noon I reckoned myself to be E. from the gulf, whence we last departed, 205 leagues and two-thirds.

Monday, November 21st. Last evening we caught a small and white land-fowl, and saw two or three more; and also this morning. This sight afforded us good hopes we were not far distant from some coast or other, yet none could we see in all this long and tedious voyage. In the night past we had a calm; and all this morning a great fog with much snow and rain. We reckoned an E. by N. way, and 10 leagues. At one in the afternoon we had a fresh gale that sprang up at E., and at E. by N.

November 22nd. Most part of this day was calm. In the meanwhile we could observe our ship to drive E. My reckoning was an E.N.E. way, and thereby 13 leagues and one-third. At one in the afternoon we had a small gale at W.S.W., our course being N.N.E. and N.E. by N.

November 23rd. This day we had a gale at N.W. and

freshening still more and more; so that we were forced to take in our top-sails and sprit-sail. The wind was not a settled gale, but often varied from point to point. At noon it came at N.E., and our course was then N.N.W. By a N. way we reckoned 16 leagues.

November 24th. Both last night and this morning was foggy weather, with some calms between times. But at eight in the morning the sun broke out, though notwithstanding the day was not clear. By a N.N.E. way we reckoned 15 leagues. This morning the wind came about to E., and by noon it was again at N.E. We had a clear evening and a fresh gale.

November 25th. All last night we had a fresh wind at E. and E.N.E., insomuch that at eight in the morning we took in our top-sails. But at noon the wind was not so fresh as it had been before. I reckoned a N.N.W. half W. way, and by the same 20 leagues.

November 26th. Last night the wind was not altogether so fresh as before; but this morning it was again very high. The weather was both dark and cloudy, and brought now and then rain and snow. We made a N.N.E. way, and hereby 30 leagues. The wind all along E. by S. and E.S.E. In the evening we had fair weather again. We experienced for the last ten days a great Western sea, and saw in the same time several seals.

Sunday, November 27th. All the past night we enjoyed a fresh gale and clear weather. I reckoned 36 leagues by a N.E. by N. way. By observation lat. 52° 48′ S. And I judged myself to be E. from the gulf 285 leagues. In the evening of this day we had a very exact sight of the sun, and found above 30° variation of the needle; whence ought to be concluded that it is very difficult to direct a course of navigation in these parts. For in the space of only 25 leagues sailing we have experienced eight or nine degrees difference of variation, by a good Dutch azimuth compass.

November 28th. All last night we had a fresh wind at E.S.E. Towards morning we had but little wind, all the day being hazy weather. This day we saw a whole flight of land fowls, of which sort we killed one before, as was mentioned above. This sight gave us occasion to believe that, neither then nor at this present, were we far distant from land, and yet we descried none in the residue of this whole voyage. We made by a N.N.E. way 33 leagues. Yesterday in the evening we set a new sprit-sail, and about three this morning we also set our main-sail. At one in the afternoon the wind came about N.E. and N.N.E., which in the evening blew very fresh, with cloudy weather.

November 29th. The night proved very cloudy, and the wind blew very fresh at E.N.E. and N.E. by E. This morning it was at E., with both snow and hail. Towards noon the weather cleared up, and we found by an observation taken lat. 49° 45′ S. Our reckoning was a N. way, and 30 leagues. This day we had a short E. sea, and withal a very cold evening. I took the sun, and hereby I found variation 26° 30′ to the N.E. This night the wind came about W. and W.N.W., continuing so all the night.

November 30th. This day the wind was N. and N.N.E., with some clouds hovering in the sky. At this time we had already almost four hours of night. The morning of this day was very fair and clear. Hereupon, to give myself satisfaction in the point, fearing the truth of Spanish books, I worked the true amplitude of the sun, and found his variation to be 26° 25′ to the N.E., being very comformable to what I had both read and experimented before. Hereabouts also we experienced a current to N. Moreover, this day we saw much rock-weed, which renewed our hopes once more of seeing land. We reckoned a N.E. way, and by the same twenty-two leagues. By an observation made we found lat. 48° 53′ S. This day also we saw several of those fowl-fish afore described called *paxaros ninos*, and these of a larger size than any we had seen before. In the afternoon the wind came about at N.N.E. whereby we stood N.W. by W., with a fresh gale and smooth water. The weather now began to grow warmer than hitherto, and the evening of this day was clear.

Tuesday, December 1st. The latter part of last night was very cloudy, and also sometimes rainy. About midnight we had a furious and violent tornado, forcing us in a moment to hand in our top-sails. At five in the morning we set them again, and at eleven we had another tornado, forcing us to hand our top-sails the second time. We made a N.N.E. two-thirds E. way, and thereby 13 leagues and two-thirds.

The afternoon of this stormy day proved very fair, and the wind came to W.S.W., our course being N.E. by N. In the evening the wind freshened, with cloudy weather.

December 2nd. Last night we experienced a very furious whirlwind, which, notwithstanding, it pleased God, did pass about the length of our ship to W. of us. However, we handed in our top-sails, and hauled up our low-sails, in the brails. After the whirlwind came a fresh storm of large hail-stones in the night, and several tornadoes; but, God be thanked, they all came large of our ship. We now made great way under a fore-course and sprit-sail. At four o'clock this morning our fore-sail split, whereby we were forced to lower our fore-yard. At half-an-hour after ten we hoisted it again with a furious S.W. wind. We made a N.E. by E. way, and by the same 47 leagues and a-half. By observation we now had lat. 46° 54′ S. We reefed our fore-sail in consequence of the violence of the wind. But in the evening this rather increased, and we had a very great sea. Our standing rigging, through the fury of this gale, gave way in several places, but was soon mended again.

December 3rd. The wind all last night was very fresh, with several flaws both of wind and rain at S.W. and S.W. by S. We enjoyed now very warm weather. This morning we set our fore-top-sail. Our reckoning gave us a N.E. half E. way and 45 leagues. We found lat. by observation 45° 28′ S. This day at noon a large shoal of young porpoises came about our ship, and played up and down.

December 4th. All last night we had a fresh gale at W.S.W. The night was clear, only that now and then we had a small cloud affording some rain. In the morning from four o'clock till eight it rained; but then it cleared up again, with a S.W. wind and a very smooth sea. We made by a N.E. one quarter N. way, 39 leagues. By observation we found lat. 44° 01′ S. At noon the wind came to S.S.W., our course then being N.N.E. This day we agreed among ourselves, having the consent of our Commander, to share the eight chests of money, which as yet were remaining unshared. Yesterday in the evening we let out the reef of our fore-sail and hoisted up our fore-yard. This evening I found variation 17° N.E.

Monday, December 5th. All last night a clear night, and

this a fair day, with a fresh wind at S.S.W. We reckoned a N.E. 5° N. way, and by the same 42 leagues. An observation gave us lat. 42° 29′ S. This afternoon we shared of the chests above-mentioned 300 pieces-of-eight each man. I now reckoned myself to be E. from my departure 471 leagues and one-third. At night again we shared 22 pieces-of-eight more to each.

December 6th. We had a clear starlight night the last, and a fair morning this day, with a fresh gale at S.W. At noon we took in our fore-top-sail. We reckoned a N.E. half N. way, and hereby 50 leagues and two-thirds. An observation taken afforded us 40° 31′ S. This evening was cloudy.

December 7th. The night was both windy and cloudy. At one in the morning we took in our top-sails, and at three handed our sprit-sail, and so we scudded away before the wind, which now was very fresh at West. This morning a gust of wind came and tore our main-sail into a hundred pieces, which made us put away before the wind till we could provide for that accident. My reckoning was a N.E. three-quarters E. way, and by the same 33 leagues. By observation we found lat. 39° 37′ S. We had now a great sea, and a fresh wind. At three in the afternoon we set another fore-sail, the first being blown to pieces. Moreover, at the same time, we furled our sprit-sail. At five the wind came at W.S.W. with very bad weather. This day our worthy Commander, Captain Sharp, had very certain intelligence given him that on Christmas Day, which was now at hand, the company, or at least a great part thereof, had a design to shoot him; he having appointed that day some time since to be merry. Hereupon he made us share the wine amongst us, being persuaded they would scarce attempt any such thing in their sobriety. The wine we shared fell out to three jars to each mess. That night the wind increased.

December 8th. Last night was both cloudy and windy, the wind often varying between N.W. and S.W. This morning it varied between W. and N.W. by W. About noon this day we brought a new main-sail to the yard, but did not set it then because there blew too much wind. I reckoned a N.E. half-N. way, and by the same 30 leagues. By observation lat. 38° 29′ S. In the afternoon we had one or two squalls of wind and rain; but the violence of both fell astern of us.

In the evening it blew again very hard. I observed this day the rising and setting of the sun, and found the exact variation to be 12° 15′ N.E.

December 9th. The night was starry, but withal very windy. About the break of day the wind came to N.W., and at seven we set our fore-top-sail, and stood N.N.E., with not much wind. We made since our last reckoning a N.E. quarter-E. way, and 29 leagues. We found by observation lat. 37° 30′ S. The sea was much fallen, but our ship now began to complain of several leaks, through our tedious and long voyage. This afternoon we hoisted up our main-yard and set up back-stays and main-swifter, whose ring-bolt gave way, but was mended. In the evening of this day we had but little wind.

December 10th. The night was very clear, but till ten o'clock this forenoon we had no wind. Then a small breeze sprang up at N. and N. by E. We made an E.N.E. one-third N. way, and hereby 21 leagues. An observation gave us lat. 37° 01′ S. In the afternoon of this day our chief surgeon cut off the foot of a negro-boy, which was perished with cold. Now it was like to be bad weather again. Hereupon we furled our top-sails, and lay under a pair of courses. But in the evening we lay under a fore-sail and mizzen, with misty weather.

Sunday, December 11th. All last night we had a fresh wind at N. and sometimes at N.N.W. The weather was very cloudy with drizzling rain. We made an E. way, and thereby 25 leagues. This day brought a great sea. About ten in the morning one of our main-shrouds gave way. In the evening fell some small rain.

December 12th. All last night we had misty rain and but little wind—yea, in the morning a perfect calm. At noon came up a small gale at E.S.E. and S.E., bringing with it cloudy weather. We reckoned a N.E. by E. way, and by the same 18 leagues. Yesterday died the negro-boy whose leg was cut off by our surgeon, as was mentioned the day before. This afternoon also died another negro, somewhat bigger than the former, named Chepillo. The boy's name was Beafero. All this evening but small wind.

December 13th. All night the wind was at E.S.E., our course being N.N.E. At three in the morning it came about at S.S.W. and at nine at E. by N. I reckoned a N.E. by N. way, and 15 leagues. The weather was hazy. In the afternoon the wind was at N.E. our course being N.N.W. We enjoyed now a very smooth sea, and saw multitudes of grampuses, whales, and porpoises every day as we sailed along.

December 14th. Last evening was cloudy; as also the night foggy. Hereupon we took in our top-sails. At half-an-hour-after-three this morning, we stood N.E., the wind being then at N.N.W. At five we put out our top-sails again. At seven of the morning we saw a turtle floating upon the sea. We reckoned a N.N.E. way. This day's observation afforded us 34° 32 S′. At this time we had very hot weather, and great dews in the night. My whole easting I reckoned to be now 675 leagues and one-third.

December 15th. Last night was fine with a great dew. The wind in the interim was between N. and N.W. I reckoned a N.E. half E. way, and by the same 31 leagues. We had an observation that gave us lat. 33° 46′ S. At noon the wind came about at N.N.W., our course being N.E. We had this day a very clear evening, and at the same time a fresh wind.

December 16th. We had a fair night and wind at N.N.W. and N.W. by N. This morning I took the sun at its rising, and found N.E. variation 20° 30′. My reckoning was a N.N.E. way, and 36 leagues and one-third. By observation I found lat. 32° 09′ S. At noon this day the wind came about to N.W.

December 17th. Most part of last night the wind was at N.W. as before. But towards morning a fine and easy gale sprang up at W.N.W. This morning we saw several dolphins playing upon the sea, which made us hope they would at last befriend us and suddenly show us some land or other. We reckoned a N.E. by N. one-third N. way, and by the same 25 leagues. An observation gave us lat. 31° 04′. A fair evening.

December 18th. We had a clear night, together with a smooth gale at N.W., which this morning was at W. by S. We had now a smooth sea for several days past. Our reckoning was 25 leagues, by a N.E. by N. way. By observation we perceived lat. 29° 48′ S.

December 19th. A clear night and a fresh breeze at S.S.W. and S.W. by E., lasting until nine in the morning. Then sprang up a wind at S.E. by E. I reckoned this day a N.N.E. half E. way, and upon the same 30 leagues. By observation, lat. 28° 29′ S. The day was very fair, and a smooth sea, with weather that was very hot. My whole easting I reckoned now to be 760 leagues. This evening I found variation 02° 50′ N.E.

CHAPTER XXV

The Buccaneers continue their navigation, without seeing any land, till they arrive at the Caribbean Islands in the West Indies. They give away their ship to some of their companions that were poor, and disperse for several countries. The author of this Journal arrives in England

December 20th, 1681. The night before this day was somewhat cloudy, but the weather was fair and the wind but little. At noon the wind came about N. by E., our course being W.N.W. We made a N.N.W. way, and thereby as I reckoned 22 leagues. By an observation made we took lat. 27° 25′ S. The evening of this day was cloudy, and now and then there fell a shower of rain.

December 21st. At eight o'clock last night the wind came N.W. by N., but with such dark weather that we were forced to take in our top-sails. The night was somewhat rainy, and the weather this morning calm and rainy. About ten we had a small breeze at N.W. We reckoned a N. by E. way, and by the same 16 leagues. The afternoon of this day was calm and still.

December 22nd. We had a fair and clear night which produced this day a smooth sea and extremely hot weather, and very little wind near the sun; so that no observation was made.

December 23rd. The night was very fair. At midnight, or thereabouts, a fresh gale sprang up at S.E. and E.S.E., which sometime was E. This freshened by degrees. We had in the day very hot and clear weather. By a N. way I reckoned 15 leagues.

December 24th. Last night we had both a fresh gale and a clear night. The wind was at E. by S. We reckoned a N.E. by E. way, and by it 31 leagues.

Sunday, December 25th. This day being Christmas day, for celebration of that great festival we killed yesterday in the evening a sow. This sow we had brought from the Gulf of Nicoya, being then a sucking-pig of three weeks old, more or less, but now weighed about fourscore-and-ten pounds. With this hog's flesh we made our Christmas dinner, being the only flesh we had eaten ever since we turned away our prizes under the equinoctial and left the island of Plata. We had this day several flaws of wind and some rain, but the weather otherwise was pretty clear. I reckoned a N. by E. way, and 33 leagues by the same. It was now also extremely hot weather, as we signified before.

December 26th. We had this day several gusts of wind, which forced us to stand by our top-sails. Yet were they but very short, and all the rest of the while we enjoyed an indifferent fresh gale at E. and E. by S. We reckoned a N. by E. way, and 28 leagues.

December 27th. We had fair weather, and a fresh wind at E. and E. by S. I reckoned a N. by E. way, and upon the same 32 leagues. The evening of this day was cloudy.

December 28th. Last night was cloudy, with a fresh wind. We reckoned a N.E. way, and by the same 46 leagues. We found by observation lat. 15° 30′ S. My whole easting I reckoned this day to be 825 leagues. Now we saw much flying fish, with some dolphins, bonitos, and albicores; but they will not take the hook.

December 29th. All last night was cloudy, with a fresh wind between E. and E.S.E. The weather all the afternoon was hazy. I reckoned a N. by E. way, and hereupon 40 leagues and one-third. In the afternoon we had a S.E. by E. wind, which blew very fresh. The evening was clear. At sunset I found variation to N.W. 04° 19′.

December 30th. Last night was cloudy. Towards morning the wind came about at E. At six it came E.S.E., and at ten to S.E. by S. We made a N. by E. way, and 43 leagues. By observation lat. 11° 03′ S. The evening of this day was clear.

December 31st. We had a cloudy night, but the morning was hazy. We came now to a strict allowance of only three good pints of water each day. We made a N. by E. way, lat. by observation 08° 55′ S. In the afternoon we had an E.S.E.

and S.E. by E. wind. My whole easting I reckoned now to be 884 leagues and one-third. At noon we stood away N.W.

Sunday, January 1st, 1682. All last night was cloudy, as this day also, with some showers of rain. We made a N.W. one-eighth N. way, and 40 leagues. In the afternoon came about a fresh wind at S.E. and E.S.E.

January 2nd. The weather this day was both dull and cloudy. We reckoned a N.W. one-quarter N. way, and by the same 32 leagues. By observation lat. 06° 06′ S. The wind came pretty fresh at S.E.

January 3rd. We had several squalls of wind, and some rain. But withal a fresh wind at S.E. and E.S.E. Our reckoning was a N.W. one-quarter N. way, and 34 leagues. The afternoon was clear, but the evening cloudy.

January 4th. All last night was very cloudy, but this forenoon it cleared up. Yesterday we put abroad our main-top-sail studding-sails; but took them in at night. At four this morning we set our larboard studding-sail, and before noon fitted up top-gallant masts and yards. We made a N.W. way, and by it 40 leagues and two-thirds. By observation, lat. 03° 09′ S. This afternoon also we set our top-gallant sail, being forced to make out all its running rigging. The wind was pretty fresh at S.E. and S.E. by E.

January 5th. Most part of the past night was clear and starlight, though with some rain towards the morning. This being come, we put out our top-gallant sail, and both our top-sail studding-sails. At noon likewise we put up our fore-top-gallant mast and yard. We caught an albicore this day, weighing about 120 pounds. The wind was at S.E. by S. and S.S.E. We made a N.W. way, and reckoned thereby 35 leagues. By observation, lat. 02° 03′ S. We had now mighty hot weather.

January 6th. Yesterday in the evening we caught another albicore, which weighed only eight or nine pounds. We made a N.W. way, and reckoned 35 leagues as before. By observation, lat. 00° 49′ S. The evening of this day was very clear.

January 7th. The wind was variable between S.S.E. and S.S.W., though not altogether so fresh as before. Our reckoning was a N.W. one-quarter N. way, and 36 leagues by the same. This day an observation gave us lat. 00° 32′ N. of the equinoctial, which now we had passed again. In the afternoon of this day we caught another albicore, which weighed more than the first we took, that is between 135 and 140 pounds. But little wind stirring this afternoon.

January 8th. Last evening we had little better than a calm. At nine this morning we had a fresh wind at S.S.E. with dark weather, so that we thought it convenient to take in our main-topsail. But at noon we set it again, and also our larboard top-studding-sail, with both top-gallant sails. We made a N.W. way, and by it 34 leagues. By observation lat. 01° 55′ N. We had now extremely hot weather, and a very small allowance of water.

January 9th. Last night we took in top-sails all night, the wind then whiffling between S. and W. We had notwithstanding for the most part very little wind. The morning of this day was rainy, and thereupon with good diligence we saved a bumpkin of water[1]. There was now a great rippling sea, rising very high ; and it is reported that sometimes and somewhere hereabouts is to be seen an enchanted island, which others say, and dare assert, that they have sailed over. I reckoned a N.W. by N. one-quarter N. way, and 25 leagues. This afternoon we had very dark and calm weather, looking as if we should have much rain. Now, reckoning up my meridian, I found myself E. from my departure 702 leagues. In the evening we had very rainy weather and a cockling sea.

January 10th. All last night was cloudy. About midnight sprang up a small breeze varying all round the compass. At five this morning we had a breeze at S.E. and a very clear sky, which afterwards continued to freshen, with the same clearness as before. We made a N.W. by N. one-quarter N. way, and by the same 2 leagues and two-thirds. By clear observation lat. 03° 16′ N. At four this evening the wind was at E.S.E., the weather being violent hot, insomuch that our allowance of water was tedious to us for its shortness. At the same time we had an indifferent smooth sea from the E.

January 11th. All last night we had little or no wind. But about two in the morning the wind freshened again at

[1] A nautical term for a vessel for carrying water : here, used for the amount it would hold. Cf. Dampier, *Voyages* (1697), ed. 1729, i, 2 : " Another canoa which had been sawn asunder in the middle, in order to have made bumkins, or vessels for carrying water."

E.N.E., and brought both a clear and hot day. We made 23 leagues by a N.W. one-quarter W. way. This day's observation gave us lat. 04° 06′ N. In the afternoon we had a shower of rain, and afterwards a fresh wind at E.N.E. But the evening grew dull.

January 12th. Last night we had two or three squalls of wind and some showers of rain. In the meanwhile the wind blew fresh at N.E. and N.E. by E., as it also continued to do in the day. I reckoned a N.W. way, and 44 leagues and one-third. Our observation this day gave us 05° 49′ N. Yesterday and to-day we set our main-top-sail. Now I could not find much variation of the needle.

January 13th. We had a fresh gale all last night, but more northerly than before, for now it was N.E. by N. We reckoned a W.N.W. way. An observation showed lat. 06° 41′ N. We had a N.N.E. sea and very clear weather.

January 14th. We had a clear night, and a fresh wind at E.N.E. We made a N.W. one-fifth W. way, and 38 leagues. By observation lat. 07° 46′ N. We had a smooth sea; and now we were come to only three horns of water a day, which made in all but a quart allowance for each man. The evening was clear, and we had a fresh wind.

Sunday, January 15th. Last night was clear, and the wind fresh at E.N.E., and again at N.E. by E. very fresh. At about eleven o'clock at night there died one of our companions, named William Stephens. It was commonly believed that he poisoned himself with *mançanilla* in Golfo Dulce, for he never had been in health since that time. This forenoon was cloudy. We reckoned 44 leagues and a N.W. way. An observation gave us this day 09° 18′ N. All last night we kept out our top-gallant sails. We saw hereabouts many flying fish, being very large in size. This morning also we threw overboard our dead man, and gave him two French volleys and one English one. I found now again very small variation.

January 16th. We had a clear night and a very fresh wind at N.E. and E.N.E., with a long, homing sea. My reckoning was a N.W. one-seventh W. way, and thereby 48 leagues and one-third. The observation made this day gave us lat. 10° 48′ N. I reckoned myself now E. from my departure 553 leagues. We had a very cloudy evening.

January 17th. All last night we enjoyed a fresh wind, and so this day also, at N.E. by N. We made a N.W. half W. way, and thereupon 47 leagues and one-third. By observation we found lat. 12° 19′ N. We had now a long north sea. At noon this day we steered away N.N.W. The day was very hot, but the night both cool and dewy.

January 18th. All last night was both cloudy and windy. At six this morning our sprit-sail top-mast broke. I reckoned a W.N.W. way, and 48 leagues by the same. We found by observation, lat. 13° 12′ N. At noon we steered away W., the wind being at N.E. fresh, with a clear evening.

January 19th. We had a clear night and a fresh wind at E.N.E., which sometimes came in pushes. Our reckoning was a W. half S. way, and by the same 46 leagues. We found by observation lat. 13° 01′ N. Yesterday in the evening we put up a new sprit-sail top-mast ; with a fine, smooth gale at N.E. by E.

January 20th. Last night was clear, and not very fresh, but at daybreak it freshened again. Last night we saw a great shoal of fish, whereof we caught none, by reason the porpoises frightened them from us, as they ofttimes had done before. Yesterday in the evening also we saw a man-of-war fowl[1], and that gave us good hopes we should e'er long see land. These hopes, and the great desires we had to end our voyage, gave us occasion this day to put in, or stake down, each man of our company a piece-of-eight for a reward to him that should first discover land. We reckoned a W. one-sixth N. way, and by it 38 leagues. An observation gave us this day lat. 13° 11′ N. The wind was at N.E. and E.N.E. This day we passed over many ripplings, and also saw many multitudes of fish ; but the porpoises did always hinder us from having any good of them.

January 21st. We made a W. way, and reckoned 47 leagues. By observation we found lat. 13° 07′ N. The wind at E.N.E. ; thence came a long sea. The evening very clear.

January 22nd. We had a fair and a clear day, the wind being at E. We reckoned a W. by N. one-third W. way and 40 leagues. An observation showed us lat. 13° 17′ N. We had a clear evening, and a fresh wind at E.N.E.

January 23rd. This day was both clear and hot, with a

[1] The frigate-bird ; also called the sea-hawk.

fresh wind at E.N.E. My reckoning was a W. way, and 46 leagues. Our observation this day afforded us lat. 13° 15′ N. In the evening we had some rain.

January 24th. This day brought us likewise clear weather, such as the day before. I reckoned a W. way, and 40 leagues and one-third. By observation we found lat. 13° 12′ N. The afternoon was cloudy, and had some rain, the wind freshening at E.N.E. and at E. by N. I reckoned now that I was E. from my departure 311 leagues. We had a cloudy evening.

January 25th. Both last night and this morning the weather was cloudy. This morning we saw several tropical birds of divers sorts. Our reckoning was a W. three-quarters N. way, and 43 leagues. We found by observation lat. 13° 29′ N. This afternoon we saw a booby[1] flying close aboard the horizon. The weather was hazy. But now we began to look out sharp on all sides for land, expecting to see it every minute. I reckoned myself to be E. of my departure 268 leagues.

January 26th. Last night was indifferent clear. Yet, notwithstanding, this morning we had a smart shower of rain, and it was very windy. Hereupon we furled our sprit-sail, the weather being very hazy to W. We reckoned a W. way, and thereby 46 leagues and one-third. By observation, lat. 13° 17′ N. At noon this day we had a very fierce tornado and rain together, but a clear afternoon. We had a high E.N.E. sea, and saw multitudes of flying-fish, and amongst these two or three boobies. The evening was hazy.

January 27th. All last night we had a fresh wind, and clear weather. This morning our fore-top-mast backstay gave way, and at daybreak the star-board sheet of our fore-top-sail broke. We had several tornadoes this day, and dark weather. Our reckoning was a W. way, and 48 leagues by the same. We had a clear evening and a dark night. This day also a certain bird called, a noddy[2], came on board us, which we took for a certain token that we were not now very far from land.

Saturday, January 28th. We had a very clear night. About an hour before day one of our company happened to descry land, which proved to be the Island of Barbados,

[1] The brown gannet, *sula cyanops*.
[2] The tern, *sterna stolida*.

at S.S.W. from us, and at 2 leagues and a-half distance, more or less. Hereupon we clapped on a wind, N. and by W. At daybreak we were only 4 leagues distant from Chalky Mount, at which time we stood S.W. by S. As we sailed we saw several ships at anchor in Spikes Road. Soon after a shallop passed by, between us and the shore, but would not come within call of us. Hereupon we stood in, within a mile of the shore, and made a wiff to a pinnace which we saw coming out of the road aforementioned. She came close aboard us, and, as it should seem, was the barge of one of his Majesty's frigates, the *Richmond*, then lying at the Bridgetown at anchor. They told us of peace at home, but would not come on board us, though often invited thereto. Neither dared we be so bold as to put in there at Barbados, for, hearing of a frigate lying there, we feared lest the said frigate should seize us for privateers and for having acted in all our voyage without commission. Thus we stood away thence for the island of Antigua.

Here I cannot easily express the infinite joy we were possessed with this day to see our own countrymen again. They told us that a ship which we saw in the offing to leeward of the island was a Bristol-man, and an interloper; but we feared that same vessel to be the frigate aforementioned. I reckoned a way of 25 leagues, so that I was now by my account to eastward of my departure 150 leagues. Now we stood N. by W., and by observation found lat. 13° 17′ N., we being then N.W. from the body of the island of Barbados between 7 and 8 leagues. This afternoon we freed the negro who was our shoemaker by trade, giving him his liberty for the good service he had done us in all the course of this voyage. We gave also to our good Commander, Captain Sharp, a mulatto-boy, as a free gift of the whole company, to wait upon him, in token of the respect we all were owing to him for the safety of our conduct through so many dangerous adventures. This being done, we shared some small parcels of money that had not as yet been touched of our former prizes; and this dividend amounted to 24 pieces-of-eight each man.

At one o'clock this day from our fore-yard we descried the island of St Lucia, being one of the Western Islands, not far distant from that of Barbados. I had omitted to tell a passage which happened in our ship on Thursday last, which was the 26th day of this month and just two days before we made the island of Barbados. On that day, therefore, a little Spanish shock-dog[1], which we had found in our last wine-prize taken under the equinoctial and had kept alive till now, was sold at the mast by public cry for 40 pieces-of-eight, his owner saying that all he could get for him should be spent upon the company at a public merriment. Our Commander, Captain Sharp, bought the dog, with intention to eat him, in case we did not see land very soon. This money, therefore, with 100 pieces-of-eight more, which our boatswain, carpenter, and quartermaster had refused to take at this last dividend, for some quarrel they had against the sharers thereof, was all laid up in store till we came to land, with the intent of spending it ashore at a common feast or drinking-bout. At sunset the island of St Lucia bore W.S.W. from us, and was at 10 leagues distance. Also the island of Martinique bore N.W. by W. of us at 12 or 13 leagues distance. We had this day a very clear evening.

Sunday, January 29th. We had a clear night, and a fresh wind at E. by N. and at E.N.E. Our reckoning was a N.N.W. half-W. way, and hereby 46 leagues. By observation we took lat. 15° 46′ N. At noon this day we saw the island named La Desirade, or The Desired Island, which then bore N.W. from us, and seemed to be at 8 leagues distance, more or less. At six o'clock in the evening we saw likewise Mariegalante, another of the Caribbee Islands, at S.W. by W. from us, and that of Guadaloupe, streaking itself in several hummocks of land, both W. and N.; as also La Desirade above-mentioned at S.E., which from there shows like tableland, and at each end has a low point running out. At six this evening it was W.S.W., and at 5 or 6 leagues distance from us. At the same time we saw the island of Montserrat at a great distance from our ship and making three round hummocks close together. This evening likewise we caught an albicore of twenty pound weight.

Monday, January 30th. We had a fair night all the last past, and a fresh wind. Hereupon all night we hauled up our main-sail in brails, standing at the same time N. by W.,

[1] A small rough-coated dog: cf. "What a terrible bandog [bound-dog; for fierceness] do's she make of it, | Which other ladies play with as familiarly | As with their shocks or Bononia dogs."—*Erminia* [1661].

with the wind at E.N.E. At midnight we stood N.W. At three in the morning we lay by until five. Then we stood away W.N.W. until six, and at that hour we stood W. At eight o'clock we saw the island of Antigua, called by us Antego, to the S. of us, making three round hummocks of land, and a long high hill to N. Hereupon we stood W.S.W. for it. At noon we found lat. 17° N., the island being then just W. from us.

We came about to the S. of the island, and sent a canoe on shore to get tobacco and other necessaries that we wanted, as also to ask leave of the Governor to come into the port. The gentry of the place and common people were very willing and desirous to receive us. But on Wednesday, February 1st, the Governor flatly denied us entry—at which all the gentry were much grieved, and showed themselves very kind to us. Hereupon we agreed among ourselves to give away and leave the ship to them of our company who had no money left of all their purchase in this voyage, having lost it all at play; and then to divide ourselves into two ships, which were now bound for England. Thus I myself and thirteen more of our company went on board Captain Robert Porteen's ship, called the *Lisbon Merchant*, and set sail from Antigua on February 11th, and landed at Dartmouth in England, March 26th, anno 1682.

INDEX

Alternative spellings of personal names are given—e.g. Alleston (Allison)—where the spellings vary in different parts of the text and the correct spelling cannot be traced.

abelcoses: 33
acajou: 32; 15 (& n.), 31
Acapulco: 339
achioc: 235
acoma: 32
adders: 300—*v. also* snakes
'a-drough': 445 (& n.)
Aguada Grande: 179
Ahorcados, Los (rocks): 437
albicores: 339 (& n.)
'*alcatraces*': 25 (& n.)
Alexander, John: 420
Alleston (Allison), R.: 298, 299
alligators: 335
aloes: 15—*v. lignum aloes*
Alonso, Capt.: 435
Alonzo del Campo y Espinosa: 160–70
d'Alvarez, Cape: 57
'*Amirricide*': 53 (& n.)
Andræas, Emp.: 262, 267, 302, 304, 308, 314, 329
Antigua: 278, 474
Aperovaco: 250
apricot-trees: 30
de Arganonda, T.: 270, 272, 366, 389
Arica: 270–1, 274, 344, 354, 374, 406–9, 410
Armadilla, La: 264–5, 321
arrows (Indian): 229, 231–2, 237
articles of association (of Buccaneers): 59–60
Assientos, Capt.: 435
Augustin: 262, 264, 266–7
azagayas: 201 (& n.), 235, 237
bacones: 16
Bahama, Channel of: 56
Ballona, Gulf of: 290, 309, 315, 332
Baltazar, Don: 366, 389
bananas: 48, 114, 115, 235
'baptism' at sea: 10–11
de Barahona, Jacinto: 322
Barbacoa: 196
Barbados: 12, 119, 252, 281, 472–3
barco d'aviso: 259, 432
Barfleur, Cape of: 9
'bark-logs': 356 (& n.), 363
Barracoa: 128
Bartholomew Portuges: 64–70
de Basco, Michael: 87
Bayala: 87, 101
Bayame: 128
Berlingues (rocks): 11
Bête rouge: 33 (n.)
Bettesa: 53
bilby-trees: 399
Binkes, Jacob: 247, 249–52
Blanco, Cape: 362, 422, 423, 438
Bleevelt, Bay of: 230
'blemishing': 292 (& n.)
de Bliniac, Gov.: 250, 252
Boca del Dragon: 227
Boca del Toro: 227, 260, 297
'*Bonête d' Oro*'—*v.* Augustin
bonitos: 339, 340, 417
booby (brown gannet): 472
'boots and tops,' pair of: 436 (& n.)
Borrica, Island of: 90
Bournano, Capt.: 297, 298, 299
Brasiliano, Roche: 70–6
bravos: 90
brazil-wood: 32
Brest: 252
Brodely, Capt.: 185
brûlots: 16
Bull, Mr: 319
Bullock, Mr: 434
'bumpkin' of water: 469 (& n.)
cabalas: 237
cabreros: 43
cacadores de moscas: 34–5
cacao: 100
Cadiz: 247
cagazons: 99 (& n.)
Caicos: 56
calarodes: 34
California: 268, 339
Camerones (river): 404, 405
Cammock, William: 392
Campeche: 67, 68, 69, 73, 81, 82, 119–20 129, 254
Campeche wood: 111 (& n.), 129, 254
Canary Islands: 128
candlewood: 15
caneletas (pagayos): 228 (& n.)
Cannis (a Buccaneer): 377
Cano, Island of: 418, 424
Caquibacoa, Cape of: 89
de Carabaxal, Don Diego: 322
Caracas: 62, 129, 147, 248
Caracas: Governor of: 90
carasoles: 16
'carbonadoed': 202 (& n.)
caremites: 30
Caribbee Islands: 9, 53, 81, 237, 474
carpenteros: 43
Cartagena: 63, 67, 77, 116, 129, 136, 175, 178, 227, 229, 257
cassava (plant): 15 (n.), 47–8, 235
cassia lignea: 31
'cat in the pan': 282 (& n.)
Cavallo, El: 276, 421, 434
Cayboa, Island of: 332, 333, 335, 336, 361
Caymanes Islands: 62
caymans: 35–8
Cayona: 14, 249, 250
de Cazeres, Lieut. Frances: 125
Chagre, Castle of: 211, 214, 222
Chagre, River of: 120, 185–9, 226
Chandy Point: 357
Chappel, James: 435
Chepillo, Island of: 319–20
Chepo: 297

Chero: 275–6
Chiquisaca: 344
Chira (island): 419, 420
Christmas Day: 462, 467
Christoval, Don: 366, 389
Ciavone, Capt.: 251
citrons: 27
Ciudad de la Serena—*v.* Serena
cochineal: 111
cochinillas: 34
coco-nuts: 67, 88, 270, 357, 365, 418, 427, 430
Colan: 440
Colla: 120
Comana: 172
comet, a: 382
Company of Negroes, The: 136
Conception, La: 167
conchs: 343
Conquet, Bay of: 10
Cook, Capt. E.: 254–6, 298, 319, 328, 333, 398
Cook, W. (his servant): 398, 411
copal: 109 (& n.)
Coquimbo: 271–3, 390–1
corlabados: 244
de Corrientes, Cape: 64
de Corrientes, port: 128
Cortadura gate: 125, 126
Costa Rica: 112, 120, 121, 129, 135–6, 224
Courland, Prince of: 249
Cox, Capt. John: 273, 336, 340, 346, 351, 357, 361, 377, 397
Coxon, Capt. J.: 257, 266–7, 268, 298, 300, 303, 308, 319, 323, 329
crab-lemons—*v.* limes
crabs: 17 (& n.), 235
crickets: 34
crocodile, ferocity of: 239—*v. also* caymans
Croxen (Coxen), Capt. J.—*v.* Coxon
Cruz de Juan Gallego: 192, 221
Cuba: 128 *sqq.*
Cul de Sac, Tortuga: 46
Curaçao: 148, 248
customs (Indian)—*v.* Indians
Damascene Plums: 30 (& n.)
Darien: 260 *sqq.*
Darien, King of: 302–3, 308, 322, 329
Darien, King of, Daughter of: 307
Dartmouth: 475
Davis, Capt. John: 77
De la Barra fortress: 92
De la Hacha river: 63, 174, 175–8
De la Plata river: 63
De la Vaca Island: 143, 174
De las Pertas (islands): 113, 116
De los Brascos: 192
De los Cayos: 82, 85, 128
Debaucheries of Buccaneers: 100, 142
Desirade, La: 474
Dieppe: 9, 56
'disembogue': 309 (& n.), 426
division of booty: 222, 434, 461, 462, 473
dolphins: 339, 340, 355, 417
Donna Maria, Cape of: 26
Drake, Sir Francis: 414
'Drake's Island'—*v.* Plate, Isle of
Duke of York's Island(s): 280–1, 448, 453–4
Dulce, Golfo: 276, 424, 425, 427
Equipment of vessels: 59–60
Espiritu Santo: 128
Esquemeling, John: 7–8
Essex, Cornelius: 257
Estera Longa Lemos: 137
Estevan del Campo, Don: 123
de Estres, Mons.: 249, 250–3
'experiment,' to (experience): 214 (& n.)
faisanes (pheasants): 230
Fall, John: 397
False Wild Harbour: 395
Farol de Plantanos: 318
figs: 376
Finisterre, Cape: 12
fire-flies: 34; -ship, *v. brûlot*
Florida: 78, 129
flota: 56 (& n.)
flying-fish: 470
Forlorn: 303
French Buccaneers in Isla de la Vaca: 99
French in Hispaniola: 26, 43 *sqq.*
French in St Christopher: 17–21
Friar, Murder of a: 360
Friars and nuns sent in front of attack: 139, 274
Fuerte (Forta): 257
Gabaret, Mons.: 250
Gabriel, Josephe (pilot): 343–4
Galapagos, De los: 269, 340, 353
Galeno, Capt. John: 125
Gallo, Island of: 346–7, 361
genipa-trees and fruit: 30–1
Gibraltar: 90–1, 92, 94–100, 154 *sqq.*
gimbes: 49 (& n.)
glow-worms: 34
Goat Key, The: 361
goat-keepers (bird): 43
'goblets' (morsels): 202 (& n.)
God Almighty, etc., Thanks given to: 53, 109, 116, 117, 395, 411, 447–8, 461
Godolphin, Sir William: 5
gold-dust: 272
'Golden-Cap, King'—*v.* Augustin
del Golfo Tristo, Cape: 68, 69, 73
Gorgona: 269, 341–4, 345, 437
Gorgonilla (island): 346–7
Gracias á Dios: 102, 113, 116–7, 233
grampuses: 343, 464
grillones: 34
'grimp,' to: 96 (& n.)
Groningen: 70
Guadaloupe, Island of: 12, 474
Guadanillas: 243
guaicum: 15, 25, 31
Guasco: 275, 412–3
Guatemala: 107, 112
Guayaquil: 270, 273, 344, 357, 365
guines agudos: 48
gummi elemi: 15, 31
Guyones, Cabo de: 423
de Guzman, Don John: 122–4
Haiti: 13 (n.)
hanegs: 176 (& n.)
Hansel, Capt.: 172
harquebuses: 358 (& n.)
Harris, Capt. P.: 260, 297, 298, 300, 319, 323, 325
Havana: 57, 67, 85, 101, 128, 129, 136, 247
Havre de Grace: 9
heronsetas: 43
He lo he—*v.* Ylo
hides: 128, 129
Hilliard, John: 397
Hilo, Point of: 372–3, 375–9, 380, 414–5
Hispaniola: 12 (& n.), 23–54, 81, 87, 99, 174, 175, 176, 245

Honduras: 129
,, Gulf of: 62, 102, 113; Indians: 110
Horadada, Pena: 439
'howting': 198 (& n.)
hoys (coasting-vessels): 17 (& n.)
Indian houses: 302
Indians: 260, 264, 362, 450–1
,, Customs of: 233–8
,, Encounters with: 200–1, 226, 228–9, 231–2
,, of Darien: 116, 267–8, 297, 302–3, 304
,, of De los Pertas: 113–4
,, of Golfo Dulce: 425–6
,, of Gracias á Dios: 233–8
,, of Iquique: 403–4
,, of Yucatan: 109–10
,, 'Wild': 90
'indifferent': 87 (& n.), 383, 418
indigo: 49, 107 (& n.), 111
Indios bravos (Wild Indians): 224–5
Insects of Hispaniola: 33–4
Iquique, Island of: 402–5
Isla de la Vaca: 99
Jacmel: 32
Jamaica: 70, 74–5, 77, 119, 121, 134, 143, 172, 173–4, 239–40, 257, 279, 281, 282
Jaquina: 32
Jardines (rocks): 70
Juan, Capt.: 336, 389
Juan Fernandez Island: 273, 393–400
junta: 161 (n.)
Lacumba: 414
Lampsius, A. & C.: 249
Lapina: 357
Le Cort: 253
Le Maire, Strait: 278, 279
Leeward Islands: 279
lemons: 27, 376
lenna de peje palo: 32
de Lesi, Governor: 250, 251
Le Leyra, Capt. J. R.: 125
lignum aloes: 31; — *sanctum*, *v.* guaicum
Lima: 261, 270, 277, 328, 352, 376, 431, 432, 437—*v. also* Paita
limes: 27, 376
Lisbon Merchant: 475
Loa river: 414
Lobos, C. de: 26, 145, 172, 416, 439
logwood—*v.* Campeche wood
L'Ollonais, François: 81–118
Lopez, Capt. Diego: 433
Mackett, Capt.: 298, 299
macoa: 108
Magdalen: 167
Magellan clouds: 369, 452
Magellan, Strait of: 262, 278, 279–80, 440, 448, 452
magniot—v. cassava
Maintenon, Le Sieur: 248
mamayns (mammees): 16 (& n.)
man-of-war fowl: 471 (& n.)
mançanilla: 32
mandioca: 47
manentines (manatees): 227 (& n.)–8
manitas: 234
Mansvelt, Mr: 76–7, 120–1
Manta, Port of: 350, 435
mapore: 32
Maracaibo: 63, 67, 74, 148
Maracaibo, Bay (Lake) of: 89, 92
Maracaibo City: 89–91; captured: 92–4, 98–9, 148–52
Maracaibo, Port of: 86, 89
marascite (iron pyrites): 231 (& n.)
Marcy, Cannis (interpreter): 421
Margarita: 62
Mariegalante: 474
Marquesa, La: 167
Marquis, James: 276
marriage and birth-customs—*v.* Indians
Martinique, Isle of: 12, 252
Mata Ricos (port): 128
Matamana: 101, 130
matales: 20
Mayflower: 273
Merida: 91
mestizos: 25 (& n.)
Mexilloner, Bay of: 414
millipes (insect): 35
Monges Island: 89
monkeys: 230–1, 343
Monte de Christo: 349
montera: 161 (& n.)
Montgomery, Robert: 366
Montserrat: 474
Moor, The old (pilot): 352–3, 389
Mora de Sama: 373–4, 375, 414
Moranto Port: 257
Moreno, Capt. Juan: 366
Moreno, Nicolas (pilot): 362, 366
Morgan, Capt. H.: 119–223, 225, 239–40, 292–5
Moro de Horse: 413
Moro Moreno: 413–4
moscas de fuego (fire-flies): 34
mosquitos and gnats: 33–4
mulattos: 25
mussel-bank: 448
Na Sa de la Soledad: 167 (& n.)
Na Sa del Carmen: 167
Nata: 120, 330
'Neptune's post-horses' (boats): 31
New England: 281
New Granada: 77
New Spain: 88, 129, 247
Newfoundland: 9
Nicaragua: 77–91, 101; River: 115
Nicoya, Gulf of: 275, 418, 421, 422
noddy: 472
Nombre de Dios: 136, 227
'No prey, no pay': 60
Nuestra Señora del Alta Gracia: 24
'occur unto,' to: 187 (& n.), 197
Ocoa, Port of: 146
Ogeron, Bertram: 21, 40, 242–7
'old wives': 339
olives: 376
ollas: 28 (& n.)
d'Ollone, Les Sables: 81
oranges: 27
Orega Island: 89
Ornay, Isle of: 9
osnaburgs: 365 (& n.), 367
Ostend: 10
Otoque, Island of: 331–2
oysters: 336, 343
Paffao, Cape: 277–9
pagayos: 228 (& n.)
Paita: 277, 280, 363, 439–41
Paita, La Silla de: 363–4, 439
palm-trees (Hispaniola): 27–30
palmettos; palmites: 16 (& n.)
Palmit, Bay of: 251
Palomas, Isla de las: 89
Panama: 178, 192, 200–19, 263–6, 274, 277, 307, 318, 321–30, 431, 432
Panama, Bay of: 332

Panama, Bishop of: 331; Governor of: 120–1
paquayes: 16
pardelas (bird): 395
Paria: 248
Passao, Cape: 348–9, 351, 431, 434
Paxaros, De los: 391, 412
paxaros ninos: 456, 460
payments for wounds, etc.: 60, 177–8
pearl-bank: 63; -fishery: 332
pedreros: 102 (& n.)
penguins: 451
de Peralta, Capt. F.: 272, 322, 323–5, 326, 336, 341, 352, 361, 366, 389
periagua: 309 (& n.)
Perico, Island of: 321, 324, 328, 330
periwinkles: 343
'*petite piracy*': 256
Philipinas Islands: 339
le Picard, Pierre: 112–3
pieces-of-eight: 60 (n.); *passim*
Pierre François: 63–4
Pierre le Grand (pirate): 56
Pigeons, Isle of: 89
pigeons: 43
pine-apples: 16 (& n.), 114, 235
Pinos, De los: 70, 102, 130, 238, 257
pintadas: 42–3
Pitch lake of La Brea, Trinidad: 108 (n.)
Piura: 439
de la Place, Mons.: 81
'planch': 226 (& n.)
plantanos: 197 (& n.), 230, 235, 236
planters, cruelties of: 52–4
Plantin Isle: 264
Plate, Isle of: 269–70, 273, 351–4, 355, 416, 435, 436
Pocatauro, Gulf of: 77
Ponce, Admiral: 437
porcupines: 230
porpoises: 461, 464, 471
Port Couillon: 174
Porteen, Capt. Robert: 475
Porto Bello: 120, 126, 135–42, 222, 243, 245–6, 247, 258–9, 420
Porto Rico: 12, 88
potatoes: 15, 46–7, 114, 235
Potosi: 274, 308, 344
priest subdues lions and tigers: 361–2
Puebla Nueva: 268–9, 333–4
Pueblo del Aso, El: 25
Puerto Caldero: 419
Puerto Cavallo: 102
Puerto de Santa Maria: 130
Puerto de Velas: 424
Puerto del Principe: 128, 130–4
Puerto Mariano: 128
Puerto Pontin: 136–7
Punta Borrica: 424–5, 428
Punta de Mero: 437
Punta d'Espada: 88, 146
Punta Parina: 363
'purchase,' to: 67 (& n.)
Quiblo, Isles of: 268
Quicara: 338
Quita Signos: 124
Quito: 357, 364
racoven: 114, 115, 235
radix Chinae: 15, 31
Rancherias: 63
raquelles: 104
Ras: 10, 11
rasp-houses: 45 (& n.)
Richmond: 281, 473
Ringrose, B., 276, 282, 290–4, 313
Rio de Juan Diaz, El: 374
Rio de Zeura: 229–30
Rochelle: 9
rojados: 34
Romney Marsh: 283
de Ronquillo, Don Pedro: 282
Rosario, El Santo: 277–8, 282, 433, 434
Row (Rose), Jno.: 257, 298, 299
Roxo, Capo: 245
Rubia: 254
saetia: 111, 156, 157
Saint (St) Antony, Cape of: 67
" Augustine of Florida: 78
" Catharine, Isle of: 77, 120, 121, 127, 178, 179–84, 189–90, 240
" Christopher, Isle of: 53; French in: 17–21
" Faucher, Mons. de: 250
" Helena, Point: 356, 437
" John de Puerto Rico: 242, 245–6
" Jerome, Castle of: 126
" Lawrence, Cape: 314, 350, 351
" Lucia: 473–4
" Maries River: 263, 275
" Martins: 9
" Nicholas, Cape of: 26
" Peter, Isle of: 12
" Roman, Cape: 89
" Teresa, Castle of: 125
" Vincent, Straits of: 456
St John: 9
St Lewis: 167
St Peter: 125, 270
St Rose: 259
St Vincent: 125
Samana: 245
Sambale, Isle of: 111
San Domingo: 13 (n.), 24, 146
San Francisco, Cape of: 276, 348, 431
San Juan de Goave: 24
San Matteo: 347–8, 429, 430
San Miguel, Gulf of—*v.* Ballona
San Pedro: 103
San Francisco: 399
San Pedro: 430
Santa Clara: 437
Santa Cruz: 128, 129, 198, 244
Santa Maria: 128, 262–3, 327
Santiago: 128–9, 347
Santiago, river of: 430
Santo Christo, El: 399
Savona, Isle of: 88, 144–7
Sawkins, Capt. R.: 260, 268, 297, 298, 300, 303, 322–5, 307, 329, 331, 333–6, 361, 398
scolopendria: 35
scorpions: 35
Scot, Lewis: 76
'sea-cow'—*v.* manentines
'sea-lions': 396 (& n.)
seals: 395, 396, 455, 459
Senegal: 9
Serena, La, 384–9, 413
Sharp, Capt. B.: 257–83, 298, 303, 319, 329, 333–6, 340, 346, 353, 376, 377–8, 398, 404, 408, 419, 433, 456, 473, 474
'Sharp's Isle': 342; *v. also* Gorgona
Shergall, Henry: 280, 447
shock-dog: 474 (& n)
Simon, Le Sieur: 121, 122–4
sloth: 343
snakes: 148, 300, 343
Solango, Isle of: 355, 436
Sourdis, Chevalier: 9

South Sea : 264 *sqq.*, 289–90, 309, 435
spiders : 35, 148
Springer, Capt. : 323
stantions : 328 (& n.)
Stephens, William : 470
storms, etc. : 12, 311–2, 336–7, 395, 397, 418, 421, 442, 445, 447, 449–50
sugar : 49, 128 ; sugar-works : 376–8
tabaco de sacerdotes : 91
Tablazo, El : 89
Tavoga, Island of : 202, 213, 216, 330–1, 426
Tavogilla, Island of : 202, 213, 216
Terra Australis Incognita : 1, 281
Terra Firma, Kingdom of : 122, 234
'terre-pleined' : 185 (& n.) ; terrepleins : 7
Tiburon, Cape : 26, 56, 146, 179
tobacco : 48–9, 90, 91, 128, 129
Tobago, Island of : 249, 251–3, 256, 266, 268
Toca Mora : 260–1
Torna Cavallos : 195
toronjas : 27
tortoises : 35, 61–2, 339, 353
Tortuga : 9, 12, 13, 14–22, 88, 112, 121, 174, 241, 242, 245–7, 248
Trinidad : 128, 129, 248
Trinidad, La : 266, 269, 273, 281, 325, 328, 334, 336, 428
Trinity Isles : 62
Truxillo : 330, 430
Tucames, Port of : 429
Tumbes : 361–2
turtles : 343, 417, 464
Ushant : 10
Van der Graef, Capt. : 251
Van Dongen, Capt. : 251, 253
Van Vin, Moses : 103
Vanclein, Moses : 112–3
Vanero : 421
Venezuela, Gulf of : 89, 92
Vera Cruz : 178
Veraguas, river : 112 ; mines : 113
veycou : 48
Vigilias, Isla de las : 89, 92
Villa de los Cayos, La : 240
Virginia : 281
volleys, funeral : 366, 420, 448, 470
,, for Christmas day : 394
Wagenaer : 278
Wapping : 291
'Wankers' : 313
Water-Key (island) : 298
Watling, Commander J. : 273–4, 398, 402, 407
whales : 343, 464
wheat : 115
wild-boars : 16, 30, 32, 39–40, 45
,, bulls and cows : 17, 25, 39, 42
,, dogs : 39–42
,, geese : 448
,, goats : 353, 394, 399, 435
,, horses : 39, 42
,, pigeons : 16–17
Xagoa (port) : 128
Xagua (river) : 102
Ximenes, Capt. J. S. : 123, 124, 125
yams (yannas) : 16 (& n.)
ycao (tree) : 32–3
yellow saunder : 15
Ylo (He lo he) : 273, 275
Zavallos (Zambullos) : 257